Renaissance Essays

Renaissance Essays

by

Hugh Trevor-Roper

The University of Chicago Press

The University of Chicago Press, Chicago 60637
Martin Secker & Warburg Limited, London WIV 3DF

© 1961, 1962, 1971, 1972, 1975, 1977, 1978, 1979,
1980, 1981, 1982, 1985 by Hugh Trevor-Roper
All rights reserved. Published 1985
Printed in Great Britain
Photoset by Rowland Phototypesetting Limited
Bury St Edmunds, Suffolk

94 93 92 91 90 89 88 87 86   5 4 3 2 1

Library of Congress Cataloging in Publication Data
Trevor-Roper, H. R. (Hugh Redwald), 1914–
Renaissance essays.

Includes index.
  1. Europe—History—1492–1648—Addresses, essays,
lectures.   2. Renaissance—Addresses, essays, lectures.
I. Title.
D210.T79 1985   940.2'1   85-2775
ISBN 0-226-81225-1

Contents

Preface

The essays in this volume all deal, essentially, with aspects or episodes of European history between the Renaissance and that great historical and intellectual watershed which can be seen as the end of the Renaissance, the Thirty Years War. Historical periodization is notoriously dangerous and perhaps unreal. The Renaissance has been discovered before 1400 and the ideas of the sixteenth century did not all perish in the seventeenth: some ideas, after all, are permanent acquisitions. But nobody, I think, would deny that the Thirty Years War marked a change in the intellectual as well as in the political structure of Europe: that it ended a chapter which had begun with the revival of ancient letters and the growth of princely power in the fifteenth century: two processes which had begun in Italy and had been carried to, and transformed in, the rest of Europe. This period, and these topics, provide such loose unity as is all that I would dare to claim for these essays. They begin in Renaissance Venice and the renewal of culture at the Habsburg court, and they end with the explosion of the 1620s in Europe, and the observation of the whole theatre of Renaissance man, as seen by Robert Burton from his private box in that 'most flourishing college in Europe', Henry VIII's foundation of Christ Church, Oxford.

Within this period I have, like Robert Burton himself, ranged freely, as accident or opportunity has led me; but my principal interest has been in intellectual and cultural history which I have tried to see not in isolation but in its relation to, and expression in, society and politics: in the realization of ideas, the patronage of the arts, the interpretation of history, the social challenge of science, the social application of religion. On all these subjects I have touched, sometimes lightly, sometimes less lightly, as the occasion has seemed to me to demand. This the reader will remark, the critic perhaps criticize. It remains for me to note the several occasions which have called forth these essays and, sometimes, and in some form, their previous publication.

The essay on the Doge Francesco Foscari (no. 1) was first published in the *Book of the Renaissance* (ed. J. H. Plumb, 1961); those on the Emperor Maximilian as Patron (no. 2) and the outbreak of the Thirty Years War (no. 13) in *Horizon* (1977, 1962). The essay on Sir Thomas More (no. 3) is, in its present form, new, although its *disjecta membra*, now reassembled, were published in two articles commemorating the fifth centenary of the birth of More, one in *The American Scholar* (winter 1978–9) and the other in the *Atti dei Convegni Lincei* (1980): the latter being the record of a conference on More held at the Accademia Nazionale dei Lincei in 1979. The essays on Erasmus (no. 4) and the Lisle Letters (no. 5) were first published as reviews of two notable works of scholarship, the six volumes of *The Lisle Letters*, edited by the late Muriel St Clair Byrne (University of Chicago Press, 1981) and the latest volumes of *The Correspondence of Erasmus*, published in English, since 1974, by the University of Toronto Press. The former review appeared in the *Times Literary Supplement* (10 February 1984), the latter in *The American Scholar* (summer 1982). The brief essay on John Stow (no. 6) was delivered as an address at the annual commemoration of that great antiquary in his parish church of St Andrew Undershaft, London, on 30 April 1975: it was printed in the *Transactions of the London and Middlesex Archaeological Society* Vol. 26 (1975). The essay on Richard Hooker (no. 7) was also first delivered in a church – in the National Cathedral of Washington D. C. – in order to commemorate the publication of the first volumes of another great work of transatlantic scholarship, the Folger Library Edition of *The Works of Richard Hooker*, edited by W. Speed Hill, and published by the Harvard University Press in 1977. It was printed in the *New York Review of Books* (24 November 1977). The essay on Camden was the second Neale Lecture in English History delivered in honour of Sir John Neale in the University of London on 2 December 1971. It was printed as a separate pamphlet by Jonathan Cape. The long essay on the Paracelsian Movement is new and here printed for the first time. As a pendant, or footnote, to it I have included the essay on the sieur de la Rivière, which was first printed in a *Festschrift* in honour of that great scholar, the late Dr Walter Pagel (*Science, Medicine and Society in the Renaissance*, edited by Allen G. Debus, New York, 1972). The essay on the Culture of the Baroque Courts was delivered as the opening lecture at the Conference on Baroque Studies held in the Herzog August Bibliothek in Wolfenbüttel in September 1979 – the fourth centenary of the birth of its founder, Augustus, Duke of Brunswick-Lüneberg. It was published in the proceedings of that Congress (*Europäische Hofkultur im 16 und 17 Jahrhundert*, Vol. 1, Hamburg 1981). The essay on Robert Burton again was inspired by a centenary – the fourth centenary of his birth in 1577. I am grateful to these centenaries which prod me into reading unread or re-reading half-forgotten works. At that time I gave a brief broadcast on Burton and his *Anatomy*. But how can that irresistible polymath – irresistible at least to a scholar of the English Renaissance – be cramped into so narrow a compass? Having once turned back to him, I soon found myself writing more diffusely upon him, and the present essay is new.

I am grateful for the stimulus, or the permission, of the publishers who have previously commissioned or printed several of these essays, and to my present publishers and those personal friends who have encouraged me to reprint, and thus forced me to revise them: especially to Mr Blair Worden in one capacity and Mr T. G. Rosenthal in another; and to my wife who, not for the first time, has not only tolerated much when I have been exasperated by lost texts and missing references but also done the real work of the index.

I

The Doge Francesco Foscari

The doges of Venice are, in general, impersonal figures. In the age of the Renaissance we think of the great Venetian artists, but their local patrons have not the same colour. Contemporaries admired the Venetian political system and Venetian policy, which preserved the independence of the Republic; they admired the University of Padua – one of the great intellectual centres of Europe; but the politicians who operated that system, and had been produced by that university, were concealed in the shadows; and none was more shadowy than their elected prince, the Doge. When we look back through Venetian history we see a succession of these shadowy princes with recurrent aristocratic names. None of them seems to have much substance or identity till we come to the mid-fifteenth century. Then we meet the Doge Francesco Foscari whose long and, in the end, dramatic reign has won him a place in history and literature; for it coincided with a turning-point in Venetian history and captured the imagination of Byron. Among those alternating phantoms he seems like Tiresias in Hades: he alone has breath and life, they are flickering shades.

The story begins in 1423, when the old doge, Tomaso Mocenigo, lay dying. The prosperity of the city was then at its height: this indeed was the golden age of the Republic. But for a generation grave problems had hung over it, and now it seemed at the parting of the ways. The problem could be expressed simply, even if the answer was not so simple: should it concentrate on its empire abroad, or on its base at home? The choice was not easy, for both alike were threatened.

The empire abroad was centred in the Aegean Sea, though it extended to the factories in Constantinople and the routes to the Middle and Far East. Here the threat came from the Ottoman Turks,

I

now settled in Europe, with their capital at Adrianople, and pushing into the Balkans. All the efforts of Venice were needed to keep them out of the Aegean, and for years that had been the prime object of Venetian diplomacy. The threat to the home base came from closer quarters: from ominous new powers which were growing up in and around Italy.

Hitherto, Venice had been able to build up its empire abroad because its neighbours at home had given little trouble. Bishoprics, communes, petty princes – they could not be ignored, but equally they offered no temptations compared with the huge profits of the Levant. So the Republic had practised a policy of the balance of power, involving the minimum of direct intervention. But now these petty neighbours were becoming part or projections of greater powers, and these greater powers were threatening the very life of Venice. The kings of Hungary and Naples were closing in on the two ends of its Adriatic lifeline. Above all, a menacing new state was pressing down the valley of the Po. For this was the time when the free republics of Italy were gradually being converted into despotic princely states; and the greatest of these states was the new duchy of Milan, under the Visconti family. Having crushed the liberties of Milan, the Visconti were creating around it an even larger hinterland or *retroterra*. In the south they had absorbed the great mercantile republic of Genoa, which, being squeezed between the Ligurian Alps and the sea, lacked such a *retroterra* in which to fight. In the east they were pushing towards another great mercantile republic, squeezed between the Lagoons and the sea, Venice.

How could Venice ensure its survival? The answer, according to some Venetians, was to enlarge its own *retroterra*, the Venetian *Terraferma*. This process had already begun, with the annexation of Padua, Vicenza, Verona. But others distrusted this policy. Land wars, they said, were costly; they distracted the city from its real task, in the east; they created a new class of landed nobility and made the city dependent on *condottiere* generals; and was it not precisely out of landed nobility and *condottieri* that the new power of the princes, which threatened the liberties of all Italian cities, was rising?

The Doge Mocenigo was one of these others. As he lay dying he summoned to his bed the ducal councillors and there delivered a famous speech. The war for the *Terraferma*, he said, had shattered the finances of the Republic. It could not be continued. The wealth of Venice lay in manufacture, trade and shipping: by keeping to that, and to peace, the city would master the wealth of Christendom. Therefore they must be careful to appoint a sound successor to himself. Then he went in turn through the possible candidates. Bembo, Loredan, another Mocenigo, Contarini, the political members of the great mercantile families who formed the closed aristocracy of Venice, there was something to be said for them all. But at the end he warned them explicitly against one man. Francesco Foscari, he said, was proud, ambitious, unscrupulous: if he were doge, it would mean war, war, war. . . .

To us there may seem something unbalanced in such a warning. Already by now the Republic had achieved its perfect aristocratic form: a form which was to be final (in all essentials) for centuries. Gone were the days when the people had power of election: since 1292 the Greater Council, the legislature and electorate of the Republic, had been 'closed' – that is, confined to the nobility, who in turn kept careful control over their own membership. Gone too were the days when the doge, however elected, had exercised personal power. By now successive 'ducal promises' – the conditions which the nobility, after observing the faults of each doge, imposed upon his successor – had reduced the doge to a mere figurehead. If offered the dogeship, a Venetian nobleman was unable by law to refuse it. Once elected, his power was narrowly circumscribed. He was unable to travel outside Venice. Neither he nor his sons could be married except to Venetian women. Neither his sons nor his personal officers could hold public positions under him, and his official councillors, without whom he could do nothing, not even open a formal letter, could not be chosen by him. His income was curtailed, his expenses limited, lest he should raise a party by bribery. His authority over the citizens was reduced lest he should raise a mob in his support. He was not even allowed to give himself social airs. He could not set up his escutcheons in public places, or answer to honorific titles. To foreigners, as representative of the greatest, richest republic in Italy, he might be *Serenissimo Principe*; at home, in that republic, he was only *messer il doge*. And finally, he could not even lay down his office at will: except with the consent of his six councillors, ratified by the approval of the Greater Council, he could not even abdicate. Why then should an ambitious man want to be doge, and what could an ambitious man do, even if he were doge?

Nevertheless, Mocenigo's warning cannot have been entirely groundless. The Venetian constitution may have been completely aristocratic, and its aristocratic character may have been jealously preserved by a perpetual subdivision of authority, indirect elections and a complex tissue of checks and balances. But even the most perfect constitution is operated by men, with human passions, and the more complex a constitution is, the more certainly it falls into the hands of skilful politicians; and skilled politicians, even with the old rules, may play a new game. In the fifteenth century, a new game was being played in all the republics of Italy. Faced by new problems, their old constitutions were crumbling, and new men – sometimes patricians rising out of their midst, sometimes *condottieri* in their service – were building up despotic rule. This had already happened in Milan, with the Visconti; it would happen again, with the Sforza. Soon it would happen in Florence too. Cosimo de' Medici might begin as *pater patriae*, 'the first citizen' of the republic; he would end by founding a grand-ducal dynasty that would last for centuries. When we remember this we cannot assume that even the Venetian constitution was proof against overthrow from above by an ambitious doge who, as a war-leader, might build up a new form of patronage and power. Such at least may have been the fear which inspired the Doge Mocenigo to warn his fellow-noblemen against electing, as his successor, Francesco Foscari.

And who was the man who aroused these fears? The great Venetian aristocrats are always somewhat impersonal figures. The very system, with its intense jealousy of individual power, tended to depersonalize them. For it was the essential character of the Venetian Republic that all personality was ruthlessly subordinated to the state. Instead of the cut-throat private enterprise of Genoa, or the brilliant individualism of Florence, here we see only an impersonal state-capitalism, an implacable 'reason of state', an official state culture entirely hostile to 'the cult of personality'. So the official records of Venice do not bring to life even a controversial personality like Foscari. And yet he certainly was a controversial character. His whole reign shows it. And it is shown, first of all, by the battle over his election.

For Foscari, it is clear, was determined to be doge. Moreover, from the point of view of Mocenigo and his friends, he was an outsider. That was why they so feared him. He was young – at fifty he was the youngest of the candidates. He was also regarded as poor by the great 'nabob' families, though he had enriched himself by marriage. He was experienced: after sharing his father's exile in Egypt, he had held most of the great elective offices of state. Above all, he was – what Venice particularly distrusted – ambitious and head of a party. Moreover, this party was particularly suspect to the great mercantile families like the Mocenigo who customarily ruled Venice, for it was a party of 'the poor nobles', the lesser noblemen, the radicals, the 'Westerners' who favoured war by land, as distinct from the Easterners with their Levantine interests. We are told that, as Procurator of St Mark, Foscari had used the large cash balances in his hands to create this following; he had relieved the wants of poor noblemen, given portions to their daughters, and made himself dangerous by their support. No doubt he had won other support by his merits too. And finally, as was soon to be shown, he was a consummate election-manager.

For when the forty-one electors met, Foscari was not the favourite. He was too impulsive, too controversial, too committed to a policy. The favourite was Pietro Loredan, the Admiral of the Republic, who was also determined on office. But Loredan made the mistake of speaking confidently on his own behalf, which lost him votes. Foscari was much more prudent. Although his rivals did not know it, he had already, from the beginning of his election, nine votes safely in his pocket. These voters acted as a bloc, and they did not reveal themselves until they had quietly contributed to shoot down all other candidates. Instead, they allowed it to appear that they too were opposed to Foscari. Then, suddenly, at the ninth ballot, they all plumped for the outsider and carried him into the ducal chair.

Thus began the longest ducal reign in the long history of the Venetian Republic. Foscari, who always liked *panache*, hastened to celebrate his victory. For a whole year he dazzled the city with feasts and pageants. The new *Sala Maggiore* was opened with splendid ceremony. At the end of the year he fetched his wife, the *Dogaressa*, in triumph to the Palace in the ducal galley, the *Bucintoro*, attended by the noblewomen of Venice. These spectacles, incidentally, were something of a sop to the non-noble citizens of Venice who, in that year, lost their last vestigial rights in the government of the Republic; but their personal emphasis may not have pleased the aristocracy. Then the Doge settled down to the business of government.

What was the character of Foscari's reign? We can describe it under three heads. First, there were pageants, feasts and spectacles of unexampled magnificence. Secondly, there was, as Mocenigo had prophesied, constant war for the *Terraferma*. Thirdly, there was the undying jealousy and hatred of those whom he had defeated, and particularly of the Loredan family whom he had pipped at the post. The pageantry made the outward splendour of the reign; the war its real content; the hatred of the Loredan brought it to a tragic end.

The outward splendour was shown in many ways. New palaces, public and private, rose by the Grand Canal and the Lagoon. The Rialto bridge was rebuilt. Paolo Uccello worked in S. Marco, Vivarini in S. Pantaleone. Famous visitors were received with ever greater pomp and show. In 1428 it was the Prince of Portugal whom the *Bucintoro*, escorted by a fleet of boats, fetched in to a banquet among 250 ladies dressed in cloth-of-gold and silk and jewels. In 1438 the Emperor of Byzantium himself, in his great need, condescended to come in person to Italy, with his brother the Despot of the Morea and the Patriarch of Constantinople, ready to accept the supremacy of the Roman Church in return for Western aid. When the *Bucintoro*, covered with red silk and golden emblems, carried the imperial party from the Lido, the whole Lagoon was full of boats, flaunting banners and playing music, with oarsmen clad in cloth-of-gold. In 1452 even this event was eclipsed when the Emperor of the West followed the Emperor of the East to Venice, and was drawn in triumph by the *Bucintoro* and the gaily-coloured boats up to the Grand Canal. Next year the last Emperor of the East had perished in the sack of his capital and the Doge Foscari would receive in Venice the fugitive scholars and salvaged treasures of Byzantium.

In Byzantine eyes, the fall of Byzantium was due to Venetian indifference. All through the reign of Foscari (it was said) the military resources of Venice had been turned too exclusively to the west. But this was hardly a fair judgement. The threat from the west was a real threat, as the fate of Genoa showed. And besides, in the first year of Foscari's reign there had been a great success in the east. In that year the Greek governor of Salonika, the emporium of Thessalian corn (Venice lived on imported corn) and the northern watchtower of the Aegean, gave or sold the city to Venice rather than lose it to the Turks. So the east, it seemed, was safe. Meanwhile, the Republic had obtained an invaluable ally for war in the west. It happened that at this time the greatest *condottiere* in Italy, the man who had himself recreated the power of the Visconti in Milan, now, on some slight, deserted his master and offered his services to Venice. This was Francesco Bussone, known as Carmagnola. The Venetians could hardly resist such an opportunity. They hired Carmagnola as their general. It was in the double security provided by Salonika in the east and Carmagnola in the west that the Republic, in 1425, made a league with Florence and declared war on the revived, aggressive power of the Visconti.

Thus within two years of his accession, Foscari was carrying out the policy that had always been associated with him. There can be no doubt that it was his policy: we have the speech with which he persuaded the Republic to make war. Of course, given the Venetian constitution, we can be sure it was not his policy alone. He had only influence, not authority. Nevertheless, it seems that it was his influence, combined with circumstances, which turned and held the scales. Even twelve years later, in 1437, we see how powerful that personal influence was. In that year the Doge had sat, day after day, at the bedside of his son Domenico, dying of the plague. His supporters feared that he too would catch the infection, and then what would they do? The lives of many, they said, depended on his: if he were to fail, the fortune of the state would be in peril. . . . Clearly, if men could say this, the Doge was no mere chairman. The forward policy of the state depended on him. Perhaps it depended particularly on him in 1437 when the initial advantages, which made the western war popular, had gone.

For in fact neither Salonika nor Carmagnola lived up to their promise. Salonika was the first to go. In 1430 the Turks captured and sacked it. The slaughter was terrible, the loss final. From now on the Aegean Sea lay open to the Turks, with the wealth of Venice in it, scattered among subject islands whose Greek inhabitants preferred (or thought they preferred) Turkish conquest to Venetian exploitation. In the same year an attempt was made to assassinate the Doge. As for Carmagnola, like so many *condottieri*, he proved thoroughly unsatisfactory. At the head of the greatest army that had been seen in Italy, he somehow failed to be as victorious in Venetian as he had been in Milanese service, and he remained suspiciously familiar with his old employer, his present enemy, the Duke of Milan. The Venetians offered to make him lord of Milan if he would only conquer it, but still he consumed time and money in mere parades or took cures at the baths of Abano. Finally the Venetians lost patience. With their usual circumspection, they did nothing rashly or openly. They invited Carmagnola to Venice to meet the Doge and discuss future strategy. He never saw the Doge. Instead, he was whisked from the palace to prison, tortured, tried and condemned. When his sentence was discussed, the Doge voted for mercy, but was overruled. Carmagnola was sentenced to death and beheaded. That was in 1432. After that the Republic employed other, less dangerous *condottieri*.

So by 1432 Foscari's policy was in difficulties on all fronts. He sensed the difficulties, and next year asked to resign his office. It is said that he asked again in 1442 and again in 1446: we can see that he was an impulsive man, impatient of obstruction, easily discouraged by defeat. But the Venetian aristocracy, or perhaps his supporters in it, would not allow him to resign. On each occasion they reminded him that, by the constitution, he could not resign except with the assent of the six Councillors and the Greater Council. It was an answer which he was later to remember and use, against his enemies.

Meanwhile the forward policy continued. The war for the *Terraferma* went on. It was very long: it lasted, with brief interludes, for thirty years. It was also very costly: the first ten years alone cost seven million ducats. There were dramatic incidents in it: the bringing of Venetian ships over the mountains from the river Adige to Lake Garda was such an incident. There were disappointments too: the Florentines, out of commercial rivalry, gradually slid over towards the side of Milan. But in the end it was successful. It carried the westward frontier of the *Terraferma* to its furthest and final limit: the provinces of Brescia and Bergamo were incorporated in it, and the Doge solemnly received them as imperial fiefs. He also obtained Ravenna as a papal fief. And before his death he inspired and signed a new treaty: a league with Florence and Milan, Rome and Naples, to preserve the liberty of Italy. It would have been a great triumph had it lasted. All we can say is that at least it outlasted Foscari.

So the pageants and the war went on. But meanwhile what of the third feature of Foscari's reign, the enmity of his rivals? That too was very long – long and bitter, as Venetian enmities always were. For if Venice, with its exaltation of state service, was free from the strife of parties which ruined every other Italian republic, it was enlivened, even more than they, by fierce personal and family feuds. In particular, the Doge Foscari never escaped the bitter hatred of the Loredan family. He had defeated them in 1423. They remembered their defeat, and in after years, with their allies the Donà and the Barbarigo, mercilessly persecuted him at his weakest point: his family.

At the time of his election, one objection to Foscari had been his large family, who, it was suggested, would feed on the resources of the state. This danger did not materialize, for of his five sons, four died young of the plague. The last survivor, who alone had heirs, and to whom the Doge was devoted, was Jacopo, a young man of cultivated tastes – a Greek scholar and collector of manuscripts – but indiscreet ways. In 1441 his marriage to Lucrezia Contarini had been one of the most magnificent of the many spectacles which the Doge gave to the city. There had been boat-races, feasts and illuminations, scarlet and cloth-of-gold, a great tournament before 30,000 people in the Piazza San Marco, and 300 horsemen had ridden in cavalcade over the Grand Canal on a specially built bridge of barges. But in 1445 Jacopo Foscari was secretly denounced for receiving gifts from Filippo Visconti, the Duke of Milan. At that time Francesco Loredan, the nephew of the defeated candidate, was one of the three chiefs of the Council of Ten, the secret political police of the Republic. His ally Ermolao Donà was another. At once the Ten decided to act. They ordered the arrest of Jacopo. The Doge and his kinsmen were excluded from all deliberations on the matter. Then sentence was pronounced: Jacopo was exiled to Nauplia in Greece, a Venetian colony, and all his goods confiscated. In vain the Dogaressa begged to see her son: the orders were given, and the name of the Doge himself was placed, with ruthless, impersonal irony, at their head. In the end there was a hitch and then, on grounds of health, the place of exile was changed to Treviso, which was both nearer and more comfortable; but the humiliation to the Doge was no less. It was after this humiliation that Foscari made his third attempt to resign; but he was forced to stay and drink the dregs of the cup.

At first the Doge scored a point. In 1447, he made a moving appeal to the Ten, and the Ten consented, not on grounds of humanity but (a typically Venetian reason) 'because it is necessary at this time to have a prince whose mind is free and serene, able to serve the republic', to remit the exile of Jacopo, now sick in body and mind. But the reunion of the Jacob and the Benjamin of the house of Foscari did not last long. In 1450 the Loredan family found another pretext, and began again.

For in 1450 one of Jacopo Foscari's judges, Ermolao Donà, was murdered, and Jacopo was at once suspected. Again the Doge's son was arrested; he was even tortured; and although nothing was proved and he was probably innocent (another man afterwards confessed to the crime), the Ten, having gone so far, were afraid to go back. They sentenced him, without proof, to exile, and this time there were no second thoughts: he was carried off to Crete. But even in Crete his movements were watched, his indiscretions observed; and in 1456 it was reported to the Ten that he was planning, or at least discussing, revenge with foreign help. The Ten (of whom Jacopo Loredan was now one of the chiefs) immediately decided that the matter was 'of the greatest importance'. So once again the Doge's son was fetched back for a third trial.

And now began the final tragedy of the Doge's reign, the tragedy which Byron converted into his drama *The Two Foscari*. At his trial it was admitted that Jacopo's projects were entirely academic, and that, being in Crete, he could do little or nothing to harm the Republic; but that made no difference. He was tortured, and judged guilty, and the remorseless Jacopo Loredan urged that he be publicly beheaded as a traitor between the columns of the piazza. Even the Ten drew the line at this, and the prisoner was sentenced to renewed exile in Crete, this time in prison. Before returning to Crete, he was allowed to see his father, now eighty-four years old. He begged the Doge to intercede for him. 'Jacopo,' replied the old man, 'go and obey your country's commands, and seek no more.' But when his son had gone, he threw himself upon a chair, weeping and crying, 'O pietà grande!' Within a few months he was shattered by the news that his last son had died in Crete.

The Doge's distress was his enemies' opportunity, and they now decided to complete their victory. The Doge, they said, was too old; he was distracted by grief – the grief they had caused him; he could no longer attend to business. Therefore he must go. The Council of Ten met and decided to demand his abdication. Their message was brought to the Doge by his enemy Jacopo Loredan. But now the old man had his revenge. He turned on them the argument they had used against him in the past: by the law, he said, he could not abdicate unless the Councillors proposed and the Greater Council agreed. Here, too, he obeyed his country's laws. Baffled, the Ten consulted again, reinterpreted the law to suit their convenience, and told the Doge of their reinterpretation; but still he kept to the old interpretation and would not move. Finally they sent him an order: he was to resign and clear out of the ducal palace within eight days. If he did so, he would receive an adequate salary and a doge's burial; if not, he would be driven out and all his goods confiscated.

It was a completely illegal demand, but the Doge was powerless. He gave in. The ducal ring was taken from his finger and broken, the ducal cap from his head. He promised to leave the palace. Then, seeing pity in the eye of one of his visitors, he called to him and taking his hand said 'Whose son are you?' 'I am the son of messer Marin Memmo' was the reply. The Doge said, 'He is my old friend. Ask him to come and visit me so that we may go in a boat at sunset to visit the monasteries.' Next day he left the palace. Wearing his old scarlet robe of state, he stepped forth, bent but unaided except by his staff. As he went to the stone steps leading down to the water, his brother Marco urged him to go to his gondola by the covered stair. 'No,' replied the Doge, 'I will go down by the same stair by which I came up to my dukedom.' A week later he died: of rage, it was said, on hearing the bells announcing the election of his successor.

The people of Venice were indignant at the indecent deposition of the Doge who had reigned so long, who had enjoyed all the publicity of government, whose figure and personality were so striking, whom the Emperors of East and West had visited, and who had given them such splendid shows. There was much murmuring against the usurpation of the Ten, and even the Doge's enemies were now a little ashamed at not waiting another week for a natural death. When Foscari was dead they gave him a splendid funeral, in spite of the protests of the ex-Dogaressa at this solemn humbug. He was buried in the church of the Frari, and a

majestic Gothic-Renaissance monument commemorated his achievement: the conquest of the *Terraferma*. Then the Ten withdrew a little
from the invidious limelight. Nevertheless, they had won, even if they
had indecently rubbed in, a notable victory. From now on the constitution was not only clearly oligarchical: it was also absolutely clear
where the centre of oligarchical power lay. It lay with that inner ring of
(for practical purposes) self-elected councillors who could mobilize,
even against the doge, the Council of Ten.

Thus ended the long reign of Francesco Foscari. It had ended, as it
had begun, in bitter personal controversy, and even today historians
dispute its significance. It has been said that it was Foscari who
diverted Venice from east to west, sacrificing Salonika and Constantinople to Bergamo and Brescia: a diversion (it is added) which led to
disastrous consequences, fifty years later, when the powers of Europe
united against what the contemporary French historian Philippe de
Commynes called 'the insatiable cupidity of the Venetians and their
lust for power'. And yet, we may answer, could any other doge really
have acted differently? Already before Foscari the dilemma had been
there: if the land-powers of Europe would not unite against the Turks, a
sea-power could not defeat them alone; and could Venice ignore the
western threat, or the warning example of Genoa? Other historians
have dwelt on the fear of princely despotism: they have represented the
Loredan as incorruptible republicans, Catos inexorable in the cause of
the constitution. But is there in fact any evidence that Foscari ever
entertained thoughts of altering the constitution? Perhaps in his early
years he did (though we can only judge from the suspicion he inspired);
but how could an old man of eighty have threatened the established
power of the oligarchy? In the end it was not he but his enemies who
broke the constitution. He submitted to its most humiliating rules,
malevolently applied; they broke through its last restraints in order to
humble him.

Nevertheless we must admit that, in Venetian history, Foscari's
reign was crucial. Whatever his personal aims, they were in the end
subordinated to and absorbed by the impersonal Venetian system.
In his reign the Milanese republic gave its last gasp; the
duchy of the Visconti foundered only to be replaced, in the end, by the
duchy of the Sforza. Meanwhile the great Florentine republic was
converted into the duchy of the Medici. But the jealous republicans of
Venice, whatever their motives, and whether they were right or wrong
in their personal suspicions, positively strengthened their Republic.
They accepted the policy, and then crushed the personality, of the one

man who might conceivably have recreated the old ducal power, so long undermined. And their victory over him was final. After 1457 the Republic no longer feared the doge. Up to that date, seven doges had been assassinated, nine had been blinded and exiled, twelve had abdicated, one had been sentenced to death and beheaded, two had been deposed. But after that date all is peace. The Venetian constitution survived intact through the era of the native princes. It kept its independence when the other Italian states fell under foreign rule; it resisted the Counter-Reformation Papacy; and in the seventeenth century it would be praised, by English Republicans and English Whigs, as the most perfect model of government for any mercantile state which aspired to be free, effective and independent.

Sources

Marino Sanudo, *Vite dei duchi di Venezia*, in Muratori, *Rerum Italicarum Scriptores*, Vol. XXII (Milan, 1733). *Francisci Barbari et aliorum ad ipsum epistolae*, ed. A. M. Quirini (Brescia, 1743). S. Romanin, *Storia Documentata di Venezia* (Venice, 1855). Charles Yriarte, *La Vie d'un Patricien de Venise au 16e siècle* (Paris, 1874). Remigio Sabbadini, *Centotrenta Lettere Inedite di Francesco Barbaro* . . . (Salerno, 1884). Horatio Brown, *Venice, an Historical Sketch* (1903). Horatio Brown, *Studies in Venetian History* (1907), Vol. I, 'The Venetian Constitution', and 'Carmagnola, a Soldier of Fortune'. H. Kretschmayr, *Geschichte von Venedig*, Vol. II (Gotha, 1920). Percy Gothein, *Francesco Barbaro Frühthumanismus u. Staatskuust in Venedig* (Berlin, 1932). Roberto Cessi, *Storia di Venezia* (Venice, 1944). F. C. Lane, *Andrea Barbarigo Merchant of Venice 1418–1449* (Baltimore, 1944). Yves Renouard, *Les Hommes d'Affaires Italiens du Moyen Age* (Paris, 1949). Nino Valeri, 'Venezia nella Crisi Italiana del Rinascimento', in *La Civiltà Veneziana del Quattrocento* (Florence, 1957).

2

The Emperor Maximilian I, as patron of the arts

In the sixteenth century the Habsburg dynasty was the greatest power in Europe. From its several capitals in Madrid and Brussels, Vienna and Prague, Augsburg, Milan and Naples, it dominated the continent. It also dominated the arts. Literature and music, painting and sculpture all received their impulse from it. This great power and patronage, which was exercised continuously till the Thirty Years War, was founded by a man who, at his death in 1519, was generally regarded as a complete failure, the Emperor Maximilian I.

Historians have never agreed about Maximilian. The greatest of German historians, Leopold von Ranke, described him as 'a prince of whom we possess many portraits, and yet all seem different'. Maximilian himself began the trouble. No ruler of his time took such trouble to present himself to contemporaries and his image to posterity; and yet the character which he presented was never the same. Nineteenth-century German historians, less cautious than Ranke, found what they sought in this fascinating but enigmatic personality. So he was presented by some as the first modern ruler and by others as the last medieval knight; as the 'new monarch' who founded archives, patronized humanists and reformed universities, and as the romantic dreamer whose life was enclosed in a world of antique chivalry; as the forward-looking champion of German imperial unity and as the reactionary enemy of German constitutional freedom. He has been cried up, not least by himself, as the model humanist prince, the universal man of the Renaissance. He has been ridiculed by posterity as a feckless adventurer, a Don Quixote whose head was full of magnificent fantasies and unattainable ambitions and who, in the end, achieved nothing – or at least nothing except a myth.

For at least the myth remains.[1] The learned humanists of his court began it; but they were not its sole authors, or it would have perished with them. It survived among the unlettered German people who would always look up, and back, to 'Kaiser Max' as a folk-hero. To the sharp-eyed officials of the Italian cities – to Machiavelli who visited him as a diplomat and to Guicciardini who observed him as a historian – he was a feckless politician, unpredictable, prodigal, indecisive and, above all, penniless, never able to finance his successive extravagant schemes. But to the Germans his virtues always triumphed over his faults. He was martial, generous and brave. He 'lived in the saddle' and showed himself everywhere to his people, giving them splendid shows: pageantry, tournaments and feasts. He was also a great hunter, 'one of the greatest hunters of all times', courting personal danger in the chase and stalking the chamois among the precipitous Alpine crags. It was because he wasted his substance in such absurd sports, said Pope Julius II, that he never had enough money for serious things. Above all, he was just, tolerant, accessible, able to charm. So his fame lived on. Even his prodigality became a virtue. He would not, he told his father, be 'a king of money' but 'a king of men'. And men remembered him, as he wished to be remembered; for, as he wrote, in the true spirit of the Renaissance, 'if a man, in his lifetime, does not provide for his own memory, he will not be remembered after his death, but will be forgotten with his passing-bell. Thus the money which I spend for the perpetuation of my memory is not lost. On the contrary, to spare such money would be to stifle my future memory.'

Maximilian certainly perpetuated his memory. He lived on in popular record, popular poetry, and always as a just, brave, generous, romantic prince. Luther loved him, pagan Catholic though he was. Myths clustered around him. He was soon woven into the Faust legend: did not the famous abbot Trithemius, the great scholar-magician of his time, conjure up for him the ghosts of Alexander the Great, Julius Caesar, and the bride whom he had vainly sought, Anne of Brittany? The young Goethe introduced him, somewhat pitilessly, into his early tragedy of *Goetz*; but afterwards, in the second part of *Faust*, he weakened, as we all weaken, towards that imperial charmer who was also, beyond his aggressive, flamboyant politics, a great artist: a figure, as a German scholar has said, 'from Shakespeare's royal dramas rather than a powerful, determined ruler'.[2]

But Maximilian's myth was not a popular myth only. It was also a dynastic myth. Though he achieved so little in politics and war, it was he who, by his dynastic marriages, laid the foundations of Habsburg greatness, and it was he who, by harnessing all the arts, gave to his dynasty an aura which, till then, it had lacked. Consequently it was to him, always to him, that his successors looked back for their inspiration. They saw him as the second founder of the dynasty, the first creator of its legend: a legend which transcended politics, nationality, even religion.

For before him, what could they find? Maximilian's father, Frederick III, who reigned for fifty-three years, was a cold, unromantic man, without culture or charm, 'almost stupid' as the humanist pope Pius II called him, a mean, puritanical egoist whose main achievement had been to concentrate in his hands, and pass on to his son, the whole Habsburg inheritance in Austria together with the Holy Roman Empire, now practically hereditary in his house. In the court of his father, at Wiener Neustadt, Vienna or Linz, Maximilian could have learned little of the arts. Frederick III built fortresses for defence, and walls covered with his coats-of-arms, and one fine chapel at Wiener Neustadt to be his own mausoleum; but he was uninterested in the new humanism, in books or works of art, and if he collected jewels, it was in rough, uncut state, as a financial investment. His greatest monument was the splendid tomb which was to preserve his memory, but which he would not see finished and which would prove too big for the chapel for which it was designed.[3]

All this world of his father, with its torpid, kill-joy conservatism, its careful accounting, its narrow defensive aims, was repudiated by the young Maximilian. But where could he discover an alternative to it? Brought up in Wiener Neustadt, he studied and hunted. His mind was quick, his interests wide; but he could hardly discover a taste for art in that fortress city, or indeed, at that time, in Austria. The great centres of European art, as of learning, were in the courts and cities of Italy and Flanders, or in the capitalist cities of South Germany, the imperial free cities of Augsburg and Nuremberg, the home of the new German school of Albrecht Dürer.

As emperor, after 1493, Maximilian would discover Augsburg, the city of Augustus, the imperial city *par excellence*. War and politics would bring him into Italy. But his first introduction to the high art of Europe was in Flanders. It came with his betrothal to Mary, the only child and heiress of Charles the Bold, the last and most flamboyant of those great patrons of all the arts, the Valois dukes of Burgundy.

To his father, the old emperor Frederick III, this marriage had seemed eminently desirable, for the Duke of Burgundy, ruler of all the Netherlands, was the richest prince in Europe. Others, however, had similar appetites. In particular, Louis XI of France wished to annex Burgundy to his crown, and when its duke was killed in battle, he claimed it as his inheritance and its heiress for his son. But the Netherlands stood by their promise and called on Maximilian, then eighteen years old, to come and claim his bride and defend her inheritance. He came, he married, he conquered; and he was in turn conquered both by the charms of his bride and by the splendour of this rich and civilized Burgundian world, where the proudest chivalry in Europe was sustained by the trade and industry of the Netherlands. 'Had we but peace,' he wrote, 'we would sit here as in a rose-garden.'

Unfortunately, he did not have peace, and the idyllic life in Flanders would not last long. After five years of nuptial bliss, Maximilian's young bride was killed by a fall from her horse and the proud nobles and rich burghers of the Netherlands refused any further rights to the widowed Austrian prince-consort. At one time they even imprisoned him and threatened to kill him, and he had to be rescued by his father. They also secured control of his two children – his son Philip the Fair, their new duke, and his daughter Margaret, who, after the death of her brother and two husbands, would remain there as regent for her nephew, the Archduke Charles, afterwards the greatest of all the Habsburgs, the Emperor Charles V.

After these disagreeable experiences, Maximilian would turn his back on Flanders. He would be recalled to Vienna to defeat the Hungarian invaders. His father's death would make him emperor – for the election was almost a formality. As emperor, he would have to wrestle with German princes and cities, wage war – unsuccessful war – in Switzerland and Italy. Nevertheless he would always look back with nostalgia to that brief taste of Burgundian splendour, and to his first bride whom he would love till his death. In his restless, even aimless, career of strife, he would recall the wonderful stability of court-life in Burgundy, with its castles and chivalry and pageantry, its hierarchical aristocratic society, crowned and consecrated by the Order of the Golden Fleece. In Burgundy, his life had had a purpose. Thereafter, its substance had gone: exiled from that stable world, he would pursue phantoms of grandeur, and seek compensation in empty rhetoric, gestures and postures. Instead of self-fulfilment, there would be self-aggrandisement, self-dramatization, self-pity.[4]

If Maximilian's career was one of continuous war, we must admit that this was largely by his own choice, for he was generally the aggressor, or could be seen as such. His marriage with the heiress of Burgundy posed a threat to France, for Burgundy and Flanders enclosed France from the north and east. Soon afterwards, Maximilian perpetrated another matrimonial attack: having lost his Burgundian bride, he married, by proxy, Anne, the heiress of the Duke of Brittany, and thus threatened France from the west also. Louis XI reacted promptly. He got the Pope to declare the marriage void and then caused his own son to repudiate his marriage to the Emperor's daughter and marry the heiress of Brittany instead. Outwitted, Maximilian had to accept defeat. He consoled himself by marrying into the family of Sforza, dukes of Milan, and thus gaining an entry into Italian politics, which would soon turn to long, expensive, unprofitable Italian wars.

Maximilian's matrimonial schemes never ceased. They were an instrument of his vast ambitions. But there were other instruments too. When his own second wife died, he saw an interesting opportunity. It happened that, at that time, the Pope, his old enemy, the wicked warrior-pope Julius II, was very ill, at death's door. So Maximilian, as he explained to his daughter, decided not to marry again 'or ever again pursue naked women', but to lobby the cardinals and have himself elected pope. This prospect he found very attractive. He enjoyed the idea of 'becoming a priest, and afterwards a saint, so that after my death you will have to worship me; of which I shall be very proud'. Three thousand ducats, he reckoned, would suffice to square the cardinals, since some of them already favoured him. He signed his letter, 'your good father Maxi, future pope'. Unfortunately Pope Julius recovered, and Maximilian's ambition of being the first pope-emperor was not fulfilled.[5]

Nor was his other ambition, of leading a crusade against the Turks. This was a project which haunted him all his life. His father, the mean and practical Frederick III, had himself been on a pilgrimage to Jerusalem, but had spent his time going incognito round the bazaars buying jewels and making bargains; after which he had returned to Austria, ignored all appeals from the Pope, and allowed Constantinople to fall to the Turks without lifting a finger. Maximilian longed to redress that wrong. He dreamed of leading a crusade and becoming Emperor of the East as well as of the West. Unfortunately, by his time, the Popes were less interested, and the affairs of Flanders, France, Switzerland, Germany and Italy kept Maximilian in Europe. Nevertheless, the idea of a crusade never left him. It would become almost a fixation, the ideal mission of his dynasty, part of the ideological inheritance which he would bequeath to his successors.

Seen politically, Maximilian's career is not impressive. Pushed out of Burgundy, outwitted by France, blocked in Germany, defeated in

Switzerland, unsuccessful in Italy, unable to establish imperial power in the West, disappointed in his dreams of conquest in the East, he seems a universal failure. He did not even succeed in being crowned in Rome, as his father and earlier emperors had been. That was not for lack of trying; but always there had been some obstacle: funds had run out, or the Venetians had refused him transit. So he simply declared himself 'elected emperor' in his own city of Trent. Here too his successors followed his example: they gave up that ceremonial coronation in Rome which he had been unable to achieve. For in this, as in so many other things, Maximilian imposed himself on his successors. He imposed himself by his very illusions: illusions to which he gave reality and force by his propaganda – that is, by his patronage of the arts.

To Maximilian, all the arts were propaganda: dynastic and personal propaganda. He was not an aesthete, a lover of art for its own sake, like some later members of his family. Always he saw a purpose in art, and patronized it for that purpose; and as his ambitions failed, so his propaganda became more intense: so intense that, like his matrimonial policy, it bore rich fruit in succeeding generations.

Where did it begin? Whence was it nourished? Not, I think, in Burgundy, although the 'joyous entries' and chivalric pageantry of the Burgundian court inspired some of the forms which it took. Nor in Italy, although the Sforza family, the patrons of Leonardo, may have suggested some ideas: the great equestrian statue which Maximilian planned for himself in the church of SS. Ulrich and Afra in Augsburg may well have been inspired by Leonardo's proposed statue of Francesco Sforza, of which Maximilian had seen the model. Precisely because Maximilian's love of art was so functional, so dynastic, it grew out of dynastic – that is, Austrian and German – sources and was only enriched by foreign contacts. It began, perhaps, at Innsbrück, the capital of Maximilian's favourite province, Tyrol.

Tyrol had been ruled, until 1490, by his uncle the Archduke Sigmund who, being childless, declared Maximilian his heir; so Maximilian ruled there as effective prince before he came to the empire. It was there that he first applied his new ideas of government and war, and there also that he was introduced to the arts which had been developed and patronized by his uncle. For Tyrol, on the route to Italy, was open to foreign influence, and Sigmund, who had artistic tastes, had made the court at Innsbrück a centre of culture.[6] From him Maximilian inherited artists, musicians and craftsmen, especially (since Tyrol was a land of mines and forges) metal-craftsmen, engravers, armourers, makers of exquisite weapons, elaborate coats of mail, rich saddles, harness and caparisons. He also inherited the mint which his uncle had established at Hall, near Innsbrück. Maximilian exploited all these opportunities. He built hunting-lodges and towers, learned the techniques of the craftsmen, himself invented new weapons and new bits for horses, and used the mint to disseminate his own effigy throughout the country. Later, as Emperor, he would flood Germany with his coins and medals. No other ruler took such trouble over his own likeness. Like a Roman Emperor, he used his coins as imperial propaganda; and he insisted that every detail, every new stamping of his portrait or his arms or his seal, should be submitted for his personal approval.

Like a Roman Emperor. . . . Always Maximilian remembered his imperial mission and his imperial pedigree, and the function of the arts, as he saw it, was to represent and glorify both the mission and the pedigree. Within those dynastic limits, he was a universal patron. He himself drew up the programme for his artists, he himself drafted the propaganda, he himself suggested, checked, corrected the details.

He was also himself an author. In the notes which he wrote, or caused to be written, throughout his active life, he described his various literary plans. He proposed to write a whole library of 130 books, and of these he noted that 30 had been written. Some of the work he would delegate to his secretaries, or to the humanist scholars whom he patronized, but always he would himself supervise the execution and correct the detail. The books were to be historical, genealogical, autobiographical and technical. They were to glorify the house of Habsburg; to set out its aims, and his own; to describe his own life, ambitions, and political maxims; and to present his encyclopaedic knowledge of the arts and crafts, the geography, history and resources of his hereditary dominions. All these books, moreover, were to be illustrated and published in Germany. For Maximilian, with his technological interests, was quick to see the usefulness of the new art of printing, and German printers and woodcut-artists were the best in the world. In his travels, Maximilian carried with him his notes, manuscripts, drafts and illustrations. He distracted himself from state affairs to dictate plans of his work to his secretaries. At one moment of the Swiss war, while crossing Lake Constance in a storm, he dictated his autobiography, in Latin, to the humanist scholar Willibald Pirckheimer. In his will, he urged his executors to see to the publication of his complete works.

The most famous of Maximilian's works, predictably, are monuments to his own glory and that of his house. The least egotistical of them are the *Hunt-book* and the *Fishing Book*,[7] which were compiled on his orders by his Chief Forester and Chief Fish-warden. These describe all the game and fish to be found in all the provinces of Austria, beginning with his favourite Tyrol. Delightful illustrations in colour portray peasants catching crayfish in nets or fishing with rod and line in Alpine waters, and adventurous huntsmen pursuing the chamois with hounds and spears on dizzy snow-clad slopes. More personal are the autobiographical romances – the poem *Teuerdank*, published in 1517, and the prose romance *Weisskunig*, which remained in manuscript for 250 years. These were written by Maximilian with the aid of his secretaries. The former describes, in allegorical form, his adventures in search of his Burgundian bride. It has been called 'a literary monument of almost unrelieved heaviness'.[8] The latter sets out his educational and political maxims for the benefit of his two grandsons, the future emperors Charles V and Ferdinand I. Both these works are illustrated with woodcuts, mainly by Hans Burgkmair of Augsburg and Hans Schäuffelein of Nördlingen, a follower of Dürer. Some of those in *Teuerdank* are by Dürer himself. Other artists employed regularly by Maximilian were Leonhard Beck of Augsburg and Dürer's pupil Hans Springinklee.

The most formal of Maximilian's personal works are his designs for triumphal arches, solemn processions and imperial pageantry. Three of these are famous: the *Freydal*, which portrays the tournaments and masques in which he had taken part in Burgundy; the *Ehrenpforte* or 'arch of honour', a huge three-dimensional work composed of ninety-two sheets under the direction of Dürer and published in 1517; and finally, greatest of all, the *Triumphzug*, a magnificent procession illustrating all the Emperor's ambitions, achievements and tastes: his battles, hunts, tournaments, music, mechanical inventions, visionary plans. This *Triumphzug* was first designed by Jörg Kölderer of Innsbrück, one of the artists whom Maximilian had taken over from his uncle Sigmund, but the completed work was by the Regensburg master, Albrecht Altdorfer. The designs may have been based on Mantegna's famous *Triumphs of Julius Caesar* – the Emperor regarded Caesar as one of his 'ancestors'. It too was published, in 1526, after Maximilian's death.[9]

These were the principal works written or commissioned by Maximilian. But there were many others for which he supplied the inspiration and commissioned the illustrations. There were histories, like the Latin lives of his father and himself, written for him by the humanist Joseph Grünpeck and illustrated in colour by South German artists. There were *Zeugbücher*, illustrated catalogues of the arms in his armouries throughout Austria. There were also works of devotion, like the prayer-books which he designed, in German and Latin. One of these – made for his favourite order, the Knights of St George – was illustrated by Dürer, Altdorfer, Burgkmair, Lucas Cranach, Hans Baldung Grien, and other artists.[10] These and such works created around the Emperor a continuing group of artists to whom he gave special privileges and sometimes titles of nobility. Apart from those already mentioned, we should single out his chosen court-painter, Bernhardin Strigel of Memmingen, who painted numerous portraits of the Emperor and his family, and Ludwig Konraiter, whom, like Kölderer, he had inherited from the Archduke Sigmund. There were also armourers and saddlers, metal-workers and medallists; he brought the great sculptors of Nuremberg into dependence on him; and we should not forget his musicians – Paul Hofhaimer, whom he had inherited from uncle Sigmund, the Fleming Heinrich Isaac, and Isaac's pupil the Swiss Ludwig Senfl – who made the court, first of Innsbrück, then of Vienna and Wiener Neustadt, famous throughout Europe for its Flemish polyphony.[11]

It has been said of Maximilian that if he had had a fixed capital, he would have made it a museum of the arts unparalleled in Northern Europe. But even if he had completed all his projects, one thing would have been lacking. Unlike the princes of Flanders and Italy – unlike his own descendants, who would inherit both Flanders and Italy – Maximilian did not commission great religious pictures. His priorities were different. His heroes were not the heroes of the Church but of the dynasty. His saints – for he did commission a series of saints – were 'the saints of the kinship of the house of Habsburg'. His buildings were not churches but monuments to the house of Habsburg. If he extended his loyalty beyond the house of Habsburg, it was only to include, among his 'ancestors', the earlier 'Roman emperors' – Julius Caesar, Charlemagne, and the German heroes and kings. He planned, had the funds not run out, a great monument to the previous German emperors in the cathedral of Speyer. But, ultimately, all these 'ancestors' looked forward to him. He longed to see his own statue dominating the church in Augsburg. The most famous of Dürer's paintings commissioned by him – his last commission, unfinished at his death – was the face which he preferred above all others: his own.

For we cannot escape the egotism of Maximilian. In his youth, he portrayed himself as a hero: the romantic *Teuerdank*, the young 'white king'. In his old age, when so many of his plans had gone awry, he saw himself as a martyr. 'No man since Christ,' he once declared, 'has suffered as I have done'; and when he faced death, he emphasized that martyrdom, ordering that his corpse be covered with lime 'and exhibited to the whole world' as evidence of the vanity of human life. However, this temporary humility did not divert him from his old ambition of posthumous fame. He had already taken steps to ensure for himself a massive, magnificent tomb.

For fifteen years Maximilian had been planning his tomb.[12] At first he entrusted the work to a newly appointed court artist, Gilg Sesselschreiber of Munich. The tomb was to be on a huge scale. His own figure, kneeling on a bronze sarcophagus adorned with twenty-four reliefs of his great achievements, was to be surrounded by thirty-four life-size statues of his mourning 'ancestors', while a hundred smaller 'saints of the house of Habsburg' looked on. Such a tomb would have been without parallel north of the Alps: only Michelangelo's tomb of Pope Julius II would have rivalled it. Unfortunately, the scale was too huge for a single artist. Maximilian had no Michelangelo at his disposal, and the unity of the plan was soon lost in the execution, which, through lack of funds and changes of mind, was also slow. So the work fell apart, different details being assigned to different artists. Jörg Kölderer, the Innsbrück artist, took the principal part, but the statues of the Habsburg 'ancestors' were allotted to various workshops. The greatest of German sculptors, Peter Vischer and Veit Stoss, both of Nuremberg, were among those employed; but Stoss's work is lost, and the two splendid statues by Vischer – King Arthur of England and Theodoric the Goth – had to be pawned to the Bishop of Augsburg to pay the Emperor's debts. When they were redeemed, thirty years later, it was too late for them to influence the companion statues. Meanwhile the city council of Nuremberg forbade the local artists to accept the imperial commission for fear of being left with the bill. When the Emperor died, the tomb was not ready: it was completed nearly a century later, by Maximilian's art-loving great-grandson, the Archduke Ferdinand of Tyrol.

That, perhaps, tells us something. It was a commonplace in the sixteenth century that if a man did not provide for his own tomb, his heirs could not be counted on to build it generously. But the heirs of Maximilian, to the fourth generation, honoured his wishes and revered his name. They were, after all, the beneficiaries of his matrimonial policy. It was thanks to him that they ruled over Spain and Flanders, Milan and Naples, Bohemia and Hungary. And it was he who had given to the dynasty its sense of identity, of history, of mission, and had consecrated that sense in propaganda which made its appeal through all the arts. So they owned him, and looked back to him as to no other member of their house. And indeed, how often they remind us of him! His grandson Charles V reminds us of him with his imperial symbolism, his passion for music, his crusade against the infidel at Tunis. His great-grandson Philip II of Spain, so different in many ways, recalls him by his pedantic love of detail in artistic matters, his encyclopaedic gazetteers of his kingdoms and their natural resources, and the egotism of his vast mausoleum. On the other, Austrian, side, Ferdinand I and Maximilian II continued his interest in the details of nature and science; and Rudolf II, Maximilian *redivivus*, consciously imitated him in all his aims: in his 'crusade' against the Turks, in his dream of a revived Byzantium, in his collection of the works of Dürer, in his Tyrolean landscapes, in his universal artistic workshop in Prague. At his death in 1519 Maximilian might seem to foreigners a universal failure; but the ideas which he had failed to realize in politics still dominated his dynasty a century later because he had converted them, for the sake of propaganda, into the forms of art.

Sources

1. See G. E. Waas, *The Legendary Character of Kaiser Maximilian I* (New York, 1941).
2. Ludwig Baldass, *Der Kunstlerkreis Kaiser Maximilians* (Vienna, 1923).
3. For Frederick III see A. Lhotsky, *Aufsätze u. Vorträge*, II, 119ff and 239ff.
4. See Andreas Walther, 'Die neuere Beurteilung Kaiser Maximilian I', in *Mitteilungen der Institut für österr. Geschichtsforschung* (1912).
5. On this episode see Aloys Schulte, *Kaiser Max. I als Kandidat für den päpstlichen Stuhl 1511* (Leipzig, 1906).
6. See David Schönherr, 'Die Kunstbestrebungen Erzherzog Sigmunds von Tirol', in *Jahrbuch der Kunsthistorischen Sammlungen . . . in Wien*, I (Vienna, 1883).
7. See *Das Fischereibuch Kaiser Maximilians I*, and *Das Jagdbuch Kaiser Maximilians I*, both published by Dr Michael Mayr (Innsbrück, 1901).
8. A. W. Ward, '*Teuerdank* and *Weisskunig*', in *An English Miscellany presented to F. J. Furnivall* (Oxford, 1901). The text of the *Weisskunig*, edited by Alwin Schultz, is printed in *Jahrbuch* VI (Leipzig, 1887).
9. Franz Schestag, 'Kaiser Maximilians I Triumph', *Jahrbuch*, I, 154–81; Walter Koschatzky and Franz Winzinger, *Triumphzug Kaiser Maximilians I* (Graz, 1973). 1973).
10. Eduard Chmelarz, 'Das Diurnale oder Gebetbuch Kaisers Max. I', in *Jahrbuch* III (1885).
11. See Louise Cuyler, *The Emperor Maximilian I and Music* (Oxford, 1973).
12. See Vinzenz Oberhammer, *Die Bronzestatuen am Grabmal Maximilian I* (Innsbrück, 1943).

3

Sir Thomas More and Utopia

Thomas More is one of the heroes of our age. Everyone venerates him now. Catholic and Protestant, Conservative and Socialist, traditional-ist and reformer, all are united in his praise. Sweetness and light, spirituality and good humour, scholarship and wit, emanate from his portrait, whether painted in colour by Holbein or in prose by Erasmus. He is a man of marvellous completeness. And naturally all of us, or at least all of us except Professor Elton, are very indignant with King Henry VIII and Thomas Cromwell who sent him to the block.

Such unanimity has its dangers. There is a risk that the image of More may be made dull by the thick patina of so much praise. Some of his writings, let us face the fact, *are* rather dull. Nor are they always good-humoured. How many of his admirers have really read those laborious works of his later life: those tedious and often ill-tempered tracts against Luther and the early English reformers, Frith and Tyndale, Barnes, Bilney and Fish, which entitled him to canonization? For it was not the works which we admire, and which give him his place in intellectual and literary history – it was not *Utopia*, nor *Richard III*, nor the translations from Lucian, nor the 'merry jests' – that qualified More for the company of the saints. Those works, or some of them, qualified him rather to join Erasmus, his lifelong friend, in more interesting, or at least more exciting company, on the Index of Prohibited Books.

Let me then begin this essay by trying to save More from the saccharine praise of his unanimous admirers. This is not too difficult an operation. All we have to do is to move back a little in time. For More was not always an uncontroversial pattern of wisdom and virtue. He was not always praised for transparent simplicity, honesty, wisdom,

24

tolerance, respect for the rights of conscience, etc. His death was not always regarded as the martyrdom of the human spirit. Indeed, it is only in the last half-century that this character has been given to him. For the first four centuries after his death he was a much more controversial, more mysterious figure. Had it been otherwise, he would surely not have had to wait four centuries for his ultimate canonization.

For it was only in 1935, on the fourth centenary of his death, that the Church of Rome gave to More that final sign of approval. This, on the face of it, is surprising. In the generation after his death, his fellow Catholics confidently prophesied such canonization. In those years biographies of him were written or inspired, and his works published, by the survivors of his family circle. However, nothing happened. The biographies remained unprinted; the memory of More became an introverted family cult* sustained largely by the wealth of the Roper family;† and in the next century it died away. The Roper family did not forget their connexion with More, but by the later seventeenth century they were more interested in their older connexion with Archbishop Chichele. That secured them some concrete advantages: it qualified them, as Founder's Kin, for hereditary fellowships of All Souls College.‡

Why, we may legitimately ask, did More have to wait so long for such

---

* We should be grateful to this cult. Not only did it ensure the transmission of the MS. biographies of More – Roper (first published in 1626); Cresacre More (1631); Harpsfield (1932); Ro. Ba. (1950); to it also we owe the existing versions of Holbein's famous painting of the family, the original of which is lost (probably destroyed by fire in 1752), although the sketch, which belonged to Erasmus, survives in the Kunstmuseum, Basel. There are two surviving versions of the final portrait, both painted for the family by Rowland Locky in the 1590s. One, an exact copy, has descended through the Roper family to Lord St Oswald and is at his home, Nostell Priory, Wakefield. The other is an expanded portrait, including the next generation of the family. It is now in the National Portrait Gallery. On these works see Stanley Morison, *The Image of Sir Thomas More* (1963).

† William Roper, the husband of More's devoted daughter Margaret, lived to be 83 (he died in 1578) and gave financial support to the More circle: *see The Lyfe of Syr Thomas More . . . by Ro. Ba.* (EETS, 1950) p. 148. In addition to his estates in Kent, he had a profitable legal office as Protonotary of the King's Bench, hereditary in his family.

‡ At Sotheby's on 26 June 1974 there was sold a 'Roper Roll' which I examined. It is a lengthy pedigree from the thirteenth to the later seventeenth century, presumably based on the roll which the Roper family produced at the Heralds' Visitation in 1619 (see 'The Visitation of Kent 1619' in *Proceedings of the Harleian Society*, 1898) and which found its most splendid form in the great Roper Roll compiled by John Philipott, Somerset Herald, in 1629, now in the possession of Lord St Oswald at Nostell Priory. Its purpose is clear; it is to claim kinship with the founder of All Souls College. The claim was successful: see G. D. Squibb, *Founder's Kin, Privilege and Pedigree* (Oxford, 1922) p. 48; but the privilege was, unhappily, abolished by Act of Parliament in 1854.

obvious recognition? The answer, I believe, is not far to seek. For centuries after his death, he was a totem figure of the English Catholics, and particularly, being himself a layman, of the English Catholic laity. The English lay Catholics were not, in those centuries, either very popular or very influential at Rome. They were also regarded as tainted in their ideas: ever since the reign of James I, they had appeared dangerously 'protestant', more English than Roman. Since they were unpopular, there was no desire, and since they were weak, there was no need to humour them. No rich and powerful regular order supported them. Even in the nineteenth century, when they grew in strength, they remained suspect, 'cisalpine' not 'ultramontane', supporters of Newman against Manning, of Acton and Döllinger against the 'Vaticanism' of Pius IX. It was not till the conciliatory reign of Pope Leo XIII that peace was made. Significantly, it was then, in 1886, that More was beatified. His beatification can be seen as a sop to the English Catholic laity, comparable with the cardinalate of Newman, the reconciliation with Acton. The English Protestants, meanwhile, looked on with indifference. They had never shown much interest in More.

Then came the canonization of 1935. At first this episode too was treated with indifference by English Protestants. The British Government took no official notice of the event, regarding it as an internal Catholic affair. Nevertheless, from that date, More's historical character changed. From a recusant figurehead he became a great Englishman in whom Protestants as well as Catholics could take pride; and Protestants and Catholics vied to revive his fame, his works, his history.

First of all, in the very year of the canonization, came the classic biography by the Anglican scholar, R. W. Chambers. In the ensuing years, the early biographies of More – almost all written in the generation after his death, and in his family circle – were printed or reprinted. So were some of his own writings. His statue was set up in the borough of Chelsea, where he had lived; and this time, even Protestants were allowed (somewhat grudgingly) to join the celebration.*

Meanwhile, this English cult was being overtaken by another, wider movement. The More industry, from being English, was becoming international. In 1963 the 'More project' was launched at Yale, and the complete works of More, unpublished since the mid-sixteenth century, began to reappear, edited and annotated with devoted scholarship.[1] In

---

* I was myself invited by the Committee to write the appeal for this statue, and was responsible for the inscription on it. But the Catholic priest of the parish, and his bishop, protested (in vain) against this impropriety, and when the statue was unveiled, I was not invited to the ceremony.

the same year the abbé Germain Marc'hadour in Angers founded an international association, the *Amici Thomae Mori*, whose membership now extends across the world and whose publication, *Moreana*, has appeared regularly ever since. At the same time More was made famous by Mr Robert Bolt's play and Mr Zinnemann's film. Now, to commemorate his fifth centenary, there have been conferences and colloquies on More everywhere. From a great Englishman he has become again, as he had been in his own lifetime, a universal genius, a great citizen of the world.

This last stage in the revival of More, it should be noted, is quite independent of his Catholicism. This is shown by the simultaneous revival of More's greatest friend, Erasmus. In the previous four centuries, Erasmus had hardly been regarded as Catholic at all. For most of them his works had been published only in Protestant countries. Today he has been brought out of his cramped Protestant cupboard just as More has been brought out of his narrow Catholic niche. To him, too, great works of scholarship have recently been devoted. His complete works too are now being republished, in Latin in his native Holland, in English in Canada.[2] His name has become a symbol of the new cosmopolitanism. There is an Erasmus prize for those who serve European unity. There is even an Erasmus international train passing, as he did, but more swiftly and luxuriously, up and down the Rhine.

The reason for this double revival, this re-convergence of two long-separated friends, is clear enough. It springs less from their times than from ours. More and Erasmus, constant friends in their lives, were torn apart, after death, by warring ideologues. Thus severed, they shrank in stature and in the nineteenth century both were devalued. Erasmus was censured for his lukewarmth when not denounced for his heresy. No nineteenth-century English historian, not even the Catholics Lingard and Acton,* thought much of More. If the two men have been reunited in our time, and thereby restored to their original greatness, it is, partly at least, as symbols of that ecumenical movement which, after four centuries of division, seeks to restore the spiritual unity of Christendom.

Of course, there is some danger in seeing the past through the

---

* Lingard represents More as an admired scholar and successful lawyer, but a 'timorous' and imprudent man who should have kept out of politics, for which, owing to his 'delicate conscience', he was not fit. (J. Lingard, *History of England 1825–31*, VI, 218, 288.) The Protestants Gilbert Burnet and Sir James Mackintosh are more sympathetic than this. On Acton see R. J. Schoeck, 'Lord Acton's views of Sir Thomas More', *Moreana*, XII, 47.

present. The modern glass through which we look may show us new aspects, but it may also discolour or distort. The English Catholics who, at home, in the England of Mary Tudor, or abroad, in Catholic Flanders during the reign of Elizabeth, narrated his life and published his works, omitted certain aspects of both which seemed to them incompatible with the new orthodoxy of the Council of Trent.[3] Modern liberals similarly slide over his rough handling of Protestants in London and credit him with views on the absolute liberty of conscience which he did not hold. If we are not to make comparable errors, we must try to see him in his own context, not ours.

Even within that context, he is mysterious enough. For in spite of the innocent simplicity which he cultivated, in life as in writing, More was not an easily intelligible character. Great men seldom are. He fits into no convenient category. To contemporaries, even to his own household, he was an enigma. Why did this open enemy of mortification and of superstitious observances secretly wear a hair-shirt next to his skin? Why did he refuse to take the oath of supremacy at which none of his devoted household boggled? Why did he give no reasons for that mortification or this martyrdom? What, above all, is the meaning of *Utopia*? While his friends were bewildered, his opponents, of course, were positively exasperated by the complexity of his character. In particular, they were maddened by his apparent levity, the indecent flippancy (as they thought it) which masked his purpose and enabled him to evade serious discussion. The same charge, of course, was brought against Erasmus by his critics, who described him as a sophist, a changeling, an amorphous polyp, a slippery mouse.

In an attempt to grasp this Protean spirit, I propose, in this essay, to look at More in his own intellectual context, to identify the tradition to which he attached himself, to watch, if possible, the formation of his mind, and its ultimate expression in the greatest, most original of his works. This cannot be done from purely biographical evidence. We have very few contemporary sources for More's early years. We know little of his studies. We have very few of his books, no personal papers; for all such property was confiscated when he was declared a traitor. His papers have all mysteriously disappeared. Almost all that we know, on this subject, is retrospective, from his own writings or those of Erasmus. We must therefore rely largely on deduction, implication, association. This method is necessarily tentative. However, it is more fruitful, I think, than to see him anachronistically, retrospectively, through an iridescent halo, or mist.

The outline of More's early career is clear enough. He was born in

1478, and sent to school in London. Then he lived for a time as a page in the household of the Archbishop of Canterbury, Cardinal Morton. Morton afterwards sent him to the University of Oxford. From Oxford he went to the Inns of Court to study law. All this reveals nothing of his mind. Then suddenly, in 1499, we have a shaft of light. In that year Erasmus comes, for the first time, to England, and in his letters reveals the new world he has discovered there.

In some ways, this first English visit of Erasmus, which was to have such large consequences, for him and for us, was an accident, a deviation. Erasmus, at that time, was based in Paris. He had not intended to come to England. His overriding aim was to learn Greek, or rather, to improve the Greek which he had begun to learn at Paris, and for that purpose he had planned to go to Italy. Italy, at that time, was the centre of Greek studies: there, as he wrote, 'the very walls speak Greek'. But Erasmus did not, in the end, go to Italy – at least not yet. He was diverted by his English pupil Lord Mountjoy, who persuaded him to come to England instead. So he came to England, to London, to the royal court, and then spent three winter months in Oxford, perfecting his Greek. In London and at Oxford he met English courtiers, clergy and scholars. At Oxford, in particular, he came to know William Grocyn and Thomas Linacre, and listened to the lectures of John Colet on the Epistles of St Paul. The whole experience delighted him. At the end of his stay he described it to another of his pupils: how, to his surprise, he had discovered

a climate at once agreeable and extremely healthy, and such a quantity of intellectual refinement and scholarship, not the usual pedantic and trivial kind either, but profound and learned and truly classical, in both Latin and Greek, that I have little longing left for Italy except for the sake of visiting it. When I listen to Colet it seems to me that I am listening to Plato himself. Who could fail to be astonished at the universal scope of Grocyn's accomplishments? Could anything be more clever or profound and sophisticated than Linacre's mind? Did Nature ever create anything kinder, sweeter or more harmonious than the character of Thomas More? . . .[4]

Today Erasmus is famous, More is famous, their friendship is famous, and we take it all for granted. But pause and consider. More, whom Erasmus thus cites, was then a young law student, twenty-one years old. He had written nothing. He had never been abroad. And yet here we find him cited, naturally, even automatically, in this company of much older men whose names were already established. For Grocyn, at that time, was fifty-three years old, Linacre thirty-nine, Colet thirty-three. Moreover, this company had clearly accepted him as one of themselves. Soon afterwards, Colet would pay a remarkable tribute to More: he would describe him as the unique genius among the many talented men of England.

And what was this company in which the young Thomas More already shone as a uniquely brilliant star? First of all, Grocyn, Linacre, Colet were all Greek scholars. All had studied Greek in Italy. That is what drew Erasmus to them, and More also. After Erasmus' departure, we find More too studying Greek, first under Grocyn, then under Linacre, whom he described as his 'master of learning'. With him, as a fellow-pupil, was Grocyn's godson, William Lily. Lily too had begun these studies abroad: he had been on a pilgrimage to Jerusalem, had learned Greek from a Greek teacher in Rhodes, and had improved his knowledge in Italy. Afterwards Colet would appoint him as the first high master of his own foundation, St Paul's School. In 1504 More described Colet and Grocyn as the only masters of his life, Linacre as his present tutor, Lily as his beloved companion. Together, these five men – to whom we should add William Latimer who had also studied in Italy – were the founding fathers of Greek studies in fifteenth-century England.

However, it was not Greek studies alone which united these men. They also have something else in common, and it is this something else which I wish to emphasize. They were all Platonists. They had become Platonists in Italy because Italy, and especially Florence, was the centre of Platonic studies in Europe. Those studies had been brought thither in the last days of Byzantium by the last great Byzantine Platonists, the pagan George Gemistus Plethon, whom his admirers described as a reincarnation of Plato, and the Christian Bessarion who became a Catholic and a cardinal. There they had flourished, and become christianized, or re-christianized, in the Platonic Academy founded in Florence, at the suggestion of Plethon, by Cosimo de' Medici. The great teachers at that academy were Marsilio Ficino, the editor of Plato and Plotinus, and his disciple Giovanni Pico della Mirandola, the prodigy of his age. It was through Ficino's work that these Englishmen discovered Plato, and it was to hear Ficino and Pico that some of them had gone personally to Florence; and it was their Platonic doctrine, as well as the Greek language, that they taught on their return. The ideas of Pico were preached in London by Colet, who corresponded with Ficino and whom we have heard Erasmus compare with Plato himself. The first publication of Linacre was a translation of the Greek Neoplatonist Proclus, a pagan of the fifth century. The earliest surviving letter of More describes his attendance at Grocyn's lectures in St Paul's Cathedral. The lectures were on 'Dionysius the Areopagite'. 'Dionysius' – the pseudo-Dionysius – was a Christian Platonist of the sixth century who plagiarized Proclus; but since he was wrongly identified with the Dionysius whom St Paul converted at Athens, his 'pious plagiarism', 'one of the most momentous in history',[5] had become the fountainhead of Christian Platonism throughout the Middle Ages. When Grocyn lectured on him in London, he may have used the new edition of his work by the great French humanist and reformer, Jacques Lefèvre d'Etaples, who had himself visited Florence in order to discuss Plato with Ficino and Pico.

Thus the little group of men to whom More listened in Oxford and London was united not only by its interest in the Greek language and Greek studies, but also, more specifically, by Platonism. It was in fact the English seminary of Florentine Platonism. And in 1499 it won an important recruit: Erasmus himself. When he came to London in that year, Erasmus was a humanist, a poet, a man of letters, a student of Greek literature. When he left, he was a Platonist. For the rest of his life he was committed to Platonism. 'Is there anything in the world', he would write next year to his pupil Lord Mountjoy, 'more splendid than Plato's philosophy, or more eloquent than his style?' 'Seneca and Plato', he would write to another disciple sixteen years later, 'if you converse with them often, they will not let your spirit lie down'; and to one of his patrons, a humanist prince and bishop of Utrecht, he would sing the praises of 'Plato, that man of exquisite and almost godlike judgment'.[6]

Formed in the same school, in London and Oxford, More too was a Grecian. He too believed that the Greek language was the necessary means of intellectual and spiritual revival. Some of his most urgent intellectual writings – his long letter to the Louvain theologian Maarten van Dorp in 1517, his letter of remonstrance to the University of Oxford in 1518 – are pleas for Greek studies, which he defends against all comers. For was it not through the Greek language, and through it alone, that the science and philosophy of Antiquity, the true faith of the New Testament and the Fathers, and 'all the other branches of learning' had come down to us, and, if lost, could now be recovered? Greek literature, he argued, even secular literature, 'prepared the soul for virtue'.[7] But within that literature, More too, like his masters, is committed to a particular philosophy. He too is a Platonist, a Christian

Platonist inspired, like them – but, like Erasmus, indirectly – from Florence.

This he showed clearly in his first published work which appeared in 1505. It was a translation into English of the biography of that 'singular layman', the Florentine Platonist Pico della Mirandola, whose life (we are told) he had chosen as a pattern for his own. The biography was the work of Pico's nephew, Gianfrancesco Pico. More published his translation in order to present it as a New Year's gift to a woman friend who had entered a nunnery as a Poor Clare. The significance of this publication cannot escape us. More himself had recently passed through a religious crisis. He had contemplated the monastic life for himself. As a law-student he had lived for a time among the Carthusians of London – the most austere and uncorrupted of monks, the only monks whom Erasmus admired. But, in the end, he had decided to marry and live, like Pico, as a religious layman, in the world. More's *Life of John Picus Earl of Mirandula* is in fact the apologia of a Christian Platonist addressed to one whose still tempting example the translator has decided not, after all, to follow.

More's interest in Plato is, of course, well known. *Utopia* is, in form, an imitation of Plato's *Republic*, and Plato is often cited in it. But the biographers of More have tended to treat this as a mere literary model. I believe that this is wrong, demonstrably wrong. I believe that if we study More's thought in his early years, we must see that his mind was not merely dipped, it was steeped in Platonism: the Platonism of Pico; the Platonism of St Augustine, who had brought Neoplatonism into Christianity; the Platonism of Plato himself. The life and ideas of Pico, says Signor Gabrieli, exercised 'a seminal influence on his mind', and many of Pico's ideas can be found in his later works.[8] At the age of twenty-three we find him lecturing on the philosophy of St Augustine in Grocyn's church in London. In his fidelity to Plato himself he went beyond any of his contemporaries, for we are told by Erasmus that 'while still a youth, he attempted a dialogue in which he maintained a defence of Plato's community, even in the matter of wives'.[9]

This Platonism of More will no doubt be disputed by some. It will be said that, in some respects, he was a Thomist, an Aristotelean. Some commentators have called him, since he commended innocent pleasure, an Epicurean. But these, I think, are superficial judgements. Platonism does not exclude some aspects of Aristoteleanism: Aristotle was, after all, a pupil of Plato, Roman writers from Cicero to Boethius sought to 'reconcile' them, and the great mediator of Greek Platonism in the fifteenth century, Gemistus Plethon, was careful to insist on the area of agreement, as well as of dissent, between the two philosophers.[10] The Florentine Platonists continued to embrace Aristotelean ideas – Pico della Mirandola tells us that he spent every morning 'conciliating Plato and Aristotle' – and their English disciples always expressed respect for Aristotle: it was only with the later revival, and petrifaction, of scholasticism, and the elaboration of Hermetic Platonism, that Aristotle and Plato became irreconcilable. More himself suffered some petrifaction too. As for Epicureanism, More accepted it only where it did not conflict with Platonism: that is, superficially. If the Utopians believed in the innocence of pleasure, it was certainly not on Epicurean premises, which, as we shall see, were explicitly condemned.

Once we recognize the profound influence of Plato on More we can understand (I believe) some other aspects of his character which puzzled contemporaries. For instance, there is his 'Socratic' technique. For behind Plato stands Plato's own master, Socrates, and Plato's Socrates was a model for both Erasmus and More. Erasmus' prayer, 'Sancte Socrates, ora pro nobis', shocked the orthodox, and More was known as 'our Christian Socrates'.[11] Both Erasmus and More used the Socratic method. They also used 'Socratic irony', that disconcerting affectation of ignorance and simplicity which was Socrates' most effective dialectical weapon.* And then there is the Socratic, or Platonic, raillery. That teasing wit, that gentle mockery, that vivid sense of the absurd which animate the writings of both Erasmus and More, are in the Platonic tradition. The obvious example is Erasmus' *Encomium Moriae*, 'the praise of Folly', inspired by More, written in his house and dedicated to him. Grave scholars were shocked by the frivolity of that work, but when they attacked it, More rushed to its defence: he gladly accepted Folly as his advocate, and he and his friends regularly played on his own name, μωρός the fool, '*oxymorus* or rather μωρόσοφος', as the great Greek scholar Guillaume Budé called him.[12] Even in his greatest work of devotion, his *Dialogue of Comfort*, written during his last imprisonment, he happily claimed to be 'of nature even half a giglot and *more*'. 'I would', he added, 'I could as easily mend my fault as I well know it, but scant can I refrain it, as old a fool as I am.'

The comic spirit of Platonism is not often emphasized or perhaps even noticed by scholars, but in the nineteenth century Lord Macaulay recognized it: Plato, he remarked, was one of the greatest comic writers;[13] and the most perceptive exponent of Platonism, Walter

---

* 'This only I know,' said Socrates, 'that I know nothing.' 'Et scientiae pars est quaedam nescire' wrote Erasmus. (Allen, *ep.* 337, 419).

Pater, acknowledged it when he cited, as one of the greatest examples of the Platonic tradition in later Greek literature, the comic dialogues of the second-century satirist Lucian of Samosata.[14] For this reason I do not find it in any way strange that More and Erasmus, with their friend William Lily, should practise their newly acquired Greek by translating, in 1505–6, the works of Lucian. On the face of it, Lucian should not have appealed to More, for he was an Epicurean philosopher who ridiculed all religion, including Christianity, and would afterwards be condemned by the Church. But the Platonic tradition, which he too represented, could triumph over these differences.

More and Erasmus, then, were both Platonists, committed Christian Platonists, inspired directly by the teaching of Florence; but they were also real Platonists, disciples of the pre-Christian Plato himself. This qualification is important, for there are several kinds of Platonism, and there is, in particular, one kind of Platonism with which neither of them had any sympathy: what we now know as 'Renaissance Platonism'. This Renaissance Platonism, which would become even more extravagant in the sixteenth century, did indeed have some roots in the work of Plato, but it was largely a later development, launched by the Neoplatonists of the Roman and Byzantine empires. In the sixteenth century it would acquire a new momentum and assume extravagant forms. It would be encrusted with Egyptian mythology, Spanish Lullism, Jewish Cabala, and would become a form of astrological and numerological magic. Those who opened the way for this new development were the same Florentine scholars who had transmitted Platonism, through Grocyn and Colet, to England and, through England, to Erasmus and More. Ficino infused its magical content and Pico blended it with Jewish Cabalism. But although their continental followers – Lefèvre d'Etaples in France, Reuchlin and Agrippa in Germany – would spread the new doctrines in Europe, their English disciples either repudiated or ignored them. Their Platonism was simpler, purer, more authentic: direct from the source.*

* It seems important to make this point because the fashionable interest in the Renaissance Platonism of Ficino and Pico has already begun to engulf their English disciples. Thus Maria Cytowska, in her article 'Erasme de Rotterdam et Marsile Ficin son maître', *Eos*, lxiii (Warsaw, 1975), p. 172, while admitting that Erasmus was untainted by Ficino's own doctrines, adds 'l'absence d'influence réelle de Ficin sur Erasme, *en dépit de Colet*, est assez remarquable' (my italics); and Frances Yates, in *The Occult Philosophy of the Elizabethan Age* (1979), p. 38, says that 'a link between Agrippa and Colet may well have been Cabala, *in which Colet was certainly interested*' (my italics). I know of no evidence to suggest that Colet was particularly interested in Cabala. His own comments suggest the reverse (see below p. 73). The link between him and

What then is the Platonism of Plato? In its simplest form it is idealism, the determination to identify the universal spirit which informs matter and, having identified it, to disengage it from the bewildering variety, the inert machinery, the practical compromises in which, in practice, it is trapped and buried. In religion, the Platonist seeks the animating spirit and is impatient of theological discipline and mere ritual. In secular life also, if he interests himself in secular life, he seeks an ideal society which can preserve itself against corruption and, by a stable constitution, dispense with the sordid trivialities of day-to-day politics. The quest for such a spirit, the demand for such an ideal stability, arises most naturally in an age of hectic change, a time of apparent corruption, disintegration, decay.

Plato himself grew up in such a time. His youth coincided with a disastrous war, in which the greatness of his city was destroyed. In the wake of that disaster, he saw his revered master, Socrates, judicially murdered. He came to hate the free, competitive society around him, and, hating it, he rebelled against those earlier philosophers who, in more stable times, had envisaged, without discomfort, a world of perpetual mobility. So in his greatest political work, his *Republic*, and in its sequel, the *Laws*, he imagined an ideal form of society which, at whatever cost in freedom, would preserve itself for ever, without change.

Platonism was thus essentially anti-historical, as it was also anti-theological. In religion it insisted on the immortality of the human soul and the divine guidance of the world. In politics it pursued the mirage of an ideal state, preserved alike against political corruption and historical change. Fortunately, perhaps, most Platonists did not go in for politics. They were artists, visionaries, mystics, saints; and their function was to illuminate, not to govern. But when they speculated in political matters, the result was always the same. Whatever the culture within which they lived and thought – whether ancient or modern, eastern or western, pagan, Christian or Muslim[15] – they invariably produced totalitarian systems, repellent to liberal men.

All this can be seen in More: indeed this is what separated More and

---

Agrippa was more probably evangelical Christianity. For Colet's relations with Ficino, and their limitations, see Sears Jayne, *John Colet and Marsilio Ficino* (Oxford, 1963); and see F. Secret, *Les Cabalistes Chrétiens de la Renaissance* (Paris, 1964). Erasmus positively repudiated Cabalism as Jewish mumbo-jumbo (see passages from his letters quoted below, p. 73). The difference between the Platonism of Florence – i.e. of Ficino and Pico – and that of Oxford – i.e. of Erasmus and More – is emphasized by A. Renaudet, *Erasme et l'Italie* (Geneva, 1954).

Erasmus from their fellow 'humanists', from those whom we now call 'civic humanists'. The civic humanists believed that Antiquity, which they studied, offered an ideal of public spirit and that the highest duty of a scholar was to serve his city or his prince. The humanist court of Henry VIII attracted many such men, headed by Thomas Cromwell.[16] But More, as a Platonist, never believed that political life was the ultimate good to be derived from classical learning. To him the world of the spirit came first, and ideally he would have kept out of politics altogether, as Erasmus always did, preferring poverty with scholarship and freedom to the golden servitude of court life. In fact he did not do so; and this is what makes him a more complex, a more mysterious, and in the end a more tragic figure than the undivided saint of European scholarship, Erasmus.

For in the end More rejected the life of scholarship as he rejected the life of the cloister. He studied the law. The law led to civic duties, Parliament, the royal service. In all these spheres of action, he discovered, and exercised, great practical abilities. He was a powerful lawyer, a formidable diplomat, a tough negotiator, secretive and strong-willed, as his foreign rivals reported, 'full of craft and subtlety' concealed 'by smooth speech and calm expression in the English way'.[17] As the climax of his career, he would achieve the highest office of all, becoming Wolsey's successor as Lord Chancellor, the first lay Lord Chancellor in English history. That career was not achieved by mere saintliness. But always, beneath the surface, there was tension. Even at the height of his success, his heart was elsewhere, in Plato's Academy, in the London Charterhouse, in Utopia. The secret hair-shirt betokened that internal tension, the Epicurean façade concealed it, the public 'fooleries' protected it. In 1505 his model was Pico della Mirandola who, though a great aristocrat, had fled from all 'worldly business' and had ended as a devotee of the puritan friar Savonarola. In 1516, when he was called to office by the King, he publicly expressed his anxiety, in the first book of *Utopia*. Erasmus, who refused to be inveigled into the service of the Emperor, rallied him for being 'haled to court', 'lost to literature and to us'. 'I will do anything rather than become enmeshed in that kind of business', he wrote; 'and how I wish you were at liberty!'[18] More felt the force of the criticism. In 1522, when he was already high in office and no cloud could be seen on the horizon, he wrote his essay on 'The Four Last Things' in which he likened civil life to a prison in which all worldly authority is 'no better but one prisoner bearing a rule among the remnant, as the tapster doth in the Marshalsea'. As Mr James McConica says, 'Nothing could be more at odds with the tone of common humanist opinion concerning the vocation to public service'.[19]

Divided souls have long agonies, but they also have moments of productive fusion. More's moment of fusion came in 1515, and its product was his greatest work, *Utopia.* For four centuries men have argued about the meaning of that work, and at the end there is still no agreement about it. Some have seen it as an expression of nostalgia for medieval traditionalism, others as a blueprint for modern socialism, or even for modern imperialism, others as a mere *ludibrium,* a *jeu d'esprit,* a holiday exercise. This last view was encouraged by More himself (but we must remember his Socratic irony). I believe that, to understand it, we should set it in the context of his mind: a mind which was, both in its melancholy and in its serious character, fundamentally Platonic. But if Platonism dictated its general philosophic content, it owed its form, I suggest, to the particular circumstances which brought it forth; and to these circumstances we must now turn.

Consider the circumstances in which More wrote *Utopia.* In 1515 he had been engaged for some two years on a serious work of modern history. His subject was the reign of Richard III, which he saw as a type of tyranny. Here too he was following a Platonic model. Plato had seen tyranny as the corruption of monarchy, and any Platonist who lived in a monarchical age was obliged to ask himself how the society around him could be preserved from that corruption. Both Erasmus and More were much exercised by this problem. One of the works of Lucian which they had translated together was specifically devoted to the moral problem of tyranny and tyrannicide. Both of them also wrote replies to it. According to Erasmus, the idea of writing such replies came from More. More, Erasmus would write later, had formerly 'disliked the court and the company of princes, because he always had a special hatred of tyranny and a great fancy to equality'. So did Erasmus himself. It was one of the subjects which united them; and never were they closer to each other, or more concerned with this topic, than in 1515. It was in that year, while More was deep in his history of Richard III, that Erasmus wrote, and dedicated to the young ruler of the Netherlands, the future Emperor Charles V, his *Institutio Principis Christiani* with its fierce attack on the tyranny of kings: birds of prey living on the bodies of their subjects, birds of ill omen heralding useless wars and the destruction of the patient work of peace. In the same year Erasmus published a revised and reorganized edition of his *Adages.* In this new edition the first adage is on the community of property, as advocated by Plato. 'It is extraordinary how Christians dislike this Platonic community of property', he there writes, 'and how they throw stones at it, although nothing was ever said by any pagan philosopher which comes closer to the mind of Christ.'

Against this background we can see that More's *History of King Richard III* was not written merely as a work of Tudor propaganda – although of course it would become such and, through Shakespeare's *Richard III*, which was based on it, would supply the stereotype of Richard in literature. It was written as an illustration of the evil of tyranny. More chose this particular illustration not to flatter the memory of Henry VII, or to serve the policy of Henry VIII, but because he had had particular opportunities, as a page in the house of Cardinal Morton, to learn the facts from a primary source. For Morton had lived through that dangerous reign and liked to entertain his household with his reminiscences; and More, an impressionable boy of thirteen or fourteen, had listened eagerly to the dramatic descriptions of his venerable master's shocking experiences and narrow escapes.

Such was the original stimulus for the historical work on which More was now engaged. It was an ambitious project of humanist history, and he took great pains about it. He sought out personal and historical sources and wrote the text in two independent versions, one in English, the other, for European readers, in Latin. But as his public duties increased, his work became intermittent, and the book would never be finished, or published in his lifetime. For our purposes it is important because he was engaged on it from 1514 to 1518 – that is, over the period within which he would write *Utopia*.[20] Indeed, we may say that it was not finished or published by him because it was overtaken and replaced by *Utopia*.

For in the end More would find the historical answer to his problem unsatisfactory. Historically, the tyranny of Richard III had been ended by his defeat and death at the battle of Bosworth Field and the creation of the Tudor monarchy. But what guarantee did that give for the future? The Tudor monarchy, like any other monarchy, could be 'corrupted' – and indeed More himself would be a witness, and a victim, of that corruption. To a politician, such an answer might be satisfactory, sufficient for his day, but a philosopher looked for a profounder solution of the problem. The question which he asked was, how could the process of corruption be arrested and tyranny not merely corrected when it occurred but so excluded from the system of government that it could never, in future, return?

It was while he was reflecting on these problems that More was sent by Henry VIII on a commercial embassy to the Netherlands. This mission necessarily interrupted his historical work. Cut off from his documents, he could not continue it. But the same mission – it was his first visit to the Continent, always an education for Englishmen – introduced him to a new world which changed the direction of his ideas. For in the Netherlands he discovered a new society, more highly developed and sophisticated than he had ever seen before: a society of prosperous, well-ordered urban republics, loosely federated under the rule of a young and, as yet, merely titular prince. This was very different from the Tudor monarchy in England. Was it not also a better and better organized society? So almost every Englishman thought who visited the Netherlands in the years of their prosperity. It was also, incidentally, the society which had produced Erasmus. Indeed, it was Erasmus who now introduced More to it. For Erasmus recommended him to one of his own closest friends and admirers in Antwerp, Peter Gillis, humanist scholar and town clerk of the city; and it was in Gillis's house that More stayed during the negotiation of the treaty.

It was there too that he began to write *Utopia*. Gillis himself appears as an actor in that book; the finished work would be dedicated to him; and he would arrange its publication. Afterwards, as a memorial of their friendship, Gillis and Erasmus would have their portraits painted by the Flemish artist Quentin Matsys and sent, as a diptych, to More. The portraits are now severed, one in the Queen's collection at Hampton Court, the other in a private house in England.[21] Clearly Gillis played a large part in the conception of *Utopia*. We can assume that it was in conversation with him that the central idea was developed. We can also assume that so profound a work was not a mere fantasy, thought up from scratch during a period of enforced leisure. Whatever More, in his self-mocking way, might say about it, it was not really a *ludibrium*, a holiday exercise. It may have been written as such, but what seems to have come off the top of a man's head has often been fermented at the bottom. Some of Plato's own works have been regarded, by some, as mere 'poetic fancies'.[22] Once we see *Utopia* in its context, its real depth becomes clear. It is a new answer to an old question: the application to a particular problem, in particular circumstances, of a long-excogitated philosophy.

Utopia did not achieve its final form in the Netherlands. What More wrote there was what is now the second of its two books, or chapters; but that book is the central part of the work, the description of the island of Utopia. Having written it, More returned to England, to the press of legal business and to the offer of more permanent royal employment. In

the intervals of such business, and while hesitating over such employment, he wrote a second chapter, which would afterwards constitute
Book I of the completed work. This new chapter did not alter the
substance of the work, but it gave it a form and a context: it turned a
philosophic treatise *de Optimo Reipublicae Statu*, on the ideal form of a
commonwealth, into a Platonic dialogue, set out in the manner which
Plato had made so effective. Platonic humour, Socratic irony, Lucianic
satire, Erasmian ambiguity, were all combined in the final version of
Utopia. Like the work of Plato himself, it has fascinated and tantalized
posterity, which, while agreeing that it is a work of genius, has never
made up its mind quite what to think of it. This, of course, is one
definition of greatness.

So much for the external, circumstantial history of More's most
famous work. Let us now look at its content in order to see how far it
reflects, and may be explained by, these circumstances.

Formally, *Utopia* is the tale of an Ancient Mariner, a Portuguese, whom
More and Gillis have met in Antwerp; for Antwerp, at that time, was
the great emporium of the world commerce then almost monopolized
by the Portuguese. The mariner claims to have sailed on several of the
four journeys of exploration of which an account had recently been
published by the Florentine Amerigo Vespucci. From the last of these
expeditions, he says, he did not return with his companions but set off
on a long, independent journey which ultimately brought him to
Calicut, the Portuguese station in India, whence a Portuguese ship took
him home. In the course of his wanderings, he came upon the island of
Utopia, whose system of government he now describes.

Utopia means Nowhere. All the names of places and persons in the
book indicate non-existence in the real world. There are Achorians,
people of no country; Polylerites, talkers of much nonsense; Anemo-
lians, wind people; Nephelogetae, cloud creatures. The capital of
Utopia is Amaurotos, dim city, and its river is Anydros, non-water. The
Ancient Mariner is called Hythlodaeus – in English, Hythlodaye –
learned in nonsense. However, behind these names, which are non-
names, the island of Utopia clearly has some resemblance to England;
the river of Non-Water is the Thames; the city of Dimness is London.
Utopia is England, not as it is, but as it might, ideally, be.

For what is England today? Look, says More, at our present society:
its inherent injustice, its competitive greed, its social exploitation, its
enclosures and depopulation, the prime cause of that epidemic of theft
and vagabondage which is so insensitively and unjustly punished by

death and persecution. At the root of all is the avarice of the rich, which is fostered by the very motor of society, the money economy, and which the law, being weak and partial, does nothing to correct. . . . In describing these evils, More does not explicitly refer to Richard III but it is clear that he has him in his eye. He refers to his own past in the household of Cardinal Morton and he quotes the conversation at that table; he dwells on the wasteful ambition of kings, the internal feuds of the ruling oligarchy, an evident allusion to that time; and he digresses in particular on the evils of sanctuary – a topic which he would set forth, in a speech ascribed to the Duke of Buckingham, in his history of Richard III. Thanks to these evils, says More, the modern state, in England as elsewhere, is not, properly speaking, a 'commonwealth' at all: it is, 'so God help me, . . . nothing but a certain conspiracy of rich men procuring their own comforts under the name and title of the commonwealth'.[23]

How different from this is Utopia! There, says the ancient mariner Hythlodaye, such exploitation simply cannot exist, for its essential motor, the money economy, has been taken away, and the very structure of the state prevents it from being established. For Utopia, like Plato's Republic, is built, from the beginning, on stable foundations. Everything there is planned, uniform, almost geometrically regular. The population is static, the towns identical, the way of life prescribed, even the clothes are uniform. There are no usurping kings, no idle gentry, no monopolizing merchants. The laws are short and clear and the lawyers, consequently, few. The necessary work of society is equally divided so that a six-hour day suffices for all. Thus men are left free to cultivate their minds. This they do in a suitably austere manner, going before daybreak to edifying public lectures; for more vulgar forms of entertainment they despise – nor are there any opportunities to indulge them. There is no freedom of travel, no trade in luxuries or frivolities, no hunting, no gambling, no taverns, no rendezvous where enemies of the people might conspire, no stews. Fornication is illegal. Above all, since covetousness is the root of all evil, there is no private property, no money. Gold and silver are despised and used only for base purposes, as in Sparta or Plato's ideal Republic.

Utopia is in fact a communist society. The citizens live in common and hold their resources in common. Even their houses and furniture are not private: 'every man that wills may go in, for there is nothing within the houses that is private or any man's own; and every tenth year they change their houses by lot'. 'These features', we are told in a marginal note, 'smack of Plato's community.' Necessary services are naturally all public. There is socialized medicine, public sanitation, communal meals. These public meals, we are told, are of a high quality, so that nobody wants to dine privately at home: the meals there are bound to be worse. They also have other advantages: everything that is said there is overheard, and so 'the sage gravity and reverence of the elders' inhibits 'the younger from wanton licence of words and behaviour'. This also is like Sparta and Plato's Republic.

Utopia, it is clear, is a very high-minded society. The aim of its government, we are told, is virtue; and both religion and politics serve that end. Consider religion. At first sight, the religion of Utopia is very liberal. There is no established church, and any religion is tolerated provided that it respects certain essential principles. These principles are simple: that the soul is immortal and that virtue is rewarded and vice punished hereafter. The Utopians, being a rational people, 'think it right' that these essential beliefs – which were brought into Christianity by Platonism – should be 'confirmed by proofs of reason'; but they do not insist that these proofs be believed, nor do they positively punish unbelievers, 'because they are persuaded that it is in no man's power to believe whatever he wishes'. However, those who do not believe must expect to suffer some inconvenience. In particular, 'if anyone should conceive so vile and base an opinion as to think that souls die and perish with the body or that the world runs by chance, governed by no divine providence' – i.e. the cardinal beliefs of the Epicureans – he is denied citizenship, 'deprived of all honours, excluded from all offices, and rejected from all public administration in the commonwealth'. This severity is justified on social grounds: for a man who disbelieves in divinely ordained rewards and punishments after death will hardly be deterred from breaking the laws of society. For the rest, Utopian religion is rational, non-sectarian, 'Erasmian'. Vulgar forms of superstition are deplored, and there are no sacrifices, only 'unharmful and hurtless' ritual and decent respect for God's work and power. For 'they think that the contemplation of Nature and the praise which grows out of it are to God a very acceptable honour'.

These are the common features of the various religions tolerated in Utopia. But there is also a superior religion professed by the wisest of the inhabitants. These men believe 'that there is a certain divine power, unknown, everlasting, incomprehensible, inexplicable, far above the capacity and reach of man's wisdom, dispersed throughout the world, not in size but in virtue and power. Him they call the Father of All.' This spiritual God, immanent in Nature, is more like the Platonic *anima mundi*, the soul of the world, than the anthropomorphic God of Christianity with his Holy Family and complicated theological properties. We are told that this Platonic religion of the Utopians prepared the way for their conversion to Christianity; so presumably, from Platonists, they too became Christian Platonists.

In general, the religion of Utopia can be described as a vague and variable deism whose common doctrines are enforced not because they are true but because they are necessary to social discipline. But it is also a positive religion, preaching, like Protestantism, a gospel of work. The Utopians, we are told, hate and avoid idleness, 'thinking felicity after this life is won and obtained by busy labours and good exercises'. There are monks of a sort, but very different from the monks of More's own time. They are divided into two sects: one celibate and austere, the other married and living in the world, but both hard-working. The Utopians count the latter sect the wiser, the former the holier. . . . 'They have priests of exceeding holiness, and therefore very few.'

So much for religion. What of the political constitution? This too is designed to protect the ideal society from any kind of corruption. The form of the state, More tells us, is laid down in advance. It is not historical, the continually flexible result of continuing, conflicting pressures: it is the perfect work of a single, timeless legislator. Just as Lycurgus, at some unrecorded and now irrelevant date, laid down the immutable constitution of Sparta, which Plato so admired, so King Utopus, long ago – at least 1,760 years ago, but the time is immaterial, for time, in Utopia, stands still – laid down the sacred, immemorial constitution of Utopia, which has ever since, by its own virtue, been maintained, perfect and unchanged, indeed unchangeable.

What is this constitution? There is a 'prince' – a very shadowy figure, for old King Utopus, who saw to everything, has left very little for his successors to do. The prince is selected for life; he must govern with the consent of his council, who are elected; and he can be deposed if he aims at tyranny. Some details of his rule are unclear – it is not even clear that he reigns over the whole island: perhaps he is merely mayor of a city and Utopia a federation of cities. But the point is of no importance, for real power is in the hands not of this remote prince but of his councillors, or 'tranibores'. These 'tranibores' are elected by lower officers or 'syphogrants'. The syphogrants in turn are annually elected by constituencies consisting of groups of families, and by the priests, who are also elected. Thus the system is essentially elective, and therefore, at first sight, democratic. However, on looking closer we soon see that it is an elitist democracy, or perhaps we should say a democracy in appearance only; for real power is in the hands of an oligarchy, a party. This party, described as the Order of Literati, consists of 500 mandarins, exempt from common labour, out of whom all the effective rulers, 'ambassadors, priests, tranibores, and finally the prince himself', must be chosen. These mandarins are persons carefully selected, often in childhood, for special education. They are selected by the priests. They are, in fact, a self-perpetuating humanist oligarchy. There are indeed safeguards against abuse of power; but those who are to enforce the safeguards are the same mandarins who might abuse the power. This renders the safeguards somewhat academic.

The same mandarins also enforce the rules, which are strict. The constitution is sacred, and any political activity conducted outside official channels is punished by death. The function of those who are not members of the party is simply to work, and the syphogrants are there to make them work: 'their chief and almost only function', we are told, is 'to take heed that no man sit idle'. To do this, they live in special buildings, like Bentham's Panopticon, equally spaced throughout the cities, and they preside over and regulate all the activities of the thirty families under the rule of each. They organize collective farms, watch, from a place of vantage, over communal meals, and control all movement. The priests also exercise great power. Though the theological doctrine of Utopia is liberal, the moral discipline is firm. The strongest weapons of the priests are rebuke and excommunication; but these, in static societies, can be very effective. 'There is almost no punishment more feared', we are told, than excommunication, and those who incur it 'fall into very great infamy'. They 'are inwardly tormented and do not long escape free with their bodies. For unless by quick repentance they prove the amendment of their lives to the priests, they are taken and punished by the Council, as wicked and irreligious.' They are handed over, in fact, by the Inquisition to the Secular Arm.

A grim collectivist tyranny, we may say; but no: there is light somewhere. Provided he conforms in the essentials of public doctrine, and keeps out of politics, and obeys all the rules, and does not hanker after the wrong kinds of pleasure, or think too much, a Utopian can have a jolly life, 'for they are much inclined to this opinion: to think no kind of pleasure forbidden wherefrom comes no harm'. They live according to Reason, and Reason, which kindles the essential truths of religion, also 'moves and encourages us to lead our life free of care in joy and mirth'. Accordingly, 'they set great store by fools' whom they protect, taking innocent pleasure in their foolishness. . . . Here we are reminded of More's own irrepressible taste for 'jesting' which would so enrage his grim Protestant assailants and which had inspired

Erasmus' *Praise of Folly* and thereby equally enraged grim Catholics; and we remember that More himself kept a fool, Henry Pattenson, who features in Holbein's portrait of the family.

Folly, licensed folly, that is the safety-valve of Utopia, the harmless substitute for dangerous, disruptive thought or bold imagination. Just as Plato, though himself a poet, banned poets from his Republic, so More, though himself a philosopher, banned philosophers from his Utopia. For neither of them was there any place in his own ideal commonwealth – except, of course, as king. Plato saw himself as the philosopher-king. More, in his daydreams (as he wrote to Erasmus), saw himself as 'marked out by my Utopians to be their king for ever'.[24] He would not have fitted easily as a mere citizen into that jolly socialist commune; still less as a non-citizen.

For not all the inhabitants of Utopia were citizens. In every society there are problems besides those of government, and even the most perfect system of government is sometimes in danger of attack, from without or from within. Who preserves the perfect constitution of Utopia from such attacks? Who does the dirty work by which it is sustained? More was a practical man and a consistent thinker. He did not evade these questions. His answers reveal some of the less agreeable aspects of the perfect commonwealth.

First, the dirty work. The citizens of Utopia, like those of Sparta, rely on a class of helots: *'servi'* More calls them bluntly, 'slaves'. For although there are religious orders which devote themselves to manual work and voluntarily choose 'the most unpleasant, hard and vile work ... the labour, loathsomeness and desperation of which frighten others', there are clearly not quite enough of these idealists to go round. So the functioning of Utopian society depends on the enslavement of criminals and prisoners-of-war condemned (since there is no death penalty except for political activity) to 'continual work and labour, but also in bonds'. These chained slaves also include native dissidents, who (we are told) are treated most harshly of all; for the Utopians 'judge them more desperate, and deserving of greater punishment, because, after being so godly brought up to virtue in so excellent a common-wealth, they could not for all that be restrained from misdoing'. The slaves clean the streets, sweep away 'the filthiness and ordure' from the market, butcher animals, and in general do all those disagreeable but necessary public tasks which the free citizens are forbidden to do, lest their pure minds be corrupted. There is also household slavery. Every Utopian household has two slaves as domestic servants.

Thus the communist workers' paradise is discovered, on closer inspection, to rest on the forced labour of disfranchised slaves, including political prisoners. Nor are these slaves the only unprivileged class in the new Sparta. A glance at foreign relations and necessary defence reveals another.

In general, the Utopians are pacifists. Resting comfortably on their own superior virtue, they 'detest and abhor war or battle, as a thing very beastly, although by no kind of beasts is it practised so much as it is by man'. However, precisely because other men are less high-minded, occasions of quarrel must sometimes arise, and on such occasions the Utopians soon show that they have little to learn from less virtuous peoples. If they are bent on a quarrel, we are told, they seldom lack a pretext, and their pretexts have a familiar ring. Their own country, they say, is being attacked, or their allies are threatened, or they wish to deliver oppressed peoples 'from the yoke and bondage of tyranny' – of which they, of course, are the sole judges. They also allow that it is legitimate to conquer land that is not being fully exploited by its present inhabitants. Nor do they lack the economic means for such imperialism. Communists at home, they are capitalists abroad. Thanks to state control of all economic activity, they dispose of vast financial resources. Some of these they invest in foreign loans, thus acquiring 'an infinite treasure abroad'. The rest they keep in hand for use as occasion may require.

Thus, in the event of an international crisis, the Utopians may exercise their economic power by calling in their foreign loans. That soon brings debtor nations to heel. Or they may try economic subversion: they will bribe enemy statesmen to commit treason, or encourage pretenders, 'the Prince's brother or some of the noblemen, to hope to obtain the Kingdom'. Alternatively, 'they stir up the neighbours of their enemies, and them they set on their necks under colour of some old title or right, such as Kings are never without'. For although they despise money in private transactions, the Utopians know how to use it for purposes of state. 'They know that, for money enough, their enemies themselves many times may be bought and sold, or else through treason set together by the ears among themselves.' For this purpose they keep 'an inestimable treasure', and because they have no other use for it, 'they lay it out frankly and freely'. Finally, if all these political methods fail, leaving no alternative but resort to force, the Utopians do not shrink from war; but even so they still contrive to preserve their own pacifist virtue. As More puts it, 'they had rather put strangers in jeopardy than their own countrymen'. So, like the pacifist Quakers in Pennsylvania two centuries later, they hire mercenaries.

Where are these mercenaries to be found? Fortunately, Nature has provided a very convenient supply of them. In particular, 500 miles to the east of Utopia – about the distance from London to Zurich – there is a people called the Zapoletes, 'the men who are for sale'. These Zapoletes 'are hideous, savage and fierce, dwelling in wild woods and high mountains', tough, primitive herdsmen, born warriors, who sell themselves very cheap and willingly fight 'for the Utopians against all nations', because the Utopians, being so rich, 'give them greater wages than any other nation will'. . . . Thus money-power, denied to individuals, is applied nakedly by the state in its own interest, and the human beings who are bought by it are ruthlessly expended. The Utopians, we are told, who are so careful of their own blood, are very free of that of the Zapoletes. They 'do not care how many of them they bring to destruction. For they believe that they would do a very good deed for all mankind, if they could rid the world of all that foul stinking den of most wicked and cursed people.' We recall that we are in 1515, the year of the battle of Marignano, the battle which rid Europe of the detested Swiss mercenaries. As if the parallel was not clear enough, More's text here has a marginal note: '*gens haud ita dissimilis Elvetiis*', 'a nation not so unlike the Swiss'. When *Utopia* was reprinted in Basel in 1518, this marginal note was tactfully omitted.

Such is Utopia, 'that commonwealth', as More tells us, 'which verily in my judgment is not only the best, but also that which alone of good right may claim and take upon itself the name of commonwealth or public weal'. It may do so principally because it is founded on 'community of their life and living' without any use – at least in internal affairs – of that money by which all other societies 'are utterly overthrown and destroyed'. Already, when Hythlodaye arrived there, it reminded him of 'those things that Plato imagined in his *Republic*'. All that was needed to make it perfect was that the Utopians should be both fully platonized and fully christianized; and this, we learn, is now happening. Hythlodaye taught them Greek – fortunately, being a passionate hellenist, he was well supplied with Greek texts (there being 'nothing extant in the Latin tongue that is to any purpose, saving a few of Seneca's and Cicero's doings') – and they took to it instantly. They have now, we are told, 'most of Plato's works', and of course 'they are delighted with Lucian's merry conceits and jests'. As for Christianity, that was already on its way, and the Utopians, we are told, are the more inclined to it because 'they heard us say that Christ approved among his followers that all things be held in common. . . .' Having discovered that they were Platonists, and having made themselves Christians, they would be a model for sixteenth-century Christendom: a model not only of a perfectly organized, perfectly just society, but also, what was no less important, of a society that was immune to corruption – that is (since it was already perfect), to change.

This is of the essence of Platonism in politics: Platonism which, in religion, in literature, in art, has always been a source of inspiration, but which in politics has always been not only communist and totalitarian, but also essentially static, unhistorical, indeed anti-historical. Politics, to the Platonist, are not an autonomous science: they are an inseparable and subordinate part of an all-embracing metaphysical system which they have no other function than to subserve and sustain.

Consider the record of Platonism in politics, beginning with Plato himself, and particularly its relation to history. Plato, at the turn of the fifth century BC, looked at Greek history and did not like it. He saw the defeat of his city, the disintegration of its ideals, and, finally, the judicial murder of his revered teacher. He wished to stop this process, to fix this endless flux in which the earlier philosophers had taken pleasure, to create an ideal society which would be proof against such change. He turned his eyes from Athens, with its freedom, its competition, its demagogues and revolutions, towards Sparta, victorious Sparta, and there he saw a form of society which had learned how to preserve itself against change. The Spartans ascribed this to their constitution, which in turn they ascribed to its semi-mythical founder, Lycurgus. But Plato was not content merely to borrow a foreign constitution. No mere political constitution, copied from Sparta or from some other *de facto* form of government, was sufficiently strong for his purposes. As a philosopher he would deduce his ideal society not from reality, empirically observed, but from first principles, securely embedded in a comprehensive *Weltanschauung*, a world-picture. So his Republic was to be communist, caste-bound, without money, ideologically protected. If this meant that freedom, individualism, poetry – everything which had been the glory of Periclean Athens – should be sacrificed, so be it: first things must come first.

Plethon, eighteen centuries later, saw Greece crumbling between the Latins and Turks. He too saw history, recent history, as a tale of decline. He too wished to stop the process, and, being a philosopher, looked to philosophy to supply the corrective to history. He too found his philosophy in Platonism, and the constitution which he proposed to the princes of the house of Palaeologus to preserve Byzantium in its last agony was communist, caste-bound, ideological.[25]

When Platonism came from Byzantium to Florence, its application was similar. The Florentine humanists were captivated by the fashionable doctrine and followed it, at first, into strange, semi-pagan byways. But then, at the close of the fifteenth century, they found a new hero, who re-christianized it for them. At the invitation of Pico della Mirandola, who had become his devotee, the Dominican friar Girolamo Savonarola returned to Florence and began his campaign of preaching. His aim was to stay the ferment of defeated Florence, as Plato had sought to stay the ferment of defeated Athens, by imposing upon it an intolerant, messianic, puritan republic. Thereupon the whole group of Platonists became enthusiasts for his cause. Savonarola was not himself a Platonist, though he was familiar with the works of Plato; but Platonists saw in him, while he lived, the man of destiny who would achieve their aims.[26] Visiting Platonists from England were carried away by him too. John Colet, who was in Florence in those years, was deeply influenced, according to Erasmus, by 'some monks, really prudent and pious' – a reference, it is generally thought, to Savonarola.

I have said that Platonism is essentially unhistorical, anti-historical. More was not unhistorical. He was himself a historian, and his history of Richard III shows that he had studied the ancient historians with care.[27] But history to him, as to the humanists in general, was not a constructive science: it was a storehouse of moral examples, some good, mostly bad. He did not seek, in past history, a means of controlling the future: he looked to philosophy for a means to end history: to end it altogether. Like Plato, like Plethon, like Savonarola, he sought a social form which would be proof against historical change – that is, against history itself. His island of Utopia had no history. Since the time when King Utopus imposed his constitution, over 1,700 years ago, nothing had happened there, and nothing would happen in the future; for the Utopians, as More wrote, had 'laid such foundations for their state as shall continue and last not only happily but also, as far as man's wit may judge and conjecture, endure for ever'. And an admiring reader and friend, the Burgundian humanist Jerome de Busleiden, wrote to him that if only the famous cities of Antiquity had adopted such a system, 'they would be flourishing today'.[28]

Perhaps they would, although 'flourishing' may not be the word we should use of an Athens in which all intellectual life had been frozen and from which the poets and thinkers had been expelled. For Platonism is not necessarily unpractical, provided that all its essential conditions are observed, all its rules kept. This point was made in the nineteenth century by the historian George Grote. The Platonic constitution, he wrote, had been dismissed as unpractical by Aristotle and others, but this was simply because it affronted established prejudices: its 'supposed impossibility' is merely 'the mode of expressing strong disapprobation and repugnance'. If it were once established and brought into operation on its own terms, there is no reason to doubt that it could continue to operate indefinitely.

The difficulty, of course, lies in the original establishment, which presupposes 'a motive, operative, demiurgic force, ready to translate such an idea into reality'. Could such a force arise? Not, Grote thought, in modern times. 'A new originating force', he wrote, 'is a very rare phenomenon', and by now the various states of the world are so set in their historic grooves that the imposition of a new form of society is out of the question. But in Antiquity it was still possible. Look at Sparta. The Spartan constitution, which Plato so admired, was extraordinary, unique. So, 'if Sparta had never been actually established, and if Aristotle had read a description of it as a mere project, he would probably have pronounced it impracticable'. But 'once brought into reality, it proved eminently durable'. Therefore, though we may fairly argue that such institutions are unlikely now to be established, we 'cannot fairly argue that they would not be good, or that they would not stand if established'.[29]

How agreeable, and how chastening, it is to see the wisdom of the modern world refuted by the wisdom of the past! Grote was a Benthamite utilitarian mandarin. He believed, like Plato, in a functional élite. He despised the traditional upper classes and (according to his wife) 'could not exchange a word with a common vulgar man without disgust'. He read Plato in Greek while waiting for his less punctual colleagues to arrive at committee meetings.[30] He could therefore entertain without dismay the thought of a radical re-ordering of society on an abstract philosophical model. But he believed that such a transformation could not now be achieved. It required a revolution; and no such revolution, no such 'originating force', could be foreseen by a historian – even a highly intelligent historian like himself – writing in the stable bourgeois world of the 1860s.

But we are running ahead. We must return to More's *Utopia*. Once published, the book immediately became famous. One of those who read it was Henry VIII's young kinsman Reginald Pole, afterwards Archbishop of Canterbury and Cardinal of England. Pole was a great admirer of More, and when he went out to Padua to study Greek philosophy under the Platonist Nicolas Leonicus – an old man who had once taught Greek to Linacre and Latimer – he spoke so warmly of *Utopia* that his teacher wrote to More, sending him a tributary volume and begging, in return, for a copy of the work. It duly came, brought out by More's protégé John Clement, who happened to be visiting Italy. Leonicus was delighted by it and wrote to Pole expressing the wish that such an ideal state could be realized: a sentiment with which Pole, as a fellow-Platonist, could agree.[31] However, the days of Platonism, that kind of Platonism, were numbered, as Pole himself was soon to discover.

For in 1530 or thereabouts, having returned to England, he was received by Henry VIII's newly risen minister, Thomas Cromwell, and was bold enough to sing in his ears the praise of Plato and the Platonic Republic. Cromwell, after all, had himself been in Florence when young, and might be supposed to have drunk at that fountain. Pole soon discovered his mistake. Cromwell puffed his recommendation aside and drew his attention to a far more useful work which had also come out of Florence. It was not yet printed, indeed, but was circulating briskly in manuscript. It was Machiavelli's *Prince*. Pole read it and was deeply shocked. That book, he declared, was written by the finger of Satan. Afterwards, having seen the effect of Cromwell's rule in England, he would ascribe it all to the teaching of that infamous book which, he would write, 'had poisoned England and would soon poison all Christendom'.

We do not know how Pole came to praise Plato to Cromwell. Perhaps they were merely exchanging Italian reminiscences. But that encounter is interesting as a belated English echo of the intellectual controversy which had divided Florence a generation earlier. For Machiavelli was himself a rebel against the fashionable Platonism of the 1490s. He had rejected the rule of Savonarola, the 'prophet unarmed' and so doomed to failure. He had become a disciple of Epicurus, a reader of Lucretius, the philosopher and the poet of anti-Platonic materialism. And he had come to believe that the key to politics lay not in heaven but on earth, not in metaphysics but in history.*

* Machiavelli, when young, had been a member of the *Compagnacci*, who opposed Savonarola and professed an Epicurean philosophy; and he copied, in his own hand, the text of Lucretius: see Sergio Bertelli (ed.), Machiavelli, *Opere* I (Verona, 1968). His claim of originality at the beginning of his *Discorsi* – 'ho deliberato entrare per una via la quale, non essendo suta ancora da alcuno trita . . .' – is an obvious echo of Lucretius' similar opening claim – 'Avia Pieridum peragro loca, nullius ante Trita solo'. Lucretius had been specifically attacked by Ficino in his *de Religione Christiana*.

Platonists like Pole were shocked by Machiavelli's realism, his 'reason of state'. But this was not the real difference between them. Thomas Cromwell had a concept of a good society which was not disreputable; it drew on some of the ideas of Erasmus. And were the methods by which Utopian society was preserved entirely un-machiavellian, in the vulgar sense of that word? Machiavelli at least apologized for the methods which he thought necessary in politics. He regretted the necessity of force and fraud and did not call them by any other name. Plato and More sanctified them, provided that they were used to sustain their own Utopian republics. Their successors, whom Machiavelli had made conscious of the problem, sought to escape from it, but only involved themselves in intolerable casuistry.

Their dilemma is illustrated most obviously by another, later seeker after Utopia. Tommaso Campanella was, like Savonarola, a Dominican friar. He was also, like More, a Christian Platonist, though a Platonist of a different kind, whose Platonism was shot through with magic and astrology. He too believed in a perfect system of government, with community of all property (including wives), common meals (with larger helpings and more delicate dishes for the élite), no money, no private trade, no cosmetics, the death-penalty for rouge or high heels, ideological brain-washing, universal espionage, slaves to do the dirty work, and authoritarian rule by a philosopher-king. His City of the Sun was in some ways grimmer even than Utopia: it allowed no room for innocent fools or organized jollity. On the other hand, there was less emphasis on hard work. It was also less hypocritic-al: its inhabitants were not pacifists, like the Utopians, but, like the Spartans, highly trained fighters. They even sent their children into battle, to accustom them to the sight of blood; for they were a conquering race, systematically and eugenically bred (all sexual rela-tions controlled by the state), and were convinced that their institutions would one day prevail throughout the world. Like the Utopians they professed a religion of Nature which could easily be adjusted to Christianity (of a kind), for it included the essential Platonic doctrines of divine Providence, the immortality of the soul, and posthumous rewards and punishments.

Unlike More, Campanella actually sought to realize his political ideals by direct action. His attempt to create a utopian republic in Calabria failed; he would be seized and tortured, and would spend twenty-seven years in a series of prisons in Naples and Rome. But he never ceased to recommend his Platonic political philosophy, or the 'machiavellian' methods by which it was to be achieved and perpetuated. While ritually denouncing Machiavelli as an impious 'Achitophel' who misled and corrupted princes by his infamous 'Reason of State', he protested that the same reason of state would be perfectly acceptable if it were re-named 'reason of good government' and applied to support not secular power but his own millenarian theocracy. And so he too, like More, recommends Machiavelli's methods, the methods which have given Machiavelli a bad name, in order to create and preserve for ever – *aeternare* – his utopia.

Between Platonists and Machiavellians there is no difference of method. Both are machiavellians in the vulgar sense of the word. Both are prepared to use 'reason of state' and to justify its use for the purposes which they approve. Where they differ – and they differ fundamentally – is in those purposes, and in their attitude to history. The crucial question is, shall 'reason of state' be used to deny history or to profit by its lessons, to arrest it or to control it? Having put it thus, perhaps we may venture to answer it. Perhaps, in the end, Plato and Plethon, Savonarola and More and Campanella, the idealists who sought to freeze history, are not the best guides in the real world. Perhaps Machiavelli, who responded to the challenge of history, who broke with the Platonic tradition of Florence, who repudiated his fellow-Florentine Savonarola, who stepped boldly forward and sought not to end history but to use it, to tame it, to make it work for him, is a better guide for our time, for all time.

The confrontation between Plato and Machiavelli, which had begun in Florence in the 1490s and was re-enacted in England in 1530, marked the end of the intellectual world of Thomas More. In 1516, the year of the publication of *Utopia*, he had appeared as the heir, the most brilliant, most attractive exponent of a long tradition. In the same year Erasmus too reached the acme of his fame: 1516 was his *annus mirabilis*, the year of his New Testament, his *Education of a Christian Prince*, his edition of St Jerome. And as each enjoyed his celebrity, their friendship became closer than ever. It was in 1517 that Erasmus sent the tributary portraits of himself and Gillis to More. 'I send you the pictures', he wrote, 'so that you may still have our company, after a fashion, if some chance removes us from the scene. . . . Farewell, my dear More, whom I love best of mortal men'; and More replied in kind: 'You would hardly believe, my most lovable Erasmus, how my affection for you, which I was convinced would admit of no addition, has been increased by this desire of yours to bind me still closer to you. . . .'[32] Every mention of More by Erasmus, in these years, is lyrical in his praise. It would culminate in his famous letter to Ulrich von Hutten which is the earliest character sketch of More – the precursor of all those hagiographical biographies – presenting him as 'a man for all seasons . . . born and made for friendship, of which he is the sincerest and most persistent devotee'.[33]

The friendship of More and Erasmus, which reached such intensity in those years, was not only a personal friendship: it was the expression of a common ideal. And never did that ideal seem so close to realization as in those years when both had achieved European recognition. It was expressed succinctly by Erasmus in the letter which he sent, in the spring of 1517, to Pope Leo X, the humanist pope of whom he expected such great things. 'I foresee', he wrote, 'the restoration to the human race of three of its greatest blessings': that true Christian piety which in so many ways is now decayed; the study of the humanities, in part neglected hitherto, and in part corrupted; and that public and perpetual harmony of the Christian world which is the fountain and parent of religion and learning':[34] in short, that fusion of Florentine Platonism with a re-spiritualized, reformed, ecumenical Christianity which Erasmus himself would describe as 'the philosophy of Christ'.

Ironically, it was in that very year that the fatal blow was struck: or rather, the stone was loosed which brought the enchanted castle down. For it was in 1517 that Martin Luther, following the innocent example of Pico della Mirandola himself, posted his challenging theses in his local church. As Erasmus foresaw, that frontal challenge, and the frontal resistance of the established Church, split the unity of Christendom, and neither Erasmus, by refusing that challenge, nor More, by accepting it, could save that unity. It was broken for centuries, perhaps for ever.

Nor was it only the unity of Christendom that foundered in those years. Less spectacularly, but no less finally, the Platonism which had given its last glow to that unity was also being undermined. It was undermined in theology by the revived scholasticism of Reformation and Counter-Reformation; it was undermined in politics by the new historical outlook of Machiavelli and his disciples; and in philosophy it was transformed. For the Platonism of More and Erasmus was a particular synthesis, tied to time and place: a synthesis of evangelical piety with the pure Platonism of Plato. But that English synthesis, which had drawn so critically on its Florentine models and which Erasmus, who had learned it in England, had carried back to Europe, was now overtaken there by a very different synthesis: the Hermetic, magical, Cabalistic 'Renaissance Platonism' of Reuchlin and

Agrippa, Cardano and Dee, Bruno and Campanella which was to have such a fortune in the later sixteenth century. In this form it would continue to offer, for those who could accept it, a means of reconciling Catholic and Protestant theology and re-creating an ecumenical church. But it was not the church of Erasmus and More: it was the church of a few esoteric adepts whom Erasmus and More would not have recognized: for, far from being evangelical, they were hardly Christian at all.

With the dissolution of More's intellectual world, there was dissolved also the spirit which had animated it, the spirit of confidence, gaiety, good-humoured raillery and love of life. As Marie Delcourt has written, the ideological tempest of the 1520s would carry away both the great hopes of the previous generation and the bold and genial spirits behind them. 'Neither the *Praise of Folly* nor *Utopia* could have been written after 1520. Thereafter, only Rabelais would triumph over the intellectual depression which had settled upon Europe.'[35] Rabelais, we may remark, was also a Platonist, like Erasmus and More; he too was an admirer and translator of Lucian – would indeed be known as 'the French Lucian'; he was the avowed disciple of Erasmus 'to whom I owe [as he wrote] *quicquid sum et valeo*, all that I am, all that I am worth'; and he borrowed some of his ideas, and names, openly from the *Utopia* of Thomas More.*

In the new age marked by the division of Christendom after 1520, Erasmus fared better than More. The Platonic 'philosophy of Christ' might have foundered, but Erasmus' scholarship and his implicit heresy – his rationality, his unflinching textual criticism, his scepticism – continued to keep his ideas alive. He looked forward to the scholars and thinkers of the next century: to the Arminians of Holland, the Socinians and deists of England. The work of More lacked these preservative ingredients, and so it dissolved, leaving only the indefinable quality of saintliness and the fact of martyrdom. *Utopia*, that Platonic political idea, with its uncomfortable social criticism and radical formula of stability, was disowned. After the Peasants' Revolt in Germany, it won no support in Europe: a Europe increasingly frightened of social radicalism.† Only a few Spanish clergy dreamed of

---

* See Rabelais's letter to Erasmus of 30 November 1532, inspired by the attack on Erasmus by J. C. Scaliger, in Allen, *Opus Epistolarum D. Erasmi*, X, 130. Rabelais's interest in *Utopia* is shown by his allusions: Gargantua's letter to Pantagruel is sent 'de Utopie' and his wife Badebec is 'fille du royaume des Amaurotes en Utopie'.

† Five Latin editions of *Utopia* were printed in 1517-19, and a German translation in 1524. Thereafter no edition or translation appeared till 1548.

applying that idealist blueprint to the unresisting conquered society of America, as Oliver Cromwell would afterwards dream of applying the equally utopian schemes of his followers to the 'blank paper' of conquered Ireland. But their voices were not heard in Europe.* There the book continued to be read as an agreeable fantasy, but in the political philosophy of the time it marks a dead end.†

As for More himself, from 1522 onwards he became a mere religious controversialist. In many ways, as he saw the need to fight for his ideas, he silently denied some of them. He became a bigot, a blind persecutor of heresy. After his martyrdom he shrank into a provincial saint, cultivated only in a dwindling family circle. In England, outside the family, he was hardly mentioned, and the biographies which that family wrote or inspired remained largely unpublished. Ironically, it was in Spain and Portugal – the countries in which the name of Erasmus was most ruthlessly blotted out – that the name of More was most warmly cherished.‡ But it was cherished only as a symbol. In the capital of Counter-Reformation Catholicism, More was seen as the most exalted critic and victim of Protestant England and its hated, heretical Tudor dynasty. So in Spain, Portugal and the Spanish Netherlands, his name was revered and his descendants pensioned,§

---

* The most famous of such projects is that of Vasco de Quiroga, on which see Silvio Zavala, *La Utopia de Tomás Moro en la Nueva España* (Mexico, 1937). See also Silvio Zavala, 'Sir Thomas More in New Spain', *Diamante*, III, London, 1955; F. B. Warren, *Vasco de Quiroga* (Washington, 1963); and cf. *Moreana*, III, Vol. V, pp. 27, 380; Vol. X, p. 87. Another Spaniard who saw Utopia as a model for New Spain was Solorzano Pereira, the author of *Política Indiana* (1648). See Silvio Zavala, 'Solórzano Pereira et l'Utopie de Thomas More', *Moreana*, XVII, 15.

† More's *Utopia* is dismissed summarily by Bodin in his *Methodus* and in his *Republique* and by Bacon in his *New Atlantis*. Alberico Gentili occasionally quotes it (generally critically) in his *Commentaries* (see Philip Dust in *Moreana*, No. 37, p. 31), and Robert Burton treats it with respect, but fundamental disagreement, in his *Anatomy of Melancholy*. Otherwise it is seldom cited in serious works.

‡ The martyr More was adopted in Spain and Portugal at an early date. In 1550 George Buchanan, defending himself before the Inquisition at Lisbon, pretended that his tragedy *Baptistes* was a sound Catholic work: Herod, he inferred, was Henry VIII, Herodias Anne Boleyn, and John the Baptist More. Presumably he thought that this unplausible evasion might be accepted in Portugal. (Guilhermo J. C. Henriques, *George Buchanan in the Lisbon Inquisition*, Lisbon, 1906, p. 28.) About the same time More's holograph MS. of his *Expositio Passionis* was obtained by Pedro de Soto, the confessor of Charles V, probably from More's granddaughter Mary Basset, and conveyed to Spain. It is now in Valencia. In 1588 the Spanish Jesuit Pedro de Ribadeneyra praised More in his *Cisma de Inglaterra*, and in 1592 Fernando de Herrera published his *Tomás Moro* at Seville. Neither of these writers appears to have read anything by More.

§ In 1614 the Spanish ambassador in London, the famous conde de Gondomar, sought the King of Spain's permission to pay a pension to one Catherine Bentley, whose but his books were not read. The greatest of them, *Utopia*, was on the Index.*

Sources

1. *The Yale edition of the Complete Works of St Thomas More* (Yale University Press, 1963–).
2. *Opera Omnia Desiderii Erasmi Roterodami* (Amsterdam, 1969); *Collected Works of Erasmus* (Toronto, 1974–).
3. On this subject see J. K. McConica, 'The Recusant Reputation of Thomas More', in R. S. Sylvester and G. Marc'hadour, *Essential Articles for the study of St Thomas More* (Archon Books, 1977).
4. Erasmus to Robert Fisher 5 Dec. 1499. *The Correspondence of Erasmus* (Toronto, 1974), I, 235.
5. R. Klibansky, *The Continuity of the Platonic Tradition during the Middle Ages* (n.d.), p. 19.
6. *Correspondence of Erasmus*, I, 258; IV, 97; V, 23.
7. E. F. Rogers (ed.), *The Correspondence of Sir Thomas More* (Princeton, 1947), pp. 63–4, 115.
8. Vittorio Gabrieli, 'Giovanni Pico and Thomas More', *Moreana*, Vol. IV (1967), No. 15, pp. 43ff.
9. Erasmus to Ulrich von Hutten [before 1519] in P. S. Allen, *Erasmi Opus Epistolarum*, IV, No. 999.
10. See F. Masai, *Pléthon et le Platonisme de Mistra* (Paris, 1956).
11. Harpsfield, *Life of More*, p. 119; Ro.Ba. *Life of More*, p. 250.
12. Rogers, op. cit, pp. 126, 132
13. G. O. Trevelyan, *Life and Letters of Lord Macaulay* (World's Classics), II, 434.
14. Walter Pater, *Plato and Platonism* (Caravan Library, 1934), p. 173.
15. On Platonism in the Muslim world see Richard Walzer 'Aspects of Islamic Political Thought: Al-Fārābī and Ibn Xaldūn', *Oriens*, Vol. 16 (1963), 40–60.

---

husband, having been condemned to death under Elizabeth, had had to flee to the Spanish Netherlands and had left her in England with thirteen children. According to Gondomar, 'she has a great qualification, for she is a granddaughter [*nieta*] of that great man Thomas More'. The King approved a pension of 1100 *reales*. (*Correspondencia Oficial de D. Diego Sarmiento de Acuña, conde de Gondomar*, Madrid, 1936–45, I, 190; III, 298–9.) Catherine Bentley was in fact the great-granddaughter of More. She is recorded in Lord St Oswald's Roper Roll as the daughter of Thomas Roper, second son of William Roper, and of his wife Lucy, sister of Anthony Browne, Viscount Montague (another great patron of recusants). For her husband Edward Bentley of Derbyshire, 'lately condemned for treason, but at liberty', see *Cal.S.P.Dom.* 1591–4, p. 372, *Hist MSS. Commission, Marquess of Salisbury*, IV, 272, and cf. XX, 55, where 'one Bentley, a young gentleman' who had lately come from Flanders to Madrid is probably a son.

* No early Spanish edition of *Utopia* is known. The book was placed on the Index in Portugal (1581) and Spain (1583), 'nisi expurgetur', by the Archbishop of Toledo. An expurgated edition in Spanish was published at Córdoba in 1637, with an introduction by Quevedo. From this edition the whole of book I is omitted. Quevedo's own copy of *Utopia* shows that the book was condemned as full of foul and impious Erasmianism. See R. O. Jones, 'Some Notes on More's *Utopia* in Spain', *Modern Language Review* (October 1950), 478–82.

16. On this see especially Gordon Zeeveld, *The making of Tudor Policy* (Harvard, 1949).
17. See V. Gabrieli, 'Tomaso Moro, *Le Quattro Cose Ultime*', in *La Cultura*, XV (1977), 453.
18. *The Correspondence of Erasmus*, V, 129, 401, 410.
19. James McConica, *Thomas More* (National Portrait Gallery), p. 57.
20. Richard S. Sylvester (ed.), *The Complete Works of St Thomas More, Vol. 2, Richard III*, lxiii–iv.
21. For the identification of the portraits see Lorne Campbell, Margaret Mann Phillips, Hubertus Schulte Herbrüggen and J. B. Trapp, 'Quentin Matsys, Desiderius Erasmus, Pieter Gillis and Thomas More', *Burlington Magazine*, CXX, (1978).
22. e.g. by John Stuart Mill, *Autobiography* (World's Classics), p. 19.
23. Quotations from *Utopia* are from the English translation by Ralph Robinson, 1551, as published by the Classics Club (New York, 1947).
24. *Correspondence of Erasmus*, IV, 163.
25. Masai, op. cit., esp. pp. 66–100.
26. On Savonarola and the Florentine Platonists see D. P. Walker, *The Ancient Theology* (1972), pp. 42–62.
27. Sylvester, op. cit., lxxxi–xcviii.
28. Rogers, op. cit., p. 83.
29. G. Grote, *Plato and the other companions of Sokrates* (1865), III, 218–19.
30. M. L. Clarke, *George Grote, a Biography* (1962), p. 63.
31. Rogers, op. cit., p. 303; F. Gasquet, *Cardinal Pole and his early Friends* (1927), 69–71.
32. *Correspondence of Erasmus*, V, 105, 147.
33. See above, note 9.
34. *Correspondence of Erasmus*, IV, 311 (Toronto, 1974).
35. Thomas More, *L'Utopie* . . . ed. Marie Delcourt (Paris, n.d.), iii.

4
Erasmus and the Crisis of Christian Humanism

The years 1516–19 were critical in the history of Christian humanism. At the beginning of that brief period it seemed unchallengeable; or at least it was opposed only by the disreputable obscurantism of monks, friars and theologians. At the end, new intellectual or at least ideological forces had been liberated which would carry away some of its own leaders and force it to change both its form and its course. Its apparent triumph and the gathering of the forces which would ultimately overwhelm it are vividly illustrated in the correspondence of its acknowledged leader, Erasmus.

What a position Erasmus held in 1516! Outwardly he was a poor scholar dependent on patronage. Not all that poor, as he tartly observed when his English friend Richard Pace described him as such: he had 300 ducats a year of his own 'besides what I get from the generosity of my patrons and as the fruit of my own labours', and he could have more if he wished; but still far from rich, unable to afford both clothes and a horse, and living frugally on casual offerings laboriously solicited. Every journey had to be financed by the grant-awarding bodies of the time: princes, bishops, publishers, friends. But intellectually he towered over Europe. Popes honoured him, kings, princes, cardinals, archbishops, pressed him to accept their patronage, to become their client, to give lustre to their names.

Early in 1517, Erasmus paid a brief visit to England, which had been his home, or at least his base, for the five years 1509–14, until he had been driven out by the sound of 'the Julian trumpet' – Pope Julius II's call to war. Now he was welcomed back with open arms. Henry VIII received him 'with the greatest kindness' and offered him a distinguished post with 600 florins a year and 'a splendid house'. Cardinal

Wolsey, 'who is not easy and affable to everyone', pressed his patronage
on him. Back in Europe, rival offers poured in. The Prince-Bishop of
Utrecht, Philip of Burgundy, twice approached him with tempting
proposals. The Prince-Bishop of Liège, the great humanist magnate
Erard de la Marck, offered to come and visit him in Louvain if Erasmus
would not visit him in Liège. The Archbishop Elector of Mainz,
President of the Electoral College of the Empire, wrote 'a whole letter in
his own hand' to express his admiration. The Duke of Bavaria begged
him to come and lend glory to his university of Ingolstadt. Cardinal
Ximenes offered him one of the best bishoprics in Spain. The King of
France, François I, offered him 'mountains of gold' if he would come to
Paris to adorn his new Collège de France. His own sovereign, Prince
Charles, Duke of Burgundy, now also King of Spain and soon to be the
Emperor Charles V, was lavish in his offers. Having given him a
pension and made him his privy councillor, he pressed him to be the
tutor of his brother, the Archduke Ferdinand, soon to be King of
Hungary. He offered him benefices in the Netherlands, in Spain, and a
bishopric in Sicily; and, wrote Erasmus, 'I am dreadfully afraid . . .
designs to make me bishop of the Indies'.

However, Erasmus wriggled out of all these gilded traps. He 'would
do anything', he wrote, 'rather than be enmeshed in that kind of
business'. He wished for patronage without strings. He would accept
sinecures, canonries, titular benefices without duties, such as were so
usual in the unreformed Church, especially in the Netherlands, but he
was determined not to be 'swept into the strong seas of politics' like his
friend More, who had been 'carried away by the whirlwind of court
favour' and was now 'lost to literature'. So he evaded the offers of Henry
VIII and Wolsey: 'I took the middle course,' he wrote, 'between
accepting the conditions offered and rejecting them.' Though devoted
to Prince Charles, he refused to accompany him to Spain and passed on
the tutorship of the Archduke to his friend the émigré Spanish Jewish
humanist Juan Luis Vives. Though he liked Paris, where he had
learned Greek, and shared the aims of François I, he dodged the royal
offers: 'I have sent a letter in reply', he wrote, 'designed to give no
definite answer.' This exasperated his friend, the great Greek scholar
Guillaume Budé, who had been the King's intermediary in the affair.
But evasion was, to Erasmus, a necessity, even a way of life. Anyway,
for the moment at least, his fate, he believed, tied him to the Netherlands, to the still lingering freedom of its city republics where he could
continue his quiet work of scholarship, now recognized and in full flow.

For the year 1516–17 was Erasmus' *annus mirabilis*. In it he published his editions of Seneca, of St Jerome's Letters, his *Institutio Principis Christiani*, and, above all, his greatest achievement, as contemporaries believed, his *Novum Instrumentum*, the New Testament newly translated direct from the original Greek and accompanied by annotations setting out both his methods and his aims. These works spread his fame all over Europe and stimulated new editions of his earlier writings. His journeys up and down the Rhine to see to their printing in Basel had revealed groups of enthusiastic 'Erasmians' in every city, who turned out to welcome him, and it was now that his works crossed the Pyrenees and made their astonishing conquest of Spain and Portugal. After that, he could reap the harvest of fame.

He also obtained freedom from an old personal worry. Pope Leo X, to whom he had dedicated his New Testament, granted him all the dispensations which he needed, and which he had been seeking through his friend Andrea Ammonio, the papal nuncio in England. That made him safe from attack on grounds of defect of birth, apostasy from his order, and disuse of clerical habit, and free to hold a plurality of benefices, in England as elsewhere. It was to receive this dispensation that he paid his brief visit to England in April 1517. Then he returned to the Netherlands to resume his scholarly work. That meant, primarily, to produce a second, revised edition of his New Testament; for he was not now satisfied with the first edition which, as he said (not without some justice), had been 'rushed into print' and needed to be 'taken to pieces and re-fashioned'. But he also had further plans: he was working on his paraphrases of the epistles of St Paul. All this was part of his systematic programme for the renewal of Christian spirituality. The Gospels, he believed, were simple and needed only to be accurately set out and commented for their message to be clear. The epistles were not: they needed to be rewritten in lucid language, their sense to be extracted and set out, if they were to be intelligible to ordinary men.

For this purpose Erasmus settled in Louvain. Louvain was convenient for his duties, such as they were, as a counsellor of his prince. It was also useful as a university city with libraries and scholars: he remembered with gratitude his stay in the English universities. On arrival, he lived in the house of Jean Desmarez, public orator of the university. Then he moved to the College of the Lily, as a paying guest. At first he was welcomed by the established theologians of Louvain. They co-opted him as a member of their Faculty, although he was not a doctor of the university, and treated him, as he admitted, 'with the greatest kindness'. He attended their Faculty meetings, 'at which' – as at so many Faculty meetings everywhere – 'they do the same thing over and over again'. This was their honeymoon period. Moreover, an unexpected accident suddenly gave him the opportunity of achieving in the Netherlands that educational ideal which he was reluctant to pursue under royal patronage in France: the creation of a humanist college to propagate the New Learning.

The opportunity came through the death, in August 1517, of Jerome de Busleiden, a rich Burgundian official of humanist learning, a friend of Erasmus and More. He died at Bordeaux, on his way to his master's new kingdom of Spain, and by his will he provided for the foundation, at Louvain, of a College of the Three Tongues – Hebrew, Greek and Latin. Erasmus, who had inspired the idea, was a driving force behind its realization: he was determined that the college should fulfil the founder's intention and not be diverted to mere theological purposes. 'Take my word for it', he exclaimed, 'there will always be enough colleges for theology, but this most noble project, unless it goes forward in accordance with Busleiden's intentions, will not be set on foot, as far as I can see, by anyone else.' So, though himself cool towards Hebrew studies, he discovered a professor of Hebrew – a Marrano from Spain – and set about finding professors of Greek and Latin. These were the tongues that were important to him: Greek, the language of Plato, the New Testament, Origen, Chrysostom, Basil, in which the 'Philosophy of Christ' was to be found; Latin, the language of Cicero, Jerome, Augustine, in which it was now to be disseminated. Hebrew was of interest to him only in order to understand the Jewish context which that philosophy had repudiated, the Rabbinical sophistries from which it must be protected. To find a Grecian, a native Greek for preference, he consulted John Lascaris at Rome. Perhaps he hoped to capture Lascaris himself; but if so, he failed: the King of France had got in first.

Thus happily installed, happily occupied with his own work and the new college, to which he proposed to bequeath his own library, it seemed that Erasmus was finally settled in Louvain. His letters purr with satisfaction: there need be no more of that ceaseless and uncomfortable travel, for which he was so often criticized, no more uncertainty, only a labour of love yielding a reward of fame. It is the dream of the scholar, seldom realized. And indeed it would not be realized for Erasmus; for scarcely had he established himself in Louvain when the trouble started.

To begin with, there were the ordinary occupational inconveniences of collegiate life. Erasmus was a European figure, a prince of the Republic of Letters. The theologians of Louvain moved, or stayed still, in a more limited parish. They were great circulators of the bottle.

Erasmus found their 'continual drinking parties' very trying. There were also more fundamental differences. For among these theologians were critics who challenged his whole philosophy, men of abject but aggressive conservatism, who, with familiarity, gradually became more and more outspoken. These men repudiated humanist studies; they disliked the whole concept of the new college, as a threat to their monopoly and a challenge to their ideas; and they denounced the very idea of using, or publishing, or translating, the Greek New Testament: what, they asked, was wrong with the Vulgate? Finally, since they had rank and status in their little corporation, and took themselves seriously, they objected to the levity of Erasmus' style: in particular, of course, to that disconcerting satire, the *Moria*, the *Praise of Folly*. Some even ascribed to him the wicked dialogue *Julius Exclusus*, on Pope Julius II shut out of Heaven. This had long circulated in manuscript; now, most inopportunely, it slipped into print. Erasmus always primly disowned it; but his disavowals have not convinced scholars, now or then.

The most difficult of the Louvain theologians was 'that stupid fool' Maarten van Dorp, who blew now hot, now cold, 'as inconstant as any woman', and was not brought to see sense even by an immense letter in support of Erasmus from Thomas More; but there was also a nasty young Englishman, one Edward Lee, who had arrived with the grandest of testimonials but had then tried to make his name, as young scholars do, by attacking established reputations. Lee's strategy was to pick holes in Erasmus' New Testament, and then to point out, peering through them, the ugly features of heresy. He would cause Erasmus a great deal of trouble, but would serve himself well in the process: he would end as Archbishop of York. Finally, behind all these, waiting their chance, were the irreconcilable enemies of the new learning and religious reform, the disciplined army of friars, Dominicans and Carmelites, impossible either to satisfy or to silence. They would never spare Erasmus, nor he them.

It was particularly unfortunate that, just at this time, Erasmus felt obliged to enter into controversy with the great French humanist and Christian Platonist, Jacques Lefèvre d'Etaples, who had accused him, among other things, of denying the divinity of Christ. Lefèvre had used strong language against such a heresy, and Erasmus, in his reply, exclaimed no less strongly against such an imputation. The friends of Christian humanism were aghast at this open breach in their ranks, which ought to be closed against their common enemies, and Erasmus protested that he was a most unwilling controversialist; but once involved, he insisted on winning the controversy. Thus his energies were diverted against a natural ally just when they were needed for the common fight against the natural enemy. For it was precisely at this time that the Dominicans in Germany launched their great attack against the New Learning, and particularly against Hebrew studies, in the person of Johann Reuchlin.

Erasmus had met Reuchlin at Frankfurt, on his return journey from Basel, in 1515, and his sympathies were immediately engaged on his side. 'Who is there anywhere with any tincture of learning or religion', he wrote, 'who does not support him?' He described Reuchlin's enemies as 'a nest of hornets', and their leader, the converted Jew Johann Pfefferkorn, who attacked Hebrew studies with all the ferocity of a renegade, as an unspeakable monster. But he did not wish to take sides publicly in the controversy, especially when it had been sharpened by the publication of the famous satire *Epistolae Obscurorum Virorum*. He disapproved of the satire from its first appearance because it had personalized and embittered the battle, and he did his best to restrain his allies. 'That scholars are supporting Reuchlin', he wrote, 'is a sign of enlightenment; but that they should dispute in writing with that kernel of mischief' – i.e. Pfefferkorn – 'the Furies' trumpeter, the tool of certain theologians in disguise and Satan's true lieutenant – of this I cannot approve'; and he urged them to leave the Dominicans to be censured by the authorities, clerical and lay, rather than be pushed, by the necessities of controversy, into anti-clerical postures which incidentally might (and in fact did) alienate those authorities. So he concentrated his attacks on the dreadful Pfefferkorn: 'half a Jew? No: a Jew and a half' who had been converted only in order to infect Christianity with his 'Jewish poison'.

Erasmus' refusal to be dragged into the battle over Reuchlin had several motives. For one thing, though the battle ground was the New Learning, the immediate front was Hebrew studies, towards which he was himself lukewarm. On this front he did not wish to fight. Judaism, to him, represented everything of which he wished to purge Christianity: formalism, ceremonialism, rabbinical pedantry. The Church, he wrote, in a particularly explosive letter, paid too much attention to the Old Testament, 'a thing of shadows, given us for a time', but now superseded, and he attacked the Jews as 'a nation full of the most tedious fabrications, who spread a kind of fog over everything: Talmud, Cabala, Tetragrammaton, *Gates of Light*, words, words, words. I would rather have Christ mixed up with Scotus than with that rubbish of theirs.' Scotus, Duns Scotus, was to him the very type of futile scholastic subtlety, the letter which killed the 'philosophy of Christ'.

There was also his own position to consider. The epicentre of the storm was Cologne where the Faculty of Theology, led by the Dominican Jacob van Hoogstraten, organized the attack against Reuchlin while the Faculty of Arts, led by Erasmus' friend and patron, the young clerical aristocrat Count Hermann von Neuenahr, defended him. Both sides appealed to Erasmus for support. But if Erasmus were to come off the fence, and declare his true opinion, how would his colleagues at Louvain react? 'I support Reuchlin as a very learned man,' he wrote when the battle began, 'but in such a way as to have no quarrel with Hoogstraten or others of his party'; and again, 'I get on reasonably well with the theologians in Louvain. Cologne university is torn by unlovely strife. . . . Those Preachers in their cowls run to and fro, spreading false rumours among the common folk and lying brazenly.' He was well aware that his real battle was with the friars, but he was not ready for a frontal struggle with them, especially on this issue. He quoted the remark of Pope Alexander VI, that he would rather offend some powerful monarch than one of those mendicant friars who, 'under that humble name,' tyrannized Christendom; and he wished that 'our young eaglet' Neuenahr would 'keep his talons off such frightful stuff, from which he can get nothing but corruption and filth. A man who takes on the Preachers has mob-warfare on his hands.'

Bibulous monks, querulous theologians, obscurantist friars, Jewish renegades, unwanted controversies. . . . After nine months Erasmus was beginning to find his sojourn in Louvain much less agreeable. But he was sustained by his sense of mission: his determination to produce a new and improved edition of his New Testament and to continue his Paraphrases of St Paul's epistles. Thus, he hoped, he would rescue Christianity from its 'Jewish' inheritance, set out the 'philosophy of Christ' in its irresistible simplicity, liberate the thought of St Paul from his barbarous Hebraized Greek, and make him speak to the modern world 'in the Roman tongue, and more intelligibly than was his wont'. For he had no great respect for the Greek style of the apostle, or indeed of the evangelists. As he explained, following the method of Colet, they had learned their Greek 'not from the speeches of Demosthenes but from the conversation of ordinary men'; consequently, their literary standard was not high. This of course was a very shocking opinion. As the famous theologian of Ingolstadt, Johann Eck, sharply reminded him, the apostles learned their Greek not from Greeks but from the Holy Ghost: 'a sufficiently well-meaning and well instructed preceptor'. Who was Erasmus to set up as the instructor of the evangelists, the corrector of the Holy Ghost?

Erasmus could ignore these cavils – or at least he thought that he could – for had he not powerful allies and a powerful machine? Thanks to the new Erasmian élite throughout Europe – that ruling class of highly educated princes and their humanist officials in Church and State – and to its new instrument, the printing press, he hoped quietly to side-step the reactionary theologians and populist monastic orders and prepare the way for Enlightenment and Reform. For this purpose, the purpose of his life, he must avoid unnecessary controversy and work, work, work. For time was short; while he was giving 'fresh vigour' to the New Testament, he was growing old himself: while 'I rescue it from senility', and restore it to its original splendour, 'I cover myself with dust and cobwebs'.

By the spring of 1518 Erasmus had almost completed his work of revision and it was time to carry his book to the publisher. But to which publisher? Should it be Aldus in Venice, with whom he had lived during his Italian journey, ten years before, and who had published the enlarged second edition of his *Adagia*, or Froben in Basel whom he had first visited in 1514 and who had published the third edition of the same work, as also his Seneca and his Jerome? Erasmus was not sure. On the whole, he preferred Venice, because his trusted bookseller in Basel, Wolfgang Lachner, Froben's father-in-law, who had financed the printing of Jerome, had died, and also because the plague, which was raging in Germany, was said to have reached Basel. But on one thing he was clear. After the works were printed, he would not now settle in Louvain. He would return to England, there, 'in one of the furthest recesses in the world', to find 'a secret and remote retreat' and be free, in his old age, 'to sing to myself and the Muses'.

For England still fascinated him. How could he ever forget the country which, twenty years before, had introduced him to Christian Platonism, the motive force of all his subsequent work? For it was not in Italy, its primary source, which had now dried up, but in England, and more particularly in Oxford, that he had discovered that living stream, the intellectual nourishment of his classical learning. Since then, England had been his alternative base, perhaps his spiritual home. Every reference to it, in his letters, is lyrical. Henry VIII – the young, still uncorrupted Henry VIII – is 'the most intelligent of the monarchs of our time and enjoys good literature'. Henry's great officers and close friends are all men of culture, of the New Learning: 'that most remarkable man', Cardinal Wolsey; Archbishop Warham; Bishops Tunstall, Foxe and Fisher; Dean Colet. . . . How different were these clergy from the theologians of Louvain! And then the laity. . . . Pace, so incredibly gifted, so learned in Greek and Latin, 'a man made expressly for friendship and popularity'; Lord Mountjoy, earliest, best and most generous of patrons; and, of course, 'my dear More, whom I love best of mortal men': More who was 'not only the Muses' darling but the pattern of all charm and grace'.

For it was in the laity, the educated laity, rather than the clergy, that Erasmus ultimately put his trust: they were the true carriers of the new learning, the new piety. 'How astonishing', he wrote, to an English friend, 'are the revolutions in human affairs! In the old days, zeal for literature was to be found among the religious orders', but now 'the dinner-tables of clergymen and divines are sodden with drink, they are infected with scurrilous jests and loud with intemperate uproar or full of poisonous backbiting'. It was at the tables of princes and their lay courtiers that one found serious, elevated discussion, and above all among the English courtiers of Henry VIII. 'What university or monastery anywhere contains so many men of outstanding integrity and learning as your court can show?' 'You know', he wrote to an Italian friend, 'how averse I have always been to the courts of princes. It is a life which I can only regard as gilded misery under a mask of splendour. But I would gladly move to a court like that.' Henry VIII's palace was, to him, 'a shrine of the Muses', 'more like an academy than a king's court. What Athens or Stoa or Lyceum' could be compared with it? More's defection from literature, 'under such a king and with so many educated colleagues and acquaintances', could be forgiven, even commended.

With such ideas, or illusions, Erasmus prepared to leave Louvain in order to publish his New Testament and then, on his return, to escape from warring Europe to an idealized England. The journey, of course, would be costly, and he wrote to his English friends not only to prepare his final retreat but also to secure immediate contributions towards his expenses. Would Fisher, for instance, provide a strong English horse? He would need three horses altogether: for himself, his servant, and the luggage. How far could Mountjoy and More go? The two themes – the immediate journey and the ultimate retreat to England – are of course related. But what we particularly note is the despondency of Erasmus' tone. Partly this was personal: he was apprehensive of the journey. Travel in 1518 was neither comfortable nor safe. But he was depressed also by the course of public affairs. Could it be that the forces of reaction would prevail, that his labours would prove vain, that the spiritual renewal for which he was working would be snuffed out?

So there is also, in these letters, a note of resignation. When his business was done, he wrote to Fisher, he had a mind 'to retire from this accursed world', in which 'the cunning of princes and the effrontery of the Roman curia' had reached its limit: 'I shall turn therefore entirely to you, as a people on the edge of the world, and perhaps the least infected province of Christianity.' And to Colet he wrote, in an even more resigned spirit:

> I am obliged, for the printing of my *New Testament* and other reasons, to go either to Basel or, what seems more likely, to Venice . . . 'What?' you say, 'an old man and an invalid like you undertake such a journey, and that in an age like ours, the most lawless for many centuries, with robbery so common everywhere?' But what would you? Such is the destiny to which I was born. If I die at my work, it will be at work not wholly bad, if I mistake not. If, after finishing the last act of this play as I wish, I am so lucky as to return, I have decided to spend the remainder of my life with you. This will be my retreat from the corruption of the whole world. Theologians in disguise hold sway in all the courts of princes. The Roman curia has abandoned any sense of shame. What could be more shameless than these constant indulgences? And now they put up a war against the Turks as a pretext, when their aim really is to drive the Spaniards from Naples. . . . If this turmoil goes any further, the rule of the Turks will be more tolerable than the rule of Christians like them.

'These constant indulgences' . . . The words sound a new note. Erasmus had recently received from Basel a printed copy of the ninety-five theses which Luther had nailed to the church door of Wittenberg five months before. It was with that radical voice echoing in his ears that he prepared to set out on his journey to a yet undetermined publisher.

When the theologians of Louvain heard of his intention, the tongues at their high table began to wag. They accused him, once again, of inconstancy, 'infirmity of purpose', illustrated by his wandering life: why could he not settle down and become respectable like themselves? Other old criticisms were revived too: the levity of the *Moria*, the danger implicit in Greek studies, the sinister import of his textual and contextual criticism. In a letter to a Burgundian friend Erasmus dealt roundly with all these criticisms. He was particularly incensed by the charge of inconstancy. 'Infirmity of purpose indeed!' he exploded. Did they think that he was undertaking this costly and perilous journey for his pleasure? Never, he protested, had he moved house except to avoid the plague, or when compelled by ill health, 'or for some honourable business reason' – to meet learned men, or visit libraries, or publish his work. 'If this was infirmity of purpose, I have yet to regret it.' His purpose was his work: to that he was constant. Had he not resisted the call of kings and princes in order to be free to publish his message to the world? If the virtue of firmness consists in immobility, 'first prize must go to stocks and stones, and after them to barnacles and sponges . . . They call me infirm of purpose because I have not spent forty-five years in the same town drinking with them – like a lot of sponges fixed on a rock, whose life consists in drinking . . .' Having delivered this broadside, he set off, on an English horse provided by More, undeterred by the prospect of plague, robbery, and, worst of all, the terrible 'Black Band', the dispersed soldiers who had turned to banditry and were terrorizing the lower Rhineland. Between Venice and Basel he had plumped, in the end, for Basel; and there he arrived on 13 May 1518.

All through that summer Erasmus stayed in Basel seeing to the printing of his works: not only the revised annotations on the New Testament but new editions of the *Institutio Principis Christiani* and of the *Enchiridion Militis Christiani*. This last work, the popular exposition of the Philosophy of Christ, had been in print since 1503, but its great influence dates from this second edition, which was carried everywhere by the fame of its author. It also contained a new dedication, addressed to one of his Rhineland admirers, a learned Benedictine abbot of Selestat in Alsace. In this new dedication Erasmus spelt out his message in clear, uncompromising terms; for he saw, in this old work, a new tract for the new times.

Erasmus' new dedication was a radical manifesto, the expression of a new radicalism of temper. Hitherto, as in the dedication of the first edition, he had attacked only the monks. *Monachatus non est pietas* had always been his message. He had spared the Church and the Papacy, to which he still looked for support. Indeed, even now he was cultivating the Pope – hence his unwillingness to admit authorship of *Julius Exclusus*. He had dedicated his New Testament to Leo X, had secured an expression of his approval of it, and was pleased to confound the critics of the *Moria* by reporting that His Holiness had laughed at the wit of that pungent but profound satire. Leo X, he admitted, was personally a cultivated man, of civilized, gentle manners, a patron of art and letters, his court 'a flourishing home of literature no less than of religion'. But could the Papacy be altogether separated from its institutions: from the bureaucracy by which it was imprisoned, from the army of monks and friars with which it could not dispense or quarrel, from the necessities of Reason of State?

In his new dedication of the *Enchiridion* Erasmus came dangerously close to criticism of the Papacy itself. He attacked the 'Philistines' who blocked the pure wells of truth, the theologians with their 'thorny and impenetrable thickets' of scholastic argument, the machiavellian politics of the Italian curia, the pretended crusade against the Turks, 'the traffic in indulgences, compositions, dispensations, and such like merchandise', relics, pilgrimages, and all the apparatus of 'mechanical religion'. By which we are reminded of Erasmus' letter to Colet before leaving Louvain. In retrospect we can see that we are now in a new historical phase. Erasmus, at the height of his fame, is being overtaken by a new ally, soon to become a new enemy, the man who would ultimately frustrate, for four centuries, his dream of ecumenical reform: Martin Luther.

Luther's ninety-five theses had been published at Basel at the end of 1517 and Erasmus, as we have seen, had received them at Louvain shortly before setting out on his journey. It was then that he had mentioned them to Colet. He had also sent a copy of them to More. Then he had left for Basel. So far, he had had no contact with Luther, nor did he, even now, mention his name: perhaps he did not yet know it, although Luther had been seeking to engage his interest since December 1516. In Basel he had had little time for correspondence and none for controversy. He was there till September; then, his editorial work with Froben being completed, he set out on the return journey to Louvain.

It was an eventful journey, on horseback, by boat, and by carriage, whose ups and downs he would describe in many vivid letters. The high points were his recognition and entertainment by the Erasmian customs officer at Boppard and the 'five delightful days' spent in 'tranquillity and comfort' at the castle of his clerical friend the Count of Neuenahr at Bedburg near Cologne. But the discomforts were many and great. The 'strong English horse' collapsed at Speyer. Erasmus was himself taken ill. At first he made light of it: the five days at Bedburg revived him, and he set off thence in restored spirits. He had planned 'a visit to the Bishop of Liège and a lively return to my friends in Brabant. The dinners, the parties of welcome, the long talks I was promising myself. . . .' And then there was the more distant mirage of England in the autumn. 'But how deceptive are the hopes of mortal men! . . . From all these dreams of felicity I was plunged headlong into utter disaster.'

Between Cologne and Aachen he was taken seriously ill and by the time he reached Louvain he expected to die, 'so relentlessly did one disaster succeed another, each worse than the last'. Three physicians who visited him diagnosed the plague, and one of them, having done so, immediately took flight. But Erasmus refused to despair, or to stop working, and after a month he recovered. He finished the final version of his New Testament and continued working on his Paraphrases. He also found himself, once again, threatened by controversy: controversy with the theologians, with the monks, with the dreadful Englishman Lee, with the enemies of Greek studies; and in the background there loomed up the beginnings of the greatest controversy of all, with Luther.

How Erasmus hated those controversies, contending with 'this scum'! He wished to get on with his work. Again and again he urged his humanist friends to ignore the critics: it was more important to continue Greek studies, he said, than to waste time and energy defending them. But the critics were not content to criticize such studies: they were determined to kill them; and so they could not be ignored: they must be resisted. The *Collegium Trilingue* at Louvain itself was in danger. 'The Philistines', Erasmus wrote, 'everywhere have put their heads together' and were determined 'to suppress humane studies' altogether. Hating alike Greek studies, Hebrew studies and Reform, they 'confound the cause of the humanities with the business of Reuchlin and Luther, though there is no connexion with them'. So Erasmus found himself pushed into the same camp as Luther and, though pressed to disavow him, was unable to do so. This made his position at Louvain extremely uncomfortable. 'This university,' he wrote, once 'the peaceful home of literary studies, has been racked by extraordinary turmoil, the like of which I have never seen in all my life.' It seemed to be 'a sworn conspiracy . . . against the classical languages and the liberal arts'. How different from England, where Greek was taught in both Oxford and Cambridge: 'in Cambridge without disturbance' because its Chancellor was Erasmus' friend, Bishop Fisher, in Oxford because the old guard had been routed by the interposition of More, supported by the King.

These troubles at Louvain caused Erasmus to sigh again for England and his English friends; so he wrote to Henry VIII, to Wolsey, and others, to see if the way was clear. They also forced him to consider his relations with Luther. Luther, of course, longed to use Erasmus' great name and authority, and in order to secure it he mobilized his most powerful allies. In November 1517, shortly after posting his theses, he had persuaded George Spalatinus, the Elector of Saxony's secretary and librarian, to write a flattering letter; but the letter was entrusted to a court-chaplain who took two years to deliver it. Meanwhile Erasmus watched developments anxiously. On the one hand, he was unwilling to be drawn into the battle and feared Luther's intemperance; on the other, Luther's enemies were his enemies, the enemies of literature and reform, and he was himself becoming more critical of papal abuses: 'I perceive', he wrote indiscreetly to a German friend of Luther in October 1518, 'that the absolute rule of a certain high priest you know of, as that see is now run, is the curse of Christianity; and yet the preachers bow down before it and are quite shameless.' A little later, when Luther was reported to be in danger, Melanchthon wrote on his behalf to Erasmus: 'Martin Luther, who is a keen supporter of your reputation, desires your good opinion at all points'; and Wolfgang Capito, the Hebrew professor of Basel – Erasmus' adviser on Old Testament matters – followed suit, urging him not to be held back by fear of the theologians of Louvain: it was better, he said, 'to make enemies of all the theologians' than of Luther's supporters, who included princes, cardinals and bishops throughout Germany. Meanwhile Luther himself wrote direct to Erasmus. It was a letter of fulsome flattery and nauseating humility, begging 'Erasmus, my glory and my hope' to 'accept this younger brother of yours in Christ', and come out openly in his support.

Erasmus was cautious. To these German correspondents he replied expressing his exasperation with the court of Rome, his respect for Luther's character and life, his sympathy with his aims. In an attempt, perhaps, to mediate, he dedicated his edition of Suetonius' *Lives of the Caesars* to the Elector of Saxony and engaged him in correspondence. In his dedication he urged the Elector to support Luther and humane letters. To his English friends he was more reserved. While insisting on the need for reform, he deplored hasty measures and avoided any commitment. He had not read Luther's works, he explained, or had read them only in snatches. 'On Luther', he wrote to Colet, 'I will write at more length another day.' To Luther himself he replied prudently – though not prudently enough to avoid a storm when the letter was published. He admitted their common enemies and common aims, but also their difference of method: 'as for me, I keep myself uncommitted, so far as I can, in hopes of being able to do more for the revival of good literature. And I think one gets further by courtesy and moderation than by clamour. That is how Christ brought the world under his sway. . . . It is more expedient to protest against those who misuse the authority of bishops than against the bishops themselves; and I think one should do the same with kings. The universities are not so much to be despised as recalled to more serious studies. . . .' Clearly, by this time – May 1519 – Erasmus was alarmed by Luther's radicalism. But he was equally alarmed by the reaction against it. Already the chasm had opened in which 'Erasmianism', now apparently at the height of its success, would ultimately founder.

But Erasmianism was not merely a middle way of reform between Luther and the Papacy. It was also a positive philosophy: a synthesis of the evangelical Christianity of the Netherlands and the new Christian Platonism of Florence, filtered and purified by its passage through England. That was what Erasmus meant by 'the philosophy of Christ'. And in the same year, 1517, in which Luther issued his challenge, a challenge which would distort and ultimately doom Erasmian re-form, another German published a book which would similarly dis-tort and ultimately doom the Christian Platonism of Erasmus and his English friends. The author was that same Reuchlin into whose quarrel, as into that of Luther, Erasmus had been so reluctant to be drawn.

For in 1517 Reuchlin published his book *de Arte Cabalistica*, the result of his too deep immersion in those Hebrew studies which Erasmus distrusted. He dedicated this book, as Erasmus had dedicated his New Testament, to Pope Leo X. Reuchlin did not indeed invent Christian Cabalism – that honour, if it is an honour, must go to Giovanni Pico della Mirandola – but his work has been described by Frances Yates as 'the first full treatise on Cabala by a non-Jew'.[1] Erasmus, who was so troubled by the controversy over Reuchlin, naturally received a copy of this book, and Reuchlin sent him a second copy to be given to his English friends. So it passed through the hands of More and Colet, to Fisher. But we have seen Erasmus' own opinion of Cabala – a Jewish fog of meaningless 'words, words, words'. 'Personally', he wrote to Cardinal Wolsey, with specific reference to Reuchlin, 'I have never felt the attraction of Cabala or Talmud.' It was indeed entirely foreign to his unmetaphysical mind. Nor, it seems, did his English friends show much interest. More made no comment on the book. Colet read it but was unimpressed by it. This 'Pythagorical and Cabalistic philosophy', he wrote, was beyond him: it was not the way to enlightenment or piety: 'let us therefore leave all these complications behind us and take the short road to truth' by 'fervent love and imitation of Christ'. Fisher did not read it. But it was to prove an influential work. Just as Luther, an admirer of Erasmus, sought to strengthen, and in fact destroyed,

Erasmian reform by the injection of the new, explosive force of justification by Faith alone, so Reuchlin and his successors sought to
strengthen, and in fact destroyed, Erasmian Platonism by the injection
of the new distorting force of Jewish Cabalism.[2] What we now know as
'Renaissance Platonism' – that bizarre farrago of Neoplatonism, Lullism, Hermeticism, Cabalism – would drive out the purified 'Oxford'
Platonism of Colet and Grocyn, Erasmus and More.

However, if these years bred the forces which destroyed Erasmianism as an immediate movement, they also gave it a new base for its
ultimate survival. In 1518 Erasmus was still in doubt whether to go to
Venice or Basel in order to publish his work. But he had no doubt about
his later plans. He intended, on his return, to escape from Louvain and
its theologians to England. In due course he would indeed escape from
Louvain, where the pressure upon him had become intolerable. The
all-powerful imperial confessor demanded that he declare himself:
would he join the inquisitors or the heretics? Erasmus would do neither.
He would not openly support Luther; but equally he would not support
the Papacy against Luther. So he left. 'I have regretted many things', he
would write long afterwards, 'but I have never regretted that departure.' But he did not now go to England. He would never again visit
England. That romance was now over, to be replaced by another. He
had fallen in love with Basel.

For eight years after his flight from Louvain, Basel, a civilized
Catholic city, would be the home of Erasmus, and thither, in 1534,
when it had become a Protestant city, he would return to die. In the
end, he found, a free city republic provided a more congenial society
than any monarchical country; and how could he have found peace in
the England in which Henry VIII, the perfect Renaissance prince
corrupted into a petulant and capricious tyrant, would send his closest
friends, More and Fisher, to the block? Basel served him well, and
would remain, for the rest of the century, 'the worst century in history'
as he called it (and it would be worse still after his death), the Erasmian
city *par excellence*, the home of his spirit as of his body and his monument.

These crucial years of Erasmus' life are documented by the two latest
volumes of the great Toronto edition of his correspondence in English.[3]
Of this work I can only repeat what I have already said: that it is a
marvellous work of organization, erudition, and presentation. The
scholarship is perfect; the editorial apparatus economical but entirely
sufficient; the translation easy, colloquial, fresh, like Erasmus'
own Latin. This is a splendid enterprise: I cannot commend it
enough.

Sources

1. Frances Yates, *The Occult Philosophy in the Elizabethan Age* (1979), p. 24.
2. Ibid., pp. 37–41.
3. *Collected Works of Erasmus*, Vols 5 and 6 *The Correspondence of Erasmus 1517–1519* (University of Toronto Press, 1979, 1982).

5
The Lisle Letters

The English historian G. M. Young once wrote that the historian
should read the documents of an age until he could hear the people
speak. That was all very well for the Victorian age of which he wrote,
but how can we penetrate, in that depth, those earlier periods for which
private correspondence hardly exists? Fifteenth-century England
seems to us infinitely remote, its anarchy almost unimaginable, until we
read the Paston Letters and see the daily problems of a Norfolk family
during the Wars of the Roses. Publicly, an age may be well
documented; but it is by its private character, by the attempts of
individuals to lead conventional lives even in the midst of revolution,
that we sense its reality and seem, while we read, to share its life.

The public character of the reign of Henry VIII is well documented.
That too was an age of revolution. Not anarchy, as in the fifteenth
century, but controlled revolution, revolution from above. The seven-
year period from 1533 to 1540 – the seven years of Thomas Cromwell –
witnessed the breach with Rome, the dissolution of the monasteries, the
Pilgrimage of Grace, the creation of a new state church and a new
'despotic' state. Politically, the process was continuous, legalized in
regular institutions, but it was accompanied, and indeed driven forward, by a reign of terror. All who opposed or obstructed it, even
involuntarily, were ruthlessly eliminated: More and Fisher, Anne
Boleyn, the Carthusians, the Pilgrim leaders, the Pole family, finally
Cromwell himself; and even after him the process would go on, though
more untidily: Cromwell's revolution in government had the true
character of a revolution: it devoured its children.

Are there any documents which reveal the private character of this
hectic period as the Paston Letters revealed that of Henry VI? There

are, and thanks to a lifetime of devoted study, some two-thirds of them have now been edited and presented in readable form, with a copious running commentary, by Miss Muriel St Clare Byrne, and published in six ample volumes, beautifully printed, by the University of Chicago Press. They are the Lisle letters, and they cover exactly those seven years in which Thomas Cromwell both ruled and transformed England in the name, and at the mercy, of Henry VIII.

The Lisle Letters are not a new discovery. They were calendared long ago, in the great nineteenth-century collection, *Letters and Papers of Henry VIII*, begun by John Brewer and continued by James Gairdner (who also edited *The Paston Letters*). Historians have always used them, picking out what they wanted, but it was left to Miss Byrne to see that they had a coherent unity, which was lost by such piecemeal use: that they could be used, not merely incidentally and individually to illustrate the course of politics, but collectively in their own right, to bring back to life the self-contained human world which had created them – the world of a prominent but essentially unpolitical family which chance had involved (and in the end nearly ruined) in this formidable Cromwellian revolution.

Who was Lord Lisle? He was the illegitimate son, by the daughter of a Hampshire gentleman, of King Edward IV. As such, he was a Plantagenet, the last survivor, in the male line, of the 'White Rose', i.e. the Yorkist, dynasty in the Wars of the Roses; but his illegitimacy, which debarred him from the throne, made him politically harmless. His own character, like that of his father, was agreeable and easy-going, and Henry VII, having married Lisle's legitimate half-sister in order to appropriate her Yorkist claims, could afford to be indulgent to this unambitious and inoffensive kinsman. Henry VIII continued the indulgence. Under him, Lisle became Keeper of the royal forests of Clarendon and Bere, Privy Councillor, and Vice-Admiral of England. Finally, in 1533 when he was about seventy (if we accept Miss Byrne's calculations, which seem here to be questionable), he was appointed the King's Deputy, or Governor, of Calais, the last relic of English rule in France. His predecessor had been Lord Berners, the translator of Froissart. Lisle took over his official residence, the old Staple Inn, and his private furniture and plate. With him went his second wife, Honor.

Lisle's first wife, by whom he had three daughters, had been a Grey, Baroness Lisle in her own right (hence his own choice of title), widow of Edmund Dudley, the minister of Henry VII and first victim of Henry VIII. He was thus stepfather of John Dudley, afterwards Duke of Northumberland, who would be executed for seeking to place his family

on the throne. Through her, he acquired land in ten counties. His
second wife was a Grenville, of a famous and dynamic Cornish family.
She too had been married before, to a West Country gentleman of very
ancient family, Sir John Basset, and her Basset children were still
young when she went to Calais. She was then in her early forties and
still hoped to bear a male heir to the name of Plantagenet; but in this she
would be disappointed. Her continuing ambitions were to preserve and
enlarge the ample Basset estates in Devon and Cornwall and to ensure
the worldly success of her Basset children.

Lisle's government of Calais has generally been dismissed as lax and
inefficient. This view was expressed categorically by the American
historian R. B. Merriman, the biographer of Cromwell, and has been
repeated since. It irritates Miss Byrne, who protests – perhaps too
much – against this 'Merriman myth'. Lisle's correspondence does not
suggest a forceful personality, but let us concede that he was a
conscientious official, worried by his duties and his debts – he was
always short of cash, and lived, as was expected of him, far beyond his
means – and that the compliments which he received from Henry and
from Cromwell were genuine. Certainly everyone agreed that he was
'gentle': 'the gentlest heart living', said the King; 'of a most gentle
nature', wrote the Protestant martyrologist John Foxe. Lady Lisle was
not gentle. Some thought her a termagant, others a busybody, others
(like Foxe) a popish bigot. She knew what she wanted and was
determined to get it. She knew all the details of her own estates and of
her husband's business, which she did not hesitate to mind. Those who
wanted something from the Lord Deputy either enlisted her aid or, if
she were unwilling, got at him alone.

Lisle's duties at Calais were to ensure the defence and provision of
the town, to see that the soldiers' wages were paid, and – most difficult
of all – to keep the peace among the English officials, all of whom were
on the make and some of whose families had been entrenched there for
generations. In time of war between its neighbours, the King of France
and the Emperor, he had to preserve the neutrality of Calais, and of
course he had to entertain visiting grandees on their way to or from
England: the Admiral of France, for instance, on his embassy in 1534,
or the Elector Palatine, coming to fix the Cleves marriage in 1539. To
assist him in these tasks he had a council of officials and a retinue,
whose officers were known as 'Spears'. Commissions as Spears were
highly valued. They provided the basis for profitable sidelines, and
local officials coveted them for their sons. So did courtiers in England.
This competition was not the least of Lisle's worries.

Theoretically such commissions were in the gift of the Lord Deputy, but in fact well-placed young men, with powerful backing, were always seeking to jump the queue. Lisle's greatest trouble came from Sir Richard Whethill, Mayor of Calais. He came from an old Calais family and claimed priority for his son, Robert. When Lisle resisted, there was a long quarrel in which all Calais took sides. Sir Richard abused Lisle in the Deputy's own garden, and Lady Whethill made a disgraceful public attack on Lady Lisle in church, screaming insults at her 'in Pilate's voice' (Pilate and Herod, Miss Byrne explains, were the two shouting partners in mystery plays). The dispute was carried to London where the Whethills boasted of their influence, and young Robert exhibited himself at court 'in a coat of crimson taffeta, cut and lined with yellow sarcenet', velvet breeches and shoes to match, and a scarlet cap with red and yellow feathers. The King was thoroughly bored with the whole affair, but the two ladies kept it going, at the highest level, for years.

Another great Calais battle involved Sir Robert Wingfield. He, too, came from an entrenched official family and was on Lisle's council. He had used his position to invest in a marsh, which he had 'improved', but which the King now insisted should be reflooded in the interest of defence. This battle, too, was carried to London and went on for a long time. In the end Lisle prevailed; 'Wingfield's Marsh' was successfully 'drowned' and, although Wingfield vowed revenge on Lisle, it remained drowned.

To drown Wingfield's marsh in Calais in the interest of defence was one thing. To pull down Lady Lisle's weir on the river Tawe at Umberleigh in Devon in the interest of navigation was, of course, quite different. In 1535 the Crown ordered a general destruction of weirs on navigable rivers. Landlords, whose weirs enabled them to corner the fish, were indignant, and none so indignant as Lady Lisle. She demanded, first, that the weir be spared, then, when it was down, that it be rebuilt. Like Lady Whethill, she became a great bore on the subject, but the weir, like the marsh, was not restored.

Although a royal commission in 1535 vindicated Lisle's government, he soon realized that he had made a mistake in accepting the post. The local troubles were endless and were being inflamed by religion. At home, his interests and his wife's estates were being threatened, and he was not allowed to leave Calais except by royal licence. He was also missing great opportunities at home – opportunities in which his rivals were investing. It was all very depressing, especially when Cromwell, who was now clearly in command of everything (he was Mr Secretary, Master of the Rolls, and Lord Privy Seal), reproved him for troubling

him with trifles. The man who was changing the structure of England
did not wish to be bothered by the internal squabbles of a garrison
town.

Fortunately for Lisle, and for us, there was John Husee. Husee is
Miss Byrne's hero, and rightly so. But for him, the correspondence
would be an amorphous mass. He is 'the unifying, energising agent who
is ultimately to weld the material into a whole, and to give it momentum
and direction'. For Husee was Lisle's agent, his secretary, his universal
factotum, the man who watched his interests, served him at every turn,
knew everybody, had the entrée everywhere, was prepared to do
anything: to buy supplies, order clothes, argue with lawyers, transport
children, arrange travel, deliver presents, handle creditors, and, above
all, to report regularly in writing.

Husee was a young man of thirty at the time. He had begun as a
London merchant – 'citizen and vintner' – and Lisle evidently found
him in Calais where he was already a member of the retinue although
clearly he was not tied to his post. He reveals himself as a man of great
energy and charm, and infinite resourcefulness. He is the sharpest of
observers, quick to note who is moving up or down at court, and
generally the first to report it. Everyone knows him, welcomes him,
speaks freely to him. 'Here cometh my Lord Lisle's man,' says Cromwell to the King, smiling benevolently as Husee enters the presence
chamber with his master's New Year's gifts in 1538. He has no enemies,
except perhaps the Abbot of Westminster, a lordly and exacting
creditor, and Sir Richard Rich, of whom no one has ever said a good
word. He is a natural diplomat, and warm and sympathetic too. How
disarmingly he protests when his employers (for Lady Lisle, of course,
treats him as her servant: she is the real boss), in their anxiety, rebuke
him for unavoidable delays! How sympathetically he consoles Lady
Lisle when the expected Plantagenet heir, for whom he has obtained
everything – a cradle, a display bed, 'a holy-water stock with sprinkler
and casting bottle' – turns out to be a 'phantom pregnancy', or rallies
Lord Lisle when the frustrations of Calais politics drive him into
melancholy or despair! And then, to crown all, he is a brilliant letter
writer, with a sharp eye for detail, a nice sense of humour, a pretty turn
of phrase, a delightful irony. He is the most memorable character in the
whole story, for it is he, above all, who brings all the rest to life.

As we read these letters, we are staggered by Husee's ubiquity and
resourcefulness. But Husee, we soon find, is not alone. He is the
organizer of intelligence, but there are other agents too: 'fee'd men', or
'privy friends', as they are called, men who are formally and officially

employed by other great men at court or in the country, but to whom Lisle pays regular secret 'fees' – generally £10 a year – to keep him informed whenever his interest is, or might be, involved. Lisle had at least two fee'd men in Cromwell's service – William Popley, Cromwell's man of business, and Ralph Sadler, one of the ablest of Cromwell's young protégés – and several in the country. In Devonshire, he had Sir Richard Pollard, the surveyor general and sheriff. But the most dramatic coup was achieved by Hugh Yeo, the agent for the Basset lands in the west. Through two privy friends in the employment of Lord Daubeny and one in that of the Earl of Hertford (afterwards the Protector Somerset), he discovered the secret plot that these two were hatching, whereby the Basset heir would lose a substantial estate for their benefit: Hertford to have the property and Daubeny to pay for an earldom with the proceeds. This plot nearly succeeded, and Daubeny, in expectation of triumph, came up to London accompanied by eighty horsemen all dressed in 'new liveries of my Lord Privy Seal's colour'; but Husee, thus warned, was able to get to Cromwell in time, and Cromwell (at a price) got the King to intervene and save the property. All great men, it seems, kept these privy friends in other great men's service: that, after all, was how Cromwell built up his marvellous intelligence service, so envied by the French ambassador, and how Shakespeare's Macbeth secured his own interests:

> There's not a one of them but in his house
> I keep a servant fee'd.

Apart from such outright espionage, there was another no less necessary method of self-protection which is vividly illustrated by these letters. This is the regular, almost ritual, distribution of gifts in kind. Here again Husee is the central figure. It is he who advises who should receive gifts, and what they should receive – how large a gift will suffice, what would be most acceptable, or perhaps has already been hinted; he who collects and delivers. The most frequent gifts are of game or wine, hawks or hunting dogs. The best wine is claret from Gascony, but tastes differed. Whereas the Earl of Sussex would only look at 'mighty great wines', Henry VIII, who had simple tastes (he was 'wondrous pleased' with Lady Lisle's homemade marmalade), was content, like Lisle himself, with 'hedge wine', which was apparently 'a good *vin ordinaire*'. Among the items of game are boars' heads and wild swine, baked cranes and sturgeon, venison of red and fallow deer, storks, egrets, guinea-fowl, herons and snipe, herrings, salmon, sprats, partridges, dotterels, peewits, quails and puffins. Sometimes they are distributed alive, like the quails, which were bought wholesale in Calais or Flanders and killed on arrival at Dover, or the dotterels, of which Anne Boleyn was very fond, and which were put in her garden in Greenwich until it was time to eat them. The fish came in barrels, as did the congers supplied by a Cornish parson and the puffins (which were regarded as fish, owing to their taste) sent regularly from the Basset estates in the west. Sometimes the game was made up into pasties or pies, like the lamprey pies, 'baken after our Cotswold fashion', sent by a Gloucester-shire gentleman, or a partridge pie which was unfortunately misshapen by immersion in the Channel, 'but they found good meat in it'. Once Lisle sent a porpoise, of which a section was gratefully acknowledged by Cromwell; but the more prestigious gift of a seal proved less successful. It was destined for the Lord Admiral, perhaps as an aquatic symbol, but Husee had great difficulty in delivering it. He had to keep it alive for five weeks at Wapping, where it cost him sixpence a day in fish 'and yet she had not dined'. When he finally presented it, the Admiral said that he had nowhere to keep it, and told him to kill it and have it baked and sent to his wife, 'and so it is done'.

Traffic in game entailed traffic in the means of catching it; so the gifts include every kind of hawk and dog: goshawks, gyrfalcons, merlins, greyhounds, lanyers, water spaniels. Red-and-white spaniels passed from France to England; English greyhounds and mastiffs were in great demand in France. The birds were liable to all kinds of accident en route: hawks escaped, or were stolen; an unspecified bird sent to Lord Hertford survived shipwreck only to be eaten by a cat at Billingsgate, 'which my Lord of Hertford took right grievously'. Sometimes we find more recondite gifts. The Lord Admiral of France sent Lisle two minuscule marmosets from Brazil and 'a long-tailed monkey, which is a pretty beast and gentle', with instructions for care and feeding. Lady Lisle thought to gain favour by sending one of them on to Queen Anne Boleyn, but this proved a gaffe: 'the Queen loveth no such beasts,' Husee reported, 'nor can scant abide the sight of them'; on the other hand she appreciated a linnet, which delighted her with its incessant song. Lisle loved birds, and he and his wife seem to have kept a small menagerie: a monk of Canterbury sent Lady Lisle, by the hand of 'a singing child' for whom he sought patronage, an unspecified 'beast, the creature of God, once wild but now tame, to comfort your heart at such time as you be weary of prayer'. One does not get the impression that Lady Lisle wearied herself much with prayer.

This constant flow of gifts is the most striking feature of the correspondence. Some of them, of course, were real gifts, in our sense of the word. Such, no doubt, was the touching present which Lady Lisle sent to the Elector Palatine after he had been her guest at Calais. She had noticed that he had picked his teeth with a pin, so she sent him her own toothpick, which she had used for seven years. Some were commissioned purchases. But most of them were an essential part of the system of patronage. Gentlemen did not give bribes. Of all the officials whom we meet, only one – Sir Thomas Pope, treasurer of the Court of Augmentations, which handled the sale of monastic lands (and afterwards founder of Trinity College, Oxford) – declined 'wine or other pleasure', saying bluntly that he wanted 'ready money . . . yea, and doth look for the same'. But there was no undue delicacy in defining what would be acceptable, and whether it gave satisfaction when it came. Cromwell let it be known that 'a pretty dog' would not come amiss. Others specified particular kinds of hawk. The King complained that Lisle's quails were not fat enough. Husee insisted on this again and again: 'Let them be very fat,' he wrote, 'or else they are not worth thanks.'

Lisle specialized in quails, buying them up in vast quantities. They were 'a prime delicacy' and could be used to sweeten requests, to attract attention, to turn away wrath. Husee was continually advising that such and such a person be remembered with wine and quails. Mr Skut, for instance, the King's tailor, with whom Lady Lisle ran up huge bills, and who sometimes became impatient for payment, received a regular tribute of quails. On one occasion Husee did not dare call on him with twelve yards of satin to make up for Lady Lisle 'because the quails be not yet come'. This of course merely shifted the debt: there is a plaintive letter from the Calais poulterer begging payment, long overdue, for forty-three dozen quails. But the operation was worthwhile, as one episode emphatically proved.

Lady Lisle, naturally, wished to do the best for her daughters, Katherine and Anne Basset. After the usual beginner's course under the eye of a local abbess, they were sent to live with a grand French family near Calais. This entailed some agreeable correspondence and a constant commerce of hawks, dogs, salmon, marmalade, etc. It also introduced a French cousin, an aristocratic abbess whose disciplined army of nuns knitted vast quantities of nightcaps, male and female, in elegant lozenge patterns. She supplied Lady Lisle with a steady and copious flow of nightcaps and family gossip. After that, the girls were on the market. Then Lady Lisle's competitive instincts were aroused. On hearing that two of her Arundell nieces had been accepted as maids of honour at court, she decided to launch Katherine and Anne in the same warm water. So she mobilized two dexterous dowagers, the Countesses of Sussex and Rutland (the latter a great oracle on court and society) and set the quails in motion. The moment to strike came when the two countesses were in waiting and the Queen was actually dining off Lord Lisle's quails. The concurrent pressure of the ladies and the birds was irresistible, and the Queen agreed to see both girls and choose one of them. She chose Anne, whom the King so fancied that at one time she was tipped for the dangerous honour of being the fifth queen of Henry VIII. Katherine stayed on with Lady Rutland.

Lady Lisle also had Basset stepdaughters. They, of course, were older. The most enjoyable is Jane, a spinster in her forties. She had no great love for her stepmother's family, but she loved her old home at Umberleigh and begged for two rooms in it, and pasture for one cow, in order to live there with her unmarried younger sister, Thomasine. Once established there, she found herself at loggerheads with the vicar, an elderly man who acted as Lady Lisle's agent. Each wrote to Lady Lisle denouncing the other. Jane accused the vicar of embezzling the fish; the vicar retaliated by intercepting and suppressing her letters. Finally, sister Thomasine decided that she had had enough and bolted. Rescued before dawn by a raiding party led by the vicar, she fled to Cornwall, leaving her clothes behind. When we last see Jane, she is still at Umberleigh with one maid, two cows, and a horse. 'Also she hath a greyhound lieth upon one of the beds day and night, but it be when she holdeth him in her hands and that every time when she goeth to the door.'

Most important, of course, were the three Basset sons. The eldest, John, was sent to Lincoln's Inn, and then, being married to the eldest Plantagenet daughter in order to secure the lands, was on the way to being 'the diamant of Devonshire'. Miss Byrne describes him as 'a dull dog'. The second, George, was first placed in an abbey, then briefly crammed, with his younger brother, at Saint-Omer, and sent, in the usual English fashion, to 'wait' in the house of Lisle's intimate friend and ally, Sir Francis Bryan, before disappearing into Cornwall, where he founded a long-lasting branch of the family. He is described as 'self-effacing'.

So we come to the youngest son, James. He was not self-effacing. On the contrary, he was 'a precocious little horror', spoiled, charming, sophisticated, and, like his mother, determined to get his way – as he generally did. After Reading Abbey, he was sent to Paris, to the Collège de Calvi. The president of the Parlement of Paris, who had met Lisle in

Calais (he had come in the train of the ambassador-admiral), had promised to look after him in Paris, but once there, he soon forgot his promise and James was taken over by a group of English scholars at the university, of whom the principal was John Bekynsaw. They took care of him and later, when he returned to Paris from the crammer in Saint-Omer, placed him, with a tutor, in the house of a kindly French merchant, Guillaume le Gras. But James had no taste for private tuition: he was determined to go to the university, to the fashionable Collège de Navarre. There, he explained, he would get to know the sons of the Duc de Vendôme and the Duc de Guise and such persons; and of course he went. Once there, he got what he wanted in other ways too. Lady Lisle in Calais, le Gras and Bekynsaw in Paris, were all manipulated by a determined boy of ten. Since he was the youngest son, his parents had destined him for the Church, and the Lisles, with their old-fashioned notions, naturally assumed that a fat benefice would be found for him, with all necessary dispensations for tender age, non-residence, etc. He was to end, no doubt, as a grand worldly bishop, like Lisle's friend (and creditor) Bishop Sherburn of Chichester who, at the age of ninety-five, astonished his fellow commissioners for the valuation of church lands by giving them a Good Friday fish dinner for seven hundred persons – 'such a dinner of fish', said one of them, as none present had ever seen 'for the quantity and goodness of them'; or like Bishop Veysey of Exeter whom we see arriving in London to call on Cromwell accompanied by eighty horsemen in livery, and scattering twenty nobles in tips. They reckoned without Archbishop Cranmer, who absolutely forbade any cure of souls for a child, however well connected. So James had to be content with minor orders and the income from a prebend in Cornwall. He never went further in the Church. He was, as Husee noted, 'meeter to serve the temporal powers than the spiritual dignities' – as indeed, in the end, he did, passing from the household of Bishop Gardiner to that of Queen Mary. But he was not entirely worldly. Marrying Mary Roper, the granddaughter of Sir Thomas More, he was absorbed into that devoted Catholic circle; and perhaps it was for his sake that his father-in-law, William Roper, afterwards relieved the wants of his old protector John Bekynsaw, and through his influence that his great-nephew Sir Robert Bassett (if he is correctly identified) wrote one of the many family biographies of Sir Thomas More.

Such were the main interests of the Lisles in Calais. But what, we naturally ask, about the revolution going on in England? Did they not notice it? Yes, when they had to. They could hardly fail to notice the execution of Anne Boleyn, for Lisle, in effect, provided the executioner. She was to be beheaded by the sword, not the axe – a skill that was practised only by the French – so an expert was sent from Calais. Also, the affair had, for the Lisles, an unfortunate consequence. One of those who was framed and executed with the Queen, as her supposed lover, was Sir Henry Norris, Keeper of the Privy Purse, who had been Lisle's chief informant and 'faithful assured friend'. All Lisle's interests at court had been managed for him by Norris, whose services, constantly extolled by Husee, had been recognized by valuable gifts – a superlative falcon, the best horse that ever came out of Flanders, etc. When he was charged, the Lisles were dismayed. Putting first things first, they tried – without waiting for their 'very friend' to be hanged, drawn and quartered – to get a grant of his confiscated lands. But how could one put in a bid without an immediate successor to Norris himself as friend at court? Husee at first suggested Sir John Russell for this office, but then, finding Russell in earnest colloquy with Lisle's enemy Whethill, feared that he 'had taken the wrong pig by the ear' and recommended Sir Thomas Heneage. Eleven dozen quails and a hogshead of Gascon wine were quickly delivered to Heneage, and snipe and wine were sent off to Cromwell. All was of no avail. Lisle was told that he had applied too late. Russell smugly said that he could have secured something if only he had been asked in time, and it was thought prudent to recognize his retrospective goodwill with wine and quails.

Norris's execution was doubly unfortunate for Lisle, because he was at that moment seeking to pick up another windfall. His spies had given him early notice of the impending dissolution of the monasteries, and he had naturally mobilized Norris. He also wrote direct to Cromwell. The abbey of Beaulieu was his first choice, being conveniently close to the Lisle lands in Hampshire; but that was asking too much – the greater abbeys were not yet to be dissolved, and anyway one of Cromwell's young men had his eye on it. So Lisle's fee'd man in Cromwell's service discreetly suppressed the letter. But Lisle was not to be restrained. He wrote direct to the King, begging him 'to help me to some old abbey in mine old days'. If not Beaulieu, there was Southwick. Waverley, too, he was told, was 'a pretty thing'. Finally, he decided that it was necessary to accept the advice given to Lady Lisle: that she should come over in person, bringing her husband in tow, in order to sue for 'one of the abbeys, towards the maintenance of my Lord's and your good Ladyship's charges'.

In the end, thanks to this visit, and a new and closer relationship with Cromwell, who was determined to cut out intermediaries, Lisle did get an abbey: the priory of Frithelstock in Devonshire, conveniently close to the Basset home at Umberleigh; but the officials of the Court of Augmentations saw to it that there were many obstructions before he could call it his own. The chancellor of the court was the dreadful Rich, immortalized by his perjury at the trial of Sir Thomas More. 'He is full of dissimulation,' Husee reported: 'I fear that he will so handle himself that he will deserve neither thanks nor reward. He passeth all that I ever sued to.' However, in the end (Rich having received a velvet gown) all was well, and in August 1537 Husee could tell Lisle that his 'long tracted suit is finished' and 'your Lordship is now prior and Lord of Fristock'.

So far so good. In 1537 the Lisles are still living splendidly in Calais, entertaining as lavishly as 'the best duke in England'. There are indeed some difficulties. The unpaid grocer is getting impatient and threatening to cut off credit; the Bishop of Chichester is discreetly, the Abbot of Westminster stiffly, demanding repayment of their debts; the weir at Umberleigh is down and all Lady Lisle's efforts cannot rebuild it. But the property is still basically intact, its future assured by marriage; the children are placed; and although Thomas Cromwell has now apparently established a complete monopoly of power, relations with him – perpetually sweetened with quails and wine, hawks, dogs, hunks of porpoise, etc. – seem particularly close. Thanks to that special relationship, Lisle's 'back friends' in Calais – false friends who go sneaking up to London – are frustrated. Husee is constantly alert, always ready to wait on the Lord Privy Seal when he is not too busy with 'the Carthusians' or 'these matters' (that is, state trials and executions), and the Lord Privy Seal is invariably solicitous, invariably reassuring: he is 'your Lordship's unfeigned friend'. 'As long as the King's Grace doth live, and he together,' he assures Lisle, 'you shall remain the King's Deputy at Calais . . . you shall die Deputy of Calais.' And Lisle believed it. Cromwell, he wrote, was his 'special good Lord', 'my only and most assured friend and last refuge in all my suits'.

Alas for all these promises. Politics never stand still, and in revolutions the changes can be very fast. From 1537 the terms of life shift, and a course of events begins which turns these hitherto purposeless annals into a fast-moving drama – and which, incidentally, has preserved these records for us. For without it they would have been dissipated long ago; our knowledge of the public events of the reign of Henry VIII would then have been diminished; and the Lisles, the Bassets, and all their family circle would have been – as they are after 1540 – mere names in genealogical records, without human identity or voice or the breath of life.

How did things go wrong? Why did Cromwell, in the last weeks of his power, call Lisle back to London, confiscate his papers, and have him thrown into the Tower, from which he would never emerge, and from which he was expected to emerge, like so many others, only to grace the scaffold? Why indeed did Cromwell himself fall, moving, with such shocking suddenness, from apparently unchallenged authority to a traitor's death? The answer, as Miss Byrne shows, with meticulous scholarship, is to be found in three converging courses of events: the treason of Cardinal Pole; the struggle for power between Cromwell and his conservative rivals; and the religious developments in Calais.

Reginald Pole was the King's cousin on the Yorkist–that is on Lisle's – side. He had been expensively educated and amply beneficed by the King and had lived in Venice on his bounty, the centre of a Platonic circle, in contact with Thomas More and other humanists at home. Henry had hoped to have him as his Archbishop of York, after Wolsey; but the King's divorce, his marriage to Anne Boleyn, and the breach with Rome put an end to all that, and in 1536, after the execution of More and Fisher, Pole did the unforgivable thing: he recited to the King, in writing, the full catalogue of his crimes. From that moment Henry would pursue Pole with all the hatred which he felt towards those, like More and Anne Boleyn, whom he had once loved and who, in his view, had betrayed him; and Pole, on his side, became a bitter enemy in deeds as well as in words: as cardinal and papal legate, he appealed to foreign powers to unite and dethrone the heretic king. Henry sought to have Pole kidnapped in Liège, 'trussed up and conveyed to Calais'. He was resolved to lay hands on him and destroy him. Nor was that all; with his hatred of Pole was joined fear for the succession, still hanging by a slender thread, and hatred of all the remaining members of the rival house, the White Rose. That meant the Poles and the Courtenays: the Cardinal's mother, the aged Countess of Salisbury, his elder brother Lord Montague, and his cousin, the Marquess of Exeter. As Henry told the French ambassador, he was 'resolved to exterminate this house of Montague, which is still of the White Rose faction, and also the family of Pole, to which the Cardinal belongs'.

At that cannibal court, where, as Husee said, every man was for himself, two great men at least believed sincerely in what they were doing: Thomas Cromwell and Archbishop Cranmer. Cromwell might be helping the King to build up the machinery of tyranny, but it was a tyranny that was to be used for a specific policy: the reform of the

Church. In 1539 that tyranny, and that policy, had isolated Henry in Europe and had almost isolated Cromwell and Cranmer in England. With the rulers of Europe combining from without, and Pole calling for revolt from within, the politics of the English court were polarized. On one side, Cromwell urged Henry further on the path of defiance and reform, proposing an alliance with German Protestantism and marriage with a German princess, Anne of Cleves. On the other side, more conservative men – men who were happy to see monasteries dissolved and papal authority rejected but had no love of religious or social change – declared that reform had gone far enough: that it must now be stabilized on a Catholic base, and defended externally, not by confronting, but by splitting the Catholic powers. The leaders of this party were Thomas, Duke of Norfolk, now back from suppressing revolt in the north, and Stephen Gardiner, Bishop of Winchester, now back from his embassy abroad.

Between these two parties the King occupied a middle position. On the one hand, he was conservative, opposed to 'Lutheran' heresy. On the other hand, he appreciated Cromwell, the architect of his new power, the best servant (as he would afterwards admit) that he had ever had. The conservatives therefore did not openly attack Cromwell: they attacked heresy, which the King, too, hated; and Cromwell did not openly attack religious conservatism: he concentrated his fire against the King's enemies, the Papacy and the traitor Pole. The King preserved a judicious balance, and emphasized it by sending, in almost equal numbers, Catholics as 'traitors' to the scaffold and Protestants as 'heretics' to the stake.

How could Lisle avoid being drawn into this battle? Calais was itself in the centre of it. Internally divided, geographically 'exposed to all the winds of doctrine that blew', it was a refuge for heretics from France, Flanders, and Germany, and religious differences inflamed all the existing discontents. The established families who dominated the council were orthodox, but Cranmer's 'commissary', who controlled the clergy, supported heresy. As a secular-minded official, untouched by new ideas, or indeed by any kind of ideas, Lisle followed the royal line. So long as Cromwell was going slowly, destroying only monasteries and the authority of Rome, there was no difficulty. The dissolution of monasteries, after all, could be useful. So could the condemnation of Pole: Lisle tried hard to get one of his rich livings for young Master James. But by 1537 the Protestants were in trouble with the council, and the Archbishop's vigorous new commissary, their supporter, was complaining that 'much papistry doth reign still, and chiefly among

them that be rulers'. Cromwell and Cranmer took up the cause of the
heretics. At one time, a colleague reported to Lisle, Cromwell 'swore by
God's Blood we were all papists . . . and I swore by God's heart it was
not so'. When Lady Lisle interceded for a priest whom the commissary
had denounced for popish observances, Cromwell let fly. If the councillors winked any longer at such abuses, he wrote, the King would
dismiss them all, for it was against all reason that they should heed 'the
prayers of women and their fond flickerings' rather than 'his just laws'.
No wonder Husee was alarmed and begged Lisle to walk warily. As
Lisle had hopes of benefits still to come – the dissolved friary at Calais
and a pension of £400 – he did.

Next year there was a crisis provoked by the arrival from Germany of
a young English priest called Adam Damplip. He was a 'Sac-
ramentary', that is, a Zwinglian, who denied the Real Presence in no
uncertain manner: a mouse, he said, 'would as soon eat the Body of God
as any other cake'; and other such heresies. These doctrines split the
council, and both parties appealed to London. When Damplip himself
fled to London, Lisle thought it time to act. He hurriedly sent a water
spaniel to Cromwell, and in response to a hint, poor Master Basset had
to surrender his favourite hawk, 'a merlin for partridges as good as
flies'. Unfortunately the hawk, on its first flight under its new owner,
was pricked by a thorn and died. After that an uneasy calm returned to
Calais.

It did not last long. Next year the Sacramentaries returned to the
charge, more insolent than ever, and Lisle, realizing that they were
being secretly supported by Cromwell and Cranmer, began cautiously
to change sides. One man to whom he appealed was Sir Anthony
Browne, the Master of the Horse. Having secured Battle Abbey for
themselves, the Brownes would become one of the mainstays of English
Catholicism. 'I beseech you,' Lisle ended his letter, 'keep this my letter
close, for if it should come to my Lord Privy Seal's knowledge or ear, I
were half undone.' Perhaps it did come to the Lord Privy Seal's ear:
who knows whether he had not a fee'd man with the Master of the
Horse? In any case, Cromwell must, by now, have suspected. Meanwhile, in London, the struggle had become even more intense. The
conservatives secured the passage of the Act of Six Articles declaring
Catholic doctrine, while Cromwell was staking all on the German
marriage. At the end of 1539 the German bride, Anne of Cleves,
stopped at Calais on her way to London and was stuck there by bad
weather. Fortunately – since she stayed for fifteen days, with a train of
263 attendants and 238 horses – the cost of her entertainment did not

fall on Lisle. When she arrived in London and the King met her, his heart sank. He went through with the marriage, but with inward reluctance, and almost immediately began to seek a means of release by annulment.

The first task was to break up the foreign coalition that had necessitated the marriage. For this purpose the Duke of Norfolk was sent on a secret mission to France. He performed his task well. The King of France was perfectly willing to agree with his brother of England, if only his brother of England would get rid of that dreadful heretic, the cause of all the trouble, Thomas Cromwell. This of course was just what the Duke wanted too. Nor was this all. Both coming and going, the Duke, as Miss Byrne has shown, stopped in Calais and evidently concerted action with Lisle. On his return, a commission was set up to investigate the religious troubles in Calais. Rather surprisingly (since he was a party to the dispute) Lisle himself was on it. Less surprisingly, its report was a condemnation of the Sacramentaries. Thus on all sides, it seemed, the enemy was closing in on Cromwell; and Lisle was with the enemy.

Even so, Cromwell did not see himself as defeated. Admittedly, the Cleves marriage had been a mistake, but it was a mistake that could be rectified; and although he was hated in the country, no doubt he thought himself indispensable to the King. His confidence, in this dark hour, is extraordinary: we find him reassuring the Sacramentaries who had been sent in chains from Calais, promising them that they would go free (in fact they would be burnt). But then he had managed it before. Religious radicalism and royal divorce had brought him to power; why should not the same means keep him in it? What was needed, while he arranged the divorce, was an external enemy. A new conspiracy must be discovered, originating, if possible, with 'the traitor Pole'.

Luckily, just at this time, such a conspiracy presented itself. A priest, one Botolf, known as Sir Gregory Sweetlips, had bolted from Calais to France, and had afterwards told his associates that he had been to Rome, had seen the Pope and Pole, and had conspired with them to surrender Calais to the French. His story was suspect, but it served its purpose. Also, Botolf had once been Lisle's chaplain. How convenient! Of all the conservative enemies of Cromwell, Lisle was the most exposed. He was the enemy of reform in Calais, which was now revealed as 'a nest of papists'. He was a member of the White Rose faction and the family of Pole which Henry was resolved to destroy. Now he could be directly implicated with Pole himself. His destruction would be a warning to the conservatives not to join the party of

Norfolk and Gardiner; it would show who was master of the King's
government; and it would be a blow struck for religious reform.

Such, it seems, was Cromwell's plan. It nearly succeeded. In the
spring of 1540 Lisle was summoned back to London. He set out
confidently. In Calais it was thought that he was going to be made an
earl. In London, he attended the House of Lords. He was present at a
chapter meeting and feast of the Knights of the Garter. Then the blow
fell. He was arrested and disappeared into the Tower. His documents,
his goods and plate were seized. Cromwell it was who was made an earl.

Meanwhile, what about the royal divorce? Alas, it was here that the
master plan came to grief. The Duke of Norfolk had a young niece,
Katherine, daughter of his brother Lord Edmund Howard, comptroller
of Calais, recently deceased. At the house of his ally, the Bishop of
Winchester, this seductive girl was placed before the royal eye. The
operation was successful. From that moment, Cromwell was doomed.
If he did not achieve an annulment of Henry's marriage, he would have
failed, as his master Cardinal Wolsey had failed, and, like him, would
be cast aside. But now, even if he secured annulment, he would have
failed no less: for as the husband of Katherine Howard, the King would
be in the camp of an enemy from whom Cromwell could expect no
mercy. So, at the last moment, the tables were turned. It was game, set,
and match to the Duke and the Bishop.

If Cromwell had won the last desperate round in the struggle for
power, Lisle would no doubt have gone to the block along with his
equally innocent kinsmen, the Courtenays and the Poles. In the Tower,
he must have expected no less. That he did not suggests that Henry
himself thought him innocent. Perhaps the execution of the mother of
the Pole brothers, the octogenarian Countess of Salisbury in 1541,
slaked the King's thirst for blood. The faction of the White Rose was
now crushed, and although the Tudor succession was not yet firm, the
Tudor despotism had little to fear from the last of the Plantagenets.
Even so, Lisle remained in prison for eighteen months. It was only after
the execution of Katherine Howard that the King, being now at leisure,
issued his pardon. Lisle was so delighted by the news that he died next
day, still in the Tower, 'through too much rejoicing'.

Such is the story told by *The Lisle Letters*. It is told in great detail in six
very large volumes, and, on the editor's part, with great scholarship
and great art. That is, she allows the letters to tell it themselves, with as
much explanation and commentary as she thinks necessary for that
purpose. The commentary is copious, but it is sustained by an infec-
tious enthusiasm which carries even the most recondite explanation.

The scholarship, gathered in a lifetime, extends to every subject. Though sometimes repetitive, it neither holds up the story nor weighs it down, and the reader will hardly notice the range of editorial skill that has been necessary to overcome problems of orthography, paleography, dating, interpretation. Above all, I am impressed by the editor's invariable freshness and enthusiasm, which infuses the whole work. At first, the pace is slow, for we must get to know the scenario and the persons; but soon it quickens: we come to know the characters and find ourselves in the middle of a fascinating family saga, a sixteenth-century *War and Peace* or *A la recherche du temps perdu*. This book has been my companion for several weeks. I read it, at first, as a labour. At the end I would not wish it to have been a page shorter.

6

John Stow

A commemorative address in the church of St Andrew Undershaft, London

John Stow, tailor of Lime Street, in this parish, who is buried in this church and whom today, 370 years after his death, we still celebrate, was the publisher and abridger of many English chronicles, the collector and preserver of many historical manuscripts which might otherwise have perished. In his lifetime, and immediately afterwards, his chronicles were widely read, and his collection of manuscripts – 'Stow's storehouse' as it was known – was often raided by his fellow antiquaries. But his lasting fame was achieved by one work first published in 1598, when he was seventy-three years old: his *Survey of London*. It is thanks to this work that he is still remembered, and even still read. Only a few weeks ago I read his *Survey* through. I followed him with pleasure as he 'perambulated', always on foot – he went everywhere on foot, for his means did not allow him to ride – from ward to ward, recounting the character, and the history, of every gate and bridge, every conduit and watergate, church, prison and hall of his native city. For Stow, who is the first, is also the most intimate of the 'chorographers' of London, the worthy rival of 'my loving friend Mr Camden', the chorographer of Britain, and of 'that learned gentleman William Lambarde esquire', whose *Perambulation of Kent*, published in 1576, was the inspiration and model of his *Survey*.

Camden, Lambarde, Stow . . . these are the famous names, but we could easily extend the list. Is there not also Humfrey Llwyd's *Breviary of Britain* and *Description of the Isle of Man*; John Norden's *Speculum Britanniae*, his projected 'surveys', or 'chorographical descriptions', of the counties of England; and Richard Carew's *Survey of Cornwall*, and many others after them? 'Surveys', 'chorographies' and 'perambulations' were the order of the day under Queen Elizabeth and James I. So, for that matter, was that other literary *genre* in which Stow so successfully specialized: *Chronicles, Annals* and *Summaries*.

Why did Elizabethan England suddenly produce this crop of antiquaries? The answer is not far to seek. It stands out clearly in the lives of nearly all of them. In the long reign of Queen Elizabeth, Englishmen 'discovered' England – its topography, its history; and they discovered it with zeal and urgency because they had seen how, in the brief reign of her brother Edward VI, it had almost been lost.

Consider the life of John Stow. He was born in 1525, in the piping times of the young Henry VIII and Cardinal Wolsey. How stable England seemed then! How magnificently the Cardinal lived, in splendour 'passing all other subjects of his time', with 400 servants daily attending in his house, besides 'his servants' servants, which were many'. But then, while Stow was still a child, came the fall of the Cardinal, the rule of Thomas Cromwell, the Reformation. Stow could see, in London, the dissolution of the monastic houses: indeed, the Reformation came very close to him, for his father, Thomas Stow, a tallow-chandler, lived in Throgmorton Street, and one of his neighbours was Thomas Cromwell himself, who built himself a large house there and designed, around it, an ample pleasure garden. One morning Thomas Stow woke up to find how that design had been realized. Half his own garden had been sliced off, his summerhouse had been dug up and moved back twenty-two feet on rollers, and a high brick wall marked the new frontier. When he protested to the surveyor, the only answer was 'that their master Sir Thomas told them so to do'. To add insult to injury, Stow's rent, unlike his garden, remained undiminished. 'Thus much', he comments, 'of mine own knowledge have I thought good to note, that the sudden rising of some men causeth them in some matters to forget themselves': a text which may still be applied to our modern developers.

Thomas Cromwell at least controlled his Reformation. His dissolution of monasteries was a planned, constructive nationalization. If he dissolved abbeys, it was to found new bishoprics. He would have preserved the charitable and educational functions of the old foundations. He himself, in his grandeur, imitated the munificence of the old nobility, who 'lived together in good amity with the citizens' and 'gave great relief to the poor'. 'I myself,' Stow records, 'in that declining time of charity, have oft seen, at the Lord Cromwell's gate in London, more than 200 persons served twice every day with bread, meat and drink sufficient; for he observed that ancient and charitable custom, as all prelates, noblemen or men of honour and worship, his predecessors, had done before him.'

But every revolution has its own momentum, and when the strong hand slackens or is removed, the pace quickens, even to destruction. Stow was fifteen when Cromwell fell, twenty-two when Henry VIII died; and in the minority of Edward VI he saw Reformation turned into revolution: the uncontrolled rapacity of a new class of 'suddenly risen' men, the senseless destruction of corporate property and institutions, a breach in the orderly continuity of history. As church property was seized, church records were destroyed. Libraries, schools, charities, collapsed with the institutions which had maintained them. And the intellectuals of the time, the radical reformers who demanded a clean break with the past, rejoiced in the destruction. The learning of the past, they said, was 'duncery'; the records of the past were irrelevant to their brave new world; the monuments of the past were idols, to be smashed, or at least defaced.

It was the sight of this indiscriminate destruction that determined men of Stow's temper and Stow's generation. Outraged by such vandalism, which could only have happened in a society that had become indifferent to its own history, they resolved to remind Englishmen of their heritage and, by reminding them, to preserve it before it should be destroyed. This meant that they must also preach a doctrine. The doctrine was the continuity of English history, of English institutions, and, particularly – since that was the battleground – of the English Church. Against those terrible reformers who would destroy the whole substance of the English episcopal Church as an inseparable branch of the corrupt, antichristian Church of Rome, they insisted that the Church of England was historically independent, that its origins preceded the corruptions of Rome, and that reformation entailed not a wholesale repudiation of the native past, but a return to it, by the removal of those spurious charms recently borrowed from the painted harlot on the Seven Hills. This had been the policy of Henry VIII: why should it not be continued under his children?

The founder of this school of conservative, Protestant, English antiquaries was John Leland, the chaplain of Henry VIII, whom that king, the greatest royal patron of learning in our history, made, in 1533, his 'Antiquary Royal': the first and only holder of that post. As such, Leland was sent to search for English antiquities in the libraries of all English cathedrals, abbeys and colleges; and for the rest of the King's life he travelled all over England compiling that great register of its historical documents, his *Itinerary*. He was the first of our 'perambulators'; but his perambulations, which yielded a rich harvest for the King's library and for his own successors, soon drove him into a deep depression. He saw everywhere the destruction of records which, single-handed, he could not stay. When the King died and the pace of destruction quickened, his mind, by overwork, became unhinged; and by 1550 he was incurably insane. Fortunately his records were preserved. They were preserved, used and transcribed by his disciples: Camden and Stow.

Throughout the middle years of the sixteenth century, the destruction went on. Church property was gobbled up. The bishops' houses in London were pulled down by new owners. Statues, stained-glass windows, monuments, tombs, were smashed as 'idols'. Libraries, including Duke Humfrey's Library at Oxford, were scattered. In 1556 John Dee, philosopher, mathematician, magician and antiquary, petitioned Queen Mary to establish a royal library to save the records of the past. Failing, he set out to save them himself. By his own efforts he built up, in his house at Mortlake, the greatest private library in England: a library of books and manuscripts saved, by his exertions, from destruction.

Then, three years later, with the new reign, came a remarkable change. At the beginning of her reign, Queen Elizabeth settled the English Church on a firm basis: Protestant, episcopalian, traditional, claiming an independent pedigree from apostolic times. At the same time she put out a proclamation forbidding the defacement of monuments. Her new minister, William Cecil, afterwards Lord Burghley, and her new Archbishop of Canterbury, Matthew Parker, offered themselves as patrons of historical study to vindicate the continuity of English institutions. So, surprisingly enough, did the new great favourite, Robert Dudley, Earl of Leicester, the heir of the greatest and most ruthless of the Edwardian developers. Between them, these great men were the patrons of all the antiquaries of the new reign: Camden, Lambarde, Norden, Dee, Stow.

Such was the background of Stow's career as an antiquary. He was not an isolated scholar, he was one of a generation: a generation committed to the intellectual re-validation of the English heritage. All of them set out, by personal investigation, to rediscover and document that heritage. Some of them – the giants like Leland and Camden – *perambulated*' all Britain. Others, like Lambarde and Carew, concentrated on their own counties. Stow, tied by his modest trade to London, concentrated on his native city. But the inspiration of all was the same.

It was not mere antiquarianism, the self-indulgence of leisured scholars. It was antiquarianism with a purpose: the restoration of England's consciousness of its own history.

Often, in his *Survey*, Stow reveals that purpose, that inspiration. For instance, there is the continuity and independence of the Church of England. Romanist writers deduced the Church of England from St Augustine of Canterbury, the missionary of Pope Gregory the Great, who in AD 597 converted the Saxon king of Kent. They had the Venerable Bede for their warrant: Bede, whose *History* the Roman Catholic archdeacon, Thomas Stapleton, had translated in the reign of Mary, the Catholic queen. The Elizabethan Protestants avoided that trap: they traced the English episcopal church back to the legendary British King Lucius who was converted in apostolic times, before the usurpations of the bishop of Rome. The parish church of St Peter upon Cornhill, says Stow, was built under King Lucius, by Thean the first archbishop of London, with 'the aid of Ciran, chief butler to King Lucius'; and Thean's successor Eluanus added a library 'and converted many of the Druids, learned men in the pagan law, to Christianity'. That put St Augustine of Canterbury in his place. But alas, this library, which still existed in the time of Henry VIII, 'well furnished of books' and 'repaired with brick by the executors of Sir John Crosby, alderman', was now, like so many other church libraries, scattered and 'those books be gone'.

Then there were those dreadful iconoclasts, the Edwardian defacers of monuments. How Stow hated them! He is reminded of them when he comes to Ludgate, built (as he assures us) by King Lud in AD 66, restored in stone by King John out of the rifled fabric of rich Jewish houses, and adorned, under Henry III, with statues of King Lud and other old British kings. But 'these images of kings', Stow tells us, 'in the reign of Edward VI, had their heads smitten off and were otherwise defaced by such as judged every image to be an idol'. Happily, after being patched up under Mary, they had all been completely renewed when the gate itself was restored in 1586, and the image of Queen Elizabeth had been added on the other side. But even under Elizabeth, fanatics did not cease from troubling: witness the assaults in 1581 on the great cross at Cheapside, the last of Queen Eleanor's crosses before Charing Cross. Happily, the Queen's government stood firm, and in the 1603 edition of the *Survey* Stow was able to record that Cheapside Cross had now been restored. Restored, it was to brave the Puritans for another forty-five years: then, in the course of their Revolution, they would pull it finally down.

Stow felt very strongly about this Puritan vandalism. In every city church he records the 'monuments defaced' and the 'monuments not defaced', lest the iconoclasts should escape censure, or boast of victory. In the same spirit, Camden would catalogue the monuments of Westminster Abbey, and John Weever, a generation later, would record the *Ancient Funeral Monuments* of England – just in time, before the second act of the tragedy. But Stow, in his catalogues, was careful (as he afterwards told a friend) to omit all mention of certain more recent tombs, being of men 'who have been the defacers of the monuments of others, and so worthy to be deprived of that memory whereof they have injuriously robbed others'.

For Stow was not a man who forgot or forgave. Antiquaries, after all, are not designed to forget. Their function is to remember those little details which time and human indifference would otherwise wash away. Did not one of his contemporaries, the Welsh Catholic antiquary Richard Rowlands, alias Verstegan, another protégé of William Cecil – indeed, the man who persuaded Cecil to glorify his pedigree, and change the spelling of his name, in order to claim descent from the Roman family of the Cecilii – entitle his book *A Restitution of Decayed Intelligence*? So we should not be surprised if the life of Stow, like that of many other antiquaries – as of his Oxford successors Anthony Wood and Thomas Hearne – contains many a private animosity, jealously remembered. On these, in a commemorative sermon, it would be tactless to dwell. Therefore I shall pass over the running battle with his rival antiquary Richard Grafton concerning their respective *Chronicles*. But a knowledge of one quarrel is necessary if we are to extract the full relish from some of the more arcane antiquarian asides of John Stow's *Survey*.

I refer to the long feud with his younger brother Thomas: a deplorable story. John Stow did not approve of Mrs Thomas Stow, and was imprudent enough, one day in 1568, to lament to his old mother that Thomas should be matched with an harlot. Thomas Stow extracted this detail from the garrulous old lady, and the fat was in the fire. Conciliatory embassies, gifts of strawberries, pots of cream, sociable pints of ale, all were unavailing and Thomas Stow even denounced his brother to the authorities for a grave political offence: for possessing seditious documents – in particular, a manifesto by the Duke of Alba, the Spanish governor of the Netherlands, which the government of Queen Elizabeth had tried to suppress. John Stow survived this denunciation and, thirty years later, in his *Survey* he had his revenge. He there had occasion to refer to William FitzOsbert, a historical character who anyway must have been distasteful to him, for he was 'a seditious tailor'. In 1196, Stow tells us, FitzOsbert, having seized, fortified and defended the steeple of Bow against the legal authority of King Richard Coeur de Lion, was finally taken and hanged at Smithfield, 'where, because his followers came not to deliver him, he forsook Mary's son, as he termed Christ our Saviour, and called upon the Devil to help and deliver him. Such was the end of this deceiver, a man of evil life, a secret murderer, a filthy fornicator, a polluter of concubines, and amongst other his detestable facts, a false accuser of his elder brother, who had in his youth brought him up in learning and done many things for his preferment.' In the margin of the printed text Stow added: 'God amend, or shortly send such an end to such false brethren'; and in the manuscript he went further: 'Such a brother have I, God make him penitent.'

The angularities of Stow's character are no doubt, in part, occupational; and we should remember that the occupation of an antiquary was more dangerous then than now. To possess a library of recondite books was as sinister, in an illiterate age, as to conduct scientific experiments in a pre-scientific age; and Stow, like his friend John Dee, was suspect on both counts: he was accused of alchemy as well as antiquarianism. Against such dangers a scholar needed powerful patrons. Fortunately, in Cecil and Leicester – and particularly 'my especial benefactor, archbishop Parker', who 'animated me in the course of these studies' – Stow had such patrons. They stood him in good stead in the great crisis which seems to have begun with Thomas Stow's denunciation of him in 1569. For after clearing himself before the Lord Mayor on the charge of possessing seditious documents, he found himself denounced to the Privy Council on a new charge of possessing dangerous books of superstition.

In consequence of this charge, Stow's house was searched. The Bishop of London, the sour puritan Edmund Grindal, sent his chaplains to investigate, and they duly reported a number of 'unlawful books' which plainly declared their owner 'to be a great favourer of papistry': books such as Stapleton's translation of Bede, old English chronicles 'both in parchment and in paper', books of physic, surgery and herbs, and 'old fantastical popish books printed in the old time'. Fortunately Stow survived this examination too. Bishop Grindal it was who would ultimately get the boot. The Queen and Cecil would not tolerate his encouragement of puritan 'prophesyings'.

However, thirty years later, Stow's powerful protectors were all dead, and he might well feel less secure. He might reflect on the misfortunes of John Dee, who was accused of black arts, whose wonderful library at Mortlake had been pillaged and scattered by a right-thinking mob, and who was himself in disfavour at court. In Stow's last days, even history was coming to be suspect. Queen Elizabeth, in her old age, was very sensitive about her deposed predecessor Richard II – 'I am Richard II, know ye not that?' she would say to Lambarde – and King James, who was not at all sure that history supported his doctrine of the divine right of kings, caused the Elizabethan Society of Antiquaries, which Archbishop Parker had initiated and of which Camden, Lambarde and Stow were members, to be wound up.

Perhaps King James was right. Certainly the opponents of Stuart claims found support in the work of the great Jacobean antiquaries, with their emphasis on the historic rights of the subject, the corrective institutions of the Middle Ages. But these were a different species of scholar from the innocent, self-taught tailor who saw London's past not as an armoury of political rights but as a colourful pageant of civic life. Stow was a nostalgic, not a political antiquary. He loved the past, perhaps more than the present, as he loved the old English poets – Lydgate, Gower, Hoccleve, and above all Chaucer, whom he edited – rather than Spenser or Shakespeare, whom he never mentions. He loved to remember the London of his earlier years, before the developers got at it, before the population explosion of the sixteenth century. He loved to recall old buildings that had gone, old customs that had been discontinued – 'mayings and May-games', like 'the triumphant setting up of the great shaft (a principal maypole in Cornhill, before the parish church of St Andrew, therefore called Undershaft)', which was discontinued after the anti-immigrant riots of 'Evil May-day' in 1517. And when his own memory gave out, he would question ancient inhabitants – he found one who could remember Richard III – and make the dry bones of his old chronicles live again. His politics were simple and sound: sedition was always wrong. His references to the Peasants' Revolt of Wat Tyler, 'a presumptuous rebel', in 1381, or to the 'seditious stirs', 'the great and heinous enterprises', of the ex-Lord Mayor John Northampton in 1382, or to Jack Cade's revolt in 1449, leave no doubt about that. And then, apart from the seditious tailor of 1196, there was the seditious curate of 1549, who brings us back, once again, to Stow's own life and this, his own church.

This curate – he was Stephen, the curate of St Katharine Cree – flourished (need one say?) in the heady days of Edward VI, and Stow remembered how, in his own presence, this radical preacher had proposed the most outrageous novelties, changing everything: the days of the week, the feasts of the Church, the names of London churches. He had even seen him, 'forsaking the pulpit of his said parish church, preach out of a high elm-tree in the midst of the churchyard' – I am glad that practice is no longer in fashion, although even the future Archbishop Parker, in this same year 1549, had been forced to preach out of a tree to the Norfolk rebels – 'and then, entering the church, forsaking the altar, to have sung his high mass in English, upon a tomb of the dead, towards the North'. Finally, horror of horrors, Stow heard this dreadful curate preach at Paul's cross and declare that the great shaft of St Andrew Undershaft 'was made an idol'; 'and I saw the effect that followed', for that very afternoon a crowd, 'after they had well dined, to make themselves strong, gathered more help, and with great labour raising the shaft from the hooks whereon it had rested two-and-thirty years' – i.e. since Evil May-day in 1517 – 'they sawed it in pieces', and every man carried away his share as a trophy. 'Thus was his idol, as he termed it, mangled and afterwards burned.'

The shocking career of Stephen, the radical curate, did not end there. Soon afterwards he denounced the bailiff of Romford, 'a man very well beloved', and caused him to be unjustly hanged. Stow himself heard the condemned man's last protestation of innocence, 'for he was executed upon the pavement of my door, where I then kept house'. After which the curate, 'to avoid reproach of the people, left the city and was never heard of since'. And so may all with-it parsons pass into well-merited oblivion except in so far as their follies are held up to just execration by right-minded chroniclers, commemorated, with annual tributes of affection, in their parish churches.

7

Richard Hooker and
the Church of England

At first sight, it seems odd that Richard Hooker should be celebrated, and his works published, in America. Hooker is a very English figure, the Doctor Angelicus of the Church of England – that established Church which, from the first publication, in 1593, of his great work, *The Laws of Ecclesiastical Polity*, turned back the tide of Puritanism and sent its irreducible opponents to find a refuge,

> safe from the storm's and prelate's rage,

in this more hospitable land. Why then should it be in this continent, which has rejected all established churches, that his works are now being republished, more splendidly and more accurately than ever, thanks to the generosity of American patrons and the devotion of American scholars? On the face of it, it is a paradox.

It is not the only paradox. Hooker's work itself presents us with paradoxes. There is the paradox of his reputation. His great work was born of controversy. It was designed to secure the victory of a party in the bitter struggles of the Elizabethan Church. But in spite of this, he himself has always, in some mysterious way, remained an Olympian figure, standing benignly above the battle in which, historically, he had been so deeply engaged. In his lifetime, the praises of this Protestant, Anglican writer were sung, we are told, by Pope and Cardinals. After his death, King James I, arriving from Scotland to claim his new kingdom, was disappointed to find that he was too late to meet 'that man from whose books I have received such satisfaction'. A generation later, King Charles I and Archbishop Laud took up the refrain; but when the Puritans rebelled against both King and Archbishop,

Hooker, we find, does not sink with them: he rises effortlessly on the new stream. The magniloquent tirades of Milton spare the name of this more sedate, more philosophical prosaist; the radical pamphleteers of the Civil War explicitly exempt from condemnation 'the sweet and noble Hooker';[1] and the puritan Baxter claims him as an ally. When Church and King are restored, the Puritans sink again out of sight. But not Hooker. Now he enjoys his apotheosis as the patron saint of the narrow, high-flying High Tory Church of the Restoration; and there he stays – until the Glorious Revolution of 1688 when behold! while dynasty and High Tory Anglicanism go down, he surfaces again as the avowed oracle of John Locke and the Whig Party. And so it goes on. In the 1830s the last complete edition of Hooker's writings before this great American project filled six years of the life of John Keble, the founder of that Oxford movement which in some ways was the reversal of Hooker's work: for it ended by disowning the royal supremacy, which he had so uncompromisingly defended, and sending many of its intellectual leaders back from Canterbury to Rome. No wonder he has been immortalized under the misleading title of 'the judicious Hooker'!

How is it that Hooker, whose writings were hammered out in the internal party warfare of sixteenth-century religion, has so effortlessly transcended those battles? Why does his work alone survive the silent carnage of time? Who now – except the editors and commentators of Hooker – reads the controversial works of Cartwright and Travers, Whitgift and Bancroft, Stapleton and Persons? They have disappeared, and we see them only in fragmentary form: gobbets and slivers pickled in the footnotes to Hooker.

This, of course, is not unnatural. Many great works have been born in controversy, designed to serve short-term partisan ends. St Augustine, St Thomas Aquinas, Descartes, Locke, Marx, all built up their systems against now forgotten adversaries. Vulgar disputants die with the disputes which have nourished them. Great works shed their turbulent beginnings and seem, in retrospect, to rise out of untroubled thought. Nevertheless, to understand them we need to know their origins as well as their originality. Therefore let us look first at the religious controversies of Elizabethan England, out of which the *Laws of Ecclesiastical Polity* was born.

Richard Hooker was born early in 1554, a few months after the death of Edward VI and the accession of his Roman Catholic sister Mary Tudor. By that change of sovereign, the English Reformation, it seemed, had been fatally arrested. Some might say that the English Reformation had already outrun its original design; but we need not debate that point. The essential fact is that, in the next five years, numbers of English Protestants, seeing their Reformation halted, and its professors burned, fled abroad, and there, in Geneva, discovered a new model of the reformed Church very different from anything previously envisaged in England. For the concept of the Church which they had inherited was, in essentials, an Erasmian concept: they imagined a Church in which the traditional structure was purified of its abuses, and infused with a new spirit, under the protection – since the old spiritual head had been irremediably corrupted – of the lay ruler, the national Prince. But the concept of the Church which these exiles now discovered in Geneva was quite different. What they discovered was Calvin's model: a Church reconstituted on a new base, consecrated not by the gradual test of time but by the immediate authority of Scripture and the supposed practice of the apostles. This new model was fundamentally incompatible with the Erasmian model of the English reformers. That had been historical, evolutionary, continuous. This was unhistorical, anti-historical, fundamentalist. That had been adapted to the social forms of a modern monarchy. This implied another form of society: oligarchical, radical, perhaps revolutionary. That had been comprehensive, the Church of the whole Christian people. This was exclusive, the Church of a party, the Elect.

In early days, in the days of the common struggle against Rome, these differences might be obscured. Against the common danger, both parties found it best to stand together, postponing implicit differences. When the Marian exiles returned to Elizabethan England, they were ready, at first, to work within the existing structure; for they were weak and the Queen's government was indispensable. On her side the Queen, though determined to tolerate no 'innovation', no 'new-fangledness', was ready to use their services, for she was weak too, and needed them. So the parties settled down to an uneasy co-existence made possible by two things: first, by a large middle party of miscellaneous non-Calvinist lay Puritans who had no desire for revolution; secondly, by the legal supremacy of an indispensable Queen. So long as Queen Elizabeth lived, the *Via Media*, it seemed, could live too; or at least its implicit tensions could be contained.

So long as she lived. . . . But how long would she live? That was the great question. If she should die, who could deny the right of Mary Stuart, Mary Queen of Scots, to succeed her? Parliament might debar her; but Parliament had debarred Mary Tudor, and with what result? She had come in, and all these fragile paper barriers had dissolved before her. If Mary Stuart, like Mary Tudor, were to come in as rightful queen, how could either the unorganized forces of lay Puritanism or the fragile opportunism of a Laodicean Church resist the full force of legitimate, acknowledged, established power? Effective resistance requires organization, discipline, political will. It also requires firm doctrine, an ideology, a myth. If we ask who, in the 1570s, had that discipline, that myth, there is only one answer. It was international Calvinism: that international Calvinism which was able to defy Church and legitimate Crown in France; which had overthrown Church and legitimate Queen in Scotland; and which would soon overthrow Church and legitimate Crown in the Netherlands. Against the possible accession of the deposed Queen of Scots in England, the Calvinists were preparing an organization which could survive even a new Counter-Reformation. To do so, it would necessarily undermine and destroy the precariously established Elizabethan Church.

In those years of incubation Richard Hooker was at Oxford, first a student, then a fellow of Corpus Christi college, the college of Erasmus. At first he had been seduced by the appeal of Calvinism, with its high claims of doctrinal and structural purity: indeed, he had even been suspended from his fellowship on that account. But he had survived both that enthusiasm and that suspension; and having survived, he had found a new purpose in his own life. He would create a myth, a permanent intellectual and historical justification, for the still fragile and precarious Erasmian Anglican Church.

For we are now in the 1580s, that terrible decade, when England was beleaguered by the forces of the Counter-Reformation, when plot after plot was being mounted to destroy Queen Elizabeth for the benefit of Mary Stuart, when Alexander Farnese was reconquering the Netherlands for Spain, and invincible armadas were being built for the conquest of England. At any moment now Queen Elizabeth might be struck down, as William of Orange and Henri III of France were struck down; and then the great crisis would have come: a crisis for which revolutionary Calvinism had prepared itself but Anglicanism, as yet, had not.

In the 1580s, the Calvinists were indeed ready. Themselves a small minority, they were nevertheless highly organized, well disciplined, confident. Sure of themselves, sure of their ideology and their foreign support, they claimed the leadership of the uncertain English Protestants and sought to build up, behind the temporary façade of the episcopal Church, an unbreakable organization which would deal with Mary Stuart in England as their brethren of Scotland had already dealt with her there. It was then that Thomas Cartwright and Walter

Travers – the head and the neck of English Calvinism, as they would be called – set out resolutely to capture the still indeterminate Church of England from within, and it was then that the Calvinist agitator John Field – 'that Field which the Lord hath blessed' as the faithful called him – set in motion a plan to capture Parliament too. Had they succeeded, they would have destroyed one Church and created another. Their plan, Sir John Neale has written, was '*tabula rasa*, stark revolution'.[2]

These were the circumstances in which Richard Hooker sat down to write *The Laws of Ecclesiastical Polity*. As Master of the Temple, he met Calvinism at close quarters, for Walter Travers was his colleague, in the Temple itself, preaching and writing against him. How tense the atmosphere must have been in the Temple in those days, among those disputatious Elizabethan lawyers! Every Sunday morning they heard the Master preach the doctrines of pure Canterbury. Every afternoon they heard him corrected by his more famous lecturer, preaching pure Geneva. For Travers was a man of note, of influence, patronized by the great Lord Burghley. Fortunately, Hooker had a patron too. This was Archbishop Whitgift, an authoritarian churchman who, though himself half-Calvinist in theology, had already struck many a blow, both controversial and disciplinary, against the leaders of that party. Hooker could safely leave the political battle to his patron. His own task was purely intellectual. He wished to discredit the ideology of the Calvinists and replace it by an Anglican ideology strong enough to capture the intellectual leadership of the Church.

This was no parochial aim. Hooker did not intend merely to outbid the English Puritans in English Church politics or in theological controversy. His aims were far higher than that. They were general, indeed universal. He aimed to fix the Church of England not merely on a coherent doctrinal base but on an indisputable philosophical base. Nor was it for England only. For although he insisted that Church and Commonwealth were coterminous in jurisdiction, he did not accept that the Church of Christ had national or geographical limits. The Church of England was to him what the Church of Geneva was to Calvin: the model for all Christendom.

This may not be obvious to us. We look back on history and know the answers. We see that, in the end, the English Church, like other churches, became a national church. But in the sixteenth century, who was to foresee that? The medieval Church had been international, the Church of Christendom. The great reformers, in seeking to repair it, had no idea of breaking it up: they wished not to separate from it but to renew it, and to renew it whole. Luther did not mean to found a mere Germanic church, nor Calvin to end merely as the high priest of Geneva, Holland, Scotland. Similarly, if Anglicanism were to enter the fray, it too must make universal claims. It was only after a century of deadlock between rival claims to universality that Europe reconciled itself to distinct national churches.

Such claims required much more than mere controversial victory. The air of Elizabethan England was already full of controversy: disconnected and discordant cries, which swelled in volume in the 1580s, about sacraments and miracles, surplices and sabbath-days, episcopacy, liturgy, images, ceremonies, patronage, preaching, 'prophesying', the Apocalypse. Hooker resolved to go behind these slogans and symptoms and build up, not from Scriptural texts but from first principles, a coherent general system in which these particular controversies would either be resolved or wither away. He would not engage the adversary frontally in marginal disputes – those 'public disputations' to which the Puritans were such 'earnest challengers'; or at least he would only handle such disputes in their proper place, once the general issues had been set out; and those general issues would be determined by the only final arbiter which all men must recognize: that is, by reason, 'true, sound, divine reason' which was necessary to the interpretation of doctrine and discipline, even of Scripture itself. By placing the Elizabethan Church on a base not merely of tradition or prophecy or national law but universal reason, Hooker set out to be the complete rational philosopher, the Aquinas of Anglicanism.

Such was the political origin of Hooker's *Eight Books of the Laws of Ecclesiastical Polity*, of which the first four books were published in 1593. Though written in instalments, the work was conceived, from the beginning, as an orderly and consistent whole. The fifth book, longer than the first four put together, appeared in 1597. The last three books, having disappeared from view at Hooker's death in 1600, would emerge, fifty and sixty years later, trailing clouds of controversy as they came: controversy almost as great as that from which they had been born.

In this necessarily brief and summary account I have made some bold, perhaps some rash statements. Almost any statement about Hooker is rash today, when the foundations of scholarship about him have been, for a whole generation, shaken. Therefore let me hastily qualify some of my remarks. First, I must not suggest that Hooker was an isolated genius who single-handed established the philosophical base of Anglicanism. Such isolated genius, in my opinion, does not exist. It is the competition of peers which pushes genius to express itself, and then to eclipse its rivals so that it alone is remembered. Hooker could not have written without the work of other men, especially that of his two chief patrons and predecessors, Jewel and Whitgift. But as he eclipsed them in depth and range and expression, we remember him, not them. Secondly, let me amplify a little the statement that Hooker advanced for Anglicanism's universal claims: that he saw the Church of England as an ecumenical church. For this, I am sure, may be contested.

In some ways Hooker can certainly be presented as the advocate of a national rather than an international church. Did he not allow that all forms of government are equally legitimate? Did he not argue that the Church, though it was vindicated by its essential truth, was itself, in organization, 'a politic society', subject to the general laws of political and historical variation, and therefore, by a necessary consequence, plural? Did he not justify the right of the Church of England to go its own way? And did he not write in English, an obscure parochial language unknown in Europe? To all these questions we must surely answer, yes. However, if we detach Hooker's concept of church and society from the controversy which engendered it, we may see it in a different light.

To Hooker, as to Jewel and Parker and all Anglican apologists, the Church of England was historically continuous from earliest times. Unlike the Puritans, who were essentially unhistorical, he recognized the legitimacy of historical change. Secular society, he believed, changes its form, while retaining a lasting obligation to the original terms of its existence, and the Church, being a politic society too, has the same legitimate variety, and the same ultimate obligation. This variety, he believed, was applicable to both doctrine and discipline. There were of course fundamentals both of doctrine and of polity, but there were also, in both, *adiaphora*, 'things indifferent'. There were many differences between Canterbury and Rome, which need not, in themselves, lead to rupture; although modern Rome had deviated fatally from the true course, nevertheless, the Catholic Church remained 'a part of the house of God and a limb of the visible Church of Christ'. Good Puritans goggled at such statements; nor perhaps were they entirely pleased with their corollary, that the differences between Canterbury and Geneva, being merely historical, the effect of local circumstances, were equally harmless. To the Calvinists, though not always to Calvin himself, the Genevan model was of absolute validity. Hooker was a relativist. His relativism extended even to episcopacy.

Episcopacy, he believed, was of apostolic institution and consecrated by use; but it was not positively enjoined by the Law of God. Therefore, in certain circumstances, it might be rejected, as it had been in Geneva. The corollary was that, even in England, it was not an essential of faith. Therein lay a time-bomb for the next century.

However, in all this, Hooker is not arguing for distinct national churches as opposed to a universal Church. Nobody, I believe, argued thus in his time. His argument is that of Erasmus: a more constructive, less sceptical Erasmus. To him the organization of the universal Church is, and always has been, compatible with local variations, and neither the essential unity of the Church, nor the essential identity of its doctrine, need be broken over matters which are in themselves indifferent. It was to preserve the unity of the Church against schism that Erasmus had insisted on the indifference of 'external religion', and it was because the Roman Church had converted such *adiaphora* into articles of faith, that he accused it (as Hooker accused the Calvinists) of causing schism. In his relativism, therefore, Hooker is not advocating separate national churches, but rather a historically justified pluralism within a universal Church. Moreover he clearly believed that the Anglican Church was the best model for other national churches within the Christian world.

This was shown, in due course, by his two most personal disciples, George Cranmer and Edwin Sandys. Cranmer was the great-nephew of Archbishop Cranmer, Sandys the son of Hooker's former patron Archbishop Sandys. Both had been pupils of Hooker at Corpus Christi college. They had helped him when he was writing his great work, and had criticized his drafts, sharpening them up at times and pointing them more particularly at the immediate enemy, that is, at the English Puritans. Sandys also personally underwrote the cost of publishing the first four books. Immediately after those four books had been given to the printer, Cranmer and Sandys set off together on a prolonged tour of Western Europe. Their principal purpose, as Sandys wrote, was to view the state of religion 'in these Western parts of the world, their divided factions and professions, their differences in matters of faith, and their exercises of religion in government ecclesiastical and in life and conversation' . . . and, finally, to discover whether there were any 'possibilities and good means of uniting at least the several branches of the reformed professions, if unity universal be more to be desired than hoped in the present differences'.[3] In other words, having helped their master to produce his great work, and given it topicality in the context of the English controversies then raging, Sandys and Cranmer went abroad to explore the possibility of using it as a model for Christian reunion. They spent several years in travel, Cranmer returning in 1596, Sandys in 1599. On his return, Sandys presented a report of their findings to Archbishop Whitgift, the patron to whom Hooker had recently dedicated the fifth book of his *Laws of Ecclesiastical Polity*.

Sandys' report is entitled *A Relation of the state of Religion*. It is a remarkable work. In many ways it is the European political complement to Hooker's general theory. Hooker, it could be said, had prepared the way. He had taken the bitterness out of religious controversy, expounding a general philosophy for a time when 'these fruitless jars and janglings' should cease. Sandys set out the means of attainment. In Europe, and especially in France, he had discovered, he said, men 'not many in number' indeed, 'but sundry of them of singular learning and piety', who wished, 'when the flames of controversy might be extinguished and some tolerable peace re-established in the Church again', to re-unite Christendom in 'one general and indifferent confession and sum of faith, an uniform liturgy, a correspondent form of Church government'. The first nucleus of such a reunion could, he thought, be provided by an alliance of the Protestant Churches of Europe with the Gallican Catholics of France. The bridge upon which all these could meet was the Church of England; for 'in their more sober moods', European Catholics acknowledged England to be 'the only nation that walk the right way of justifiable reformation': with its unbroken continuity of form and doctrine, 'concurring with neither side, yet reverenced of both', the Church of England was 'the fitter and abler to work unity between them and to be an umpire and director, swayer of all'. Finally, although the 'papist' Catholics of Spain and Italy seemed beyond recovery, what of the Greek churches of the East, who preserved their faith under Ottoman tyranny? Sandys had not visited the East, but his knowledge of history and his experience of the Greek churches in Venice convinced him that they too should be brought in.[4] A few years later his younger brother George Sandys would make a tour of the Levant and report extensively on his experiences there.[5]

It was in 1599 that Edwin Sandys presented the manuscript of his work to Archbishop Whitgift. Nothing happened. It was not even published. Whitgift was now old and half-paralysed. Next year Hooker died, aged forty-six, the last three books of his work still unpublished. In the same year Cranmer was killed in Ireland. Five years later Sandys published his report. Three impressions were eagerly bought up in three months. Then the Court of High Commission stepped in. The book was condemned and burned at Paul's cross, and would not be printed again until Sandys was dead, nearly thirty years hence. Hooker's last three books would not see the light for over fifty.

What had happened? We do not know. We can only speculate. Perhaps the church authorities hesitated to provoke the cry of 'popery'. In the last year of Hooker's life, the English Puritans had struck back at him. They had accused him of various and horrible crimes: of exalting natural reason above Scripture, preferring Aristotle to Calvin, making light of important doctrinal differences, impiously ascribing to God 'a general inclination . . . that all men might be saved', and leading men, by his indecently sophisticated style, 'to fall either flatly to atheism or backwards to popery'.[6] And perhaps it was unfortunate that Sandys's *Relation* was published in the very month of the Gunpowder Plot. After that famous episode, agreement with Catholics of any kind was not to be thought of.

That was one possible objection. But there was also another, of an opposite tendency. In the years after the accession of the Stuart dynasty there was a gradual change in the philosophy of the Anglican Church. Whitgift gave way to Bancroft and Bancroft, ultimately, to Laud. It was the reign of the High Anglicans, the 'Arminians', organized as a party under James I, all-powerful under Charles I. In this new climate of opinion, Hooker's work began to seem weak and old-fashioned. Already offensive to Low Churchmen for its conciliation of popery, it now became suspect to High Churchmen for the modesty of its claims. In particular, these new 'Arminians' who approved of Hooker's theological liberalism, and paid lip-service to his achievement as the great doctor of their Church, had doubts about his ecumenism and strong objections to his political philosophy.

The idea of an ecumenical Church, an international alliance of some Catholics and some Protestants and perhaps the Greek churches of the East under the leadership of the Church of England, was held by many well-intentioned Christians in the reigns of James I and Charles I. One of these was the great Venetian historian and patriot, Fra Paolo Sarpi, who annotated an Italian translation of Sandys' *Relation* as propaganda for the purpose. Another was Isaac Casaubon, the French Huguenot scholar who, after the assassination of Henri IV and the end of ecumenical ideas in France, found asylum and favour at the court of James I. A third was one of the closest friends of Casaubon, a man whose name is often joined with that of Hooker, as a fellow philosopher of natural law, the Dutch Arminian Hugo Grotius. Grotius saw himself as the heir of his fellow-countryman Erasmus, and throughout his life his principal aim was the reunion of the churches, on an 'Arminian' – that is, an Erasmian – base. Like Casaubon, like Sarpi, like Sandys – whose work he afterwards read and wished to translate into Dutch[7] – Grotius too saw the Church of England as the natural head of such an alliance.

In 1613 Grotius came to England, officially in order to regulate Anglo-Dutch trade, unofficially in order to press his scheme for reunion. He discussed the project with the 'Arminian' English bishops, Lancelot Andrewes and John Overall. His letters from England are full of his plans. In one letter he refers to the exponents of Anglican doctrine and quotes a relevant passage from 'a book on Ecclesiastical Polity published in England'; that is, from Hooker. Since Grotius could not read English, this passage must have been drawn to his attention, probably by Andrewes, who now had custody of some of Hooker's unpublished manuscripts.

The plans for the reunion of the churches under the headship of the Church of England came, in the end, to nothing. Andrewes and Overall might have favoured them, but events were against them. In Europe, in the Thirty Years War, religious differences were sharpened, not reduced, and in England, in the 1630s, Archbishop Laud turned his back resolutely on the whole idea of reunion. In vain Grotius sought to engage him in his schemes. Neither foreign Protestants nor foreign Catholics were of interest to that rigid and purely English churchman. Whatever lip-service he might occasionally pay to ecumenical ideals, Laud's present aim was an exclusive, national Church.

Even more unfashionable, in those years of Laudian rule, were Hooker's ideas on government, both in Church and State. For Hooker believed with Aquinas that kings ruled by common consent, that the origin of government was by implied social compact, and that the government of the Church, even episcopacy itself, was a matter of convenience only. These ideas, implicit in his first five books, were stated explicitly in parts of the last three. They could hardly appeal to the high-flying theorists of Stuart absolutism with their insistence on the divine right of kings and the divine institution of episcopacy.

Thus, if we look into its historical context, the fate of Hooker's great work is easily explained. In the reign of Queen Elizabeth, he had advocated a tolerant, liberal, rational church within the structure of a tolerant, liberal, rational society. Although his views were expressed in English, in the context of an English controversy, they were of general application and were intended to provide the philosophy for a reunited Christendom. His disciples, who had been deeply involved in his work, sought to apply those views. Logically, the next step would have been the translation of his work into Latin, the universal language. Had Hooker lived, he would no doubt have seen to this. It was the normal practice for any philosopher who made his appeal to Europe. Bodin, Bacon, Descartes, Hobbes all wrote their main works in the vernacular, for their countrymen, but then had them published in Latin, for the world. Hooker's contemporary, the historian William Camden, urged that his work be so translated: it was, he wrote, 'set forth in the English, but worthy to speak Latin'.[8] However, any such project was frustrated by events: first by Hooker's own premature death, then by the change of climate in Jacobean, and even more in Caroline England. Hooker's *Laws of Ecclesiastical Polity*, though complete, remained only half-published; the work of his disciple was suppressed; even the published part of his work was not translated. For half a century, the clerical establishment of England, while ostentatiously venerating his name, effectively suppressed his work.

However, if the new leaders of the Church sought to bury Hooker under its tributary wreaths, there were others who sought to revive him. In 1629 a young Fellow of Trinity College, Oxford, William Chillingworth, Archbishop Laud's godson, seeking, like Hooker, a solid base on which to construct a rational belief and the model of an ecumenical Church, listened to the seductive words of a Jesuit missionary and took the plunge into popery. Then, at the Jesuit college at Douay in Flanders, he found that he was mistaken: that the claims of Counter-Reformation Rome were narrow, sectarian and illiberal. He read Grotius, and was convinced by him. He decided that the rational faith which he sought must be found, if anywhere, in the Church of England. So he returned to his own country, resumed its religion, and settled in the household of the young Lord Falkland at Great Tew in Oxfordshire. There he became the intellectual leader of a remarkable group of men who would afterwards be famous in England. There also he wrote his *credo*, *The Religion of Protestants*, a book which, though far more sceptical, rests visibly on Hooker's *Laws of Ecclesiastical Polity*.

The men who, all their lives, were held together by the shared experience of life at Great Tew were all admirers of Hooker. Some, like George Sandys, the traveller and poet, had personal connexions with Hooker's circle. They were also all distrusted by the Laudian Establishment. These two facts are interconnected. They were distrusted because, though Anglicans, and indeed Arminians, like Laud himself, they did not accept the new rigidities of Laudianism. Like Hooker, they did not believe in the divine right of kings or bishops; like him, they believed in unity with foreign Protestants, regarded consent as the basis and justification of political power, and looked, in religion, not for mystery or unarguable infallibility, but for reason. The result was predictable. In the 1630s, none of the clergy among them received promotion from Archbishop Laud, or the laity from the King. When the Long Parliament met in November 1640, all of them were opposed to the absolutism of the King and the Archbishop. They were on the side of reform.

Reform was not achieved, or not consolidated. Instead came civil war and revolution: a religious as well as a political revolution. It was the realization, sixty years later, of the crisis which Hooker had apprehended in the 1580s. The protective monarchy had foundered, and the structure of the Anglican Church had collapsed under the blows of its Puritan enemies, who had emerged to take over its authority. The question, now as then, was, could that Church survive? Had it the intellectual conviction which could sustain its continuity of spirit when its physical continuity had been so decisively broken?

As far as the Laudians were concerned, it had not. In the great storms of the 1640s the Laudian Church went down at the first gust, and those who did not sink with it, or clamber into the obscure safety of captivity, swam severally to distant shores. In the long years of Puritan rule, very few of the high-flying careerists who had flourished in the Laudian Church took any risks, or showed any faith in a future restoration. Those who believed in such a restoration, and by their belief and their active labours made it possible, were not the Laudian bishops and deans and their chaplains, but the men of Great Tew: Henry Hammond, George Morley, Gilbert Sheldon, John Earle, and, among laymen, the political leader of them all, Edward Hyde. In 1660 these men would come together again, and would restore monarchy and Church, not on the broken Laudian basis of divine right but on the old foundation of compact and consent, the philosophy of Hooker.

How much Hooker meant to them in those long years of exile and preparation! What had never been done in the years of Anglican supremacy was done in those years of defeat. John Earle, attending the exiled Charles II in Antwerp and Paris, at last translated Hooker's published work into Latin. Surely there is a certain heroic quality in that gesture. As Archbishop of Canterbury and Chancellor of Oxford University, the Maecenas of sound learning in England, Laud had done nothing to publish the work of the man whom he praised as the great doctor of his Church. He would fetch manuscripts from Europe and the East, set up printing presses, publish commentaries on the

Old Testament and homilies by the Fathers, but the manuscripts of
Hooker's work lay unprinted under his hand. But now, when the
Church, having been narrowed within national limits, had been utterly
extinguished, a little group of exiles was setting out its claims in the
universal language and thereby claiming for it universal validity.

Meanwhile, another of the same group was using Hooker in another
way. When all the mainland of Britain had been lost, Edward Hyde
began in the Isles of Scilly, and continued in the island of Jersey, his
great *History of the Rebellion*; and he too, in writing it, had the example of
Hooker before his eyes. Hooker, in those ominous 1580s, had looked
forward with apprehension to the destruction of his Church and had
begun his work with a solemn exordium, defiantly registering for
posterity the permanence of its claims:

> Though for no other cause, yet for this: that posterity may know we
> have not loosely through silence permitted things to pass away as a
> dream, there shall be for men's information extant thus much
> concerning the present state of the Church of God established
> amongst us, and their careful endeavour which would have upheld
> the same . . .

Hyde, in 1646, began his *History* in almost identical style:

> That posterity may not be deceived by the prosperous wickedness of
> these times into an opinion that less than a general combination and
> universal apostasy in the whole nation from their religion and
> allegiance could in so short a time have produced such a total and
> prodigious alteration . . . and so the memory of those few who . . .
> have opposed and resisted that torrent . . . may lose the recompense
> due to their virtue . . . it will not be unuseful . . . to present to the
> world a full and clear narration . . .

The message implicit in this formal imitation could hardly be clearer.
Hyde was stating that the crisis which Hooker had apprehended had
come to pass, and that the mantle of Hooker had fallen on him.

The resemblance does not stop there. Even in his English style, even
in his personal tricks of style, Hyde shows the ever-present influence of
Hooker: those long, serpentine sentences majestically uncoiling, clause
after clause, now smooth and sinuous, now coruscating with a sudden,
sharp, malicious flicker – how can we avoid comparing it with Hooker's
similarly articulated style: that style which Fuller described as 'long

and pithy, drawing on a whole flock of several clauses before he came to the close of a sentence',[9] and which is equally capable of grave irony and quick malice? Like Hooker, Hyde wrote a work of controversy: his *History* was directed against the Parliamentary propaganda of Tom May just as Hooker's *Laws* had been directed against the Puritan propaganda of Walter Travers. But like Hooker he was determined to rise above controversy, to look beyond present misfortunes, and to produce a long-term validation of the English monarchy that would win support from an uncommitted posterity. Such an aim entailed magnanimity to persons. Just as Hooker would praise Calvin as 'incomparably the wisest man that ever the French Church did enjoy', so Hyde would praise John Hampden and Oliver Cromwell, being resolved, as he wrote, to do equal justice to all men on whichever side they fought, or fell.

Incidentally, the fate of the two works was also curiously similar. The publication of Hyde's *History*, like that of Hooker's *Laws*, would be at the mercy of politics. It too first appeared in full over fifty years after its author's death. And in it too political partisans were quick to allege improper interpolations.

If Hooker thus supplied the inspiration of the defeated Anglicans in the 1640s and 1650s, it was natural that he should share their triumph in 1660. 'True it is', wrote Thomas Fuller, immediately after the Restoration, 'his book in our late times was beheld as an old almanack grown out of date; but blessed be God there is now a Revolution, which may bring his works again into reputation.'[10] And so we are not surprised that in 1662, when Hyde, Sheldon and Morley ruled State and Church, Hooker's great work was at last published in full; and when a new life of the author was required, that Sheldon's friend and fellow-fisherman, Izaak Walton, should be brought in to write it. Sheldon supplied the documents; the *Life* was written in Morley's episcopal palace at Farnham. Meanwhile Earle, as Bishop of Salisbury, was finishing his Latin translation, and Hyde, now Lord Chancellor and Earl of Clarendon, was waiting to ensure its publication. The great doctor of the Anglican Church had at last, it seemed, been canonized.

Alas, canonization is a ticklish process which often requires some judicious tampering with the evidence. Any revolution is a nasty business which hardens men's hearts and narrows their minds. If all had gone according to plan in 1641 – if the Laudians had been defeated and the Church saved – then, perhaps, the ideas of Hooker would have been accepted in their entirety. But after nearly twenty years of 'blood and confusion', things could never be the same, and we have to admit that, in 1660, the temper of the old liberals of Great Tew, having been soured by events, was much nearer to that of the old Laudians than that of their old selves. In 1641, even in 1647, Hyde and Sheldon, Morley and Earle, and their friends, had accepted Hooker's philosophy in full. They had believed in mixed monarchy, liberal episcopacy, comprehension, consensus, a rational faith, an ecumenical Church. After 1649, after the execution of the King and the destruction of their Church, their temper, or that of their party, had changed; and so they required that Hooker change too. In particular, they needed to disown those last three books of Hooker's *Laws of Ecclesiastical Polity* which, for half a century after their author's death, had been so zealously suppressed.

So a convenient fiction was devised. Those last books, it was now said, were not the works of the saint, but apocryphal works posthumously fathered upon him by Puritan schemers. How else could the great doctor of Anglican episcopacy have been made to utter those 'poisonous assertions' about the origin of bishops and kings? In order to explain this obvious imposture, it was necessary to look for a scapegoat; and the scapegoat which conveniently offered itself, like that timely ram which emerged from the thicket to replace Isaac on the sacrificial altar, was the unfortunate Mrs Hooker. For nearly three centuries Mrs Hooker has been immolated, a substitute victim, in the cause of high Anglican hagiography.

How can I, at the tail-end of a lecture, presume to reiterate the sad tale of the posthumous denigration of Mrs Hooker? In all mid-seventeenth-century accounts she appears as the villain of the story, destroying the peace of mind, the work, the fame of her unworldly husband. To Hooker, wrote 'honest Tom Fuller', his wife was 'neither to his comfort when living nor his credit when dead'.[11] She was foisted on him by her impecunious grasping mother, says the innocent Izaak Walton, and accepted by him because he was too saintly to recognize her moral faults, and too short-sighted to see her ill looks. She dragged him from his studies, obliged him to rock cradles and mind sheep, and when he died, 'stayed not long to bewail her widowhood', and handed his true works over to the ideological enemy in order to be turned into puritan propaganda.[12] She was, says that crusted college bachelor Anthony Wood, 'a clownish silly woman and withal a mere Xantippe'.[13]* And once she had been given a bad name, it stuck. It was so convenient. It explained all. Immortalized in Izaak Walton's *Life of Hooker*, it was reprinted, in that famous *Life*, in every edition of Hooker's

---

* Xantippe, the wife of Socrates, was a notorious scold.

works: an essential brick in the temple erroneously reared to an imaginary high Anglican saint.[14]

Happily, all that is over now. The ladies, and particularly the wives of scholars, will be glad to know that time, the mother of truth, has vindicated Mrs Hooker, at least from the gravest of these aspersions. In 1940 C. J. Sisson, by a splendid piece of scholarly research, showed how this libel had arisen, after the death of Hooker and Mrs Hooker, directly or indirectly out of a series of disagreeable lawsuits with which they personally had nothing to do.[15] Incidentally, out of those same lawsuits, Sisson produced evidence about the publication and history of Hooker's work which re-activated the whole industry of Hooker scholarship. The smooth image of three centuries, so carefully composed in the 1660s, thereupon began to crumble, and a new and truer appreciation became possible. Of that industry the solid result is this great American enterprise which we now celebrate.

Such a celebration is particularly appropriate to these ecumenical days. For the work which we are celebrating was attacked, in its own time, for qualities which we respect in ours. Today, as we look back through the history of human thought, we find Hooker and Grotius more attractive than Calvin and Cartwright or Bancroft and Laud. Like Hooker, we wish to look past doctrinal controversies to the profounder issues which they so often concealed; and we may find ourselves in agreement with that uncomfortably isolated Roman Catholic scholar of the nineteenth century, Lord Acton. In the sixteenth century, wrote Acton, as a serious quest for a set of principles which should hold good alike under all changes of religion, 'Hooker's *Ecclesiastical Polity* stands almost alone'.[16]

Sources

1. [Henry Parker], *A Discourse concerning Puritans* (1641), p. 40.
2. J. E. Neale, *Elizabeth I and her Parliaments 1584–1600* (1957), pp. 148–9.
3. [E. Sandys], *A Relation of the State of Religion* ... (1605), sig. A3.
4. Ibid., sig. S4v, T2, etc.
5. George Sandys, *The Relation of a Journey made in AD 1610* (1615).
6. *A Christian Letter of Certain English Protestants unto Mr R. Hoo, requiring resolution in his Ecclesiasticall Pollicie* (1599). Hooker was defended in the reply of William Covell, *A Just and Temperate Defence of the Five Books of Ecclesiastical Policie by R. Hooker* (1603).
7. Grotius to his brother Willem de Groot, 30 January 1637. *Briefwisseling van Hugo Grotius*, ed. B. L. Moelenbroek VIII (Hague, 1971), 65.
8. Camden, *Annales Rerum Anglicarum et Hibernicarum, regnante Elizabetha*, 1615, under year 1599.
9. T. Fuller, *The Church History of Britain*, ed. J. S. Brewer (Oxford, 1845), V, 183.

10. T. Fuller, *The History of the Worthies of England* (ed. John Nichols, 1811), I, 290 (Devonshire).
11. Ibid.
12. Izaak Walton, *The Lives of John Donne* . . . (etc.) (World's Classics), pp. 177–80.
13. A. Wood, *Athenae Oxonienses* (ed. P. Bliss) 1813–20, II. 652–3.
14. On Walton's *Life of Hooker* see David Novarr, *The Making of Walton's Lives* (Cornell, 1958).
15. C. J. Sisson, *The Judicious Marriage of Mr. Hooker* (Cambridge, 1940).
16. Lord Acton, *The History of Freedom and Other Essays* (1907), p. 45.

8

Queen Elizabeth's first historian:
William Camden

In the first Neale Lecture, delivered last year, Dame Veronica Wedgwood spoke of the Elizabethanism of Oliver Cromwell and his generation: the idealized portrait of 'that great lady' which hung, as it were, always before the eyes of the regicide Lord Protector.[1] Images often determine reality, and the seventeenth-century conception of Queen Elizabeth is an intangible historical force, but Oliver Cromwell's fixation upon it contains a certain paradox: for whereas the image of Queen Elizabeth, for all her feminine vacillation, procrastination and tergiversation, possessed for him, and has retained even for us, a certain historical consistency, that of Oliver Cromwell, the resolute man of action, the self-made master of three kingdoms, is quite remarkable for its instability. Every historian, from his own day to ours, has had a different view of him, and some historians have contrived to change their own view of him from year to year, from book to book. When I reflect on this paradox, I ask myself whether the explanation may not lie as much in the historians of these two great rulers as in their own characters. May it not be that the relative fixity of the image of Queen Elizabeth owes something to the fact that her first historian, like her last, was a master who could capture and stabilize even so variable a character as Gloriana, the English Jezebel, 'that wicked woman of England', 'good Queen Bess', 'that infamous wolf in woman's form', 'Queen Elizabeth of glorious memory'? At all events, I cannot think of a better way in which to honour Sir John Neale than by putting before you some account of his greatest predecessor, William Camden.

I shall be concerned, of course, with William Camden the historian of Queen Elizabeth, the first 'civil historian' of England, not with William Camden the author of *Britannia*, the first 'chorographer' of England.

And yet how can the two be entirely separated? The same man wrote both works: there is history in *Britannia* and 'chorography' in the *Annals*; one work grew naturally out of the other, and the mind which created the former will be seen constantly at work in the latter. Human genius is indivisible, though it may throw off distinct particles, and it was because he had shown his quality in *Britannia* that Camden was first encouraged, by the same patron, to begin his *Annals*. Therefore let me first say something, however briefly, about Camden's first work, *Britannia*, which was published in 1586.

Camden's *Britannia* was the vacation work of an active London schoolmaster. For Camden was not, like so many of the Elizabethan antiquaries, a gentleman amateur of scholarship: he was a professional, an academic. At Oxford, as an undergraduate, he had fallen in love with antiquities and had been encouraged, in particular, by his contemporary Sir Philip Sidney, to whom he would afterwards, in *Britannia*, pay a glowing tribute. After leaving Oxford, he sought to gratify that love by 'perambulating' England, as older scholars, Leland and Lambarde, had done before him. Then, in 1575, he acquired a solid base. He was appointed an under-master at Westminster School. One of the attractions of the academic life is the vacations, and in the school holidays Camden was able to continue and extend his perambulations, 'discovering' England, county by county. Sometimes he took with him a pupil whom he had interested in these studies. His most famous pupil was Sir Robert Bruce Cotton, who, much later, would accompany him on his expedition to the Roman Wall. Cotton would remain a lifelong friend of Camden. His contribution to Camden's work – as to the work of every other historian for the next century – would be immense. He would also play a curious part in the strange history of Camden's *Annals*, to which we must soon come.

The friendship of Cotton would be useful to Camden all his life. Even more useful, in his early years, was the patronage of Queen Elizabeth's great minister, Lord Burghley. For Burghley was himself a lover of antiquities, a maintainer of scholars. His interest was genuine; but it had also its political motives. As a statesman, Burghley was concerned to stabilize the rule of Queen Elizabeth, to place that trembling throne, and that delicate Protestant Church, both of which seemed so precarious in 1559, on a solid base: a base which would not only be firm in itself, politically and economically, but also consecrated, intellectually, by a continuous pedigree. The rule of Queen Elizabeth must not appear to be, as foreigners saw it, the fragile authority of an insecure young woman, the last, frail life of the usurping Tudor dynasty: it must appear as the natural, organic continuation of a robust, uncontested, ancient monarchy. Equally, the Elizabethan Church must not appear as a whimsical and heretical innovation, an ephemeral political compromise, doomed to founder in the stress of ideological war: it must appear as the true and legitimate continuation of that first Christian Church which had been planted in England centuries before the upstart Bishop of Rome had taken it over and corrupted its purity. These views of Lord Burghley were shared by his friend, Archbishop Parker. Thus Queen Elizabeth's two greatest advisers, her first statesman and her first churchman, were convinced patrons of antiquarian study in England. What we tend to see as a modern idea, the idea that history does not consist of high politics only but is contained and controlled by the whole glutinous contexture of present and past society, was felt, if not articulated, long before Hegel: it was imposed upon Elizabethan Englishmen by the knowledge that, politically, the Queen's government, in both Church and State, hung upon slender filaments and a feeble title. If it were to take root, it needed the stronger warrant of an organic theory.

This was not the case of the English monarchy only. It was equally true of the French. The dynasty of the Valois, like that of the Tudors, was visibly near its end. Catherine de Médicis, like Queen Elizabeth, was a woman, struggling to preserve the power of the Crown from being the prey of political parties and religious factions. In France too, thinking men looked for a strong impersonal basis for the continuance of government, and an intellectual justification for that basis. It is no accident that while Englishmen were seeking a justification for their Church and State which transcended the claims of the Tudors, Frenchmen were seeking a justification for theirs which transcended the claims of the Valois. The need was the same. The solution was similar. On both sides of the Channel men looked for political stability rather than religious truth. Such men were called, in France, *politiques*. The difference was that while the English *politiques* found an empirical justification in history, the continuity of *ecclesia Anglicana*, the French *politiques* looked rather to the theoretical justification of law: the stabilizing institutional law of the Roman Empire. Their greatest scholar was a lawyer, Jean Bodin; but Bodin had also written on historical method, and he was to have historical disciples who were to play an important part in Camden's life, as we shall see.

At the time when he wrote *Britannia*, Camden may not yet have been influenced by Bodin; but he was no insular Englishman. He too, like so many of his generation, looked back, for stability, to the unified Roman

Empire: the Roman Empire of the second century AD, of the Antonines. He saw his country in the context of the Roman Empire just as Bodin saw his in the context of Roman Law. The man who, more than any other, presented this context to him was the great Flemish cartographer Abraham Ortelius. In 1577 Ortelius was looking for an English scholar to supply him with authentic evidence for his map of Roman Britain. In that year he came to London and happened to meet Camden. The meeting was of great consequence to both parties. It gave Ortelius what he wanted. It also gave Camden what he needed. It brought his concept of Britain into a European framework and himself into the European Republic of Letters. Nine years later, when *Britannia* was published, it contained acknowledgments to Sir Robert Cotton, 'a great admirer of antiquities'; it was dedicated to Lord Burghley; and the first sentence of the text describes how the author had been inspired to write it by 'that great restorer of the old geography, Abraham Ortelius'.

So much for *Britannia*. Of its content I shall say nothing here. I wish to emphasize only two aspects of it: first, the coherent philosophy which underlay it – a philosophy of organic historical continuity from the earliest times to Tudor England; secondly, Camden's cosmopolitanism, the wide, European view which distinguished him from more parochial English antiquaries, and which he owed, above all, to the inspiration of Ortelius. Perhaps I should also touch more lightly on an obvious fact: the gentle – in this case helpful – pressure of patronage: the patronage of Lord Burghley. All these aspects of *Britannia* will be visible also, with significant variations, in his later work, the *Annals*.

In the twenty years which followed the publication of *Britannia*, Camden worked continuously on no second major book. He was famous; he had a wide international correspondence; he was busy as a schoolmaster, later as headmaster of Westminster; and in 1596, when he ceased to be a schoolmaster, he was Clarenceux King of Arms in the College of Heralds. Meanwhile, with his pupil Sir Robert Cotton, he founded the Elizabethan Society of Antiquaries and he continued his perambulations of England, adding ever new material, as edition followed edition of *Britannia*. He had projects indeed, in those years, but they came to nothing or little. It was not till King James was settled on the throne that a new conjuncture of forces set him to work on his second great enterprise; and this new conjuncture was similar, in general terms, to the old. Once again Sir Robert Cotton was there to help, his splendid collection of manuscripts greater, more indispensable than ever. Once again there was a highly placed patron to point the way. Once again a great international scholar provided at least part of the impetus. This new conjuncture occurred in the years 1605–7. In those years Camden suddenly called a halt to his old studies. He ceased to write Greek grammars for Westminster School and tourist guides to Westminster Abbey. He gave up collecting material for new editions of *Britannia*. Indeed he took, as it were, a formal leave of *Britannia*. And he resolved to complete a second great work, the work with which this lecture is concerned, the *Annals of Great Britain in the Reign of Elizabeth*.[2]

Before coming to the content of Camden's *Annals*, I must say something of their external history: the history of the forces which brought them into being and gave them their shape. It is indeed a strange, fascinating, even bizarre story; and like every incident of intellectual life at the court of the British Solomon, it has an irresistibly comic side. Strictly speaking, this external history is irrelevant to the content of the work, because Camden was strong enough to ignore the outward pressure that was put upon him. Nevertheless, because he was subjected to that pressure, and because he resisted it, it cannot altogether be omitted. *Habent sua fata libelli*, and the pre-natal history of Camden's *Annals* deserves at least to be summarized.

Camden himself, in his introduction to the *Annals*, as published, has given an account of their origin. He there tells us how, in 1596, his old patron Lord Burghley suggested to him that he write the history of the reign of Queen Elizabeth and, for that purpose, put at his disposal all his own, and the public, state papers. Cotton too made him free of his great library, and soon Camden was at work. But then, in 1598, Burghley died and Camden's industry 'began to flag and wax cold', and not long afterwards 'that incomparable Princess also rendered her celestial soul to God', whereupon 'I stood in expectation for some time, full of hope that some other person, haply some one of that great number of learned men who through her favour and bounty did abound with both wealth and leisure, would render her this due and deserved piece of gratitude.' Only when they declined did Camden decide to fill the gap. So he 'buckled himself afresh to his intermitted study and plied it harder than before'; and this time he brought it to a conclusion. Such is Camden's own account, as published in 1615. It is not untrue, but it is very discreet. It is discreet because it leaves out the *primum mobile* in the whole affair: King James.

At first sight it may seem odd that King James, who had no great love for history (he broke up Camden's Society of Antiquaries as a potentially subversive body) or for historians (as Sir Walter Ralegh was to

discover), should have sponsored a historical work celebrating, of all
things, the glorious reign of his immediate predecessor. King James
had been obliged to flatter Queen Elizabeth as long as she was alive, but
he had no reason to love her now that she was dead. After all, she had
kept him in continual suspense, had sent him most disagreeable letters,
and had cut off his mother's head. If she was now praised by his
subjects, that (he knew only too well) was mainly in order to imply
unflattering comparisons with himself. However, love and hatred are
relative terms and sometimes a man may call in Beelzebub to drive out
Satan. If we are to understand King James's invocation of Camden, we
must look back to its original and overpowering motive. He wished to
drive out another historian whom he particularly hated: his old tutor
George Buchanan.

It is true, James I had already taken steps against Buchanan. He had
explicitly forbidden his subjects in all three kingdoms to read the
dreadful *History of Scotland*, in which that eminent humanist had not
only advanced a consistent republican thesis but also pilloried Mary
Queen of Scots to all the world as a profligate, a murderess, an idol-
atress and a tyrant. Unfortunately, this was not enough. The King's
writ might run in England, Scotland and Ireland, but Buchanan's
works were written in Latin, published abroad and read throughout Europe. Moreover, they were, so far, the only available source for
Scottish history. However, King James had barely established himself
on the English throne when he saw a wonderful opportunity of correc-
tion. This opportunity was supplied by the sudden emergence of a new
historian, a historian of incomparable range and power, perfect style
and irresistible authority, a historian who was also the heir to Bodin as
the intellectual leader of the French *politiques*: Jacques-Auguste de
Thou.

How can one do justice, in a few parenthetic paragraphs, to Jacques-
Auguste de Thou? If Camden has fixed for succeeding centuries the
political image of Queen Elizabeth, de Thou (as some modern French
historians complain[3]) has equally fixed the historical interpretation of
the French Wars of Religion. If it is thanks to Camden that we ascribe
to Queen Elizabeth a consistent policy of *via media* rather than an
inconsequent series of unresolved conflicts and paralysed indecisions, it
is (they tell us) thanks to de Thou's great *History of his Own Time* that
Frenchmen, for three centuries, have looked upon their history, in the
same period, through the eyes of the *politiques*. In vain the Catholic
Church would condemn his work as heretical beyond the possibility of
expurgation. In vain later historians have struggled to emancipate

themselves from his influence. From the moment when the first volume appeared, in 1603, the European establishment, political and literary alike, bowed down before it. Kings and princes competed to flatter the author. The greatest writers of the day offered to supply him with raw material. Like some grand professor (if such there be) whose publications are fed by a disciplined seminar of research-students, he drew the whole Republic of Letters into his orbit. But what professor has ever ruled such a seminar as his? Hugo Grotius and Paolo Sarpi and Francis Bacon were all members of it. All wrote, or were instructed to write, essays or even theses for incorporation in the magisterial work of Professor de Thou.

Among the kings who so eagerly read de Thou's first volume was James I.[4] On the advice of Henri IV, de Thou had sent a presentation-copy to the most learned king in Europe, and the King, reading it, saw at once both the opportunity and the danger which it presented. For de Thou's first volume carried the history of Europe from 1540 to 1560. The next volume, inevitably, would deal with certain events of European significance which happened to take place in Scotland: the arrival of Mary Stuart in that inhospitable land; the Darnley marriage; the murder of Riccio; the tragedy of Kirk-o'-Fields; the deposition, defeat and flight of Mary; the indictment of her by her half-brother, the regent Moray; the mystery of the Casket Letters. . . . How, the King asked himself, would de Thou handle these delicate questions? Would he correct, or would he support, and by supporting authenticate for ever, the pitiless declamations of the infamous Buchanan?

With such thoughts as these in his mind, King James decided to court de Thou. He wrote personally to thank and congratulate him. How rare it was, he exclaimed, to discover, in these times, a historian who was so refreshingly free from that besetting sin of the tribe, partiality! He looked forward eagerly, he added, to the next volumes. It was very gratifying to de Thou to receive such royal approbation: gratifying, but also somewhat alarming; for the hint was obvious, and de Thou, who could already sense the storm that was blowing up in the Vatican, had no desire to be drenched by an entirely separate squall from across the Channel. Faced by such a prospect, de Thou decided that he needed, in his seminar, an expert on British history; and with his infallible flair for picking the ablest research-students in Europe, he turned, as Ortelius had turned thirty years before, to Camden.

It was in 1605 that de Thou, through a Huguenot intermediary, established contact with Camden. Having found him friendly, he then wrote to him direct and posed the essential question: how could he deal

faithfully, and yet without giving offence, with the history of the
revolution in Scotland? Buchanan, he observed, had written somewhat
sharply on these matters, and 'I hear that his royal pupil is angry with
him on that account. However, facts are facts and an honest man
cannot conceal them. Write, and do not grudge your help to your
perplexed friend.'

Camden duly wrote. He gave excellent advice. He urged de Thou to
understand the context of the Scottish revolution. He must realize that
neither Moray nor his rivals, the Hamiltons, were pure patriots: both
were politicians, party leaders, seeking power, though Moray undoubtedly had 'great qualities'. As for Buchanan, he too was an
interested party, the client, the agent, and the propagandist of Moray:
he was not to be accepted as a historical authority – at least not without
a careful check; and his personal judgements should never be trusted.
This was excellent advice. It was a pity that de Thou did not take it
more seriously. Unfortunately he had by now discovered another
authority on Scotch affairs, one John Colville, a Scotch émigré living in
Paris. Colville had recently become a Roman Catholic, but nevertheless supported Buchanan's interpretation. This impressed de Thou. In
fact Colville was a notorious rascal and turncoat who would say
anything to serve his present interests. King James hated him and
regarded him as a traitor. He would lead de Thou into error and
trouble. De Thou would have done better to follow Camden. As it was,
he followed Buchanan and Colville and hoped, by protestations of
objectivity and studied moderation, to satisfy King James. Then he
nervously presented the new volume to the English ambassador, Sir
George Carew – yet another member of his seminar* – to pass on to the
King.

He was sadly mistaken. On receiving the book, Carew thought it
prudent to see what de Thou had written 'touching the matters of
Scotland'. What he read so alarmed him that he did not dare send it to
the King. Instead he sent it to Cecil. It was clear, he explained, that de
Thou, 'finding Buchanan's story written in a smooth Latin style, for
want of others, hath wholly followed that'. The King would unques-
tionably be very upset. However, the book was bound to be widely read.
The best course, therefore, was to put it right; and he advised that the
truth be set forth 'by some good pen such as, among other men's,
Savile's or Camden's is'.[5]

---

* Carew supplied de Thou with material on the history of Denmark, where he had
been English ambassador.

'Savile or Camden'. . . . Curiously (but we must remember that Carew and de Thou were friends) it was precisely to these two men that de Thou now appealed to cushion the expected blow from England. 'I am afraid I have not always preserved that prudence which you recommended to me', he admitted to Camden; but facts were facts; he had good independent authorities; he had used temperate language. . . . 'If only your great Queen Elizabeth were alive,' he sighed to Savile, 'perhaps one could still write without fear on this subject'; but alas, times had changed and now one could not be so sure. . . .

The answers which de Thou received to these letters were diplomatic but not very encouraging. We all know the difficulties of writing contemporary history, replied Savile: however prudent we may be, there are some wounds which reopen at the slightest touch. Camden remained silent for a year; then, after a prodding letter from the Embassy in Paris, he sent to de Thou, as explanation of his silence, the newly published 1607 edition of *Britannia*, in which de Thou would notice (he remarked) that he had said very little about Scotland. The reason was that there is no satisfying the Scots short of saying that their country is vastly better and more important than it is. De Thou, he added, had been very prudent on that irritable nation, although it was true that King James was still harping away on the old string. De Thou found this cold comfort. He wished that Camden had written more fully about Scotland, he replied, and given an example of the safe tone for a historian to adopt in these delicate matters: then he would not have offended 'your powers'.

Thus on all sides Camden was being pressed to write about Queen Elizabeth and Mary Stuart. He was being pressed by de Thou, who wanted guidance through the treacherous maze of Scotch history; he was being pressed on the King by Carew; soon the King would be pressing too. These are the facts which Camden does not mention in his published preface. But they help to explain the sudden change in his programme in those years 1605–7. The dates alone tell the tale. It was in 1605, the same year in which he was first approached by de Thou, that he began the winding-up of *Britannia*. In that year he published his *Remains*, the over-matter of those researches, and dedicated them to Sir Robert Cotton. It was in 1607, after the appearance of de Thou's second volume, that he published the last and fullest edition of *Britannia* which he himself would edit. Then he resumed work on the reign of Elizabeth. Next year, in 1608, he recorded in his journal, *Annales digerere coepi*, 'I began to compile my *Annals*.'[6]

So much for the first impulse. What of the execution? Once again we turn to that discreet preface. It had been his intention, he there tells us, not to publish his book, but 'to bequeathe it to that honourable person' Jacques-Auguste de Thou, for use in his *History of his Own Time*; 'but in this purpose', he adds, 'I was (I know not by what fate) prevented', and although a part of it was sent to de Thou, in somewhat unsatisfactory form, and used by him, Camden decided, in the end, to publish it under his own name. Once again, the language is somewhat evasive. Once again, if we look behind it, we find a somewhat different reality. It may be that Camden, when he resumed his *Annals*, intended them to be mere raw material for de Thou. It may be that, as he told de Thou in 1612, he thought of publishing them anonymously in Germany, dedicated to de Thou. But once again he reckoned without King James.

King James, of course, was very cross with de Thou for ignoring his plain hints. However, he did not give way to impotent rage. As a practical man he saw that, in the long run, he could not win against de Thou, and therefore he must try to convert him. Perhaps de Thou could be persuaded to correct what he had published. Besides, there was more to come. De Thou's second volume, published in 1607, had only reached 1574. Mary Queen of Scots had gone on to 1587. It was more important to secure the future than to recriminate over the past.

So there began a protracted comedy which lasted altogether eight years, with King James persistently seeking to persuade de Thou to correct what he had written and adjust what he intended to write. In this comedy, which sometimes acquires the character of *opéra bouffe*, a key part was played by the great Huguenot scholar Isaac Casaubon, who, from 1610, was installed, a favoured guest, at the court of King James. Casaubon was an old friend of de Thou, and King James used him as his intermediary. The King would express himself freely to Casaubon. Casaubon would then write formal letters to de Thou, which the King would vet before dispatch. De Thou understood the system perfectly. He would reply formally to Casaubon, knowing that his letters would be shown to the King. But at the same time these two old friends would exchange private letters commenting on and explaining their own formal correspondence. The formal letters were in Latin, the private in French. By reading the two series together, we can follow the royal comedy on two levels, above and below stairs. They supply a diverting, but essential, background to the quiet, methodical scholarship of Camden.

The crisis began in 1611. In that year, when Camden had drafted a large part of his *Annals*, he received a surprise visit from the most learned, but not the most agreeable, of English noblemen, King James's confidant, Henry Howard, Earl of Northampton. Northampton told him that the King wanted to see his manuscript, and asked him to give it to Sir Robert Cotton. Camden was reluctant to do so: the manuscript, he said, was still rough and unfinished; but he could not refuse anything to Cotton and he complied: he gave to Cotton the text of his *Annals* up to 1572. Unfortunately Cotton was not in control of events. Afterwards Camden saw a copy of his work after treatment – either by the King or by Northampton or by both. It was 'full of mutilations and gaps and certain words had been effaced by the effrontery of the copyist'. This was the state in which it had been returned by the King to Cotton, with orders to send it to de Thou. De Thou received it as the work of Cotton: for some time neither he nor anyone else – except Camden and Cotton – knew that the work was really by Camden;* nor did Camden know what had been done with his manuscript.

De Thou received the manuscript with delight. If only he had received such guidance sooner! Now at last he had an expert for British affairs. He begged for more; and early next year more came. It was brought to Paris by a travelling courtier, John Pory, who called personally on de Thou, handed him the manuscript, and stayed for a little social conversation. The social conversation proved disastrous.

For in that genial atmosphere de Thou spoke freely. He told Pory, as one man of the world to another – or at least Pory understood him to say – that of course he had no intention of altering what he had already written. He was satisfied of its truth, and anyway the existing edition must be sold out first. Pory reported all this in a letter to Cotton, and Cotton showed the letter to the King. The result was a terrible explosion. The King declared that de Thou was no gentleman, that he was a double-crosser and a slanderer. De Thou, on his side, was no less explosive. What right, he asked, had the King to go up in smoke without ascertaining the facts? He was not afraid of kings. He was a free man, and would continue to live freely, like an ancient Gaul, respecting only the truth. . . . Gradually the decencies were restored and everyone agreed to put all the blame on the unfortunate Pory; but de Thou called

---

* Thus Bacon, to whom James I showed the material, and who added his own emendations, understood that it was by Cotton. On 1 July 1612, Casaubon wrote to de Thou that Cotton composed the *Annals* in English and Camden put them into Latin. It was not till August 1612 that Camden told de Thou that he was the author. Even then Camden was not sure that it was his MS which had been sent to de Thou.

for the third instalment of 'Cotton's' manuscript in vain. He was told that the King had lost faith in him, or was still too cross to send it, or had turned his attention to other things.

However, in the end it came. Early in 1615 the King returned to the matter. He decided that Camden should publish his work. That work had now reached 1588. Mary Queen of Scots had been tried and executed. The King thereupon wrote a formal letter under the signet to Cotton and Camden directing them to publish it.[7] Having made this decision, he sent his Huguenot doctor, Theodore de Mayerne, to Paris to hand over to de Thou the last instalment, up to 1587, the death of Mary. The doctor was more discreet than Pory: he reported that de Thou was very submissive, had shown him all kinds of corrections which he had already made, and would undoubtedly do all that was required.[8]

In fact, de Thou did no such thing. He had had enough of King James. Harassed from Rome, harassed in France, harassed from London, he had decided to publish no more. He would go on collecting material, would go on writing, but for posterity only. By his will, he charged his executors, Pierre Dupuy and Nicolas Rigault, to see to the publication, after his death, of his last forty-six books. When he died, in 1617, the executors secured the manuscript, which de Thou's timid heirs would have burnt, and sent it to Geneva to be published in the safety of a Protestant republic.

So James I failed with de Thou; but at least, he could feel, he had succeeded with Camden. Camden had not wanted to publish his work and, like de Thou, he clearly resented the political pressure put upon him. But being commanded, he obeyed. In the summer of 1615 the *Annals of Great Britain under Queen Elizabeth* appeared. Only between the lines, or by omission, did the author's true feelings appear: in the Aesopian, elliptical language of the preface, and in the curious dedication. For Camden did not dedicate the *Annals* to King James, their true promoter, as he had dedicated *Britannia* to Lord Burghley. He did not dedicate them to de Thou, as he had once intended: that might, by now, seem provocative. He dedicated them, somewhat defiantly, 'to God, my country and posterity, at the altar of Truth'.

On 11 June 1615, while sending the work to de Thou, Camden observed that he expected to incur as much trouble with his book as de Thou had done with his, 'for we live in an age of lying and intolerance'; but a good conscience, he added, fears nothing. De Thou gloomily assented. 'We struggle in the same sea,' he wrote, 'the same baleful stars look down on us, the same tides and storms drive us up and down, towards rock and reef.' Our appeal, he concluded, must be to posterity. They must both press on with their work; and he asked to see the sequel of the *Annals*, after 1588, in manuscript: 'If he who can command will not allow it to be published, you can still share it with your friends.'

In fact, Camden did follow, almost exactly, the precedent set by de Thou. Like him, he preferred not to publish. A chorus of praise greeted the first part of his *Annals*. Camden, wrote Francis Sweert, is the only impartial historian; therefore write on! Camden and de Thou, wrote the Huguenot scholar Jacques Godefroy, are the only impartial historians of our age: thanks to Camden, Britain now dominates the world of scholarship. So they all pressed him to go on and publish the sequel. 'I hear your work is finished,' wrote Pierre Dupuy in 1617, 'but why is it not published?' It was positively dangerous, wrote Nicolas Fabri de Peiresc in 1620, to leave such a work in manuscript. Let Camden be warned by the fate of de Thou's last volumes, which had so narrowly escaped destruction. And there were other warnings. There had now been a revolution in Holland and Hugo Grotius, escaping from prison, had fled abroad leaving unpublished the history of his country which he too had written for de Thou. 'If Grotius had only listened to our advice more than six months before his misfortune, there would be a copy of his *History* in this kingdom, outside the reach of his enemies.' The only guarantee of survival was publication, and publication now.[9]

Camden decided to behave correctly. When the *Annals* were complete, he submitted the manuscript, through a royal minister, to 'his Majesty's judicious censure, whether it please him that they should be suppressed or published, for I am indifferent'. He pointed out that some passages – the eulogy of Sir Francis Walsingham, for instance – might offend the King (for Walsingham had been the strongest advocate of the execution of Mary). But he did not offer to change anything. He made one request. If the King wished the remaining books to be published, Camden asked that they be published in Latin only, 'for I do not desire that they be set forth in English until after my death, knowing how unjust carpers the unlearned readers are'.*

The King, it seems, opposed publication. After his mother's death he had no further interest in the reign of Elizabeth. So the work remained unprinted. But Camden took his precautions. He was indeed warned by the fate of de Thou's last volume. In 1620 he wrote to de Thou's

---

* Smith, p. 351. The letter is undated, presumably a draft, and the addressee unnamed: he is merely addressed as 'Right Honourable'.

faithful executor Pierre Dupuy: 'You need not despair of seeing the rest
of my *Annals*. God willing, you will read them in due course, even if
times change.' The historian's trade is dangerous, he added, as the
illustrious de Thou had discovered, 'nor do I expect any other fate than
his. Meanwhile I am thinking of a trustee to whose safe keeping I may
commit them. What about you?'* Dupuy accepted the trust, received
the text, and undertook to publish it after Camden's death. It thus first
appeared in Leiden in 1625 and Pierre Dupuy had the honour of
publishing, in foreign Calvinist cities, the last works of both the
Catholic de Thou and the Anglican Camden.

Such was the external history of Camden's second great work. Let us
now turn to the work itself. How far did it, in its content, reflect these
external pressures? The answer, I think, is twofold. The pressure of
King James is reflected not at all.† Never did any work, whose writing
was promoted and whose publication was ordered by that much

---

* Camden to Dupuy, 4/14 August [1620]. This letter, as far as I know, is unpublished. The original was in the collection of the late Dr Albert Ehrman, who kindly gave
me a copy. It is in answer to Dupuy's letter to Camden of 9 December 1619 (Smith,
p. 193). Dupuy replied to it on 23 November 1620 (Smith, pp. 310–11).

† The history of the King's pressures on Camden has been unnecessarily confused
by an erroneous tradition, which seems to have been first published by Bishop Burnet.
In 1687, in his *Defence of the Reflexions on . . . Mr. Varillas' History of Heresies*, Burnet,
amplifying what he had previously written in his *Reflexions on Mr. Varillas' History*
(Amsterdam, 1686, p. 52), stated that de Thou, on reading the *Annals*, and finding a
discrepancy between Camden's published work and his private letters, 'writ severely'
to Camden demanding an explanation, and that Camden, in reply, 'told him the truth,
that King James would needs revise it himself, and afterwards put it in the Earl of
Northampton's hands . . . and that many things were struck out and many things
altered. This troubled Camden extremely, who took care that his second part should
not run the same fate, and therefore he sent it out of England to that great man [de
Thou] that it might be printed faithfully after his death. This is well known in
England . . .' Later writers have been at pains to refute Burnet. Sir Edward Maunde
Thompson, having compared Camden's successive drafts among the Cotton MSS, was
able to state (in the *D.N.B.*, s.v. 'Camden') that the published text showed no
alterations which could be ascribed to royal pressure. Other details in Burnet's account
are also erroneous; and some modern writers have therefore concluded that the whole
story of royal interference is untrue (cf. Camden, *The History of . . . Elizabeth*, ed.
W. McCaffrey [Chicago, 1970], pp. xxxv–vi).
In fact, Burnet's account contained some truth, which, as usual, he mishandled. The
royal intervention, and the part played by the Earl of Northampton, is proved by
Camden's own letter to de Thou of 10 August 1612, which in turn provides the key to
Camden's more guarded statement in the Preface to the *Annals*. But this intervention
did not affect Camden's own text of the *Annals* which was printed in London in 1615: it
only affected the text as sent, under Cotton's name, to de Thou. That text, as is
indicated by Camden's own statements, was a separate transcription, made for the
purpose, and not afterwards returned to Camden.

flattered king, treat its patron, and his known wishes, with such studied indifference. What, I wonder, did King James make of that severe phrase in the Preface, 'As for danger, I feared none, no, not from those who think the memory of succeeding ages may be extinguished by present power'? Like de Thou, Camden was determined to yield to no pressure, to pay no price for patronage, and it is clear that it was only King James's fear and hatred of Buchanan, and his inability to control de Thou, which forced him to sponsor this magnificently uncourtly work. If Camden in fact differed from de Thou in the interpretation of Scottish affairs, that was not because he was a subject of King James: it was because he genuinely thought – as he had long ago privately told de Thou – that de Thou was wrong.

On the other hand the influence of de Thou, as a historian, on the whole form of the *Annals* is as pervasive and emphatic as the influence of Ortelius on *Britannia*. Thanks to it, Camden wrote history, as he had written 'chorography', in a European, not an insular spirit; and that spirit, in historiography, was the new spirit of the French lawyer-historians, of the *politiques*. For first Bodin, in his philosophy – in his *Method of Reading History*, which was read by both de Thou and Camden – then de Thou in his *History*, had broken away from the two dominant traditions of the time: from the humanist, merely literary tradition, with its fictitious rhetoric and moral examples, and from the ecclesiastical tradition, which embedded history in revelation and prophecy. Both saw history as a secular study, to be pursued for its political and social lessons. 'The task of the historian', wrote Bodin, 'is above all the study of political conditions and the explanation of human revolutions.' The exponents of this new kind of history called it 'civil history'.

Between de Thou and Camden there are many similarities. Both wrote in the form of annals, by years. Both used the device of formal obituaries within those years. Both used a grave and measured language which can convey a redoubled effect and is compatible with solemn irony. But the resemblance goes far deeper than that. Both, like Bodin, repudiated equally the humanist and the ecclesiastical interpretation of history. Both were *politiques*. Both were sceptical, rational 'civil historians'. Both sought in history not moral examples or rhetorical opportunities or evidence of the workings of Providence, but explanation. In this Camden was even more resolute than de Thou. De Thou's classical models were Tacitus for philosophy, Livy for style. Camden paid lip-service to Tacitus but, like Bodin, he reserved his real veneration for the most philosophic and profound of ancient historians, the man who sought to explain the rise to empire of the Roman Republic, 'the great master of history', Polybius. In his Preface he quoted Polybius' statement of his own historical philosophy: 'Take away from History Why, How, and To what end things have been done, and whether the thing done hath succeeded according to reason, and all that remains will rather be an idle sport and foolery than a profitable instruction.'

As a *politique*, Camden, like de Thou, accepted the religion of state. To de Thou that was Gallican Catholicism, to Camden it was Anglican Protestantism. Both hated fanatics of all kinds, and most particularly those on their own side. As de Thou hated the Holy League and the Jesuits, so Camden hated the English Puritans, 'men of an unquiet spirit, greedy of novelties and too eager to root up things that were well established'. Their secular leaders were 'noblemen who gaped after the wealth of the Church . . . under the glorious pretext of religion'. Religious fanaticism, he believed (with Bodin), necessarily corrupted the truth of history, for 'persons whose minds differ in religion do far too much obscure the light of honesty and truth on both sides'. So, in interpreting his sources, he refused to heed 'the declamations and exclamations of the ecclesiastical sort of people on both sides, who for the most part are very fiery and vehement'. And he could achieve, at times, at the expense of clerical hypocrisy, an almost Gibbonian note. Thus, having described a peculiarly treacherous murder by the Irish Desmonds, he adds drily that this action was described by the English Catholic priest Nicholas Sanders as 'a sweet sacrifice in the sight of God'. On the other side, he records without comment how the English Parliament, pressing Queen Elizabeth to sign the death-warrant of Mary, reminded her 'how fearful were the examples of God's vengeance upon King Saul for sparing Agag, and upon King Ahab for sparing the life of Ben-Hadad'. He describes the Scottish Lords of the Congregation, in treaty with Queen Elizabeth's emissaries, protesting, 'with eyes lifted up to Heaven, that they had no other aim but to advance the glory of Jesus Christ . . . and preserve their ancient liberty'. On another occasion he describes the Edinburgh ministers foaming in their pulpits against the French ambassador who was at that moment being feasted by the City Council, 'so that a little more, and they had proceeded to excommunicate all the guests that dined there'. And with the same majestic disdain he comments that Francis Drake, having decided to set out on a great piratical expedition, easily found 'a divine belonging to the fleet' who 'persuaded him that it was lawful'.

As they hated sectarians, so both Camden and de Thou rejected the sectarian, ecclesiastical philosophy of history: the assumption that history was theologically determined, that its course was decreed by God, revealed by prophecy, and guided by Providence. According to this doctrine, the history of the world was comprehended in the four great Monarchies foretold in the Book of Daniel, and the modern historian, by narrow study of the prophetic books, and of the objective evidence of the stars, could place current events in their proper relation to that cosmic process. This doctrine had been openly rejected, almost alone, by Bodin; but Bodin was regarded as little better than an atheist, whom right-thinking men would do well to ignore. In England, this unrewarding theory became a favourite system of the more puritan writers. John Foxe, and many others, saw the reign of Elizabeth as a distinct phase in the process, and such celestial phenomena as the 'new star' which appeared in Cassiopeia in 1572 and the comet of 1582 conveniently confirmed whatever views had been drawn from, or ascribed to, Holy Scripture. In the next reign Sir Walter Ralegh would sophisticate the same general theory and supply this 'providential' history with credentials for another century.

This entire philosophy, which rendered puritan history ultimately sterile, Camden treated with contempt. If he thought that the reign of Elizabeth was a great age, it was not for any reason drawn out of Scripture or the stars. He never (I think) uses the word 'Providence'. He certainly never uses it in this technical sense. He never refers to the cosmological apparatus of the Four Monarchies. He is contemptuous of astronomical evidence. 'I know not whether it be worth our while to mention that which all other historiographers of our time have recorded', he says of the new star of 1572, which he had himself observed. 'Let it suffice to make mention in a word only of the comet or blazing star' which so excited men in 1582. Astrology, sorcery, magic, prophecy, whenever they come under his pen, are treated with the same polite disdain.

The other historical philosophy which both de Thou and Camden – again, like Bodin – disavowed was the literary philosophy of the humanists. To the humanists, history was a rhetorical exercise. They used historical characters as ideal types, whether of moral virtue (or vice) or political *virtù*. They made politics depend on personalities, ascribed edifying or unedifying motives, and invented appropriate speeches. They set great store by an elegant Latin style. Indeed, they were more interested in style than in objective truth, for history to them had an ulterior purpose: it was 'philosophy teaching by examples', and the examples were chosen, or adjusted, to fit the philosophy. The philosophy itself, of course, could vary. The Jesuits, those skilful adapters, used humanist history to document the Catholic thesis. Protestant humanists turned the same weapon against them. The greatest of Protestant humanist historians was King James's *bête noire*, Buchanan.

King James hated Buchanan because of his politics: because he used humanist history to support a republican philosophy. But Camden's dislike went far deeper: he would have disliked him equally if he had been on the other side. To Camden, Buchanan had all the vices of the humanist historian. He presented his characters as types: Mary Queen of Scots as a villain, the Earl of Moray as a hero; and he ascribed motives accordingly. He invented speeches to serve his purpose. His whole history of Scotland was a political thesis presented in pseudo-historical form and made persuasive not by its truth – large parts of it (as Camden knew) were fabulous – but by its admittedly incomparable Latin style.

Camden disowned this whole philosophy. He refused to fabricate speeches. 'Speeches and orations,' he wrote, 'unless they be the very same *verbatim*, or else abbreviated, I have not meddled withal, much less coined them out of mine own head.' Nor would he reduce history to the virtue or wickedness of great men. To him it was a far more complex process; and anyway, how could a historian be so sure of men's motives? 'The secrets of princes are an inextricable labyrinth. . . . Who can dive into the secret meanings of princes? Wise men do keep their thoughts locked up within the closets of their breasts.' Camden admired Buchanan as a poet, as everyone else did, but he had long despised him as an antiquary and repudiated him as a historian: he regarded him as a mere rhetorician.

What then was Camden's own philosophy of history? Where did he see its substance and motor? Here his vision was wider even than that of de Thou. Just as, in *Britannia*, he had seen the history of England embedded, contained, controlled in the continuing physical structure of Roman Britain, so, in the *Annals*, he saw the England of Elizabeth not as a series of political decisions or indecisions, not as a drama of persons (though he had a strong sense of drama), not as a morality play or the exemplification of a political thesis, but as a living political and social organism whose political acts were contained, and must be understood, within a wider context.

More than any of his predecessors, Camden was interested in

economic and social matters. Thus he is careful to describe economic legislation: laws against depopulation, invasion of commons, vagabondage, usury; laws to restrain the cultivation of woad, to set up hospitals, to relieve the poor. Among Sir Thomas Smith's services to learning, he includes his Act tying the rents of college estates to the price of corn. He emphasizes the economic hardship caused to the Church by Queen Elizabeth's Enabling Act of 1559, which King James so laudably reversed, and the abuses of those 'harpies' the Purveyors which he so lamentably multiplied. He deals in detail with the economic aspects of war: the search for copper, for brass ordnance, the opening of the Mines Royal, the embargoes on the cloth-trade and the struggle with the Hanseatic merchants. He notes the great and disturbing growth of London and describes the foundation by Sir Thomas Gresham of the Royal Exchange. He gives particular praise to Queen Elizabeth for her financial policy: her reduction of the burden of public debt; her intervention, against the wishes of both Burghley and Leicester, in the Great Farm of the Customs; and, above all, her recoinage of the currency in 1560, 'a great and memorable act' which undid the disastrous debasement of her father and gave England 'better and purer money than was seen in two hundred years before, or hath been elsewhere in use throughout all Europe'.

With these economic interests, Camden naturally records the Elizabethan journeys of discovery and commerce. He dwells with enthusiasm on the opening up of the Russian trade by the Muscovy Company and describes 'the great and memorable adventure' whereby the English, having followed the long route down the Volga to Astrakhan, 'crossed the Caspian Sea, which is very full of flats and shelves, and pierced through the vast Deserts of Hyrcania and Bactriana' to the cities of Persia. He records the founding of the Levant Company, which opened 'a very gainful trade for spices, cottons, raw silk, tapestries, Indian dye, grapes of Corinth or currants, soap, etc.', and of the East India Company which, 'to the honour of the English nation, has placed factories in Surat, in the empire of the Great Mogul, in Masilipatam, Bantam, Patane, Siam, Sagad, Macassar and also in Japan'; and he describes the search for the North-West Passage and the whaling expeditions to Spitzbergen.

Of these peaceful commercial voyages Camden approved, though he doubted whether the East India trade, which drained silver out of England, was ultimately 'to the good of the Commonwealth'. Of the semi-piratical voyages of Drake and Hawkins he writes with more reserve. He records how Hawkins, by his example, led Englishmen to

take up the slave-trade, adding the dry comment 'how honestly I know
not'; he seems to approve of the hanging of John Oxenham at Lima 'as a
pirate and common enemy of mankind'; and having described the
seizure of the great Portuguese carrack *Madre de Deus* in 1592, he relates,
without comment, how a great part of its precious cargo was embezzled
by its captors, who would swear to anything rather than surrender any
of their stolen profits, declaring 'that they had rather venture their souls
in the hands of a merciful God by perjury, than their fortunes gotten
with peril and hazard of their lives in the hands of unmerciful men'.
Nevertheless, though he may have disapproved of their motives,
Camden cannot imagine without emotion or record without eloquence
the great voyages of Frobisher and Drake: Frobisher 'tossed up and
down with foul weather, snows and unconstant winds', opposed by
'heaps of ice, like mountains', and Eskimo 'with black hair, broad faces,
flat noses, swarthy coloured, apparelled in seal-calves' skins; the
women painted about the eyes and balls of the cheek with a blue colour
like the ancient Britons'; Drake following the Pacific coast southwards
from Canada, where there was 'nothing but thick clouds, sharp cold
and naked shores covered only with snow', to California, where naked
Indians, pleasantly disposed, danced daily in a ring, offered sacrifices,
and proposed to make him their king.

These voyages brought new wealth to England, changed the attitudes of Englishmen and opened their eyes to new possibilities. Camden describes the new exotic importations of the time: the reindeer, first
brought from Russia by Queen Elizabeth's ambassador Sir Jerome
Bowes; the tamarisk, imported by Archbishop Grindal 'to ease the hard
distemper of the spleen'; tobacco, on which he shared the opinion of
King James. It was, he thought, a drug fit only for the barbarians of
America; but nothing would stop the English from imitating them,
'sucking in the stinking smoke thereof through an earthen pipe, which
presently they blew out again at their nostrils, in so much as tobacco-
shops are now as ordinary in most towns as taphouses and taverns'.
The English, he sighed, were an 'apish nation'; hitherto commended for
their sobriety, they learned, in the Dutch wars, 'to drown themselves
with immoderate drinking'; they copied from foreigners 'a wondrous
excess in apparel', quite contrary to their former habits, and 'jetted
up and down in their silks, glittering with gold and silver, either
embroidered or laced'; and they followed up these sartorial
fantasies with 'riotous banqueting and prodigal bravery in building'. The 'neat, large and sumptuous edifices' which sprang up
over Elizabethan England were no doubt 'to the great ornament of

the kingdom, but to as great decay of the glorious hospitality of the nation'.

Such, to Camden, was the Elizabethan age: *aevum Elizabetheum* – the phrase was coined by one of his correspondents.* Its glories consisted not merely in foreign policy and war but in the total activity of English society. The Queen, of course, was its heroine, and Camden placed her firmly in the centre of his account. Her popularity, which maddened King James, for it increased as his own declined, Camden emphasized. She not only came to the throne with universal acclamation, he wrote (he could have said the same of King James), but (unlike him) during the whole course of her life she never forfeited it: 'never did the people embrace any other Prince with more willing and constant mind and affection, with greater observance, more joyful applause and prayers reiterated, whensoever she went abroad'. He described too the regular annual celebration of her accession day, whose revival in his reign was another of King James's mortifications: how 'all good men, throughout England, on November 17th, joyfully triumphed, with thanksgivings, sermons in churches, multiplied prayers, joyful ringing of bells, running at tilt, and festival mirth . . . which, in testimony of their affectionate love towards her, they never ceased to observe as long as she lived'. Even in the distant Cape Verde Islands, he tells us, Drake and his sailors, in 1585, celebrated that day 'with peals of ordnance'. Sir John Neale, in an interesting essay, has described the revival of this celebration of 'Queen Elizabeth's day' from about 1610, as the popularity of her successor began to decline.[10] King James can hardly have been pleased at this added reminder.

It was by placing her in the centre of her age, embedding her firmly in it, enclosing her politics in that wide context, that Camden performed his great feat of stabilizing the waywardness of Queen Elizabeth which other historians, by isolating her again, have sometimes sought to emphasize. There were other, more personal stabilizers too. In particular, Lord Burghley, Camden's own patron, whose papers he had used and whose policy he admired. Camden admired Burghley for many reasons, but above all, perhaps, for his conservatism: he did not force the pace of change, or gamble with the life of the nation; his genuine Protestantism (and Camden too was a genuine Protestant) was controlled by political sense, his machiavellian realism by an appreciation of

* 'At tu, mi domine, licet sexagenarius, perge porro felici auspicio, et repraesenta nobis aevum Elizabetheum.' Janus Gruter to Camden, 21 September 1611, in Smith, p. 137.

the long English inheritance. For Burghley remembered the destructive years of the mid-century when so much of that inheritance – the wealth of the Crown, the lands of the Church, the libraries of the monasteries and universities – had been squandered away by radicals in a hurry: radicals who had nearly lost all by the reaction they had provoked in the reign of Mary; radicals who had been led, at that time, by that unscrupulous adventurer John Dudley, Duke of Northumberland, and who had not perished with him, for they were still active, led by John Dudley's son, Burghley's constant and dangerous rival, Robert Dudley, Earl of Leicester.

How Camden hated Leicester! When he portrays that ambiguous politician, his sedate pen seems suddenly to lose its poise. To him Leicester was 'an accomplished courtier, spruce and neat, free and bountiful to soldiers and students, a cunning time-server and respecter of his own advantages, of a disposition ready and apt to please, crafty and subtle towards his adversaries'. With such gifts, though despised by his rivals as 'a new upstart' with only two ancestors, both executed as traitors, he 'entertained boundless hopes', and since 'he preferred power and greatness before solid virtue', he succeeded beyond his deserts. By courtly arts, cunning dissimulation, and a gift for tears and feigned repentance, he won influence over the Queen, was often the only intermediary to her, and 'dived farther than any man into her secret thoughts'. But he had no scruples of conscience. When others proposed that Mary Queen of Scots be put to death by law, he 'thought rather by poison, and sent a divine' – doubtless a good Puritan – 'to Walsingham to satisfy him that it was lawful'. Finally, 'tickled with an ambitious desire of command and glory', he obtained the post of Queen Elizabeth's representative in the Netherlands, and, once there, was so 'soothed up with flatteries' – 'acclamations, triumphal arches, votive tablets, feastings and the like', as well as a guard of honour and the title of 'Your Excellency' – that he 'began to take it upon him as if he were a perfect king' and 'no doubt had it in mind to usurp the government'. However, his plot failed. The Queen was furious with his mismanagement, and in the end he was recalled in disfavour, 'and the title of His Excellency, which of all Englishmen he was the first that ever used, was exploded and hissed off the stage'. When he died, just after the defeat of the Armada, Camden tersely remarks that the public joy at that event was in no way abated by his death.

In his treatment of Leicester, and perhaps here alone, Camden allows his personal feelings, even his personal prejudices, to appear. Leicester, to him, was the personification of all the policies and political attitudes which he disliked. And this dislike is inherited, after Leicester's death, by the heir to his policy, his stepson, the Earl of Essex. Essex also had his claque of Puritan preachers; he also advocated aggression; he entertained in his house and consulted as his 'oracle' the man whom the Queen 'verily detested' and to whom Burghley 'scarcely vouchsafed to speak', the treacherous Antonio Perez who had 'divulged his King's secrets'; and in the end he too, carried away by ambition, sought military glory and, failing, attempted in an even more radical manner to 'usurp the government'. To Camden, Essex was a disturber of the peace, both at home and abroad. It is to Camden that we owe the famous scene in which, after Essex had opposed peace with Spain in 1598, the aged Lord Burghley 'said that he breathed forth nothing but war, slaughter and blood; and after a hot dispute about this matter, as if he presaged what would after be, he drew forth a Psalm-book and, saying nothing, pointed him to this verse, *Men of Blood shall not live out half their days*'. In the end Essex did not live out half his days. He died as a rebel, the leader of Puritans and Papists against the pacific, Elizabethan, Cecilian establishment which Camden supported and which King James, after his dangerous flirtation with Essex, prudently preferred to inherit and continue.

It is only fair to add that Camden's hatred of Leicester, which was extended to embrace his effective political heir, Essex, was not allowed to touch Leicester's intended political heir, Camden's friend and hero, Sir Philip Sidney. Sidney was no doubt a more cultivated, more admirable, more honourable person than his uncle; but their foreign policy was the same. We are forced to conclude that in the case of Leicester, Camden forgot or suspended his own philosophy and expressed the long-muffled resentment of his patron Lord Burghley. But such a lapse does not invalidate the philosophy which it denies: it merely shows that no man can be a philosopher all the time.

With such a general philosophy it is clear in advance, without any pressure from King James, what Camden's attitude would be towards Mary Queen of Scots. Politically, Camden must deplore Mary. How could an admirer of Queen Elizabeth's prudence and skilful government, a Protestant and a moralist, approve of that giddy Papist? Of Mary's partisans he wrote censoriously enough. The Bishop of Ross, he wrote, served his mistress well, 'but to the undoing of some and endangering of more'. Bothwell he saw as 'a wicked man blinded by ambition'. His character of Maitland of Lethington brought protests from Maitland's son, who accused him of relying too implicitly on

Buchanan's *Chamaeleon*.* Politicians like these, says Camden, were dangerous advisers, and Mary was unwise to heed them. On the other side, Moray might be an ambitious nobleman like Guise or Essex, a patron of radical preachers like Leicester: he might exploit religion in politics and cultivate John Knox 'as a patriarch'; but he had his virtues and could be justly praised by 'the wiser sort' of Protestants 'for expelling the Romish religion out of Scotland, for preserving the young king, for administering justice indifferently, and for his bounty to learned men, especially Buchanan' – that is, Buchanan the poet, not the partisan; for Camden, like James I himself, always distinguished between the two capacities of that extraordinary man. But when all these admissions had been made, there remained other factors before Mary could be judged. The world was wider and more complex than the heated philosophy of Knox and Buchanan. Mary was born a queen: it was not ambition, which must pay its own price, but accident that had placed her on that tottering throne, a woman among 'the deadly feuds and animosities which the Scots above all peoples do maintain and practise among themselves'. Finally, there was the objective situation, the complex of hard facts and conflicting pressures of which, in that difficult conjuncture of time, Mary and Elizabeth alike were prisoners.

For Camden, now that Mary was safely dead and Elizabethan England had survived, could see the tragedy of her fate as Buchanan and the Scotch lords and clergy, living perpetually in fear of a reversal of fortune, could not. He saw that, whether she was guilty or not – whether she had ordered the murder of her husband or not, whether she had personally sanctioned the plots against Elizabeth or not (and neither charge had been proved) – Mary was the victim of circumstances, just as Elizabeth, whether she approved of Mary's deposition or not, could hardly have acted otherwise than she did. He saw that Mary's aim – to rescue the Scottish monarchy from the alliance of ambitious lords and revolutionary clergy – was a natural response to

---

* *Annals*, pp. 92, 198, 303, 495. The letter in which James Maitland protested against Camden's treatment of his father is in Smith, pp. 305–6. James Maitland had not seen Buchanan's *Chamaeleon*, which was not printed till 1710, but Camden had access to the manuscript in Cotton's library (now B. L. Cotton MSS Caligula C III 265) which had probably been sent by Buchanan to Cecil, and refers to it in his *Annals* (p. 198) – a passage copied almost *verbatim* by de Thou in his fifty-fifth book. Not obtaining satisfaction, James Maitland wrote *An Apologie for William Maitland of Lethington against the Lies and Calumnies of John Leslie Bishop of Ross, George Buchanan and William Camden* (published in *Scottish Historical Society, Miscellany*, Vol. II, 1904).

the situation in which she found herself. It was not the result of her religion or her morals. After all, that was exactly what James VI had sought to do, and had done, with general approval, although his religion and his morals differed from hers. King James had succeeded, in part, because he had English support and the prospect of the English Crown. Mary lacked that support precisely because she had that prospect, and, unlike her son, had been tied, by forces stronger than herself, to a foreign cause.

For neither Mary nor Elizabeth, nor anyone else, could alter the fact that if Elizabeth were to die, Mary would succeed, all artificial restraints notwithstanding: no noble intrigues, no parliamentary exclusion, had succeeded in keeping Mary Tudor from the throne. Therefore, given the monarchical system of Europe and the royal control of religion, all the forces and interests of the Counter-Reformation required that Mary should survive Elizabeth, and all the forces and interests of Protestantism required that Elizabeth should survive Mary. Burdened with these terrible responsibilities, Elizabeth, thanks to her able ministers, played her part with skill and success; but it was an agonizing part nevertheless. In spite of her high views of monarchy, she found herself supporting rebels against legitimate sovereigns in Scotland as in the Netherlands. She might wish to restore Mary to her throne, but neither the effort nor the risk could be justified. In the end, when the enemies of the Counter-Reformation were being assassinated one after another, and the military conquest of England was being prepared, she yielded to necessity and removed the alternative ruler who waited to profit by her death. Mary had no such able ministers, no such political skill. Like her grandson, Charles I, she bungled throughout. But as the external difficulties were not of her making, was it fair to blame her? And in the end, again like her grandson, she redeemed her errors by dignity in captivity, before her judges and at the block.

So Camden, not because of the pressure of King James but thanks to his understanding of the historical context, saw the relations of Elizabeth and Mary as a tragedy in which both parties were the victims of historical necessity. There was no need of argument or advocacy: a tragedian does not obtrude his own commentary, and Camden himself had a sense of the dramatic. He would fall casually into theatrical metaphors and record theatrical episodes: the charge against Essex's steward of bringing on 'an old outworn play of the tragical deposing of King Richard II', the destruction of Drury Lane Theatre, and the death of the great actor Richard Burbage. He also had a taste for great public spectacles. He had himself attended the trials of the Duke of

Norfolk and the Earl of Essex, had watched the barbarous punishment and seen the dramatic, loyal gesture of the Puritan zealot John Stubbe, and had been present when Séan O'Neill, 'with a guard of axe-bearing galloglasses, bare-headed, with curled hair hanging down, yellow surplices dyed with saffron or man's stale, long sleeves, short coats and hairy mantles', came to England to howl for the Queen's pardon. And in dealing with the tragedy of Mary Queen of Scots, his dramatic sense does not desert him. He brings his characters on to the stage, allows them all to say their parts and state their case – Queen Elizabeth, Queen Mary, the English commissioners, the Scottish queen's friends – and so, without a word of praise, blame or interpretation, allows the insoluble dilemma to appear, the sombre finale to take place. When all is over, he describes Queen Elizabeth's real or feigned remorse, and the fate of the unfortunate secretary Davison, a poor player who was 'brought upon the court-stage of purpose (as most men thought) to act for a time this part in the tragedy; and soon after, the part being acted, and his stage-attire laid aside, as if he had failed in the last act, he was thrust down from the stage and, not without the pity of many, shut up for a long time in prison'.

When Camden's work was published, everyone recognized its novelty. He had placed historical studies on a new base of scientific documentation, and in a new context, of geographical, economic and social understanding. He had also informed it with a new philosophy which made the humanist history of Buchanan seem thin and trivial and the 'providential' history of Foxe and Ralegh superannuated and sterile. Of course the victory was not complete. Such intellectual revolutions never are. Always there is a backwash; and in this instance the backwash was driven by a powerful political force. Within a few years of Camden's death, the Puritan reaction had set in and both Buchanan and Ralegh would enjoy an unexpected recovery. But one historian of the next generation knew his master. In his enforced seclusion in the island of Jersey in 1646, where he meditated and began his great *History of the Rebellion*, Edward Hyde, afterwards Earl of Clarendon, reread and annotated Camden's *Britannia*;[11] and in the very beginning of his own work, where he insisted that the explanation of the English Revolution was to be sought not in divine Providence but in 'the same natural causes and means which have usually attended kingdoms' in like condition, he showed himself a true disciple of the first great 'civil historian'. In the splendid picture gallery which he built up to be, as it were, the Pantheon of his own historical faith, the nucleus of the

National Portrait Gallery as Cotton's library was the nucleus of the British Museum, Clarendon 'was resolved', we are told, 'on no account to lack the portrait of Camden'; and he duly secured it. It is one of the few which survived the Great Fire of 1666 and is still in the possession of the Clarendon family.*

It was in 1621, when he was seventy years old, that Camden entrusted the manuscript of the second part of his *Annals* to Pierre Dupuy. Having thus ensured its ultimate publication, he took steps to perpetuate the study of history as he had redirected it in England. In 1622 he endowed, at his own university of Oxford, a chair of 'civil history'. Two years later, his friend and patron Fulke Greville, Lord Brooke, did the same at Cambridge. Both insisted that their chairs should be of 'civil history', and Camden added, 'according to the practice of such professors in all universities beyond seas'. The friend of Ortelius and de Thou, Casaubon and Gruter, Dupuy and Peiresc, Bergier and Lingelsheim, did not wish the academic study of history to become insular. Lord Brooke showed his agreement by actually seeking his first professor in one of the most famous universities beyond seas, Leiden. Unfortunately, Brooke's chair in Cambridge did not last long. The second lecture in the series was too much for the institution and no third was ever given. I hope that these Neale Lectures, founded to commemorate our modern Camden, will follow rather the precedent of Camden's chair in the more dependable university of Oxford. Together with Sir Robert Cotton's library, now intact in the British Museum, and Camden's *Britannia*, reprinted this year – not to speak of the College of Arms, of which he was a herald, and Westminster School, of which he was headmaster – it is with us still, to remind us of that structural continuity of English history, transcending persons and politics, which he taught us to value.

* Sir Edward Maunde Thompson, in *D.N.B.*, says that Clarendon obtained for his collection the portrait of Camden surreptitiously painted while he was on his deathbed. This seems to be a mistaken inference from the Latin account by Thomas Smith ('Vita Camdeni' in Smith, p. lxxii). Smith there states that Clarendon was determined to secure a portrait of Camden and that on his deathbed a painter was smuggled into the room to paint him; but he does not say that this was the portrait secured by Clarendon. The portrait owned by Clarendon is described in Lady Theresa Lewis, *Lives of the Friends of Lord Chancellor Clarendon* . . . (1852), Vol. III, p. 284. See also Roy Strong, *Tudor and Jacobean Portraits* (HMSO, 1969), Vol. I, pp. 35–7.

Sources

1. C. V. Wedgwood, *Oliver Cromwell and the Elizabethan Inheritance* (1970).
2. The correct title, as published in Latin in 1615, is *Annales Rerum Anglicarum et Hibernicarum regnante Elizabetha*.
3. Henri Hauser, *Les Sources de l'histoire de France, XVIe siècle* (1494–1610), Vol. III (Paris, 1912), pp. 13, 15; Lucien Romier, *Le Royaume de Cathérine de Médicis* (Paris, 1922), preface, 'Les Témoignages'.
4. The story of de Thou's relations with James I and Camden can be followed in the correspondence of de Thou, Casaubon, Camden, Dupuy and their circle. Most of this is in print. See *Cl. V. Gul. Camdeni . . . Epistolae*, ed. T. Smith, 1691 (hereafter cited as 'Smith'); *Is. Casauboni . . . Epistolarum Sylloge*, ed. T. Jansen (Rotterdam, 1710); *Choix de lettres françaises inédites de J. A. de Thou*, ed. Leroux de Lincy (Société des Bibliophiles, Paris, 1877); and Vol. VII of the London edition of de Thou's *History* (*J. A. Thuani Historiarum Sui Temporis libri CXXXVIII*, ed. Samuel Buckley, 1733). Besides transcriptions of previously printed letters of Casaubon and Camden, this last volume contains documents from the papers of de Thou and Dupuy, transcribed by the Jacobite scholar Thomas Carte.
5. Carew to Cecil, 2/12 September 1606 (P.R.O., S.P. 78/53, fo. 155c). I am indebted to Mr Alfred Soman of Carleton College, Northfield, Minnesota, for this reference.
6. Camden, 'Memorabilia', in Smith, part II, p. 85.
7. Edward Arber, *A Transcript of the Registers of the Company of Stationers of London*, Vol. III (1876), p. 260.
8. Mayerne's report to the King is in B.L. Add. MS 32092, fo. 224.
9. Smith, pp. 147, 162, 169, 194, 308–10.
10. J. E. Neale, *Essays in Elizabethan History* (1958), pp. 9–20.
11. Bodleian Library, MS Clarendon 126, pp. 167–75.

9

The Paracelsian Movement

(1)

In the history of medicine in the period of the Renaissance there are several great names: Vesalius and Harvey, Fernel and Paré, Falloppio, Cesalpino, Fabricius . . . But if greatness is to be measured by public fame and the creation of a school of followers, no one can rival Paracelsus. For a century at least his very name was an explosive force. In the eyes of his numerous and vocal disciples, he was a prophet who had inaugurated a new age: thanks to a new vision of the universe, and of man's place in it, he had challenged the inveterate errors of a millennium and broken the monopoly of the rigid social caste which professed and perpetuated them. In the eyes of his enemies, he was an ignorant, self-opinionated heretic, an arrogant charlatan, the patron of revolutionary ideas which threatened the whole science of medicine and its honourable institutions: for he launched a frontal attack alike on the established medicine of Galen and on the medical faculties of the European universities.

This confrontation between Paracelsus and the traditional 'Galenists' of the medical schools was absolute. It was not only medical: it was also ideological, social and, at times, religious. The tension was at its height in the early years of the seventeenth century. Afterwards the pattern became more complex as the forces on both sides began to decompose; and in the period of the Thirty Years War Paracelsianism itself seemed to disintegrate. But it did not go quietly. In the 1650s, in revolutionary England, it made its strongest, or at least its most vocal claims. It was not till the end of the seventeenth century that its several elements had been either absorbed into medical ideas and practice or rejected and forgotten. In Pierre Bayle's great *Dictionnaire historique et critique*, that marvellous repository of the learning of the past two centuries – or rather, perhaps, that capacious acid tank in which that learning was quietly dissolved – there is no entry for Paracelsus: indeed, in all that vast work, he is only mentioned once, in a footnote, in which an absurd speculation about the bodily formation of Adam is quoted from him, at second hand, from the Dutch savant G. J. Vossius. The scepticism, the rationality, the empiricism of the age of Enlightenment could find no place for the bizarre medical dogmatist of the age of Reformation.

In this essay I wish to deal not with Paracelsus but with the movement which he launched; but in order to trace that movement I must begin by saying something about Paracelsus himself.[1]

Paracelsus was the name given (though not apparently by himself) to Philip Theophrastus Bombast von Hohenheim. He was born in 1493 or 1494 at Einsiedeln, a small country town near Zurich, chiefly famous for its great abbey, whose original Gothic grandeur inspired Zwingli to become a religious revolutionary and whose extravagant rococo restoration would dazzle and outrage the young Gibbon. His father, an illegitimate member of an ancient and noble Swabian family, was the local physician. When Paracelsus was nine years old, his father moved to Villach in Austria, and Paracelsus himself began work as an apprentice in the nearby silver-mines of Hutenberg. The mines were the property of those great captains of industry, the Fugger family of Augsburg. Afterwards he travelled widely, studying and practising medicine, in Italy, Holland, Prussia, Poland, Scandinavia, the Levant. In 1526, after fleeing secretly from Salzburg (where he had been imprisoned for his open sympathy with the peasants' revolt), he appeared in the city of Basel and had the good fortune to succeed where other doctors had failed, curing the ailments of the great printer, Johann Froben. Froben is famous as the publisher of Erasmus, and through him Paracelsus became physician to Erasmus, and was taken up by the Erasmian circle in Basel. He was appointed *Stadtphysicus*, or city physician, with the title of professor of medicine and the right to lecture at the university. But alas, his lectures were not academically respectable. To the horror of the medical faculty, he refused to lecture on the standard authorities – Hippocrates, Galen, Avicenna – and announced that he would base his lectures on his own experience. That included experience of miners' diseases, which he had seen in the Fugger mines, and of war wounds, which he had seen as an army surgeon in the pay of the republic of Venice (1522). Paracelsus afterwards (1533) published the first treatise on occupational diseases, and inspired new methods of treating wounds.

The very nature of Paracelsus' teaching was such as to oppose him to the medical faculties in established universities. These had a time-honoured structure: the physician, a scholar trained in the approved course and equipped with the necessary degrees, interpreted the science, or rather the philosophy of medicine, and the surgeon and the apothecary, men of inferior status, without university training or knowledge of Latin, carried out his orders and were limited by them. Paracelsus probably had a doctor's degree from the University of Ferrara, and he certainly had a thorough knowledge of the approved medical syllabus of his time; but his whole teaching was in fact a challenge both to the hierarchy and to the syllabus of the establishment, and he emphasized the challenge by lecturing not in Latin, with its sophisticated medical terminology, but in the vernacular, and a very low vernacular at that: his own German-Swiss dialect. He emphasized it still further on St John's day (24 June) 1527 by a dramatic public gesture: by throwing the *Canon* of Avicenna – one of the sacred texts of the faculty – on the traditional bonfire.

It was unfortunate for Paracelsus that his chief patron in Basel, Froben, died soon afterwards, and another powerful patient, a canon of the cathedral, quarrelled with him over his fee. Exposed to the hatred of the university and the Church, and lacking any powerful defenders, he fled from Basel, and for the next fourteen years of his life was a wanderer again. We find him travelling through Alsace, Austria, Bavaria, Bohemia, Switzerland. Sometimes he was fêted as a great man, a hero; sometimes he was reduced to mendicancy. He was honourably received by Ferdinand, King of the Romans, King of Bohemia and Hungary, the brother of the Emperor Charles V – who, however, soon changed his view of him. He was driven, in beggar's rags, from Innsbrück and Stertzing. He would appear at one time, in prosperity, at fashionable watering places; at another, he would be found as an itinerant evangelist preaching strange doctrines to the Swiss peasants of Appenzell (1533). His friends were alternately dazzled by his genius, for he clearly had a charismatic personality, and shocked by his behaviour. He lived high and drank deep. He wore expensive clothes, but never took them off at night, or indeed the long sword which he always carried. He slept little and spent whole days at his furnace, rejoicing in the sickening fumes. He challenged peasants to drinking bouts and left them under the table; then, apparently still lucid, he would turn aside to dictate his philosophical works. He would start up in the night, go berserk and behave like a madman. This irregular way of life was not conducive to that longevity on which he wrote a treatise. He died in Salzburg in 1541, aged about forty-seven.

During his lifetime very few of Paracelsus' works were published. These included a work on mineral waters, a work on surgery, and a short work on the cure of syphilis. This last was a subject which he had studied at Nuremberg after his flight from Basel. Here he satisfied himself that the customary treatment, by means of guiac wood and liquid mercury, was positively harmful. His full exposition of the subject (*Eight Books on the French Disease*) could not be published at the time: the City Council of Nuremberg forbade publication, probably at the instigation of the Fugger family, who held the profitable monopoly of guiac wood, and did not want it to be devalued. Apart from these works Paracelsus wrote a large number of works which he seems to have deposited in the hands of disciples as he travelled through Europe and which only came to light after his death. Their emergence played a large part in the formation of the Paracelsian movement.

The most productive period of Paracelsus' life was his brief stay at Basel from 1526 to 1527. There he had an academic post and leisure to systematize his ideas. He also had a servant and amanuensis who was qualified to be his editor and publisher. This was a young man called Johannes Herbst who, as a good humanist, grecized his surname as Oporinus. When Paracelsus fled from Basel, he left his manuscripts in the hands of Oporinus. Oporinus afterwards had a distinguished career in Basel, first as professor of Greek, then as a printer. He would become printer-in-chief to the scholars of the Reformation, and John Foxe, the English martyrologist, would spend his exile, in the reign of Mary Tudor, working as a proof-reader in his firm. But Oporinus did not, in the end, print the manuscripts of Paracelsus: indeed, as a cultivated humanist scholar, he was embarrassed by that uncouth master with his disorderly habits and his barbarous German writings. So the manuscripts lay unprinted in his hands until they were discovered by a physician who joined the medical faculty of Basel in 1558. This was Adam von Bodenstein, the son of the Protestant reformer Andreas von Bodenstein, also known as Karlstadt.

Adam von Bodenstein had begun his career as an orthodox Galenist. He was physician to a German prince, Ottheinrich, Elector Palatine, the head of the great German family of Wittelsbach. In 1556 he had himself fallen ill of a tertian fever which, with its complications, had incapacitated him for over a year. Finally, in despair, he accepted treatment from a Paracelsian physician, and found himself completely cured in a month. After this he became an enthusiastic Paracelsian and was the first, after Paracelsus himself, to teach Paracelsianism in Basel.[2] The university authorities warned him to desist, but he did not heed the warnings and in 1564 he was expelled from the Faculty for publishing 'divers heretical and scandalous books' and for being 'an adherent of the false teaching of Theophrastus' – i.e. Paracelsus. However, although expelled, he remained at Basel, forwarding the cause. He forwarded it very effectively, publishing over forty works of Paracelsus and inspiring friends and pupils who published more.

One of the pupils was Michael Schütz, known as Toxites. Toxites was a humanist and a poet who, after various misadventures as a wandering school teacher, studied medicine with Bodenstein in Basel and then, when about fifty years old, settled down as a physician first in Strasbourg, then in Hagenau in Alsace.[3] Like his teacher, he became an enthusiastic collector of Paracelsian manuscripts, seeking them out wherever the itinerant author might have left them: in Alsace, in Salzburg, in Silesia. It was he who published, in 1570, the most important chemical writings of Paracelsus: his book on 'the secrets of Antimony' and the *Archidoxa*, in which he set out his system of chemistry. Altogether between 1564 and his death in 1581, Toxites published some thirty Paracelsian works, mainly at Strasbourg. Gerard Dorn, a German of whom very little is known, but who evidently practised medicine in Frankfurt, also published over twenty works, and another twelve were printed by Theodor Birckmann, an ardent Paracelsian collector who was both *Stadtphysicus* in Cologne and a member of a well-known publishing house there.

Birckmann also encouraged others to discover and collect Paracelsian manuscripts. He persuaded the Archduke Ferdinand of Austria to advertise for them, and it was thanks to him that a huge *cache* of such documents was revealed in the castle of Neuburg on the Danube. This was the castle of the same Elector Palatine Ottheinrich whom Bodenstein had served as physician. The manuscripts had been collected by the Elector's chemist, Hans Kilian. They were afterwards acquired by Johann Huser, physician to another Wittelsbach prince, Ernst, Elector of Cologne. Huser planned an edition of the complete works of Paracelsus, and for this purpose collected manuscripts from all over Germany. His edition, in ten volumes, published at Basel in 1589–90, at the expense of the Elector, though not completed till after his death,* remained the standard text till the end of the nineteenth century.

Many of the 'Paracelsian' works which poured from the presses in the last quarter of the sixteenth century were spurious. By that time Paracelsus had acquired imitators. Soon he would be supplied with equally spurious predecessors. By the end of the century distinctive Paracelsian ideas were being ascribed to imaginary fifteenth-century alchemists called Basil Valentine and Isaac Hollandus. In fact Paracelsus was indebted to medieval precursors, but not to these. Nevertheless, Basil Valentine and Isaac Hollandus (who was soon supplied with a son, also an alchemist, called John) enjoyed a great repute for many years as the 'first discoverers' of important truths, afterwards improved and refined by Paracelsus. These imaginary precursors did not weaken the credit of Paracelsus: rather they confirmed it by fixing him more firmly in a respectable medieval tradition.

At first the dissemination of Paracelsus' work was largely confined to the German-speaking world; for he had written, as he had lectured, in German: in an obscure, mystical German which even his German contemporaries could not easily understand. After his death, some of his works were translated into Latin, especially by Gerard Dorn, but the bulk of them remained in German, including Huser's edition of his 'complete works'. Huser did indeed think it necessary to excuse himself for having left them in that language, in the 'rough and unliterary style' and 'improper' vocabulary of their author. He did so by appealing to German nationalism. German, he declared defiantly, was 'just as much a *Hauptsprach* as Latin, Greek or Arabic' – the three historic languages of medicine – and its use was justified by the age and dignity of the German Empire. This argument would hardly have been admitted by any sixteenth-century European, or indeed by Paracelsus himself who wrote in German not because German was a world language, but, partly at least, because it was not. Though his philosophy was universal, his medicine was, in one sense, provincial: he believed that every country and every age had its own diseases and provided their particular cures; and he was concerned with modern German diseases and their cures. But the German language also served his revolutionary purpose. By using it, he could break away from the established tradition and create his own. He could also present his novel doctrines

---

* Huser was unable to include the surgical works in his edition: they were first included in the edition of 1603–5, published by Lazarus Zetzner at Strasbourg. For the circumstances see Sudhoff's Introduction to *Sämtliche Werke*.

to a new class of society. He could summon the unlearned artisans of the medical profession, the surgeons and apothecaries, to invade the monopoly, and challenge the orthodoxy, of the entrenched experts. This was in itself an act of defiance as challenging, and as resented, as the action of Luther and the other Protestant Reformers in publishing the Scriptures in the vulgar tongue.

Since he was so aggressively German, and so radical in his attacks on the establishment of his time, it is tempting to describe Paracelsus as a kind of medical Luther; and indeed this is how he has often been described, especially by his Catholic opponents in the later sixteenth century. As we shall see, Protestantism and Paracelsianism had by then acquired certain common interests. However, we have not yet arrived at that stage. At present it is enough to say that Paracelsus himself cannot be fitted into any sectarian category. He certainly hated the Catholic ecclesiastical establishment; but he equally hated Luther, whom he recognized, correctly enough after 1525, as the creature of the German princes. Although he made no public profession – he was never seen to pray – he was intensely religious and believed himself to be a devout Christian. Indeed, it was as such that he denounced the 'pagan' Aristotle; for it was through Aristotle, he believed, that the true philosophy – the mystical spiritual philosophy of those *prisci theologi*, Moses, Zoroaster, Plato, Hermes Trismegistus, the authentic precursors of Christ – had been fatally distorted and materialized, and through Aristotle's disciples, Galen and the medieval Schoolmen, that first medicine and then Christianity itself had been paganized. In fact he can be described, in religion, as a radical Christian in whom the new 'natural' philosophy of the Renaissance mingled with the Teutonic mysticism of the later Middle Ages: an individualist of the cast of his German contemporaries Caspar Schwenckfeld and Sebastian Franck and their successors Valentin Weigel and Jacob Boehme.[4] His religious philosophy, like theirs, could no more easily be accommodated to that of Luther or to any established system of ideas, than its medical content to the teaching of the established schools.

What was that content? It was a content which was heavily masked by its deterrent form. Those who approached it from the established medical tradition were immediately repelled by its outward aspect. Paracelsus himself, and his disciples after him, not only declared frontal war on the established medical philosophy: they also used every means to shock their adversaries – aggressive dogmatism, wild claims, bombastic, arcane and insulting language. Into the stylized and conventional language of the medical world, they introduced challenging concepts and bizarre neoterisms: *archeus, magma, iliastrum, cagastrum, hylech, duelech*; for in order to destroy the old orthodoxy it was not enough to refute its central ideas: they needed to destroy its habits of thought, its very terminology. This in turn entailed a new vocabulary, new dictionaries. In the later sixteenth century there was a great industry of compiling such dictionaries.* But if we can once get past this new and rebarbative language, and penetrate the system of Paracelsianism, we can see that, on three levels at least, it had an acceptable message for the time.

First, on the metaphysical level, it had an appeal which could be universal – i.e. which was not necessarily confined to Germans or Protestants. That appeal was to the Hermetic Platonism of the Renaissance. Galenism, the ruling orthodoxy of the medical schools, was essentially Aristotelean: it assumed an Aristotelean cosmology. Paracelsianism was essentially anti-Aristotelean. It was both Neoplatonic and Hermetic. Its theory depended, absolutely, on belief in the Neoplatonic cosmology, as elaborated by Marsilio Ficino (for whom Paracelsus expressed his admiration). In particular, it depended on the doctrine of the macrocosm and the microcosm: that is, on the idea that the body and soul of man are a miniature replica of the body and soul of the world, and that between these two worlds, the great and the little, there are correspondences, sympathies and antipathies, which the philosopher, the *magus*, could understand and control. Paracelsus not only accepted this theory as fundamental to his philosophy: he also gave it a new and exciting dimension; for, out of his study of the medieval alchemists and his own experience in the mines and furnaces of the Fugger family, he evolved the view that the universe, the macrocosm, was chemically controlled – was, in fact, itself a gigantic chemical crucible – and that its original creation had been a chemical operation, or rather 'separation' of the pure from the impure. From this it followed that the microcosm – the human body – was also a chemical system whose condition could be altered, adjusted, cured by chemical treatment. It was by reference to this general theory, from which he deduced some new and fertile ideas, but which he also encrusted with many bizarre and inconsequent details drawn from his own imagina-

---

* e.g. Adam von Bodenstein, *Onomasticon Theophrasti Paracelsi* . . . (Basel, 1575); Leonhard Thurneyssen, ʽΕϱμηνεία, *Das ist ein Onomasticum* . . . (Berlin, 1974), etc. The best-known of such dictionaries was the *Lexicon Alchemiae* of Martin Ruland, the physician of the Emperor Rudolf II: but Johannes Rhenanus, the physician of Maurice the Learned, Landgrave of Hesse, accused him of stealing his work. (Rhenanus, *Opera Chymiatrica* . . . Frankfurt, 1635, Ep.ded.)

tion and from German peasant folklore, that Paracelsus justified his particular medical innovations: his insistence that diseases were living parasites planted in the individual human body, not merely an accidental imbalance of 'humours'; his replacement of those four 'humours' of the Galenists by his three chemical 'principles', sulphur, mercury and salt; his search for a 'universal dissolvent' – the 'liquor Alkahest' as it would afterwards be called; his detoxication of poisons to convert them into cures; his homoeopathic remedies; his distillations and 'projections' which made this revolutionary innovator a continuator, in the age of the Renaissance, of the alchemical tradition of the Middle Ages.

Secondly, on the ideological level, this Neoplatonic philosophy easily acquired a prophetic, messianic, potentially revolutionary character. For if the world, as Christians held, was finite, with a beginning and an end, and if its beginning, the Creation, was a chemical operation, would not its end be chemical too? The Bible had promised that the Prophet Elijah would return 'before the coming of the great and dreadful day of the Lord',[5] and this promise, often recalled by the contemporaries of Christ,[6] had been taken up and put in a new context by the twelfth-century Calabrian abbot Joachim of Flora. Joachim had divided the history of the world into three ages and had placed the return of Elijah, and the coming of Antichrist, at the beginning of the third and last age, soon to come. Joachim's apocalyptic scenario was taken over by the radical friars of the later Middle Ages and would be their gift to their Protestant successors: Luther himself was seen by some as Elijah. Paracelsus too adopted it, but with a significant change. He not only adjusted the dates – Elijah, he said, would appear fifty-eight years after his own death: he also introduced him in a new guise, as 'Elias Artista,' Elijah the 'Artist' – that is, in the specialized language of the adepts, the Alchemist. As an alchemist, 'Elias' was to reveal all the secrets of chemistry, showing how iron could be transmuted into gold. He was also to begin the last transmutation of the world, which was to be not an operatic epiphany or a battle of Armageddon but, once again, a chemical act of separation. The millennium was to be a chemical millennium. Thus Paracelsianism offered, to those who took it whole, the prospect of a special kind of utopian revolution.[7]

Finally, on a practical level, whether the theory was correct or not, its practitioners did in fact achieve certain results. These results were largely obtained by chemical or mineral remedies. Moreover, the Paracelsian remedies were often more agreeable to take or to endure than the time-honoured remedies of the Establishment. The Paracelsians respected the curative power of Nature: their treatment of wounds was, by modern standards, wonderfully enlightened. They used mild rather than strong doses, simple rather than elaborate drugs; they laid great emphasis on mineral waters and baths – the chemistry of Nature; and they devised narcotics and opiates to relieve pain. Paracelsus' most famous pain-killer was his 'laudanum' – another word invented by him. He also discovered how to make and use ether.

Thus, however heretical in theory, the Paracelsians could claim a growing number of supporters for the best of practical reasons: their patients were, or seemed to themselves to be, cured. Froben, after all, had been cured. Adam von Bodenstein had been cured. The orthodox doctors countered such claims by compiling lists, or at least statistics, of those who (they said) had been killed by Paracelsian remedies, especially by antimony, the most notorious of mineral cures. But they found that there was no arguing with matters of fact. Against antimony, there was always laudanum. Oporinus and Toxites both bore witness to the life-saving effects of laudanum. So did many others. At the end of the sixteenth century, the humanist scholar and bibliophile, Jacques Bongars, a Huguenot who served Henri IV as ambassador in Germany, wrote to the German physician Joachim Camerarius of Nuremberg describing his own illness and its treatment. 'Out of numberless medicines which have been poured into me,' he wrote, 'none has had any good effect except the *laudanum* of Paracelsus, which my doctors somehow allowed themselves to be persuaded to use. It never failed. It relieved my pains for six or seven hours and induced a restful sleep for two or three hours. In a word, when I was nearly dead with pain, it restored intervals of life.'[8] The claims of the physicians on both sides can perhaps be discounted. The claims of the patients cannot.

Neoplatonist 'theosophy', messianic prophecy, chemical medicine – these are the three chief ingredients of Paracelsus' philosophy, and the history of the movement is the history of their gradual separation, their periodic reunion. If the medicine could have been detached from the theology, or at least from the prophecy, it might have found acceptance within medical orthodoxy. But could it have been so detached? Did not the new medicine perhaps need the ideological force of a new metaphysic if it was to break down the resistance of the old? As we follow the course of the movement we shall see how, for a whole century, critical physicians sought to detach the medicine from the philosophy, or at least, while leaving the philosophy in suspense, to achieve a practical compromise. But the true Paracelsians would have none of this. To them, the new philosophy must be taken whole: Paracelsianism and

Galenism were fundamentally incompatible medical systems. They were contained within fundamentally incompatible philosophical and religious systems, and therefore there could be no question of piecemeal accommodation between them. So the particular Paracelsian remedies were on offer by them only as part of a package. Enthusiastically, even defiantly presented, as an inseparable element in a new total *Weltanschauung*, they became the tabloid slogans of a radical party, threatening to subvert the established ideology and institutions of the medical – and not only the medical – world. It was a frontal challenge; and naturally it caused a hardening of the philosophy which it challenged and aroused frontal opposition.

(2)

The hard core of the opposition to Paracelsianism was to be found, naturally enough, in the established medical corporations: the Faculties of Medicine in the universities and the colleges of physicians incorporated by royal charter. To these corporations, Paracelsianism was not only an intellectual heresy: it was also a social threat. For the corporations had vested interests to protect. They had rights and privileges. They were empowered to legislate in medical matters, to grant licences to practise, to disfranchise quacks, to control apothecaries and surgeons. Paracelsianism undermined all these privileges. It rejected official legislation, ignored licences. It was the charter of quacks. Above all, it encouraged the subject classes of the profession – the surgeons and apothecaries – to claim rights above their station.

Against the citadels of medical orthodoxy, the Paracelsian heretics for some time beat in vain. If they were to make any progress there, they needed to break out of Germany into Europe: to find a chink in the protective wall of the establishment, penetrate the closed, defensive academic world, speak to it in 'the general language' – that is, Latin – win the sympathy of professional men. This they began to do in the later 1560s, and they did it on two levels. On one level – the level of practice – they won the support of surgeons and apothecaries: the surgeons who followed the warring armies of Europe, the apothecaries who were the physicians of the poor. These men, like Paracelsus himself, gradually yielded to the evidence of practice, and were able, by that evidence, to win converts even among physicians. On another level – the level of theory – they found advocates who could present their case persuasively to the international world of learning. They found them, especially, in the city of Basel.

For if the University of Basel had expelled both Paracelsus and his disciple Bodenstein, the city was more liberal. It was a free city, allied to the cantons of Switzerland; it was, by now, consciously the city of Erasmus; and as a great centre of printing, it was an open source and market of ideas. Moreover, among its printers there was one who, being himself a heretic, was particularly ready to publish heretical ideas. This was Pietro Perna, an Italian, one of those 'libertine' disciples of Erasmus who, to the indignation of Calvin in Geneva, had taken refuge in this hospitable city. There he published the works of a whole series of disconcerting writers – Machiavelli, Castellio, Postel, Weyer, Ramus. He also became the greatest publisher of Paracelsus and his interpreters. Between 1570 and 1603, seventy works of Paracelsus were published in Basel, sixty of them by Perna or his son-in-law and successor Konrad Waldkirch. That was the great age of Basel as a cultural centre. After 1603 these publications ceased altogether; thereafter Paracelsus' works issued not from Basel, the city of Bodenstein, but from Strasbourg, the city of Toxites.[9]

The process whereby Paracelsus became intellectually acceptable began in 1571. It was launched by a distinguished orthodox physician, Winther (or Günther) von Andernach. He was a humanist and a Greek scholar who had translated Galen and, as professor of medicine at Paris, had been the teacher of Vesalius. At the end of his life he moved to Strasbourg. There he found Toxites and other disciples of Paracelsus; through them he became interested in the new chemistry; and in 1571 he announced his partial conversion in a solid work 'Of the Old and the New Medicine'. The book, which was published by Perna at Basel, was essentially a work of conciliation. While still advocating the old medical system, Winther sought to find a place in it for the new. In order to perform this feat, he disregarded the metaphysical basis of Paracelsus' theories, and he deplored the vulgar self-advertisement of the self-styled disciples of Paracelsus; but he accepted certain Paracelsian chemical remedies, of which he gave a very full account, and he praised Paracelsus himself, not indeed as a radical innovator, but, in agreement with Paracelsus' own claims, as the restorer of the true medicine of the ancients, that had almost been lost.[10]

In the same year, 1571, which saw the publication of Winther von Andernach's work, another more important book was published, also at Basel, by a Danish physician who was then travelling in Europe. This was Peder Soerensen, who latinized his name as Severinus, and was generally known, in order to distinguish him from the Italian physician Marcus Aurelius Severinus, as 'Severinus the Dane'. Severinus had discovered the works of Paracelsus in Germany, and became a faithful disciple – 'the most genuine and reliable expositor of Paracelsus'.[11] But he was personally very different from his master: an urbane and cultivated man such as is necessary, at given moments in the history of ideas, in order to complete the process of their reception. The rough prophet who challenges the old assumptions needs the help of a smooth evangelist who will soothe and convert the shaken establishment: the inspired eccentric George Fox is succeeded by the urbane courtier William Penn. Severinus entitled his book *The Idea of Philosophic Medicine*. After publishing it, he returned to his native country and was appointed court-physician in Copenhagen: a post which he held for thirty years under two successive Danish kings, Frederick II and Christian IV. It was thanks to him and to his writings, above all, that Paracelsianism, in the last quarter of the sixteenth century, became internationally respectable: he purged away its grossness and bombast, while preserving, organizing and presenting – in civilized Latin – its essential method.

In the next generation the work of Severinus would be widely read and admired. One of his admirers was Gui de la Brosse, the founder of the Jardin des Plantes in Paris, who described him as the first to bring the work of Paracelsus to order and as one who understood Paracelsus better than Paracelsus himself.[12] Another was Francis Bacon, who was always careful to distinguish between the uncouth prophet and his civilized interpreter. 'Only one of your followers do I envy you, Paracelsus,' he would write, 'and that is Peter Severinus, a man who does not deserve to perish with your absurdities.'[13] Indeed, Severinus can be seen as a bridge between Paracelsus and Bacon, enabling Bacon, though from different premises, to endorse the apparently empirical method of Paracelsus. In a famous passage of his *Idea Medicinae*, Severinus had urged his readers to

> sell your lands, your houses, your clothes and your jewelry; burn up your books. Instead buy yourselves stout shoes, travel to the mountains, search the valleys, the deserts, the sea-shores and the deepest recesses of the earth; mark the distinctions between several kinds of animals, plants, minerals . . . Be not ashamed to study the heavenly and earthly lore of peasants. Lastly, buy coal, build furnaces, work with fire. Thus and thus only will you attain to knowledge of things and their properties.[14]

I am not sure about the peasants, but the general message could have been uttered by Bacon.

Thus by 1571, the year in which Winther von Andernach and Peter Severinus published their commendations of his work, it can be said that Paracelsus had achieved a certain academic respectability and was a force to be reckoned with; and indeed, next year, the reckoning came. It came in the form of a swingeing attack on 'the new medicine of Paracelsus' by a fellow Swiss, Thomas Liebler, more familiar under his Latin name of Erastus: he was the prophet of 'Erastianism', the doctrine which entailed the subjection of the Church to the State. Erastus was a philosopher, a theologian and a physician; since 1558 he had held the chair of all three subjects at Heidelberg; and in all three he was soundly conservative: Aristotelean in philosophy, Lutheran (or more precisely Zwinglian) in religion, Galenist in medicine. From this firm position he set out, at the request of the Lutheran Duke of Saxony, to discredit Paracelsus' Platonist theology, to expose his philosophical inconsistencies, and to counter his medical claims. This he did to some tune, summarily rejecting all inconvenient evidence: all Paracelsus' miraculous cures, he said, had been merely temporary and had invariably been followed, after a brief interval, by the death of the patient. Erastus' four books of *Disputations*, published at Basel in 1572–3, were accepted as the classic refutation of Paracelsus, convincing to those who were already convinced, irrelevant to those who were not. Naturally they helped to advertise the works of the author whom they denounced.

Once begun, the process continued. In 1575 Perna printed at Basel, in Latin, the work 'On the Secrets of Antimony' by one of the greatest of early Paracelsists, Alexander von Suchten. It had originally been published in German, at Strasbourg, thanks to Toxites. Suchten was a native of Danzig who had studied medicine in Louvain and Italy and had become a Paracelsian while librarian and physician to that universal patron Ottheinrich, Elector Palatine; then he had gone back to Poland to be physician to King Sigismund Augustus. But his aggressive Paracelsianism had roused the orthodox against him and he had returned to Germany. He was unpopular with traditional alchemists too, for he proved scientifically that the transmutation of base metals into gold was impossible. His proof did not, however, deter his fellow alchemists, or his fellow Paracelsians, whom he encouraged to believe in the coming of 'Elias' to reveal the last alchemical mysteries.[15]

Three years later there came to Basel a young Englishman (or rather, as he described himself, Anglo-Scot) who would do for his country what Severinus had done for Denmark and Suchten for Poland. This was

Thomas Muffet, or Mouffet. Muffet had studied medicine in Galenist Cambridge under the famous Galenist physician Dr Caius; but then he had come to Basel, had discovered Paracelsus, and had been bowled over by him. The immediate result was unfortunate. In his doctoral thesis, on pain-killing medicines – i.e. on Paracelsus' laudanum, etc. – he expressed his new loyalty so provocatively that the thesis was referred back to him and he was awarded his doctorate only after he had retracted his intemperate attacks on Galen and his champion Erastus. He then spent three years travelling in Europe. After returning to England he accompanied Peregrine Bertie, Lord Willoughby, on his embassy to Copenhagen, and there became friendly with Severinus. Two years later, in 1584, he published, in Latin, a dialogue to prove the superiority of Paracelsian chemical medicine, and dedicated it to Severinus.

Like Severinus, Muffet was a cultivated man of the world who moved easily among the great and could recommend the new doctrines to them. Thanks to noble patrons, particularly the Earl of Pembroke, he had a highly satisfactory career in Elizabethan England, becoming a member of Parliament as well as a Fellow of the Royal College of Physicians and a very successful general practitioner. Among his patients were the Earls of Leicester and Essex, Sir Philip Sidney, Sir Francis Walsingham and Sir Francis Drake. All these were radicals – but establishment radicals – in politics as Muffet himself was in medicine. As a Fellow of the Royal College, Muffet played an important part in trying to bring selected Paracelsian remedies into the London Pharmacopoeia. He was also a naturalist: he compiled an illustrated work on insects which he left in manuscript – a ravishingly beautiful manuscript – at his death, and he published a poem, based on his experiences in Spain and Italy, on 'the Silkworms and their Flies'. His little daughter too is connected with entomological literature on a somewhat different level: who has not heard of the agonizing experience of Little Miss Muffet as she faced the spider, poised on her tuffet?[16]

Thus all through the 1570s Paracelsian ideas were being disseminated, in respectable academic Latin, from the presses of Basel; and the University of Basel could not escape their influence. The man who did most to convert the University – or at least to introduce Paracelsian chemistry into its curriculum – was its most famous teacher, the scholar who dominated its intellectual life in the later sixteenth century, Theodor Zwinger. Zwinger was a universal man, professor in turn of Greek, of moral theology, and of theoretical medicine. Like most of the great Swiss doctors of his time, he had taken his medical degree at

Padua and was by training a humanist, an Aristotelean and a Galenist. As such he was at first a contemptuous opponent of Paracelsus and he had played a leading part in the expulsion of Bodenstein in 1564. But gradually, in the following decade, he changed his views. Practical experience of the plague in Zurich, and his own study of Hippocrates, had caused him to read Paracelsus with care and to take up the study of chemistry. By the later 1570s he would write a laudatory epitaph of Bodenstein and would praise Paracelsus as a most gifted and enlightened man, the German Hippocrates. Zwinger would never himself be a Paracelsian, but he opened the medical school of Basel to chemical ideas; he collaborated closely with Perna as a publisher of Paracelsus; and many Paracelsians of the next generation were his pupils at Basel. Only his death prevented him from appearing as one of the editors of Huser's edition of the complete works of Paracelsus. Thanks largely to him, it can be said, Paracelsian chemistry found an academic centre from which it could claim admittance into traditional medicine.[17]

So far we have been dealing with the dissemination of Paracelsian ideas, rendered academically respectable, or at least worthy of academic refutation, mainly from the city and university of Basel. They did of course circulate on other levels too. If Paracelsus the chemical physician spoke through Severinus, Muffet and Zwinger, Paracelsus the mystic inspired Weigel and Jakob Boehme, Paracelsus the *magus* was eagerly studied by that greatest of Elizabethan *magi*, John Dee,[18] and Paracelsus the practical empiric was popularized in hundreds of publications, generally of spurious or derivative works, offering detailed recipes and remedies. And at the lowest level of all, quacks and charlatans of every kind seized upon the often unintelligible language of Paracelsus, imitated his strident manners, and claimed his authority for their pretended cures. The complaints about such 'empirics', such 'false and lying Theophrasteans' are numerous. They swarmed particularly in Germany – there were over 100,000 of them (one hostile critic maintained) in Austria, Carinthia, Silesia and Bohemia alone: doctors and apothecaries, nobles and commoners, men and women, all with their own brands of 'laudanum';[19] and they were a constant liability to those who sought to defend and clarify the real ideas of the Master. However, we need not do more than notice this fact. More interesting is the question of the religious identification of Paracelsianism: how far was it associated with any particular form of Christianity in the age of the Reformation?

Clearly there was a certain bias towards Protestantism. Paracelsianism, like Protestantism, was a philosophy of revolt against the established order. Many of the early Paracelsians were, or became, Protestants; and the same can be said of their princely patrons – the Elector Palatine Ottheinrich, the Polish prince Albert Laski. Basel too was now a Protestant city, though of a very liberal kind, and its printing presses catered largely, though by no means exclusively, for the Protestant world. Those foreigners who went thither to study were mainly Protestants, and if they carried Paracelsianism back home, it was to Protestant countries or Protestant societies. However, there was as yet no necessary connection. Paracelsianism was still, in the 1570s, undenominational, committed only to a Neoplatonic philosophy which was itself, as yet, undenominational. It was therefore perfectly capable of penetrating, and indeed did penetrate, Catholic societies, so long as those societies were open to Platonic ideas: that is, so long as their ecclesiastical and medical institutions were not determined and able to enforce scholastic theology and Galenic medicine.

In general, the Catholic Church was still tolerant of Platonism in the mid-sixteenth century – although its suspicions were growing. Therefore the resistance to Paracelsianism was professional, not sectarian: it came not from the Church but from the established medical corporations. However, these institutions, though jealous of their rights, had difficulty in enforcing them. The poor continued to resort to apothecaries who could not be controlled, and the rich, who alone patronized physicians, could hire what doctors they pleased: if they were persuaded that Paracelsian doctors could serve them better, it was in vain that colleges of physicians forbade those doctors to practise. So Paracelsian physicians – 'spagyrists' as they called themselves in the Paracelsian language – flourished at all levels, even the highest. They might be banned from university faculties and medical corporations but they were appointed *stadtphysici* of German cities and employed by noble households and royal courts. This was the position in Catholic and Protestant countries alike.

However, in the later years of the century, the attitude of the Roman Church changed. It then became less tolerant of Neoplatonism. This was one aspect of that hardening of views and strengthening of the instruments of control which followed the last session of the Council of Trent in 1564. The leaders of the Church now reasserted Aristotelian orthodoxy and looked askance at Platonism which they saw as a dangerously 'irenic' philosophy, seeking to re-unite Christendom on an erroneous, or at least highly undesirable, base of 'natural' religion. Thus the Counter-Reformation Church, protecting its doctrine, became the natural ally of the medical corporations, protecting their monopoly; and Paracelsianism, not by inherent necessity but by force of circumstances, was pushed into alliance with Protestantism. The process did not stop there: as established Protestantism, in its turn, developed instruments of control, Paracelsianism would take refuge in Protestant heresy; but Protestant control would never be as effective as Catholic control, and anyway we have not yet reached that stage.

The process can be seen most clearly in France, for there it was hastened by ideological confrontation. In the later sixteenth century, Germany and England were internally at peace. There the Interim, here the 'Elizabethan compromise', preserved the religious balance. But France was not at peace. It was rent by civil war; and that civil war caused a decisive polarization not only in politics and religion but also in medicine, or at least in medical philosophy. It was a polarization which, as we shall see, would be repeated and intensified as the same ideological struggle was carried, afterwards, to other countries: to Germany and England.

(3)

Paracelsianism came into France by two routes: one royal and one provincial. The royal route led direct to the Valois court under the regency of the tolerant, irenic, platonizing Catherine de Médicis who, in the difficult 1560s, was seeking to maintain a balance, and a consensus, between Protestant and Catholic. There a group of royal doctors, most of whom had been army surgeons, discussed Paracelsian ideas and heard them defended 'against the calumnies of many ignorant and envious men' – no doubt members of the Paris Faculty. These doctors met at the house of Leonard Botal, a Piedmontese physician who had been an army surgeon and had written on gunshot wounds. He would become *premier médecin* to the Queen Regent and to her sons. Others who attended these discussions were the reigning *premier médecin* to the Queen, Honoré Castellan, who, we are told, 'greatly approved Paracelsus as a surgeon'; Jean Chapelain, *premier médecin* to the King; and the most famous of all sixteenth-century surgeons, Ambroise Paré. But the driving force appears to have been Jacques Gohory, a cultivated and versatile man of letters who had served the Crown as a diplomat abroad before turning to natural science. It was probably during his travels abroad that he had discovered and become interested in Paracelsus. At all events, whereas others were merely interested in Paracelsian ideas, Gohory, by 1562, had become a disciple: he would be described in the next century as 'the first advocate of Paracelsianism in France'.[20] He wrote a biography of Paracelsus, describing him as the gravest physician and the most subtle philosopher of the age. He also commented on one of his works and wrote a compendium of his philosophy, which was published at Basel in 1568. In 1571 he founded a 'Lycium philosophal' – a private academy, arboretum and herb-garden – in the Parisian suburb of St Marceau, close to the academy of his friend J. A. de Baïf. This 'Lycium' was the precursor of the more famous Jardin des Plantes founded in the next century by Gui de la Brosse.[21]

Thus already, at an early date – before Severinus, well before Muffet – Paracelsianism was being advocated and critically discussed by educated men, all of them Roman Catholics, at the civilized court of Catherine de Médicis. But it was also seeping into France at another level, often in a cruder form, and in association with heresy. It was brought from Germany or Switzerland, often by Huguenots who had drunk their heresy at those bubbling springs; it was nourished in the petty colleges of the provinces which the orthodox mandarins of Paris were so eager to suppress and which were often under Huguenot control; and it flourished in the shadow of the Huguenot nobility. We find it on the German borders of France, in Huguenot fiefs, or in Huguenot enclaves in the great cities: Lyon, Paris, Orleans, Rouen. Winther von Andernach, for instance, who had taught orthodox Galenism in Paris, became a semi-Paracelsian only when he had retreated to the German-speaking free city of Strasbourg. Pierre de la Ramée – Petrus Ramus, the great enemy of Aristotelean logic – became an admirer of Paracelsus by visiting Basel: he then completed the process by becoming a Huguenot. A later convert was Bernard Penot, a native of Guienne, in southern France – the great redoubt of Huguenotism which was also, in the eyes of the orthodox doctors, the nursery of charlatans.[22] He had studied abroad and taken his doctorate in Basel, after which he began to collect and publish Paracelsian manuscripts. Then he settled in Lyon and wrote works which were published in Latin and German, but not French. Soon he found it prudent to retreat from Lyon to Franckenthal, the Huguenot city of refuge in the Calvinist Palatinate. Neither Winther von Andernach nor Penot had much direct influence in France, and Ramus was murdered soon after his return to Paris, a victim of the massacre of St Bartholomew; but Paracelsian ideas, often of a debased kind, spread among herbalists and apothecaries and were adopted by unlicensed physicians. Their advance alarmed the medical establishment, and their association with Huguenots, and with the court, alarmed those other defenders of orthodoxy, the Parlement of Paris and the Gallican Church.

For throughout the wars of religion, and indeed long afterwards, the corporate institutions of France stood firmly together in defence of orthodoxy, the law and their rights. The Medical Faculty of the University of Paris was as zealous a guardian of medical orthodoxy as the Theological Faculty – the Sorbonne – was of religious orthodoxy; and both were the more zealous, and the more intolerant, because they felt that the burden of defending such orthodoxy rested entirely on them. Betrayed from above, deserted by the natural establishment, forced to conclude that neither the feeble and vacillating last Valois kings nor the ex-Huguenot Henri IV could be relied upon to support them, they saw themselves, at least within their own provinces, as sovereign bodies, the only effective authority in Paris. For the same reason the Parlement of Paris, the highest legal authority in the kingdom, felt itself to be the sole consistent guarantor of public order. So these three bodies – the Parlement, the Sorbonne, the Medical Faculty – three self-conscious guardians of threatened order and orthodoxy, stood firmly together, sustaining each other, in those dark years, against any weakening in law, religion or medicine.

The first decisive step was taken in 1566 – that is, precisely at the time when the royal doctors were encouraging Paracelsianism in Paris. In that year the Faculty of Medicine struck back by formally declaring that antimony was a poison which was never to be used in medicine, and this declaration was given legal authority by a decree of the Parlement of Paris. The ban was entirely ineffective – it would be repeated, by both bodies, fifty years later, and the 'war of antimony' would still be raging a generation after that; but at least it was a manifesto against the courtly patrons of Paracelsianism. In the years which followed, religious passions were intensified. They culminated, in 1572, in the massacre of St Bartholomew. After that terrible outbreak of communal violence, the fears of the Parisian establishment were sharpened and in 1578 the medical faculty decided to act. The occasion for action was supplied by the arrival in Paris of a notorious Paracelsian 'empiric', Roch le Baillif.

I have written elsewhere of Roch le Baillif.* Here it is enough to say that he was a native of Normandy who claimed to have a degree from the local college of Caen. He was a professed Paracelsian, who wrote books of vulgar Paracelsianism, translating into French the outlandish

---

* See below, pp. 200–210.

vocabulary of his master. Like so many of the early Paracelsians, he was a great self-advertiser, semi-literate and bombastic. He was also a Huguenot, whose principal protectors were the greatest of Huguenot families, the Breton family of Rohan; but he would change sides at need. By 1578 he had contrived – no doubt through the Paracelsian sympathizers at court – to obtain the title of *médecin ordinaire du roi*, and he set out to conquer Paris. Thereupon the Faculty of Medicine decided to fight a test case. So, on the formal ground that he was not a doctor of the University of Paris, it forbade him to practise, and then, when he disregarded the ban, hauled him before the Parlement of Paris.

It was a spectacular trial, lasting at least three days, before a crowded court. Famous lawyers were engaged on both sides. The Faculty won, and would long boast of its victory: Roch le Baillif was duly hounded out of Paris. But it was something of a pyrrhic victory. From now on the name of Paracelsus was famous in France. A year later, Montaigne would refer to Paracelsus as 'ce nouveau venu' – that is, newly come to France; and the advocate who had defended Roch le Baillif – the great lawyer-historian Etienne Pasquier – though he had forgotten the name of his client and some details of the trial, would refer often to the great 'case of the Paracelsians', which had caused him to respect Paracelsus and his medicine. That medicine, he would write a few years later, 'is now practised openly in Germany and Switzerland and secretly in various places in this kingdom' – in great cities, in noble houses, and even, more openly, in the royal court.

In particular, in the royal court. One of the reasons why the Faculty was so fierce against Roch le Baillif was, no doubt, his title of *médecin ordinaire du roi*. The Valois court seemed positively to prefer heterodox doctors, thus letting down the cause of medical orthodoxy, just as it periodically let down the cause of religious orthodoxy by conceding power, or toleration, to the Huguenots. Being both a Paracelsian and a Huguenot, Roch le Baillif must have seemed an ideal victim. In expelling him, the Faculty no doubt thought that it was teaching a lesson not only to 'empirics', quacks, 'spagyrists', *agyrtae, circumforanei* etc. – i.e. Paracelsians and any other infringers of its privileges – but also to Huguenots and to the patrons of both classes, the wayward royal court.

The lesson, alas, was not well learned. From now on Paracelsianism was more favoured than ever at the French court. Its most famous professor was Joseph du Chesne, alias Quercetanus: a name to conjure with throughout the next century. He too was a Huguenot, from the Huguenot south of France: a Gascon from Armagnac, who had gone to

Germany and there learned Paracelsian doctrines from Dr Birckmann, the *stadtphysicus* of Cologne and publisher of Paracelsian manuscripts, whom I have already mentioned. He also travelled through Germany, like Paracelsus himself, as an army doctor. He was accompanied in his travels by a young assistant, Henri Cherlier, who worked with him 'in favo meo spagyrico', 'in my spagyric cell', and who afterwards found a niche in the Protestant academy of Nîmes before coming to Basel and marrying the daughter of the great Basel physician and naturalist Johann Bauhin. Du Chesne too went to Basel, took a doctor's degree there, and then, after a brief stay in Lyon, settled in Geneva. He published numerous works, including Paracelsian tracts on the properties of minerals and the correct treatment of gunshot wounds, and a long poem setting forth the Paracelsian cosmology in the style of the Huguenot poet, so admired at the time, so forgotten today, Guillaume Saluste du Bartas. Unlike Roch le Baillif, but like Severinus and Muffet, du Chesne was a polished man of the world, able to move in courtly circles. He became known to several German princes, who were patrons of the new medicine, and in Geneva he acted as the political agent of Henri of Navarre, combining his medical activities with diplomatic and military missions to the Swiss cantons on behalf of the Huguenot king.

Another Huguenot physician who, though not at first a Paracelsian, had adopted many of the chemical remedies associated with Paracelsus, was Jean Ribit, sieur de la Rivière. He was a native of Geneva, who had studied in Turin and then travelled widely in Europe. In the 1580s he too was drawn to the Protestant court of Henri of Navarre at Nérac, and became physician to the Huguenot grandee Henri de la Tour d'Auvergne, afterwards famous as Duc de Bouillon. La Rivière accompanied his patron on diplomatic missions to England and Germany. Then he returned with him to France and, in 1594, was appointed *premier médecin* to Henri of Navarre. La Rivière was not like Severinus and du Chesne, a committed Paracelsian: a polished courtier, he was disgusted by the vulgarity and self-advertisement of the Paracelsian empirics who swarmed in Germany. He was rather an eclectic who sought, like Winther von Andernach, to combine Paracelsian and Galenist elements in a non-ideological medical philosophy. This was an appropriate ambition at the court of Henri of Navarre, who was seen, even before he had come to the throne of France, as the conciliator who might combine Catholicism and Protestantism in a non-denominational form of Christianity.

Such views, of course, were anathema to the strict Galenists of the

Paris Faculty. To them there was no difference between the unconventional Paracelsus and the polite Severinus, between the fundamentalist bigotry of a Roch le Baillif and the open-minded eclecticism of a la Rivière. But, in reality, the difference was great, and when ideological tensions were muted, it was allowed to emerge. We have seen its emergence in the liberal University of Basel, which had rejected Paracelsian doctrine in the person of Adam von Bodenstein, but had gradually admitted chemical remedies, many of which in fact came from Paracelsus. The same process can be seen within France in another 'liberal' institution: the semi-Protestant University of Montpellier.

Montpellier was the intellectual capital of southern France: of that Languedoc which had once been the home of the Albigensian and was now the home of the Huguenot heresy. The Parisian doctors hated it – 'a stinking bog of ignorance and imposture', as one of them would call it.[23] They saw it as an upstart rival, far too successful in pushing its doctors, far too tolerant of medical as of religious heresy, far too negligent of the conventions and hierarchies necessary to a well-ordered university. In Paris, the surgeons and apothecaries were kept in their place: in Montpellier physicians worked with their hands. In Paris the greatest classical scholar of the age – perhaps of any age – the Huguenot Joseph Scaliger, had been furiously attacked for having dared, though not a doctor of medicine, to comment on the Greek text of Hippocrates; at Montpellier, the second greatest classical scholar of the age, the Huguenot Isaac Casaubon, had been positively invited to lecture on the same text and had been escorted into the University in triumph to do so. Paracelsianism was not explicitly taught at Montpellier, any more than at Basel, but the theses offered for the medical examination there show that here, as there, Paracelsian ideas had been accepted. In 1596, when Theodore de Mayerne, another Huguenot from Geneva, a friend and protégé of du Chesne, supplicated for his doctorate at Montpellier, he defended a whole series of Paracelsian propositions and actually quoted Paracelsus in his defence; and he received his doctorate.[24]

All this Paracelsianism and semi-Paracelsianism which had seeped into France from Germany through Huguenot doctors, Huguenot households, Huguenot institutions, found a focus in the court of Henri of Navarre. As Huguenot king of Navarre, Henri had always used Huguenot physicians, often from Montpellier, and when he moved to Paris, as Catholic King of France, his preference did not change. In 1594, having appointed as his *premier médecin* the semi-Paracelsian la

Rivière, he summoned from Geneva his political agent, the Paracelsian Joseph du Chesne, to be *médecin par quartier*: that is, physician in attendance for three months in the year. Soon these two heretics would be joined by a third. By 1599 Mayerne was practising in Paris. In that year he set out on a tour of Germany and Italy with his patron, the young Huguenot leader, Henri Duc de Rohan. On his return, he too became *médecin ordinaire du roi*, and so the Paris Faculty could observe with alarm three Paracelsian Huguenots from the Calvinist city of Geneva forming a close partnership round the Most Catholic King.

Imagine the tension of the situation. Henri IV had only been accepted in Paris on terms. To the Catholic establishment, which had so long kept him at bay, he was thoroughly suspect as an ex-Huguenot from the South. He was still surrounded by Huguenot grandees, Huguenot officers, Huguenot clients of all kinds; and these Huguenots were not merely individual non-conformists: they represented an alternative form of society. There was a danger of a take-over by Southern carpet-baggers, or at least of new encouragement for the Huguenots already in and around the seat of government. In order to prevent this, the Parisian establishment had insisted that the King of Navarre renounce his religion before he could be accepted as King of France. By that, of course, they did not mean that he should merely renounce his personal professions. That would not have been enough for their purpose. They meant that he must sever himself entirely from the Huguenot party, and place himself at the head of the Catholic establishment, and be absorbed by it. And the grandees, of course, were to follow him. France was to become, once again, a unitary society, conservative in doctrine through and through. There was to be no repetition, under the Bourbons, of the distressing vagaries of the last Valois kings.

In order to see the full significance of the struggle, we must look abroad. For we have now reached the time in which the Catholic Church turned decisively against the Neoplatonic movement. It was the culmination of a process which had been gathering strength, irregularly, for some time. Its irregularity was particularly obvious in Germany: after all, it was a Catholic archbishop, the Elector of Cologne, who had financed the publication of the complete works of Paracelsus in 1589, and the Emperor Rudolf II (a more nominal Catholic) was the greatest patron of alchemy in Europe. However, by the end of the century Rome made its position clear. It was then that the writings of Francesco Patrizi were condemned in Rome, then that Giordano Bruno was burnt and Campanella imprisoned. Patrizi was a

Catholic professor, Campanella and Bruno Dominican friars. All three were Hermetic philosophers. With Neoplatonic philosophy, of course, went Paracelsian medicine. In 1599, only ten years after they had been published under the patronage of a Catholic archbishop, all the works of Paracelsus were put on the Roman Index.

It was against this European background, then, that the great battle was fought in Paris. That battle was part of a general attempt, by the Catholic establishment, to win over the new Bourbon dynasty not only from one church to another, but from one ideology to another. The French court was being called upon to repudiate Huguenotism *in toto* and become the solid bulwark of a reinforced *ancien régime*. The result of the battle, so far, was a draw. Henri IV had indeed succumbed to the Catholic embrace, and he was indeed doing his best to bring his old comrades, the Huguenot grandees, over to Catholicism with him. As far as religion was concerned, he would be the Most Catholic King, with the convert cardinal du Perron as his mouthpiece and the Jesuit père Coton as his ear. But if the clerical establishment had thus prevailed, it soon became clear that the medical establishment had not. The Medical Faculty of the University was quite unable to break the ring of Huguenot Paracelsian doctors round the throne.

Chief among these, of course, was the *premier médecin du roi*. The *premier médecin* was not only an important figure at court: he also exercised great patronage in the country. La Rivière, du Chesne and Mayerne also had foreign contacts and correspondents, especially in Protestant Germany. They were used as secret agents in the 'Huguenot' foreign policy which Henri IV, to the dismay of the *dévots*, continued to pursue: a continuation of the old struggle for political supremacy against Catholic Spain. Du Chesne would be a regular agent in Henri IV's secret diplomacy with Maurice the Learned, Landgrave of Hesse, the King's main ally among the Protestant princes of Germany, and Mayerne was suspect as the political agent of the Duc de Rohan and other Huguenot leaders. In the eyes of the Paris Faculty, these Huguenot Paracelsians were dangerous enemies – far more dangerous, because far more powerful and far more successful, than Roch le Baillif a generation before. Like Roch le Baillif they were also technically vulnerable, for not one of them was a doctor of Paris. That also, of course, added to their crimes.

The campaign to break the 'Paracelsians' at court was mounted in 1604, after the publication of a challenging book by du Chesne which sought to establish Hermetic Paracelsian medicine as a new school at least equal in status to the orthodox teaching of Aristotle and Galen and

– a conciliatory gesture – capable of being harmonized with it. Mayerne
was closely associated with this book and had sought to secure for it, in
advance, the patronage of the Protestant Duke of Württemberg.[25] In
the end it was dedicated to two successive chancellors of France – just to
show that the author was not lightly to be attacked. Nevertheless, the
Faculty decided that, if its own authority was to be preserved, the
sticking point had now come. The leader of the Faculty, at this time,
was the elder Jean Riolan. Riolan was a tenacious defender of the rights
and privileges of the Faculty, and his views can be inferred from the
titles of some of his books, such as *A Philosophical Defence of the Ancient
Dignity of Medicine against the impudence of certain surgeons who wish to be the
equals of the physicians and publicly teach surgery* and *A Comparison of the
Physician with the Surgeon, to chastise the audacity of certain surgeons who can
neither speak well nor be silent*. By now, Riolan senior was an old man, and
mellowed by age, but he could rely on the active belligerency of his
young son who was on the make: he was working for his doctorate of
medicine in Paris and was only too ready to be the propagandist of the
Faculty against innovations of any kind, and the defender of the ancient
privileges which he hoped to inherit. Throughout the long battle which
followed, Riolan junior showed remarkable virtuosity as a pam-
phleteer. Sometimes he would write in the name of his father, sometimes in his own name, and sometimes as an anonymous third party
who intervened as an impartial arbiter and awarded victory, with noisy
and abusive cries of triumph, to his own side.

The battle began with a solemn meeting of the Faculty and a formal
condemnation by it, first of du Chesne, then, when he had come out in
support of du Chesne, of Mayerne. The anathemas launched against
these two doctors were formidable, not to say hysterical documents.
They condemned not only the particular works of du Chesne and
Mayerne, but also the whole 'spagyric' art and forbade any medical
practitioner in Paris to consult with the offending doctors, and any
apothecary to make drugs for them. In the pamphlet war which
accompanied the battle, and added to the noise, the young Riolan
poured out a series of vitriolic tracts, and du Chesne and Mayerne were
supported by other doctors whose character only served to emphasize
the ideological character of this ostensibly medical dispute. Their first
supporters, Israel Harvet and Guillaume Baycinet, came from a
strongly entrenched group of Huguenot Paracelsian doctors in
Orleans. These at least were Frenchmen, of a kind: Frenchmen who
had studied at Basel. Their next supporter added to their offence by
being not only a Protestant but a foreigner, for du Chesne and Mayerne

appealed to Germany and brought down upon the unfortunate Riolan the ponderous and scientific sledge-hammer of the greatest of German chemists – 'the real founder of chemistry, as a scientific and academic subject'[26] – the Saxon Andreas Libavius.

Ironically, Riolan and his friends had hoped to have Libavius on their side, and indeed Libavius' own correspondence suggested that, at first, he sympathized with them. A conservative Lutheran school-master, of traditional humanist education, he was already known as an outspoken anti-Paracelsian who never shrank from controversy. But his views were really more akin to those of la Rivière – i.e. although he hated the extravagant claims, bombastic language and bizarre cosmology of the German Paracelsians, whom he regarded as danger-ous radicals, he was equally opposed to the narrow Galenism of Paris which denied the legitimacy of chemistry itself. The whole purpose of his life, as he wrote, was to rescue chemistry from every echo of 'Theophrastia' and 'the impious pagan Hermes Trismegistus', and to establish it as an autonomous science within the traditional system of knowledge. The Parisian controversy enabled him to define his position, and in two works, first in his *Defensio Alchymiae* and then in his *Alchymia Triumphans*, he effectively defined it. Having liberated the study of chemistry from its central Paracelsian theology, and its marginal Paracelsian incrustations, he set it on a more limited base; and from that base he firmly put down the insolent claims of the Paris Faculty.[27]

Intellectually Libavius destroyed the arguments of the Parisian doctors. In practice, the dispute would ultimately be ended by a face-saving compromise: du Chesne and Mayerne would promise to comply with the regulations, 'to practise medicine according to the rules of Hippocrates and Galen . . . and not otherwise'; the ferocious anathemas would be lifted; and, 'at the command of the Most Christian King and the High Chancellor of France', outward peace would be restored.[28] But in one important respect, Henri IV decided to yield – if not to the Faculty, at least to the Church. He did not give up his preference for 'chemical' doctors, but he decided never again to have a Huguenot as *premier médecin*. In the early stage of the controversy, in 1605, la Rivière died. He was not succeeded by du Chesne but by André du Laurens. Du Laurens was disliked by the Paris Faculty as a doctor of Montpellier, not Paris, and as a friend of the new medicine and its practitioners, but at least he was a Catholic. Henri IV also appointed Jean Héroard, a Huguenot and a chemical doctor, as *premier médecin* to his son, but insisted that he become a Catholic: which he did. This was a warning signal to the Huguenots. Du Chesne, in his last years, turned away from Paris. He published his last works abroad, dedicated to German princes, and sighed for independence and Geneva. In 1609, when both du Chesne and du Laurens died, the King tried to persuade Mayerne, now the most successful 'Paracelsian' doctor in Paris, to accept Catholicism as the price of succession to the highest medical post at court. In spite of great pressure, Mayerne refused.[29] Then, next year, Henri IV was assassinated; the Catholic establishment seized its chance; under the regency of the Queen Mother, Marie de Médicis, the Catholic *dévots* recovered control; and Mayerne emigrated to England to become court physician to James I, and to treat his grand French patients by correspondence from London.

The deaths of la Rivière and du Chesne, and the emigration of Mayerne, left the field to the Paris Faculty. However, that was not the end of the story; for la Rivière, du Chesne and Mayerne had left in Paris colleagues and disciples who continued, less conspicuously, their middle way. The court continued to use chemical doctors and the converted Huguenot Héroard did not forget his old friends. An important rôle was played by the Huguenot Jean Béguin who, having begun as a Paracelsian enthusiast, quickly moved over into a more critical position. Béguin was probably the teacher, and Héroard was certainly the patron, of Gui de la Brosse, the founder of the Jardin des Plantes.[30] He too was probably a convert from Huguenotism. The Jardin des Plantes was to become the centre of chemical teaching in France; but it was not pure Paracelsianism that was taught: Gui de la Brosse was an admirer of la Rivière and was careful to distinguish himself from most other Paracelsians. He also, being a prudent man, insisted that Paracelsian doctrines, properly interpreted, were in no way inconsistent with those of 'our Mother, the Holy Church'. Others were less prudent, and in the 1630s the tension would once again become acute; for by then Richelieu (an old patient of Mayerne) was in power and, having destroyed the Huguenots as a separate force in the state and the Catholic *dévots* as a party round the throne, felt no need to compromise. Resuming the old anti-Habsburg policy of Henri IV, he relied, as Henri IV himself had done, on Huguenot agents in foreign Protestant courts and on Huguenot economic advisers at home; and, as if by a necessary consequence, he turned to Huguenot and Paracelsian doctors. He tried to lure Mayerne back to Paris,[31] and he patronized the maverick Paracelsian physician and 'gazeteer' – another Huguenot protégé of Héroard – Théophraste Renaudot.

What a battle was then joined! As we follow its course, vividly documented in the brilliant, acrid letters of Gui Patin, we feel that we are back in 1602–5. Only the persons have changed; for although Mayerne and Riolan are both still there, one in London, one in Paris, they are spectators rather than actors: they have left the action to younger men. On one side, Renaudot himself, Huguenot, Paracelsian doctor of Montpellier, is the heir of Mayerne; on the other, Gui Patin, Gallican, Galenist, doctor of Paris, is the heir of Riolan. Once again, the Faculty prevailed. In spite of his great patron, Renaudot was not allowed to practise medicine in Paris; and when Richelieu tried to compensate him for his defeat by recommending the admission of his sons as members of the Faculty, that intransigent corporation stood firm even against the all-powerful minister. In 1643, when Richelieu died, Gui Patin could boast that although the cardinal had been the most powerful minister in a century, although he had made the earth tremble, had terrified the Pope, and had shaken the King of Spain, he had not been able to impose the two sons of 'the gazeteer' on 'our society'.

The war in Paris, which had broken out in 1602, lasted as long as the warriors. As late as 1651 it would break out again. In that year, when they were both distinguished old men, Jean Riolan, who was now the *doyen* of the Paris Faculty, but who, as his friend Gui Patin wrote, 'was never at ease unless he was biting somebody', would suddenly, gratuitously and spitefully republish the violent anathema in which the Faculty had described Mayerne, nearly half a century ago, as an ignorant drunken charlatan unfit to practise in the city of Paris: Mayerne who was now eighty years old and had for forty years been the most famous physician in England. But this was, by now, a belated echo, a voice from the past. The chemical war was now over in France, the name, and the cosmology, of Paracelsus forgotten in the new age of Louis XIV.

Such was the history of Paracelsianism in France. It is of particular interest because it shows how Paracelsianism in general, and chemical medicine in particular, were driven, during the Wars of Religion, into an alliance with Protestantism which was not inherently necessary, but which became constant. If we now turn to England, we find that the history was similar although the time-scale was different. There were no 'wars of religion' in late sixteenth-century England: instead there was a policy of consensus, an 'Elizabethan compromise'; but there was a revolution – 'the Puritan Revolution' – in the mid-seventeenth century; and within this different time-scale, we shall find, Paracelsianism ran a very similar course. During the years of compromise, Paracelsianism co-existed with Galenism; during the years of political and ideological conflict, the medical consensus would also crumble, and as in France Catholic Galenism had resisted Huguenot Paracelsianism, so in England Anglican Galenism would resist Puritan Paracelsianism – though it would be Paracelsianism, in the end, in a new form.

(4)

Paracelsian chemical medicine, as we have seen, had been brought into Elizabethan England from Germany by Thomas Muffet. When Muffet became a Fellow of the Royal College of Physicians, plans were made to publish a new official pharmacopoeia, including chemical medicines. But this project was suspended; the last years of Elizabeth coincided with a period of conservative reaction after the radicalism of the 1580s, and when Muffet died in 1604, nothing had been done. However, the 'Elizabethan compromise', in medicine as in religion, continued into the reign of James I; Paracelsian ideas still circulated at all levels and the Royal College remained liberal in its attitude towards them. All that was needed was a new impetus. In 1611, when Mayerne emigrated from France to England, that new impetus was given.

Mayerne knew that he would be well received in England, for he had been there before and had secretly and cautiously prepared his way. But when he arrived, the warmth of his welcome surprised him. For he was received with open arms not merely by the King, but by the medical establishment: the university faculties and the Royal College of Physicians. Thus encouraged, he set out to resume Muffet's work and bring it to a conclusion. He was the driving force behind the London Pharmacopoeia of 1618, the first such document after the Augsburg Pharmacopoeia of 1613 to be 'decidedly influenced by chemistry'.[32] Thus, in Walter Pagel's words, he made chemical remedies legitimate, 'doing much to bring a long and galling controversy to an end and justifying the life-work and struggle of Paracelsus'.[33] In other ways too Mayerne continued Muffet's work. He discovered Muffet's apothecary, one Darnell, and bought from him Muffet's manuscripts. Among them was Muffet's splendid work on insects, complete with its dedication to Queen Elizabeth. Mayerne prepared to publish the book, rededicating it to his patron King James. In his preface, he dwelt on his own welcome in England; how he had been received by the College of Physicians, not with envious frowns and sidelong glances, but with open friendliness. The side-kick at the Paris Faculty is obvious.

Mayerne was a Paracelsian, strongly under the influence of du

Chesne. He was involved with du Chesne and another Paracelsian alchemist – a Huguenot from Orleans called Guillaume de Trougny – in secret sessions and experiments to discover the philosopher's stone. They gave themselves private names – 'Hermes', 'Druid', etc. – which sufficiently indicated their Hermetic interests. They believed in the mysterious 'Elias Artista' who had apparently already appeared and revealed some of his secrets to Trougny. But Mayerne was also an eclectic like la Rivière: his Paracelsianism was compatible with a good deal of traditional practice. Much the same can be said of Sir William Paddy, another royal doctor of whose views we know little, since he published nothing, but who, though a high Anglican, was clearly a Paracelsian and a mystic. More extreme was Robert Fludd, mystic, cabalist, theosophist, the oracular philosopher of the Macrocosm and the Microcosm. Both Paddy and Fludd were accepted as Fellows of the Royal College of Physicians, which, under James I – himself a lover of unorthodox speculation – was an open, tolerant society.

However, in the next reign, the fashion changed, at least at court. In 1628–9, the Elizabethan compromise finally broke down. It broke down in politics: Charles I, having been defeated in war with France and Spain, and having had his bellyful of parliaments, decided on a new course. He renounced the politics of consensus, scrapped the disastrous Protestant foreign policy which he had inherited, and dispensed with Parliament. At the same time he ended the compromise in religion: the Protestant Archbishop Abbot was pushed aside and complete authority in the Church was given to the uncompromising William Laud. Plato now went out of fashion and Aristotle would be declared 'paramount' in the universities. And, as if by a necessary consequence, there was a shift in the medical philosophy favoured at court. Quietly but perceptibly, Charles I withdrew his personal favour from Mayerne.

This last change was tactfully concealed. Mayerne remained physician to Queen Henrietta Maria, who liked to have a French doctor with courtly manners. But Mayerne recognized the fact. He showed it when he came at last to publish Muffet's long-delayed book of insects. Since King James was dead, Mayerne now had to change the dedication again, but this time he did not dedicate it to royalty. He dedicated it instead to his medical friend, Sir William Paddy.[34]

Charles I did not like chemical doctors: their ideology was too Protestant for him. His favoured doctor was William Harvey, a far greater man than Mayerne – and also very different. Mayerne was a Neoplatonist, a Hermetist, a chemist. Harvey was an Aristotelean, who 'did not care for chymistry' and was 'wont to undervalue its professors'.

'Go to the fountain-head and read Aristotle, Cicero, Avicenna', Harvey advised his young friends – no nonsense about Plato and Hermes – and as for 'the neoteriques', that is the Paracelsians, he irreverently called them 'shit-breeches'.[35] When civil war broke out, Harvey followed the King. He was with him at the battle of Edgehill, accompanied him to Oxford, was installed there as royalist Warden of Merton College. Mayerne remained in London, with the Parliament and his rich patients.

Thus Paracelsianism in England, as in France, was squeezed out of the establishment, and a philosopher might conclude that it had no future, for its work was now done. In the century since it had been thrust on the world, it had been received, opposed, criticized, discussed, tested. What was useful in it had been extracted, detached from the Neoplatonic *Weltanschauung* of its founder, and incorporated in traditional Galenist medicine, which had shown that it could not easily be destroyed. So was it not time now to dispose of that elaborate cosmology which had perhaps been necessary in the time of challenge but was now a mere encumbrance, preventing a rational fusion of the two systems? Such views – the views which we have seen advanced by Winther von Andernach, la Rivière, Libavius – were often expressed in the early years of the century, those years of general peace, in which so many schemes of ideological unity, or at least co-existence, were devised. Many books were then published on the compatibility of the Galenist and Paracelsian systems: that is, of course, of the details, presuming that large parts of the cosmology were shed. However, neither in religion nor in medicine was that unity achieved. There was life in the Paracelsian cosmology still, although it had been driven back to its original base, Germany – or rather, to that 'Holy Roman Empire of the German nation' which embraced not only Germany but the Netherlands and Bohemia. There it would retain its strength, its apparently inexhaustible dynamism. Thither we must now pursue it; for thence, in due course, it would return to England – in more critical times, in a more radical form.

In Germany, as we have seen, Paracelsianism, as a philosophical doctrine, had been pushed largely, though not exclusively, into Protestant courts and cities. Many princes had their own academies, their own chemical laboratories – not all of them disinterested, for chemistry included alchemy and alchemy promised the transmutation of base metals into gold. In Germany, as in France and England, there were those – like Libavius in Coburg and Daniel Sennert in Breslau – who sought to reconcile Paracelsianism with Galenism by separating it from its ideological base and purging it of its grosser incrustations. But here, as there, the true heirs of Paracelsus could not allow such a separation: to them Paracelsus was not merely the incidental discoverer of certain chemical cures, but the prophet of a total reformation – a 'chemical' reformation, in which the Paracelsians at all the courts of Europe would play a part. These men formed a Paracelsian international throughout Germany. They communicated with one another, moved from court to court. Their capital, while he reigned, was the capital of the Emperor Rudolf II at Prague; but in that fragmented polity there were many lesser centres in which they could flourish: at Stuttgart, at Marburg, at Wolfenbüttel, at the Calvinist academy of Herborn, and, above all, at the Calvinist court of the Elector Palatine at Heidelberg. In 1613 the Elector Palatine became the son-in-law of James I of England and thus a new link was forged between those two countries. It was in the Palatinate that Robert Fludd published his Paracelsian works on the 'Mosaic philosophy', the Macrocosm and the Microcosm.

The most famous of these international Paracelsians of the new century were Michael Sedziwoj, or Sendivogius, and Oswald Croll. Sendivogius was a Pole who claimed, in 1604, to have discovered the philosopher's stone and is credited with the idea, at least, of oxygen.[36] His main work, *Novum Lumen Chymicum*, would run through thirty editions and would be read and annotated by Isaac Newton. Croll came from Hesse and studied at Marburg, Heidelberg, Strasbourg and Geneva. Then he spent twenty years travelling in France, Italy, Germany, Hungary, Poland, Bohemia. He was the physician, and the secret political agent, of Christian of Anhalt, the most radical of German princes, himself a Paracelsian adept and the political adviser of the Elector Palatine, and, like so many other Paracelsians, alchemists and magicians, he haunted the court of the Emperor Rudolf at Prague. His great work, *Basilica Chymica*, was written at Prague and dedicated to Christian of Anhalt. In it he expressed his confidence not only in chemical medicine, but also in a revolution which, at any moment now, would overturn the ancient doctrines of the schools and introduce a new 'chemical' millennium: for 'Elias the Artist, who is to restore all things,' was now due to appear and reveal the hidden secrets of the universe.[37] Croll's book was published in 1609, the year of his death. At that time the Protestant Union was being organized from Heidelberg by Christian of Anhalt. Against it stood the Catholic League, dominated by Counter-Reformation Bavaria. Croll's secret mission in Bohemia was to secure the support of the great Protestant magnate, his patient Peter Vok of Rožmberk, for the Palatine cause. Peter Vok was also a

Paracelsian, a great collector of Paracelsian manuscripts. Another Paracelsian physician, the French Huguenot Pierre Asselineau, the intimate friend of Paolo Sarpi, was operating in the same interest in Venice.[38] Europe was being polarized for ideological civil war.

In the next decade, with the deposition of the Emperor Rudolf, Paracelsianism lost its imperial patron. At the same time, German Protestantism, pushed to the defensive, became more radical. The two forces were thus driven together, and their millenarian aspirations found rhapsodical expression in elusive utopian societies. The most famous, but most elusive, of these societies was the 'Fraternity of the Rosy Cross', the Rosicrucians, whose origins are in the sixteenth century,[39] whose symbolism appears in Heidelberg in 1600,[40] and whose manifestos, published in 1614–16, aroused the curiosity and the speculation of Europe. The society was professedly Paracelsian: according to its blueprints, its founder was one Christian Rosenkreutz in whose tomb, the temple of his disciples, there were preserved, next to his own writings, the books of Paracelsus.[41] All the Rosicrucian manifestos were impregnated with Paracelsian ideas. Indeed, without Paracelsus the whole Rosicrucian idea – the form of its message and the extraordinary echo of that little voice – is unintelligible. The last of the manifestos to be published, though probably the first to be written – it was evidently written in 1604 – was an allegorical romance entitled 'the Chemical Wedding of Christian Rosenkreutz'. The author was Johann Valentin Andreae, a disciple of the Paracelsian Valentin Weigel, and he wrote it in Württemberg, the most exposed bastion of Protestantism in South Germany; but the allegory appears to be sited in the castle of the Elector Palatine at Heidelberg.[42]

Prague and Heidelberg, the memory of Rudolf II lingering in his abandoned capital, and the ambitions of the Elector Palatine, driven on by his adviser Christian of Anhalt with his Paracelsian ideas of a mysterious 'chemical revolution' – all converged in the second decade of the seventeenth century. They converged intellectually in the strange personality of Count Michael Maier, the ennobled alchemist of Rudolf II who, in 1617, hurried from England to Bohemia, and dedicated his works to Christian of Anhalt and the Brotherhood of the Rosy Cross; and they converged politically in the adventure which began two years later, when the Elector accepted, from the Protestant nobility, the crown of Bohemia. At that moment the revolutionary Paracelsian Protestants throughout Germany believed that their millennium had come: the prophecies of Daniel and Revelation, of Joachim of Flora and Paracelsus, were about to be fulfilled; 'Christian Rosenkreutz' was speaking from the grave; 'Elias Artista' was about to return – if he had not already returned – to re-activate the great laboratory of the world;* and the rash usurpation of a foreign throne was hailed not merely as a politic coup which would transform the balance of power in Europe, but as the inauguration of a new 'chemical' golden age.

The golden age did not last long. In November 1620, in the Battle of the White Mountain, the millenarian dream was shattered. On that one day, when the 'Winter King' was driven from his usurped throne, a whole era came to an end. Within a few years, Bohemian independence had been lost for three centuries; Bohemian Protestantism, the most ancient in Europe, had been totally destroyed; and the vision of an immediate 'chemical revolution' in Europe had dissolved. With Prague conquered, Heidelberg sacked, and the French Huguenots totally crushed, the prophets of the Paracelsian revolution had no firm base left. They would be scattered over Europe: a Europe now convulsed by the long, untidy struggle of the Thirty Years War.

Among those exiles was one of the most famous figures in the intellectual history of Bohemia. Jan Amos Comenius had studied at Herborn under the millenarian encyclopaedist J. H. Alsted, and then at Heidelberg, before returning to his native Bohemia. A few years later the revolt broke out. By that time he had become a Neoplatonist, an admirer of Andreae and the Rosicrucian ideal, a believer in the Paracelsian reformation and the coming of the chemical Elias. After the collapse of the revolt, he fled, with his little community of the Bohemian Brethren, and took refuge on the estate of the Protestant magnate Karel

---

* Expectation of the coming of 'Elias Artista', promised by Paracelsus and, after him, by Alexander von Suchten and 'Basil Valentine', was intensified after 1604, the year of the 'New Star', which was supposed by the faithful to be a new Star of Bethlehem declaring the birth of the new Messiah. Raphael Eglinus, an alchemist of Marburg, in his *Disquisitio de Helia Artista* (1606), Benedictus Figulus in his *Rosarium Novum Olympicum* (1608) and Oswald Croll in his *Basilica Chymica* (1609) all announced the coming of Elias, and the Rosicrucian movement exploited the mood of the time, suggesting that the invisible fraternity was 'a corporate Elias' (A. E. Waite, *The Brotherhood of the Rosy Cross*, 1924, pp. 57, 241–2, 252–3). Thus the revolutionary events of 1618–21 took place in a context of expectation. It was in 1622, in the Protestant town of Sedan in which he had taken refuge, that Guillaume de Trougny (see above, p. 179) communicated to Mayerne the important alchemical secrets recently revealed to him by 'Elias Artista'. Robert Burton, in his *Anatomy of Melancholy* (Everyman edition, I, 118), was more sceptical, both about the Rosicrucians and about 'Elias Artifex, their Theophrastian master, whom . . . some will have to be *the renewer of all arts and sciences*, reformer of the world, and now living'. But those who were young in Germany in 1618 continued to believe that Elias was their contemporary, and in 1660 the self-taught practical chemist J. R. Glauber, in his arrogance, like Comenius in his senility, identified himself with Elias (see Pagel, article cited in note 7 below, pp. 13–16).

Žerotín in Moravia. Then he moved on to other Protestant protectors in Silesia, in Poland, on the Baltic sea-coast. For the rest of his life, like Paracelsus himself, he would be a wanderer, seeking, among the dangers and discomforts of constant dislocation, to reunite philosophy, prophecy, natural science and alchemy in a millenarian, encyclopaedic 'Pansophia'. Comenius has too often been seen as a merely educational reformer, just as Paracelsus has too often been seen as a merely medical reformer. In fact they were both total philosophers, presenting, with different emphasis, a continuous, comprehensive, Neoplatonic ideology.[43]

The ups and downs of politics have their influence on fashions of thought. Just as the Bohemian adventure aroused the Paracelsians of Europe to a new pitch of enthusiasm, so the Bohemian catastrophe gave to their intellectual adversaries a new opportunity. Already in 1616, after the appearance of the first Rosicrucian pamphlets, the anti-Paracelsian chemists – those who sought to separate chemistry from ideology – had found their champion. He was Andreas Libavius – the same Libavius who, ten years before, had intervened so decisively in the 'chemical' controversy of Paris. Then he had come in to defend chemistry on its right-hand flank, against the reactionary Galenism of the Paris Faculty. Now he intervened from an opposite position, to defend it on the left against his old enemies, the Paracelsian fanatics who insisted on reuniting it with a radical ideology. This had always been his purpose; he had always been intemperate in pursuit of it; and now, in his old age, he was more intemperate than ever. Personal disappointment, growing religious bigotry, and fear of revolution all sharpened the pen of this conservative Lutheran pundit against the 'madness', the 'atheism', the 'abominable impiety' of Paracelsus, of Croll, and now of these new Rosicrucians, 'the offspring of Paracelsian fantasy'.* All this was before the Bohemian adventure, which Libavius did not live to see. After the failure of that adventure the counter-attack gathered strength. In 1623 the appearance of mysterious Rosicrucian placards caused a sensation in Paris. In the same year, the Minim friar Marin Mersenne, with his massive work, *Quaestiones Celeberrimae in Genesim*, struck at all the heirs of Renaissance Platonism: the Her-

---

* Libavius had hoped to be appointed to the chair of chemistry at Marburg founded by Maurice the Learned, Landgrave of Hesse, in 1609; but it had been given to the Paracelsian Johann Hartmann. Hannaway (op.cit. pp. 93–4) suggests that Libavius saw 'an unholy alliance' of radical Calvinism and Hermetic Paracelsianism. The Landgrave had recently been converted from Lutheranism to Calvinism; Croll was a secret agent of the Calvinist leader; and the appearance of the Rosicrucian manifestos from the Lutheran centre of Tübingen may have been the last straw.

metists, the millenarians, the 'natural philosophers', the chemists; thereafter Gassendi, joining the fray, would fasten his teeth in the pretentious work of the supposed Rosicrucian, Dr Fludd; and, most formidable of all, Descartes would outline the beginnings of a new, rational system of revived scholastic philosophy.

By 1630, it might seem, Paracelsianism, as an ideology, had been destroyed. The conservative chemists, the eclectics who had detached chemistry from ideology and inserted it, in detail, into the Galenic system, were still there, eager to preserve their limited gains, but the millenarian chemical cosmology had been discredited everywhere. Condemned by the Counter-Reformation, squeezed out of Protestant England by the new conservatism of Charles I, and out of Gallican France by the victory of Catholic orthodoxy and the strength of the University of Paris, it had been ruined in Germany by association with a revolution that had failed. For a brief period, its utopian advocates pinned their hopes to Gustavus Adolphus, the Protestant saviour from Sweden; but with his death on the field of Lützen in 1632, those hopes were dashed. It might survive in petty German courts, or under Swedish protection in occupied Baltic towns, but as a revolutionary political movement it had no base left: it seemed at an end.

However, its vitality was not yet extinct. In 1640 a political change in England suddenly offered a new stage on which the last act of the long drama could be played out. The Bohemian and Palatine visionaries of 1619, scattered over Europe from Sweden to Transylvania, would turn their footsteps, or at least their eyes, towards England; and English enthusiasts, inspired by them, would come out of the cold into which they had been driven in the 1630s. In some ways, the English Puritan Revolution was the renewal of the Bohemian revolution of 1618–20. Indeed many of the actors in it were the same, or at least had learned their parts in the first act of the tragedy – not excluding the Palatine family itself, whose head, the heir of the unfortunate Winter King, would now come to England and hang, expectant to the last, around his beleaguered uncle's throne.

(5)

We have seen that, in England, Paracelsianism, in a modified form, had been accepted by the medical establishment. Apart from the eccentric Dr Fludd, most of those who professed it were critical men, eclectics in the tradition of Winther and la Rivière: they admitted chemical medicines and Paracelsian methods of surgery, but did not swallow the macrocosm and the microcosm or the Neoplatonic cosmology of the prophet. If they agreed with the conclusion of Paracelsus that experience and experiment were necessary, they did not accept the dogmatic premises upon which those conclusions were based. Rather, they would agree with their compatriot, Francis Bacon, whose philosophy, though adumbrated fifteen years earlier, began to be published systematically, in instalments, from 1620 onwards – i.e. at the same time as the general philosophical counter-attack against Neoplatonism. Bacon had no use for the metaphysical system of Paracelsus. He repudiated 'the ancient opinion that man was Microcosmus, an abstract or model of the world': an opinion (he wrote) which 'hath been fantastically strained by Paracelsus and the alchemists, as if there were to be found in man's body certain correspondences and parallels, which should have respect to all varieties of things, as stars, planets, minerals, which are extant in the great world'. Of alchemy, in general, he was very sceptical. Alchemists, he believed, might occasionally, 'by chance, not by design', make important chemical discoveries, and therefore he would not condemn their experiments, but their speculative philosophy seemed to him 'hardly sane'. Similarly he would commend Paracelsus the empiricist, guided by the 'light of Nature', but he despised Paracelsus the *magus* with his preposterous theories, which, he said, made man 'a pantomime'.[44]

In an earlier essay,[45] I have described how Bacon's plans for a 'Great Instauration' – a programme of scientific exploration, based on inductive philosophy and directed not only to the discovery of the secrets of Nature but also to 'the relief of man's estate' – was, in the 1630s, both puritanized and vulgarized. It was puritanized because it was excluded from the revived Aristotelean philosophy of the English court, and it was vulgarized because it was taken over by the continental, and particularly the German enthusiasts of 1618–20. These enthusiasts, as we have seen, were largely Paracelsians: Paracelsians on the run, seeking a new leader who might rehabilitate their discredited philosophy. Reading the works of Bacon, which were published in Latin at the time when they were reeling under the impact of the Bohemian catastrophe, they seized upon that part of them which supported their own aspirations and then, ignoring his repudiation of their metaphysical ideas, triumphantly claimed him as their own. So the name of Bacon was used to give authority to ideas some of which, indeed, he would have acknowledged, but many of which he had already explicitly repudiated. The confusion was neatly illustrated by Comenius, who, in a single breath, claimed Bacon and Campanella as the prophets of a new age. Bacon, in his writings, never mentioned Campanella, and it is difficult to see much community between their two utopias: Bacon's *New Atlantis* and Campanella's *City of the Sun*. But the very fact that Bacon wrote a utopia made him seem one of the party. For this was the age of utopias. When his Rosicrucian stunt had failed, J. V. Andreae continued to found secret societies and draft ideal commonwealths;* Andreae's friend Comenius, in his Moravian exile, wrote his *Labyrinth of the World* in imitation of him;† and in England Robert Burton, a more conservative Baconian, whose quiet life in Oxford was unruffled by the hurricane sweeping through Germany, followed the fashion, setting out, in his *Anatomy of Melancholy*, 'an utopia of mine own'.

In 1628, when the prospects of the Protestant cause on the Continent seemed blackest, the utopians of Central Europe turned their eyes to England. It was then that Samuel Hartlib fled from conquered Elbing to London and there built up his extraordinary position as the organizer and the oracle of an international movement which was at once Puritan, Baconian, messianic and, to a large extent, Paracelsian. Once again, it did not need to be Puritan, and in fact it had some Anglican patrons; but the new polarization of English politics which began precisely in that year made it effectively puritan, and it was gradually taken over by those who opposed the new, Laudian course. Hartlib, who became the agent in England of all the continental utopians, himself planned a model society which was to be realized either in England or in the English plantations across the Atlantic. He called it *Antilia*: a name which, as an ideal concept, would haunt him for the rest of his life.

During the 1630s, Hartlib's plans remained academic, although one experiment showed that they might be realized. In 1635, when Laudianism seemed all-triumphant in England, John Winthrop junior left it to found the colony of Saybrook for the 'Puritan' politicians, Lords Saye and Brooke. Winthrop was a Baconian and a Paracelsian, interested in improvement and practical chemistry, and he established successful ironworks in New England. Later, he would be joined by

---

* I refer to his *Reipublicae Christianopolitanae Descriptio*, 1619, and *Christiani amoris dextra porrecta*, 1620. In a letter to Comenius of 27 June 1642 Andreae claimed to have founded such a society, but that it was scattered by 'this conflagration which consumed all Germany' – i.e. the Thirty Years War.

† According to Červenka (op.cit.), Comenius' *Labyrinth* 'ist nichts anders als eine grossartige, poëtisch gefarbte, durch cusanischen Gedanken bereicherte Paraphrase von dessen [Andreaes] Traktaten *Peregrini in patria errores* [1618] und *Civis christiani sive peregrini quondam errantis restitutio* [1619].'

Robert Child, a Baconian physician, and by George Starkey, a Paracelsian enthusiast and alchemist from Bermuda who would claim, like Sendivogius, to have discovered the Philosopher's Stone.* This venture can therefore be seen as a Paracelsian project achieved; but it was not *Antilia*: it gave no relief to the exiled German enthusiasts who drove, even in England, the Paracelsian machine.

Then, in 1640, came the great change. Charles I's system of 'personal government' foundered; Parliament was recalled; and all the forces which had been driven together in opposition pressed home their attack. They also announced their alternative form of society – their utopia, as it turned out to be. There was to be a return to the old Elizabethan consensus, a continuation of Elizabethan policy, a reform of Church and Society, beginning again where the Elizabethans had drawn back, or left off.

To the Central European enthusiasts this was the great opportunity. Their investment, it seemed, was about to pay off. John Pym was the man of the hour, and beside him, as his intimate friend and adviser, stood their indefatigable agent and organizer, Samuel Hartlib. In 1641 Hartlib published a new utopia, a revised version of *Antilia*, now called *Macaria*.[46] In that year, as in 1619–20, his followers believed that the new age – a combination of Bacon's Great Instauration and the Millennium – was in sight; and although it soon became clear that victory would not be won without a battle, at least this time there was no Battle of the White Mountain. The Parliamentary armies survived their first defeats and would continue the struggle to ultimate victory. Throughout the long years of civil war Hartlib never lost hope. He organized his forces to realize his dream. The model for his organization – his 'Office of Addresses' – was provided by the French Paracelsian who at that time was causing such trouble to the medical establishment of Paris, the Huguenot 'gazeteer' Theophraste Renaudot.

So far, the millenarian-Baconian movement is not specifically Paracelsian. Although it drew on Paracelsian ideology – including the concept of 'Elias Artista'† – it lacked a professional medical

---

* On Winthrop as a Paracelsian see R. S. Wilkinson, 'The Alchemical Library of John Winthrop, jr.', *Ambix*, II (1963). Starkey wrote some of his work under the pseudonym Eirenaeus Philoponus Philalethes, whom he presented as a distinct person. E. I. Carlyle, the author of the article on Starkey in *D.N.B.*, accepts this distinction; but see Charles Webster, *The Great Instauration* (1975), p. 305.

† Thus George Hakewill, in the third edition of his *Apologie or Declaration of the Power and Providence of God* (1635), wrote that 'Either Elias himself, or some other great heroical spirit . . . is yet to be sent for the accomplishing of this great business in restoring of all things' (cit. Webster, op.cit. 20).

content. But in the course of the revolution it acquired that content. In England, as previously in France, the civil war was carried into the medical world. The pattern of the struggle, too, was the same: 'Paracelsian' surgeons and apothecaries launched an attack on the 'monopoly' of the 'Galenist' medical establishment.

The Puritan party, from the very beginning of the revolution, had been inspired by a hatred of monopolies. It had attacked monopolies in manufacture, trade, law, religion, education. It also discovered a monopoly in medicine: the monopoly of the medical faculties and of the Royal College of Physicians. In fact, as we have seen, the College had not been illiberal, either in its outlook or in its practice. It had admitted chemical, even Hermetic physicians to its Fellowship and chemical remedies to its pharmacopoeia. It had supported the incorporation of the Society of Apothecaries. In politics it had been cautious and non-committal. But however liberal in practice, it remained a legally defined monopoly, a privileged institution, a self-protecting élite. Moreover, by now it could be regarded as out-of-date. The population of London had more than doubled since the last years of Elizabeth, but the size of the College remained the same – thirty Fellows. The number of physicians whom it licensed to practise in the capital also remained constant – twenty-five each decade; and these physicians remained essentially the physicians of the rich: they had no responsibility for the rapidly expanding population of the poor, who relied on apothecaries and surgeons, sometimes reputable, sometimes quacks. As the revolution gathered force, and one monopoly after another was battered down, the cry was raised against this medical monopoly; and once again it was raised in ideological language: the physicians were attacked as Aristoteleans, Galenists, the guardians and the products of a false, reactionary, 'heathen' system of education; and their attackers called for a new, democratic system of public health inspired by Hermetic 'natural magic', Paracelsian alchemy, chemical remedies.[47]

The attack began in earnest with the defeat of Charles I in 1646. It reached its climax in 1653, that truly revolutionary year in which the messianic 'Fifth-monarchy men', the Anabaptists, the 'Parliament of Saints', sought to take over the government of England. In those years Paracelsian translations and radical pamphlets poured from the presses, 'a constant stream of German Hermeticists' debouched into England to be received and regulated by Samuel Hartlib,[48] and English Paracelsians, partly inspired by them, demanded a complete revolution, not only in medicine and philosophy but in the entire educational system behind it.

One of the immigrant Germans was Frederick Clodius who became Hartlib's son-in-law. He set up a laboratory in his kitchen and planned to form a 'Chemical Council' which was to discover 'the great medicinal *arcana*'. Many others followed him, and introduced (as Charles Webster writes) 'diverse, bizarre and egoistical influences' into English Hermeticism, claiming to have discovered the *liquor Alkahest*, 'the *arcanum* of the celestial liquor', the universal tincture, the Philosopher's Stone. Under the influence of Clodius, Hartlib published a collection of *Chymical, Medicinal and Chyrurgical Addresses* by various hands; the works of Sendivogius and Croll, and many lesser Paracelsians, were translated and published; and plans were laid to set up a rival College of Medicine in London. Among the English enthusiasts, the most vocal were two men who demanded a complete revolution in the intellectual and academic world. These were Noah Biggs who, in 1651, like Andreae before 1618, looked forward to a 'reformation of the universities and the whole landscape of physic', so that 'the *terra incognita* of Chymistrie' might at last be discovered,[49] and John Webster who, in the revolutionary year 1653, imagined that the time for such a revolution had now actually come.

Webster was a learned and dogmatic autodidact, who had picked up some chemical knowledge from John Hunyadi, or Huniades, an Hungarian alchemist settled in England since the reign of James I.[50] During the civil war he had served as a surgeon and chaplain in the Parliamentary army and had been rewarded with a vicarage in Yorkshire. He now put himself forward as a radical reformer of university education in England. His programme was not very coherent. A compulsive name-dropper, he uncritically sang the praises of all writers who, from whatever position, had attacked his *bêtes noires*, the 'Archsophister' Aristotle and the 'ignorant pagan' Galen. His highest praise was awarded to the prophets of 'that sublime and never sufficiently praised science of Pyrotechny or Chymistry' honoured in the past by Hermes Trismegistus and the medieval alchemists, and now revived by Basil Valentine, Isaac Holland, and 'that miracle of industry and pains, Theophrastus Paracelsus', with his 'most admirable and soul-ravishing knowledge of the three great hypostatical principles of Nature: salt, sulphur and mercury'. For good measure, he also awarded marks to Descartes, to the Catholic controversialist Thomas White, to 'the mysterious and divinely inspired Teutonick', Jacob Boehme, and to the 'highly illuminated fraternity of the Rosy Cross'. In Webster's reformed universities, science was to be based on 'the noble and almost divine science of Natural magic', and to be taught by the methods 'so judiciously laid down by our learned countryman the Lord Bacon' and in 'the elaborate writings of that profoundly learned man Dr Fludd, than which . . . the world never had a more rare, experimental and perfect piece'. On this it is enough to quote the comment of the true Baconians, Seth Ward and John Wilkins, that 'there are not two ways in the whole world more opposite than those of the Lord Verulam and Dr Fludd, the one founded upon experiment, the other upon mystical ideal reasons' – a comment equally applicable to all the 'vulgar Baconians' of that heady time.[51]

The great chemical revolution was not achieved in Puritan England any more than in the Bohemia of the Winter King. In December 1653 Oliver Cromwell turned out the Parliament of Saints and the messianic hopes of the enthusiasts were dashed. Under the increasingly conservative Protectorate the study of chemistry was not discouraged – indeed it was continued; but it was not continued on their terms. Once again it was gradually separated from the millenarian and revolutionary Neoplatonism to which it had owed its ideological force. It was continued as a specialized study within the structure of traditional society. The Royal College of Physicians, which had never opposed it on these terms, had already set up its own laboratory in 1648 and appointed its own chemist to defend it against its critics. Now it could resume its confidence. After 1660 it was joined by the new Royal Society, which looked back for its inspiration not to Fludd and Paracelsus, but, above all, to Bacon.

Indeed, by now Paracelsianism, as a total ideology, had reached its term. The English Puritan Revolution had provided it with its last opportunity. Perhaps it was already, by that time, moribund, and only jerked into a belated life by a combination of accidents. In this, as in other ways, the Puritan Revolution may be seen not as a progressive movement, but intellectually, at least, as the backlash of a dying world. For Paracelsianism was not chemistry. Although chemistry and chemical medicine were an important element in it, and would be its most lasting practical contribution, they did not supply its driving force. That force was total, ideological, potentially revolutionary. Chemistry was merely the deposit – one of the deposits – which would be left when that force had evaporated.

In its time, that force was perhaps necessary; for how else, we may ask, could the old philosophy have been broken up, its hold over science loosened? For centuries Aristotelean physics had been incorporated into Christian cosmology, and Galenic medicine, which rested on an Aristotelean base, had been institutionalized in the universities of

Christendom. In such circumstances it was not enough – it was not practical – merely to add chemical medicine to traditional medicine; to borrow the methods of the alchemists and lend them to the established physicians. The established physicians would not accept them on those terms. If they were to be accepted, the whole reigning philosophy had to be challenged, its structure loosened, its elements re-examined and perhaps replaced. This entailed a revolution not only in medicine but in science and religion: a revolution that could also, in certain circumstances, be transferred to politics.

In this essay we have witnessed the process and stages of that revolution. Intellectually, it was based on Neoplatonism, as revived by Ficino and Pico. Paracelsus – *génie barbare, mais génie quand même*, as Lucien Fèbvre described him – carried it into medicine, simultaneously infusing into it the same German mysticism which had given power to the parallel revolution of Luther. After him, successive physicians and philosophers had sought to detach parts of his ideology, to pick up, as it were, the cooling fragments cast out by that fiery volcanic eruption. But so long as the traditional world-picture remained firm, these efforts had little general effect. In the universities Galenism was positively reinforced. So its challengers fell back on the total Neoplatonic system, which resumed its radical form and appeal. By the early seventeenth century chemical philosophy was, once again, drawn back into ideology: an ideology which could indeed be purely mystical and quietist, but which also, as Libavius so clearly saw, could be, and in his time was, revolutionary.

When did that ideology lose its power? To give precise dates to major intellectual changes is impossible. Intellectual systems are not destroyed intellectually by mere disproof: they are tied to social structures which, if themselves healthy, are prompt to repair local damage and to re-fortify weakened positions. Even when they have been discovered to be socially irrelevant, they do not dissolve at once: they live on in the minds of those habituated to them and only perish when that generation has disappeared and a new generation, in different circumstances, proves immune to their appeal. Even then, their decomposing relics may linger on in corners and perhaps, in time, generate new heresies, as Platonism itself has been regenerated, out of its own *detritus*, again and again.

With these reservations we may say that the total Paracelsian ideology, together with the Neoplatonism of the Renaissance, which was its intellectual cement, crumbled in the 1620s, in the aftermath of its great bid for power in the country which had originally been, and had always remained, its home. It crumbled together with the Aristotelean cosmology which it had opposed and undermined, but over which it could not, by itself, prevail. If it did not then disintegrate altogether, but was able in the next generation, to insert itself into a new revolution, that was due in part, I suggest, to the continuity of persons. It was the generation of the 1620s which made the English revolution of the 1640s, and that generation was the last that can be called truly Paracelsian. For no new messianic or revolutionary Paracelsian writer appeared after 1620: the English ideologues of the 1640s and 1650s sustained themselves on translations of their German predecessors. Sendivogius and Croll and Boehme lived again, for a time, in revolutionary England – Sendivogius, said his translator, the English Paracelsian John French, was second only to the Bible as a source of knowledge of God and the world. All these were dead by 1640. Comenius indeed survived, and would hover distantly and ineffectively over the Puritan Revolution; but by 1650 he too was a spent force, a ghost from the past gibbering and squeaking among mad prophets in Transylvania. In his last years he would go further still and identify himself with Elias Artista, the apocalyptic alchemical renovator of the world.[52]

One man indeed, in these revolutionary years, gave a new look, and a new life, to the ideas of Paracelsus. This was the last and greatest of his disciples, but one also who, to a large extent, drained his teaching of its explosive content: Joan Baptista van Helmont.[53]

Van Helmont was a Belgian, of a Catholic landed and official family. He was born in 1579, at the beginning of a period which he would describe as 'the most calamitous for all Belgium', for it was the period in which his country was reconquered by Alexander Farnese and firmly subjected to the Spanish crown and the Counter-Reformation church. As a Belgian patriot, van Helmont detested Spanish rule, and he particularly hated the Jesuits who consecrated that rule, and by their complacent intellectual claims and their control of teaching, imposed their orthodoxy on all sciences. In revolt against this orthodoxy, van Helmont, who had studied medicine at Louvain, turned to the Book of Nature and found in Paracelsus an initial guide and interpreter. Like his Paracelsian contemporaries, he then travelled widely in search of knowledge and experience. The Europe in which he travelled in 1599–1605 was the Europe of Sendivogius and Croll, Andreae and Libavius, of the burning of Giordano Bruno, the Parisian controversies and the beginnings of Rosicrucianism. On his travels, van Helmont was wooed by the great patrons of the new philosophy – by the Emperor Rudolf and by Ernst von Wittelsbach, the Elector of Cologne who financed the great edition of Paracelsus – but he resisted their offers and returned to live on his estate at Vilvorde near Brussels. There he devoted himself to chemical research. This soon brought him into trouble. His Paracelsian views on the weapon-salve – a famous debate of the time – brought him into controversy with the Jesuits. Controversy led to suspicion of heresy; he suffered persecution and imprisonment; and for twenty years he was confined to his estate, where he practised medicine, carried out experiments, and wrote, but did not publish, his conclusions. We may note that the period of his persecution, the later 1620s and the 1630s, was the period of the general counter-attack – Catholic, Anglican, Lutheran, Cartesian – against Neoplatonic ideas. He died in 1644. Nearly all his works were first published after his death. The most important of them appeared in 1648, and some of them were translated into English in 1650 – the year after the execution of Charles I.

Van Helmont's English translator was Walter Charleton, a royalist. He had been one of the royal physicians. Now he was a somewhat controversial candidate for election to the College (the former Royal College) of Physicians: controversial because of his royalist past. His interest in van Helmont, it seems, was purely academic, or opportunist. But whatever his motives, he gave an opportunity to the English radicals, who seized upon van Helmont as a new supporter of 'the chemical revolution'. 'Helmontianism' now replaced 'Paracelsianism' in their vocabulary; Noah Biggs was (not unjustly) described by a less bigoted chemist as 'Helmont's parrot';[54] and for several years van Helmont became the patron saint of those London practitioners who continued to oppose the monopoly of the College – after 1660 once again the Royal College – of Physicians.[55] This appropriation of van Helmont by the radicals alarmed conservative physicians, and his English translator soon regretted his premature enthusiasm. So, like Libavius in the face of Croll, he beat a retreat. By 1655 he disowned van Helmont and declared himself a Cartesian.[56] Cartesianism, by now, was the approved defensive position for neo-conservatives seeking to stay and control any kind of radical mysticism.

To the English enthusiasts of the 1650s, van Helmont was indistinguishable from Paracelsus, whose own works had reached them only in vulgarized form.[57] But in fact there was a substantial difference, which van Helmont himself was careful to emphasize. Van Helmont did indeed accept many important ideas from Paracelsus – the vitalist philosophy of Nature, the individuality and spiritual origin of disease, the total repudiation of Galenic 'humours' – but he rejected altogether the metaphysical basis of Paracelsianism: astrology, the doctrine of signatures, the three 'principles' of sulphur, mercury and salt, and, above all, the central theory of the microcosm and the macrocosm, by which, as Pagel writes, 'the doctrines of Paracelsus stand and fall'.[58] This theory, which Bacon had rejected, had been accepted as fundamental by the true Paracelsians – Severinus, Fludd, the Rosicrucians, Sendivogius, Croll. Van Helmont discarded it completely, and, by so doing, removed from experimental chemical medicine, and indeed from chemistry itself, the motor which had driven it and integrated it into a radical ideology.

That integration, that ideology, had been the creation of Paracelsus himself. He had taken up the alchemy of the Middle Ages and amalgamated it with the German mysticism of the fifteenth century and the Neoplatonism of the Renaissance. By his radical, turbulent, charismatic personality he had created out of it a revolutionary force: revolutionary at first in medicine, then in philosophy, finally even in politics. In his challenge to the established world he was indeed 'the Luther of medicine' – with the difference that his message, unlike that of Luther, became more radical with the passage of time. How different was van Helmont, the sceptical, pessimist, 'internal émigré' of Vilvorde! When the last form of Paracelsian radicalism had been disintegrated in the Thirty Years War, he salvaged its scientific content and set it on a new, more modest (if equally metaphysical) base. The residue of Paracelsianism as a religious movement would now be taken over not by revolutionary Calvinism but by German pietism, and a new era of chemistry and medicine, freed from ideology, began.

(6)

When we look back on the Paracelsian movement, from its beginning in the career of Paracelsus to its disintegration in the mid-seventeenth century, we may well regard it – and it has often been regarded – as a purely medical or chemical movement. If we look from this end of its course, this is natural enough, for that was its ultimate contribution: the thin continuous stream which flowed on into our modern world after so much of the original river had evaporated or lost itself in the sand. But seen in its historical context, in that earlier stage of its course, when it was in full flow, it becomes a far greater, more comprehensive and more complex movement: a total philosophy, capable, like Lutheranism or Calvinism, of taking many forms and inspiring action, even revolution, on many levels. It could be popular or private, fundamentalist or sophisticated, messianic or scientific, radical or quietist. It was also capable of progressive change and specific medical discovery: opiates, mineral remedies, the process of digestion, van Helmont's 'gas'.

It was also essentially a German movement, one aspect of that extraordinary and still ill-documented German Renaissance whose true nature has been distorted by the overpowering figure of Luther: a Renaissance which drew not only on external influences, from Italy, but also, and perhaps more deeply, on native inspiration – on the philosophy of Cusanus and on the German mysticism of the fifteenth century. Paracelsus was produced by the same great German revival which produced not only Luther but Regiomontanus and Copernicus, Reuchlin and Agrippa, Dürer and Holbein, Schwenckfeld and Franck, the Swiss reformers and Erasmus.* Germany – the area of German culture – remained to the end the continuing source and strength of the movement. When it overflowed into other countries, it was still largely limited by its German character. It was exported from German universities by German émigrés or fetched thence by foreign visitors; and it was contained within the envelope of German Protestantism. In the Latin world, and in the area recovered by the Latin Counter-Reformation, it had very limited influence. In France it was transformed by La Rivière and Béguin; in Flanders van Helmont was persecuted. Even in the non-Latin world, outside Germany, it was accepted with a difference: it was purged of its revolutionary character, reduced to popular recipes, or converted – as by Severinus and Muffet – into more sophisticated forms. Only when the Puritan revolution had broken out did it assume its radical character in England – and that was thanks largely to an influx of defeated radical prophets from Germany; and then it soon declined into the propaganda of a local medical pressure-group. Outside Germany, it was critically disintegrated. Inside Germany, it retained its total character. There it had its popular support – the swarms of 'spagyrist' empirics who intoned the name of their prophet. There also it had its most violent enemies: Erastus, who pursued the vain, ignorant, deluded, 'grunting swine' Paracelsus through four successive books of tangled erudition; Libavius, who stood at the covert-side in Saxe-Coburg, to chop the monster as he emerged

---

* Erasmus, a Netherlander, regarded himself as a German, referring regularly to 'us Germans', 'our Germany' etc. Copernicus is claimed by the Poles, but he came of a German family in the German city of Thorn.

and rescue the pure Dame Chemistry from his stinking lair. And there, to the end, it remained not a mere science but a philosophical, even a religious movement, which transcended medicine and chemistry: the mystical movement which Paracelsus himself had inherited from the Platonic, Hellenistic, medieval past and which had been transmitted, through his non-medical disciples – Weigel, Andreae, Boehme, Comenius – in changing, dwindling form, to the German pietists and the forerunners of the German Enlightenment.

Sources

1. The indispensable sources on Paracelsus are the edition of his medical works by Karl Sudhoff (14 vols, Munich/Berlin, 1922–33) and of his religious works by K. Goldammer (Wiesbaden, 1955–). The secondary literature on him is enormous. Essential are the two books by Walter Pagel, viz: *Paracelsus* (Basel, 1958) and *Das Medizinische Weltbild des Paracelsus* (Wiesbaden, 1962) and for ideology, Goldammer, *Paracelsus, Natur und Offenbarung* (Hanover, 1953).
2. Bodenstein's account of his conversion is printed in Pagel, *Paracelsus*, pp. 126–7.
3. On Toxites see C. Schmidt, *Michael Schütz genannt Toxites, Leben eines Humanisten und Arztes* (Strasbourg, 1888).
4. See Pagel, *Paracelsus*, pp. 40–4; Alexandre Koyré, *Mystiques, Spirituels, Alchimistes* (Paris, 1955).
5. Malachi 4:5.
6. Matt. 2:14; 17:11–13.
7. See K. Goldammer, 'Paracelsische Eschatologie', in *Nova Acta Paracelsica*, VI (1952), 68–102; W. Pagel, 'The Paracelsian Elias Artista and the Alchemical Tradition', in *Medizinhistorisches Journal*, 16 (1981), 6–19.
8. *J. Bongarsii Epistolae ad Joach. Camerarium medicum* (Leiden, 1647), p. 437.
9. On Perna see the essay of A. Rotondò, 'Pietro Perna e la vita culturale e religiosa di Basilea 1570–80', in his *Studi e ricerche di storia ereticale italiana del '500* (Turin, 1974), 273–391.
10. Winther von Andernach, *De Medicina Veteri et Nova* (Basel, 1571), Praefatio; Ibid, 11, 24–30.
11. W. Pagel, *Joan Baptista van Helmont* (Cambridge, 1982), 139. Cf. Ibid., 48, 134.
12. Gui de la Brosse, *De la Nature, Vertu et Utilité des Plantes* (1628), pp. 288–9.
13. Francis Bacon, *Works* (ed. Spedding), I, 564; III, 533.
14. P. Severinus, *Idea Medicinae Philosophicae* (Basel, 1571), cap VII, p. 73.
15. On Alexander von Suchten see Wlodzimierz Hubicki, 'Alexander von Suchten', *Sudhoff's Archiv fur die Geschichte der Medizin*, xliv (1960), 64–76; also Hubicki's article on him in *Dictionary of Scientific Biography*. For his reference to the coming of Elias see his *De Secretis Antimonii* (Basel, 1575), cap. III.
16. On Muffet see Allen Debus, *The English Paracelsians* (1965), pp. 71–2; R. Blaser, 'Une rare temoignage de fidélité envers Paracelse à Bâle', in *Proc. XIX Congrès Internat. d'Histoire Medicale* (Basel, 1964); Manfred E. Welti, 'Englisch-baslerische Beziehungen Zur Zeit der Renaissance in Medizin . . .', in *Gesnerus*, XX (1963), 165–80.
17. On Zwinger and his relation with Paracelsianism see Johannes Karcher, *Theodor Zwinger und seine Zeitgenossen (Studien zur Geschichte der Wissenschaften in Basel*, III), Basel, 1956; and, especially, Carlos Gilly, 'Zwischen Erfahrung und Spekulation:

Theodor Zwinger und die religiöse und Kulturelle Krise seiner Zeit', in *Basler Zeitschrift für Geschichte und Altertumskunde*, Nos 77, 79 (1977, 1979).

18. Dee collected Paracelsian works 'with almost obsessive zeal'. See Charles Webster, 'Alchemical and Paracelsian medicine', in *Health, Medicine and Mortality in the 16th century* (ed. Charles Webster, Cambridge, 1979), pp. 321–2. Cf. John French, *John Dee* (1972), p. 52.

19. Gilly, op. cit. (1977), p. 117.

20. G. Naudé, *Apologie pour tous les grands personnages qui ont esté faussement soupçonnez de magie* (Paris, 1625), p. 394.

21. On Gohory and his group see E. T. Hamy, 'Un Precurseur de Guy de la Brosse . . .' in *Nouvelles Archives d'Histoire Naturelle* (4ᵉ serie, Vol. I, 1899); D. P. Walker, *Spiritual and Demonic Magic* (1958), pp. 96–106. The account of the meetings in Paris is given by Gohory himself (who wrote under the name of Leo Suavius) in his *Instruction sur l'Herbe Petum . . .* (Paris, 1572).

22. *Lettres de Gui Patin*, ed. J. H. Reveille-Pariset (Paris, 1846), II, 73 and 173.

23. Ibid. II, 210

24. The theses defended by Mayerne at Montpellier are in B.L. Add. MS. 20291/ 83–90.

25. B.L. Add. MS 20921/54.

26. W. Pagel, *Joan Baptista van Helmont*, p. 204.

27. On Libavius see O. Hannaway, *The Chemists and the Word* (Baltimore, 1975). The Paris dispute is described by W. P. D. Wightman, *Science and the Renaissance* (Edinburgh, 1962), II, 258ff.

28. The settlement of the dispute, in 1607, is recorded in the MS Register of the Faculty of Medicine (Paris, MSS Ecole de Medecine, X, 105).

29. *Memoires-Journaux de Pierre de l'Estoile*, ed. G. Brunet, 1875, ix, 390.

30. See Henry Guerlac, 'Guy de la Brosse and the French Paracelsians', in Allen G. Debus (ed.), *Science, Medicine and Society in the Renaissance* (New York, 1972), I, 177–99.

31. This is clear from a letter of Mayerne in B.L. Add. MS 20921/75.

32. Wolfgang Schneider, 'Chemistry and Iatrochemistry' in Debus (ed.), op.cit., I, 145–6.

33. W. Pagel, *New Light on William Harvey* (Basel, 1976), p. 60.

34. The history of the dedication can be seen in the successive title pages in the MS (B.L. MS Sloane 4014).

35. Aubrey, *Brief Lives*, William Harvey.

36. On this see Wlodzimierz Hubicki, 'Michael Sendivogius' theory, its origins and significance in the history of chemistry', *Actes du Xᵉᵐᵉ Congrès International D'Histoire des Sciences* (Ithaca, 1962), II, 829.

37. Croll's ideological Paracelsianism is expressed in his 'Praefatio Admonitoria' prefaced to his *Basilica Chymica*. It is translated in Henry Pinnell, *Philosophy Reformed . . .* (1657).

38. For Asselineau see *Dizionario Biografico degli Italiani*, s.v.

39. Rosicrucian symbolism appears in connexion with Paracelsus as early as 1567. See Pagel, *Paracelsus*, 235.

40. For Rosicrucian symbolism in Heidelberg in 1603–4 see Chr. v. Rommel, *Correspondance de Henri IV . . . avec Maurice le Savant, Landgrave de Hesse* (Paris, 1840), pp. 172–3, 178.

41. J. V. Andreae, *Fama Fraternitatis* (Stuttgart, 1973), pp. 20, 25–6.

42. Frances A. Yates, *The Rosicrucian Enlightenment* (1972), p. 67.

43. On Comenius' Paracelsianism see especially Jaromir Červenka, *Die Naturphilosophie des J. A. Comenius* (Prague, 1970).

44. Bacon's views on Paracelsus and chemistry are to be found in *The Advancement of*

Learning (Works, ed. Spedding, III, 366, 370), *Redargutio Philosophiarum* (Ibid, III, 575), *Cogitata et Visa* (III, 605), *de Augmentis* (I, 564). The intemperate attack on Paracelsus (and on almost all other philosophers) in *Temporis Partus Masculus* (III, 533) is untypical and is to be regarded as a rhetorical exercise.

45. 'Three Foreigners' in *Religion, The Reformation and Social Change* (1967). On the whole subject of Baconianism and the Puritan Revolution see now Charles Webster, *The Great Instauration* (1975).

46. Mr Webster has shown that the author of *Macaria* was Gabriel Plattes, but the inspiration behind it came from Hartlib. See his article, 'The authorship and significance of Macaria', *Past and Present*, No. 56 (1972).

47. For the Paracelsian attack on the Royal College of Physicians, see P. M. Rattansi, 'Paracelsus and the Puritan Revolution', in *Ambix*, X (1963); C. Webster, 'English Medical Reformers of the Puritan Revolution', *Ambix*, XIV (1967).

48. Webster, 'English Medical Reformers', p. 30; *Great Instauration*, pp. 301ff.

49. Noah Biggs, *Chymiatrophilos, Mataeotechnia medicinae praxeos*, 1651; cf. Debus, 'Paracelsian Medicine: Noah Biggs and the Problem of Medical Reform', in *Medicine in 17th Century England*, ed. A. Debus (Univ. California, 1974).

50. On Hunyadi, who became chemist to the Earl of Pembroke, see F. Sherwood Taylor and C. H. Josten, 'Johannes Banfi Hunyades', *Ambix*, V (1953), 44–52; G. Gömöri, 'New Light on János Bánfihunyadi's Life', Ibid., 24 (1970), 170.

51. John Webster, *Academiarum Examen* (1653), 70–77, 105; [John Wilkins and Seth Ward], *Vindiciae Academiarum* (1654), p. 240.

52. This was in his *Clamores Eliae*, a work left unfinished at his death. It has been published in *Veröffentlichungen der Comenius-Forschungsstelle im Institut für Pädagogik*, No. 8 (Bochum, 1977). See also Klaus Schaller, *Die Pädagogik der 'Mahnrufe des Elias'* (Ibid, No. 9) and Antonin Skarka's article in *Universita Karlova J. A. Komenskému 1670–1970* (Prague, 1970), pp. 60 ff, which has a summary in English.

53. On van Helmont see W. Pagel, *Joan Baptista van Helmont, Reformer of Medicine* (Cambridge, 1982).

54. W[illiam] J[ohnson], *Three Exact Pieces of . . . Phioravant* (1652).

55. P. M. Rattansi, 'The Helmontian-Galenist Controversy in Restoration England', *Ambix*, XII (1964), 1–23.

56. On Charleton's part in the affair see Lindsay Sharp, 'The Royal College of Physicians and Interregnum Politics', *Medical History*, 19 (1975), 107–28.

57. Charles Webster, 'Alchemical and Paracelsian Medicine', in Charles Webster (ed.), *Health, Medicine and Mortality in the 16th Century* (Cambridge, 1979).

58. Pagel, *Paracelsus*, p. 246.

10

The sieur de la Rivière

The sieur de la Rivière, *premier médecin* of Henri IV from 1594 to 1605, is mentioned by several contemporary writers, but not with much detail or even by an exact name. The historian Jacques-Auguste de Thou, who mentions him as one of the doctors consulted in the famous case of Marthe Brossier, the pretended demoniac, in 1599, calls him 'N. Riverius', which in the eighteenth-century French translation of de Thou's work appears as Nicolas de Rivière.[1] On the other hand, Theodore de Mayerne, who knew him well, refers to him as 'D. Ian. Riverius' ('Ian.' being presumably a misprint for 'Joan.').[2] Sully, Agrippa d'Aubigné, Pierre de l'Estoile and other writers of his time simply refer to him as Rivière, de la Rivière or, in Latin, Riverius or Riparius. These writers do not tell us much about him. More modern writers have added darkness rather than light by confusing such little identity as he has with that of another and very different doctor who happened to assume the same territorial title. The purpose of this essay is to rescue the *premier médecin* from this confusion and provide, for the first time, some account of his true character and significance.

First let us see him, as far as possible, through the eyes of his contemporaries. What they tell us can be stated very briefly. They inform us that he was a Huguenot and a Paracelsian, though not, apparently, a bigot either in religious or in medical doctrine; and that he was greatly valued by Henri IV, who genuinely lamented his death. Sully, a fellow Huguenot, though not himself the most religious of men, says that la Rivière had not much religion, but inclined more to Protestantism than to Catholicism; he adds that he was good at casting nativities, and quotes, as a particular example of his skill, his horoscope of the infant Louis XIII.[3] Agrippa d'Aubigné is more explicit. Writing somewhat satirically, in the name of the apostate Huguenot grandee Nicolas Harlay de Sancy, he describes la Rivière (who was de Sancy's doctor) as 'bon Galéniste et très-bon Paracelsiste. Il dit que la doctrine de Galien est honorable et non méprisable pour la pathologie et profitable pour les boutiques. L'autre, pourvu que ce soit de vrais préceptes de Paracelse, est bonne à suivre pour la vérité, pour la subtilité, pour l'épargne, en somme pour la thérapeutique. Partant il fait de son âme comme de son corps: étant romain pour le profit et huguenot pour la guérison de son âme.'[4] This somewhat sardonic view is confirmed by d'Aubigné's own letters to la Rivière, to which we shall refer later: there d'Aubigné implicitly though politely reproves the physician for indifference in religion, disbelief in witchcraft and demoniac possession, and a general scepticism about the supernatural. La Rivière's orthodox medical colleagues evidently looked upon him with distrust. Some of them even regarded him as little better than a quack.[5]

These views must be respected. On the other hand we must remember that the reign of Henri IV was a period of fierce doctrinal controversy, in matters of medicine as in matters of religion, and la Rivière was clearly the representative, indeed the leader, of a party. This party was the party of the 'chemical doctors' who were violently attacked by the established Galenists of the University of Paris. The two best-known members of this party, and those who, by their writings, became most deeply involved in controversy with the medical establishment, were Joseph du Chesne, who wrote in Latin under the name of Quercetanus, and Theodore de Mayerne, who afterwards became famous as court-doctor of James I and Charles I of England. Both du Chesne and Mayerne were *médecins ordinaires* of Henri IV under la Rivière; both, like him, were Huguenots and 'iatrochemists'; both worked in partnership with him in private practice. Both acknowledged la Rivière as their patron. Mayerne sang his praises as the greatest doctor of the time, 'whatever the dirty crowd of ignorant men may mouth against him' (*quicquid obganniat imperitorum coenosa turba*). Du Chesne dedicated to him his treatise on the gout and the stone, and tells us incidentally something about la Rivière's travels: how, 'not content with vulgar medicine', he travelled in Germany under the auspices of the duc de Bouillon and was greatly admired by that 'star of French genius', Philippe Canaye de Fresne, who was then acting as French ambassador in Germany.[6]

Such is the sum, as far as I know, of contemporary published evidence concerning the *premier médecin*. But later writers, thanks to a plausible speculation, have added considerably to it. For the last two centuries every writer who has sought to give any account of la Rivière has assumed without question that he was identical with Roch le Baillif, sieur de la Rivière, generally characterized as 'le fameux empirique'.

Prima facie, this identification seems probable enough. Roch le Baillif, like the *premier médecin*, was a Huguenot and a Paracelsian. Like him, he fell foul of the orthodox Galenist establishment of Paris: indeed, in 1578–9 he was chased out of Paris by it. Like him, he nevertheless penetrated court circles, and could describe himself, from 1579 to 1592, as *médecin ordinaire du roi*. Like him, he was suspected of inconstancy in religion. Moreover, the careers of the two men seem neatly to fit into a common frame. By 1592 Roch le Baillif, sieur de la Rivière, had published several works of somewhat crude Paracelsian propaganda. Thereafter we lose trace of that name, but in 1594 we pick up the trail of a Paracelsian Huguenot sieur de la Rivière who in that year is appointed *premier médecin du roi*. Such a happy coincidence of name, time and character seems irresistible, and it is natural to suppose that the persecuted Huguenot Paracelsian *médecin ordinaire* of 1579–92 is the humble caterpillar of which the established, but still unpopular, Huguenot Paracelsian *premier médecin* of 1594–1605 is the airborne butterfly. Admittedly, after 1592, the name of Roch le Baillif is heard no more, but the territorial title 'sieur de la Rivière' provides the continuity.

The assumption is certainly plausible. However, I am now persuaded that it is false, and that two quite distinct persons have been confused under one name, with consequent injustice to the reputation of the *premier médecin*. I was first driven to this conclusion by the evidence of the letters and papers of the *premier médecin* which his disciple Theodore de Mayerne brought with him to England in 1611 and which are now incorporated in Mayerne's papers in the Sloane manuscripts in the British Museum.[7] A reading of these papers has caused me to reexamine the evidence on which the identity of the *médecin ordinaire* and the *premier médecin* has been assumed, and I have found this evidence inadequate. Further study of the positive evidence has convinced me that the conclusion is anyway untenable: that Roch le Baillif and the *premier médecin* are distinct and incompatible persons. I had already reached this conclusion when the archivist at Rennes, whom I had consulted on the subject of Roch le Baillif, drew my attention to the thesis of Emmanuel Philipot on the Breton writer Noël du Fail.[8] Reading this work, I realized that Philipot, starting from a different position, had come to the same conclusion. He had shown that Roch le Baillif could hardly have become the *premier médecin*, just as I had convinced myself that the *premier médecin* could hardly have been Roch le Baillif. However, since Philipot's work seems unknown to the historians of medicine, I shall not take it for granted but will subsume his evidence in my own.

In order to disentangle the confusion, it is convenient to begin with the entanglement. The identification of Roch le Baillif with the *premier médecin* was first made, as far as I can discover, in 1693, by the Huguenot scholar Jacob le Duchat, in his commentary on Agrippa d'Aubigné's *Confession de Sancy*. Le Duchat there gives a note on the *premier médecin* la Rivière, 'que je suppose avoir été pareillement connu sous le nom de Roche le Bailly, seigneur de la Rivière'.[9] Le Duchat was a learned and accurate historical scholar, and his opinions carry weight; but since he admits that his identification is a mere supposition, it is clear that he knew of no concrete evidence to support it; nor have I been able to discover any such evidence in the material which has become available since his time. However, his admitted supposition was soon adopted by the scholars of the eighteenth century and became the unquestioned assumption of later writers.

The man who effected the change was the learned and prolific Jansenist writer the abbé Claude-Pierre Goujet. Goujet accepted the identification made by le Duchat and in 1735, in his Supplement to the *Grand Dictionnaire Historique* of Moréri, he added such details as he knew concerning the *premier médecin* to the existing account of Roch le Baillif. These details, like all the abbé's additions, were incorporated into the text of the next edition of the dictionary (1759). From this source all later works of reference repeated the confusion, and if new biographical details were discovered, whether of Roch le Baillif or of the *premier médecin*, they were immediately credited to the synthetic personality thus established. Thus Roch le Baillif, sieur de la Rivière, Huguenot and Paracelsian, born in Normandy, educated in Geneva, practising in Brittany, driven from Paris by the Faculty, brought back in triumph by the King, and dying there as *premier médecin* in 1605, appears in J.-F. Carrère's *Bibliothèque historique et critique de la médecine* (1776), in N. F. J. Eloy's *Dictionnaire historique de la médecine* (1778), in Michaud's *Biographie Générale* (1862), in the great Huguenot biographical dictionary, *La France Protestante* of the brothers Haag (1846–59), in Berger de Xivrey's *Lettres Missives de Henri IV* (1853), and in such bibliographical works as Edouard Frère's *Manuel du Bibliographe Normand* (1860) and Antoine de la Borderie's *Archives du Bibliophile Breton* (1885). Philipot's doubts, published in 1914, passed unnoticed, and the old identification, repeated from source to source and consecrated by such repetition, is included in the current third edition of August Hirsch's *Biographisches Lexikon der Hervorragenden Ärzten* (ed. E. Gurlt and N. Wernich, 1962). Thus all standard works of reference declare without hesitation (but also without evidence) that the *premier médecin* was the author of the works, and suffered the misfortunes, of the 'famous empiric' Roch le Baillif.

If we are to test so inveterate an hypothesis we must ignore all these later compilations, which assume its truth, and begin again from the unquestioned evidence. We must separate the evidence which demonstrably refers to Roch le Baillif from that which refers, no less demonstrably, to the *premier médecin*. Only when we have built up the personalities and biographies of the two persons on the basis of such exclusive material can we decide whether, in the end, they must remain distinct or can be merged in one individual. We shall begin with the earlier of the two persons, or of the two stages in the life of one person.

The life of Roch le Baillif, sieur de la Rivière, is documented by his own published works and by the records of his trial before the Parlement of Paris in 1579. To this printed evidence Emmanuel Philipot has added some further archival evidence, mainly from local sources. From these documents it emerges clearly that le Baillif was a native of Falaise in Normandy; that he claimed to have been awarded a doctorate by the local university of Caen (a claim which the doctors of Caen, when consulted by Madame de Rohan, denied); and that he was twice married. His first wife was Françoise Poret, presumably a relation of his apothecary in Paris, who bore that surname; his second was Julienne Riou, a Breton woman. The contract for the second marriage is dated 13 January 1573, before a Breton notary employed by the family of Rohan. It is thus clear that already, by this date, le Baillif was settled in Brittany as a dependent of that great Breton family.*

Le Baillif's first known patron was Henri de Rohan, Prince de Guemené, known as 'le Goutteux', who lived at the château de Blain. After Henri de Rohan's death in 1576, he was maintained by his younger brother Louis de Rohan, known as 'l'Aveugle', of whom he declared himself in 1578, 'très humble subject et vassal'. Le Baillif

---

* See the document concerning his marriage cited by Philipot, op. cit., p. 349. In 1579 le Baillif's critics declared to the Parlement of Paris that 'en toute la Bretagne . . . la Rivière n'en a pas peu guarir un seul en cinq ans', which implies that he had been practising in Brittany for at least five years.

treated Henri de Rohan for his gout; no doubt he also treated Louis for his blindness. He also treated a Madame de Rohan, and his enemies declared that he had caused the death, in childbirth, of another lady of the family. Perhaps it was on this last occasion that Madame de Rohan's suspicions were aroused and she wrote to the doctors of Caen to check le Baillif's claim to a doctorate. In 1577 he published an account of the antiquities and singularities of Brittany, which he dedicated to the nobility of Brittany. In this he gave particular prominence to the family of Rohan, which was descended (he said) from the learned astrologer Ruhan, the son of Armoreus, the founder of Brittany. Armoreus, in turn, was the son of Aeneas and carried the lineage of the Rohan family back before Abraham.[10] Le Baillif seems, at this time at least, to have been a Huguenot. His known friends were Huguenots; so were his printers; and the Rohan family were the leaders and protectors of Huguenotism in Brittany.*

He was also a committed, indeed a fanatical Paracelsist. His treatise on Brittany is Paracelsian in its emphasis on natural phenomena, mineral deposits, medicinal baths, etc. In 1578 he published his *Demosterion*, in which he claimed to reduce the science of Paracelsus into a series of 300 aphorisms. He there described himself as 'sectateur, à mon pouvoir, du divin Paracelse'. His enemies described him as 'le singe de Paracelse', which was not unfair, for his Paracelsianism is of a primitive, fundamentalist, even vulgar kind. They also said that he piqued himself, above all, on astrology; and this is compatible with the title of one of his works.[11] He also practised cheiromancy and other forms of divination, and described himself as a 'spagyrist', or Paracelsian alchemical physician, and 'edelphe', or Paracelsian seer.[12]

We do not know when, or where, or in what circumstances Roch le Baillif received the Paracelsian revelation. Paracelsianism was largely a Protestant heresy and most of the early French Paracelsians discovered it in Protestant countries – Germany or Switzerland – or through Protestant teachers who had studied there. Le Baillif himself cites Paracelsus' German admirers Winther von Andernach, Adam von Bodenstein, Gerard Dorn, Peter Hassereus. It is tempting to suppose that he must, at some time, have travelled abroad. However, we have no evidence of such travel, and possibly he received his ideas at second hand. If Roch le Baillif had studied abroad, he would probably

---

* He was evidently a close friend of the Huguenot Noël du Fail. His printers at Rennes, Julien du Clos and Pierre le Bret, were both Huguenots. In the course of his trial in 1579, frequent references were made to le Baillif's religious unorthodoxy, and the Dean of the Faculty described him as 'a Luther'.

have claimed a foreign doctorate rather than risk exposure by claiming one from the third-rate local college of Caen.* This fact alone suggests that his youth was spent in his native province. The statements – which even Philipot repeats – that he emigrated to Geneva with his father and studied there rest on no authority but seem to spring from confusion with the other la Rivière.

Some time before the end of 1577, le Baillif's relations with the Rohan family were interrupted by a violent episode. It seems that certain servants of M. de Rohan, 'esmeus d'une vengeance mal reglée', had plotted to kill him; that le Baillif turned the tables on them, denounced them to the officers of the law, and secured their execution; and that this episode was the cause, or at least the occasion, of his departure from Brittany to Paris and his attempt to practise medicine there. At all events, he now ceased to cite the Rohan family as his patrons and described himself as 'conseiller et médecin ordinaire' of the King and the duc de Mercoeur. The duc de Mercoeur was the leader of the Catholic party in Brittany and as such the natural rival and enemy of the family of Rohan. It seems, therefore, that le Baillif had found it necessary to change his allegiance. His appointment as *médecin ordinaire* to Henri III was no doubt titular and acquired for him by Mercoeur, who was brother-in-law to the King. However, even this protection did not secure him against a series of persecutions in Paris. He was accused of coining false money. He was thrown into prison. Finally his medical activities aroused the professional jealousy of the doctors of Paris.

It seems that the Medical Faculty of Paris, the guardian alike of orthodoxy and monopoly, was looking for an opportunity to strike a blow at this dangerous new heresy of Paracelsianism and that le Baillif presented himself as a convenient victim. On 17 June 1578 the first blow was struck: the Faculty forbade him to practise or lecture in Paris, not being a doctor of the university. Le Baillif ignored the ban and on 30 April 1579, at the instance of the Dean of the Faculty, who described him as 'this plague', he was haled before the Parlement of Paris. The trial was a notable show of strength. The university employed three well-known advocates, one of whom, Barnabé Brisson, *advocat du roi*, spoke so eloquently in defence of Hippocrates and ancient medicine that the Faculty, overcome by emotion, solemnly undertook to give him

---

* Cardinal du Perron wished to see the college of Caen, and indeed all medical colleges in France except Paris and Montpellier, suppressed, 'car elles ne servent que d'asyle à l'ignorance' (*Perroniana* (1740), p. 331).

and his family free, non-Paracelsian medical attention for three generations.[13] Le Baillif had an even more distinguished counsel, the famous lawyer-historian Etienne Pasquier, who had made his name defending the claims of the University against the Jesuits in 1564. Pasquier would long remember this 'case of the Paracelsists' which he had pleaded 'for three Thursdays, before a vast crowd of people':[14] it caused him to speak tolerantly of Paracelsianism afterwards, though he did not himself accept its claims. But all his forensic eloquence on behalf of le Baillif proved vain. On 2 June 1579 the Parlement issued an *arrêt* forbidding le Baillif to practise 'etiam inter volentes' and ordering him to leave the city under pain of corporal punishment. The Dean of the Faculty, Henri de Monanteuil, a man of large humanist learning and enlightened views, was so pleased with his achievement in ridding the city of this charlatan that he afterwards caused it to be recorded on his own tomb.[15]

Le Baillif now returned to Brittany and to the protection of his noble patrons there. By 1580 he was established at Rennes and was again describing himself as *médecin ordinaire* of the king and of the duc de Mercoeur. As such he published more works of vulgar Paracelsianism, dedicated to Mercoeur. In the political struggle in Brittany he was apparently an active supporter of Mercoeur. In May 1584, when the *bourgeois* of Rennes were preparing to welcome Mercoeur to their town, it was le Baillif whom they proposed to commission as their poet. No doubt it was through Mercoeur's patronage that he was appointed, in 1588, as medical adviser to the Parlement of Rennes. When war broke out between Henri III and the ultra-Catholic *Sainte Ligue*, the forces of the *Ligue* in Brittany were led by Mercoeur. Le Baillif thereupon supported his local aristocratic, not his distant royal patron. Whether he was still a Huguenot or not we do not know, but his behaviour was certainly that of a *Ligueur*. In the testimony given to the royal officers after the murder of the Guise brothers, in the spring and summer of 1589, we are told that le Baillif, being now very rich from his practice, fitted out his son, the sieur de St Martin, with 1000 *écus*, to command a company in the service of Mercoeur; and the young man, in command of forty or fifty men, horse and foot, with a trumpeter, ravaged the countryside, ransacked, pillaged and burnt the houses of the royalists, seized and sold their movable property, and held their persons to ransom.[16]

However, the father was evidently more circumspect than the son in his political loyalty. Though he frequented ultra-Catholic families, le Baillif did not over-expose himself, and when the tide turned we find him back in favour with the Huguenot party and his old patrons, the Rohan. In 1591, he dedicated a work to the new head of the family, the young Henri, vicomte de Rohan, as his 'très-humble et affectionné serviteur et vassal'.

Henri de Rohan was the nephew of Henri le Goutteux and Louis l'Aveugle and would become the great Huguenot leader of the next century. Le Baillif now claimed to have been saved by Rohan's authority from 'la dent vénéneuse des envieux'.[17] Since Henri de Rohan was only born in 1579 this can hardly refer to the Parisian prosecution of that year when le Baillif was anyway out of favour with the Rohan family and was protected by their rivals. Presumably, after the defeat of the *Ligue*, he felt in danger from the Huguenot revenge and sought refuge with the young Rohan's widowed mother. We may note that after 1589 le Baillif no longer appears as doctor of the duc de Mercoeur: he now signs his works as *conseiller et médecin ordinaire du roy et de la cour du Parlement de Bretagne*. The king was now Henri IV. The agility with which le Baillif switched from side to side in politics (and perhaps also in religion) is remarkable. The most favourable construction that we can put on it is that he was not, or not necessarily, a timeserver but could have been a *politique*. After all, even the greatest thinker of the *politiques*, Jean Bodin, had once been a Huguenot and became, for a time, a *Ligueur*. But Bodin was not able, like le Baillif, to reverse the somersault.

Roch le Baillif's last known work was published in 1592. It was dedicated to Henri IV. The dedication implies that he relies on the protection of the King. The book itself is a literary dialogue or symposium designed to show that Paracelsus, in his medical philosophy, had never departed from the teaching of Hippocrates.[18] This had always been le Baillif's thesis, although even his defenders had found it implausible.* In July of the same year, 1592, we find le Baillif, who is described as a physician of Rennes, employed by a Breton gentleman, Gilles Satin, sieur de la Teillaye, to make a steel or copper corset to correct the shoulder of his hunchbacked child.[19] That is the last glimpse that we have of Roch le Baillif, sieur de la Rivière, as distinct from his alleged reincarnation, the sieur de la Rivière, *premier médecin* of Henri IV.

---

* Le Baillif had already put forward this thesis in his *Demosterion* (1578). Etienne Pasquier, who defended him in court, and his cause in correspondence, could not swallow this part of his argument: to him the medical system of Paracelsus was 'de tout contraire en principes à celle d'Hippocrate et Galien' (*Lettres d'Etienne Pasquier*, II, 546).

From this account it is obvious that le Baillif was a man of limited horizons, both intellectual and local. Though he acquired powerful patrons and eloquent advertisers of his works, these works show very little medical knowledge as distinct from popular Paracelsian philosophy. As the eighteenth-century medical historian Eloy wrote of le Baillif's *Traité de l'homme et de son essentielle anatomie* (1580), 'on y trouve peu d'anatomie mais beaucoup de verbiage inintelligible'. His general education was also poor. No person of intellectual stature seems to have respected him. Noël de Fail, the Breton writer, who defended him in his difficulties and wrote a laudatory preface to his *Demosterion*, soon saw through his pretensions and dismissed him as a charlatan.[20] It is questionable whether he knew Latin. All his books were written in French (although the aphorisms of the *Demosterion* were presented in Latin too). His critics in the Faculty of Medicine in Paris declared that he knew no Latin and that he justified his admitted ignorance by saying 'que les maladies ne se guérissent ny en latin ny en grec: que c'est assez que la chose soit entendue et les remèdes cogneus'. Hippocrates and Galen, he said, wrote in Greek because it was their native tongue; for the same reason the 'Arabs' wrote in Arabic and he himself wrote in French. His critics would not accept this specious argument: to them Latin was by now the essential language of medicine, whose technicalities could not be discussed except with the aid of its specialized vocabulary. They therefore insisted on examining le Baillif in that language, and they took visible pleasure in recording the knots in which they tied him and the solecisms which he committed. Michel Marescot, a distinguished physician, afterwards one of Henri's IV's *médecins ordinaires* and, as such, a friend and colleague of the *premier médecin* la Rivière,* protested before the Parlement that he would gladly argue with a learned Paracelsian but that he could do nothing 'cum hoc homine plane ignaro'.

Indeed, the whole trial of Roch le Baillif seems to have been something of a disappointment to the Paris doctors. They had intended to strike a spectacular blow at the Paracelsian doctrines which, at that time, had newly invaded France. The solemnity of the occasion, the importance of the counsel employed on both sides, the lasting memories of the affair retained by Etienne Pasquier, all suggest this. But le Baillif could not sustain his part. As Emmanuel Philipot wrote, 'on avait préparé une grande machine de guerre contre le Paracelsisme et l'on fut

---

* See, for example, MS Sloane 2089, fo. 78 v. Marescot would succeed la Rivière as *premier médecin*, but died very soon after his appointment.

deçu de se trouver en presence d'un médecin surtout empirique dont le bagage doctrinal était assez léger'.[21]

Locally, le Baillif was equally limited. All such evidence as clearly refers to him indicates a career confined to Normandy and Brittany except for his brief and unsuccessful incursion into Paris in 1578–80. All his works, except during the year in Paris, were printed in Rennes. His known friends, his patients, his patrons, are all inhabitants of Normandy or Brittany. His writings also have a provincial quality. The Paracelsianism which they express is crude and repetitive and he seldom breaks out of his narrow repertoire of ritual phrases. As the Parisian doctors put it, le Baillif, 'a toute question proposée, tousjour chantoit l'une de ses trois chansons . . . à sçavoir, de ses trois principes, sel, soufre et mercure; de la séparation du pur et de l'impur; et du microcosme'. In short, he appears, on all the available evidence, to have been a monoglot provincial crank.

What happened to him after 1592? If we have no later record of his life, at least we have a record of his death. The register of burials in the parish of Saint Sauveur, Rennes, tells us that Roch le Baillif, sieur de la Rivière, was buried there on 8 January 1598. This fact alone would seem conclusive proof that he was not identical with the *premier médecin* of Henri IV. Attempts have been made to save the old theory by supposing that this entry refers to the burial of an otherwise unrecorded son of le Baillif. These attempts are not very plausible, and Emmanuel Philipot has effectively refuted them by discovering further documentary evidence of le Baillif's death at that time.* But Philipot thought it prudent to add that 'le probleme sera definitivement élucidé lorsqu'un chercheur aura pris la peine d'étudier la biographie du médecin de Henri IV, mort en 1605'. To him, therefore, we now turn.

The first question concerns his true name. Vincent Minutoli, the accurate Genevese scholar who, at the end of the seventeenth century, supplied information to Pierre Bayle, refers to him as 'M. Ribbit de la Rivière'[22] and it can be stated confidently that his original name was Jean Ribit: he normally signs his own letters, and is addressed by his correspondents, as Joannes Riverius, and at least on one occasion he signs as 'Jo. Ribittus'.[23] According to le Duchat – who on this occasion writes confidently, as one stating a fact, not merely a supposition – he was the son of one Jean Ribit who professed theology at Geneva. This

---

* Philipot, op. cit., 348–9. The document cited is an authorization signed on 25 January 1598 by Jacques le Baillif, son of Roch le Baillif, allowing his brother-in-law Olivier le Bel to deal with the inheritance of 'déffunt noble homme Roch le Baillif, sieur de la Rivière, son beau-père'.

statement has been denied by the brothers Haag, who say roundly that 'rien ne justifie cette assertion du savant critique'.[24] But the only ground which the brothers Haag give for rejecting the statement is that no professor of theology called Ribit is recorded at the University of Geneva. This ground is insufficient, for there was a well-known professor of theology called Jean Ribit at the academy of Lausanne, and clearly it was of him that le Duchat was thinking.

This Jean Ribit, the professor, was a Huguenot who had fled to Switzerland from Savoy. He had been born at Sales in the district of Faucigny, Savoy,* and had studied Greek at the collège de la Roche in Faucigny, under Hubert Louis, and afterwards at the University of Paris. In 1538 he was in Zurich, where he married Agnes Rosin of Zurich. In 1540 he succeeded his close friend Conrad Gesner as professor of Greek at Lausanne.[25] He published editions of Xenophon, Lucian and other Greek writers. In 1547, though primarily a Hellenist, he became professor of theology at Lausanne. Resigning in 1559, he became regent of the College of Geneva and then professor of biblical exegesis at Orléans, where he died in 1564.[26] There were other Ribits in Geneva at this time, no doubt of the same family. Helenus Ribit, who seems to have been a brother of Jean Ribit, practised there as a lawyer and Hippolyte Ribit worked as a goldsmith.[27] That Jean Ribit, the future *premier médecin*, came from this family of Savoyard Huguenots settled on Lake Leman is very probable, for he was born in or near Geneva and studied in Savoy, and we find him, in later life, revisiting Lausanne.† He was most probably, as le Duchat states, the son of Jean Ribit the Hellenist who, as we know from his letters, had a son called Jean.[28]

* N. Weiss, in *Biographie Universelle*, s.v. 'Ribit', denies that Ribit was a Savoyard: 'on ne sait sur quel fondement Fabricius, *Bibliotheca Graeca* [Hamburg 1717] t. VIII, 822, dit que Ribit était Savoisien: rien ne l'indique dans les titres et dans les préfaces de ses ouvrages...' In fact Ribit explicitly names himself as 'Joannes Ribittus, Sabaudus' in the table of contents of his Latin translation of Maximus, Theophilus and Tatian, *Sententiarum sive capitum theologorum... tomi tres* (Zurich, 1546).

† In MS Sloane 2089 there are several (imperfectly dated) letters between la Rivière and another doctor, Gerard Boyssonade, originally from Agen, who had studied medicine at Montpellier. In two letters, Boyssonade and Rivière regret their failure to meet in Lausanne. Rivière writes from Caumont, near Avignon. He explains that he was detained by attendance on his patron ('nam a Maecenatis latere ne latum quidem unguem discedam'). His patron was presumably the Huguenot grandee Jacques Nompar de Caumont, duc de la Force. Later we find Boyssonade established in Condom, in close and regular contact with la Rivière at Nérac. He then returned to Agen. He was known to Mayerne, who describes him as 'bonus medicus in maniacis et melancholicis' (MS Sloane 2129 fos. 109–113 v, 2080 fo. 25 v).

That Jean Ribit, the future *premier médecin*, was born in or near Geneva is clear from a letter sent to him long afterwards by Agrippa d'Aubigné.* This letter is undated, but it deals with the subject of demoniac possession: it may well have been occasioned by the case of Marthe Brossier in 1599. In it d'Aubigné reminds la Rivière of the case of 'la démoniaque de Cartigny, au pays de vostre naissance et de vos études de vous et de moy'. This demoniac had appeared in the village of Cartigny, near Geneva, and had created great excitement by answering questions in numerous languages. The professor of Hebrew at Geneva, Antoine Chevalier, had questioned her in Hebrew; three Orientals visiting the West and then in Geneva had been called in to converse with her in the eighteen different Eastern languages which they commanded, and d'Aubigné himself had put to her 'deux petites questions greques'. D'Aubigné remarks that he hardly needs to remind la Rivière of this episode since 'vous estiez lors à Genève et say bien que vous la visitiez'. This episode can be dated to the years 1565–7, when the young d'Aubigné was in Geneva and Antoine Chevalier was still professor of Hebrew there. The year of la Rivière's birth can be deduced from a letter which he wrote, on 20 June 1591, to Joachim Camerarius II, the famous Nuremberg physician and humanist, and in which he implies that he was then forty-five years old.[29] From these two documents we may therefore conclude that he was born in or about 1546, in or near Geneva. This fact alone effectively distinguishes him from Roch de Baillif, who clearly describes himself, on the title-page of his work on the antiquities of Brittany, as 'natif de Fallaize'.

The same letter of Agrippa d'Aubigné also shows that Jean Ribit had at least part of his education at Geneva. He is not recorded as a student of Calvin's Academy: probably he studied at the Collège de Genève of which his father was regent, and where Agrippa d'Aubigné also studied.† Under his father (assuming that Jean Ribit was his father), he

---

* *Oeuvres Complètes d'Agrippa d'Aubigné* ed. Reaume et Caussade (1873–1892), I., 423. Emmanuel Philipot, op. cit. p. 348, by an extraordinary misinterpretation (and misquotation) of this letter, uses it to argue that la Rivière, like Roch le Baillif, was born in Normandy, where there is apparently a village called Cartigny near Isigny. In fact the letter, with its explicit references to Geneva and Chevalier, is perfectly clear. Since Agrippa d'Aubigné was not Norman either, it is difficult to see how even Philipot's misquotation could lead to such a conclusion.

† The brothers Haag, *La France Protestante*, s.v. 'le Baillif', say of the synthetic la Rivière that he was 'né à Falaise mais élevé à Genève par son père, qui y avait cherché un asyle contre la persecution et qui y professait, dit-on, la théologie'. Jean Ribit is recognizable in all but the birthplace and Haag may have had authority for the education of Ribit by his father. If Ribit studied at the Collège de Genève, d'Aubigné's phrase 'de vos études de vous et de moy' becomes more definite.

would be sure of a good humanist education in 'philosophy', i.e. in Latin and Greek, and his letters show that he was fluent and elegant in both languages. Unlike Roch le Baillif, who wrote even his medical works in French, Jean Ribit wrote even his private letters to Frenchmen in Latin. Of his later education we know nothing except what he casually reveals in another letter to Camerarius, of 30 June 1591. Writing about the medical use of white antimony (*flores antimonii*), he there states that it was first so used 'in Turin twenty years ago, when I attended the lectures of Argenterius there'.[30] Argenterius – Giovanni Argenterio – was a native of Piedmont whom Emmanuel Philibert, Duke of Savoy, had lured back from Naples to be professor of medicine at his university at Mondovì, and then, from 1566 to 1571, when the university had been restored to Turin, at Turin. He was a humanist doctor, an advocate of novelty in medicine, and interested in chemical innovations.[31] From this evidence it is clear that Ribit studied medicine at Turin in or before 1571.

The connexion between Geneva and Turin is natural enough. Many Piedmontese had settled in Geneva, especially physicians and apothecaries: indeed, the medical profession in Geneva, at this time, was almost cornered by the Piedmontese.[32] But of course these Piedmontese immigrants were Protestants. Like Jean Ribit senior, they had fled from the dominions of the Duke of Savoy to avoid religious persecution. In these circumstances, it is a little odd that Jean Ribit junior should move in the opposite direction. Why, we may ask, did he not rather go, if he were to study medicine, to the Protestant University of Basel, one of the best medical schools in Europe, or to Zurich where Conrad Gesner himself, his father's closest friend, was professor? In this connexion we may notice a remark by le Duchat that the young Ribit was converted to Catholicism. Le Duchat gives no source for this statement, but it may well be true. If true, it would explain the somewhat censorious attitude of his old friend, the unyielding Calvinist Agrippa d'Aubigné. D'Aubigné did not approve of religious inconstancy. In any case, Ribit's conversion, if it took place, does not seem to have had a lasting effect. Perhaps, as le Duchat suggests, it was the effect of temporary worldly ambition. Perhaps it was only a brief phase, like the Catholicism through which Bayle and Gibbon would pass on their way to a mature scepticism.

Jean Ribit was at Turin in or before 1571. Of the next eighteen years of his life we know almost nothing. Only one document even refers to them. In a letter to Caspar Peucer, of 15 February 1591, Ribit states that, 'having laid the foundations of medical theory by attendance in the schools of France and Italy', he had travelled over 'almost all Europe' – except apparently Germany – in order to confirm theory by practice. The reason he gave for avoiding Germany in his travels is interesting. We shall come to it shortly. Where in fact he went we cannot even guess. Some of the most enterprising sixteenth-century doctors, like Ambroise Paré and Joseph du Chesne, attached themselves to warring armies and improved their art by practice in camps or military hospitals. Others found employment in the courts of princes. Doctors from the schools of Italy were employed in the courts of Poland and Hungary. Doctors from Piedmont seem to have been particularly energetic. Apart from the Piedmontese in Geneva, we know of one Piedmontese doctor Leonardo Botallo, or Botal, who made a very successful career in France as *médecin ordinaire* to Catherine de Médicis and her sons. He too began as an army doctor, specializing in gunshot wounds.[33] Another Piedmontese doctor, Giovanni Giorgio Biandrata, introduced medical and religious heresy into Calvinist Transylvania. Ribit's implied distinction between 'almost all Europe' on the one hand and France, Italy and Germany on the other suggests that his travels may have been in Eastern Europe. But this is mere speculation. We know nothing positive until the late 1580s, when we find Ribit equipped with the territorial title of sieur de la Rivière – presumably he had acquired a property of that name – and established in or close to the court of Henri de Navarre. In the early months of 1589 he was apparently in Genoa.* He then returned to the court of Navarre at Nérac. He was evidently patronized by Henri's only sister, Catherine de Navarre, afterwards Duchess of Lorraine and Bar and a stronger Protestant than her brother; for it was she who recommended him to the famous Huguenot nobleman, the stormy petrel of Huguenot politics, Henri de la Tour d'Auvergne, vicomte de Turenne, afterwards duc de Bouillon. Turenne had fought as a volunteer in the Netherlands, had spent eighteen months as a prisoner of the Duke of Parma, and now, on his return to freedom, had been shot in the buttock by an arquebus during a private affray on the river Garonne. He had suffered long and seriously from these and older injuries when he was told about la Rivière and called him in. On 1 October 1589, by his own account, la

---

* MS Sloane 2089 fos. 75 v-77. This is a letter from la Rivière to a Genoese physician Ottavio Boerio or Boere, dated 8 cal. Jun. 1591 (26 May 1591). Rivière there says that the tumults of France were reported to him as he was leaving Genoa for France and that these had prevented him from writing to Boerio earlier to thank him for his hospitality in Genoa. I presume that these 'tumults' were the dramatic events following the assassination of Henri III in August 1589.

Rivière arrived at Turenne's house at Mont-de-Marsan and was put in sole charge of his health.[34]

For the next five years, la Rivière was Turenne's physician. Late in 1590, when Turenne was sent by Henri IV, now King of France, on a special embassy to Queen Elizabeth, in order to seek English support against Spain and the Ligue, la Rivière accompanied him. He was evidently seriously ill in England – indeed, by his own account, nearly died there.[35] Early next year, Turenne went on from England to Germany in order to raise continental allies for Henri IV, and la Rivière accompanied him on this journey too. For him the journey had a double purpose: he went not only as Turenne's medical attendant but also, as his friend Joseph du Chesne tells us, to study chemical medicine in its native home.[36]

Turenne's travels in Germany are well documented. He sailed from Colchester to Flushing, travelled through the Netherlands, visited the courts of Dresden, Berlin, Heidelberg, Cassel, Württemberg, and the city of Frankfurt, and returned to France at the head of a German army in the autumn of 1591. In October 1591 he married, at Sedan, Charlotte, sister and heiress of Guillaume-Robert de la Marck, and thus became duc de Bouillon and prince of Sedan. La Rivière was certainly with him in Dresden and Frankfurt, for some of his letters were written from those cities. Turenne was accompanied, for much of his journey, by Queen Elizabeth's special ambassador, the Genoese émigré Sir Horatio Pallavicino, who had sailed with him from England.[37] Pallavicino also became a patient of la Rivière, who treated him, as he treated the resident French ambassador Philippe Canaye de Fresne, for gout. Pallavicino (like Canaye) evidently thought highly of la Rivière and obtained from him *consilia* or prescriptions for his old mother in Genoa.[38]

While in Dresden with Turenne, la Rivière wrote a very interesting letter which we have already quoted. This is the letter in which he described his earlier travels. The letter was addressed to Caspar Peucer, the humanist historian and reformer who was also physician first to August, Elector of Saxony, and then to Joachim Ernst, Prince of Anhalt. After describing his travels over 'almost all Europe', la Rivière admits that he had hitherto avoided Germany, a land (he allows) fertile of learned and religious men, and he attempts to explain this omission. He had been deterred, he says, by the swarms of 'spagyrists who proclaim Paracelsus as the leader of their sect'. These 'spagyrists', he explains, having first sprung up in Germany, have now invaded France too. They insinuate themselves into noble households, even into the royal court, offering quick and easy cures for all diseases, refusing rational discussion, and trumpeting their exaggerated claims with insolent rhetoric. La Rivière is careful to explain that he is not a bigot in the matter: he does not accept the arguments of the most famous critic of Paracelsus, Thomas Erastus of Heidelberg. He merely wishes to judge Paracelsian claims objectively. But this, he complains, is precisely what the Paracelsians themselves will not allow. They will not submit their method to objective tests. In fact, explains la Rivière, 'I have never yet met a Paracelsian who was a sound, learned man: everywhere I have found them garrulous impostors . . .' This long attack on the Paracelsian 'sectaries' almost reads like a description, by an enemy, of Roch le Baillif, *sectateur du divin Paracelse*, physician to the King and to the nobility of Brittany.

However, la Rivière makes it clear that if he attacks the Paracelsian fanatics, it is only in order to discover, if he can, the element of true science which may be contained in Paracelsianism. His experience of these quacks, he says, has forced him to ask certain questions. First, are the marvellous cures which are ascribed to Paracelsus true? Secondly, if true, are they accidental or scientific? Thirdly, among all the German disciples of Paracelsus is there any one who can rival his master? Finally, what is the considered opinion of the best German doctors about the whole tribe? After all, Paracelsus lived in Germany and wrote in German, and it was from Germany that his followers had spilled out over Europe, for like the Jesuits, they creep into every country, wherever money is to be made or found. . . . La Rivière is very anxious to be fair. He realizes that the active Paracelsians may be wrongly attacked by supercilious armchair physicians: 'in medical consultations those who are trained only in academic medicine often reject remedies which are proved valid by use, simply because they cannot rationally explain them'; and he gives as an example the famous weapon-salve: a bizarre concoction which, if applied to the weapon that inflicted the wound, cures the victim 'even if the patient and the medicine are many miles apart, as I have often witnessed . . .' To us, the illustration may not seem very cogent, but at least the general proposition is unexceptionable.

This objective, critical attitude towards Paracelsian medicine is further shown by another letter which la Rivière wrote almost at the same time. It is his letter of 30 June 1591 to Joachim Camerarius – the same letter in which he describes his attendance at the lectures of Argenterius in Turin. Here he discusses the chemical process whereby 'white antimony' was prepared for medical use. The method of Argenterius, he says, was by mere sublimation; but this left a poisonous residue. La Rivière had seen a second method used in France, for the cure of venereal disease. This, he said, was 'a secret remedy devised by an accomplished "dogmatic" [i.e. Galenist] physician of my acquaintance. . . . I have never used it, as I only follow safe courses, publicly known and tested.' The use of antimony in medicine was of course a badge of Paracelsianism, and all those who employed chemical remedies were accused by the orthodox of killing their patients with 'this demon of antimony'. La Rivière's caution, and his Baconian rejection of secret remedies, distinguishes him clearly from the more fundamentalist disciples of Paracelsus.

La Rivière presumably returned to France with Turenne in the autumn of 1591. He was still with Turenne (now duc de Bouillon) in 1594. Then, on the death of d'Ailleboust, the reigning *premier médecin*, Henri IV applied for his services and Bouillon released him to serve, for the next eleven years, as *premier médecin du roi*. [39] One of la Rivière's first acts, after his appointment, was to write to Joachim Camerarius in Nuremberg in order to learn from him the most up-to-date antidote to the poison upon which the King's baffled enemies were now relying to destroy him. We have the letter in which Camerarius replied. After congratulating la Rivière on his appointment, and expressing horror at the infamous designs of regicide, he offered some useful hints. There was the 'Saxon powder' which Camerarius himself had first communicated to his friends. It would work well in dry bodies like that of Henri IV. There was the liquid extract of gentian used by the late King of Sweden. But best of all was quince-juice mixed with orange. Other doctors believed in prophylactic gems, but these were not recommended by Camerarius.*

The character of Jean Ribit, sieur de la Rivière, which emerges from this admittedly scanty evidence is very different from that of his contemporary Roch le Baillif, sieur de la Rivière, and the confusion between them, based on little more than a very common territorial title, has injured the reputation of the *premier médecin*. In fact the characters and careers of the two men are quite incompatible. Their physical courses probably never crossed. One was born in Normandy, the other in Switzerland. One based his life in Brittany, the other in Navarre. The surviving writings of one are all in French, of the other in Latin. One was a provincial autodidact, the other an educated and travelled

---

* MS Sloane 2089 fo. 73 v. La Rivière also received details of the Saxon powder from Sigismund Kolreuter, physician to the Elector of Saxony (Bodl. Library, MS Rawlinson C. 512).

humanist. And in medicine, although both were Paracelsian, their Paracelsianism was very different. One was a bigot, a fundamentalist, the other a critical adherent of Paracelsianism.

Ribit de la Rivière was a Paracelsian indeed, but a Paracelsian of the second or third generation, who had rejected the mumbo-jumbo of the master and converted the original Paracelsian impulse into a critical interest in chemical remedies. Although he published nothing to be remembered by, even the few documents which survive show that he was a man of learning who moved among the intellectual élite of his time. He was a friend or correspondent of Agrippa d'Aubigné, Philippe Canaye de Fresne, Joachim Camerarius, Casper Peucer. It is unfortunate that Agrippa d'Aubigné, who was so careful to preserve the letters written by himself, did not keep those which he received, so that we do not know, at first hand, the views expressed by la Rivière in their 'disputes' about Nature and the supernatural; but it seems clear that la Rivière was a good deal more 'modern', in some ways, than his protesting correspondent. The severe d'Aubigné rebuked him for 'vos libertez et gayetez ordinaires', for his infection by the 'vanities of the court', and for his scepticism. He was particularly shocked by la Rivière's insistence that he had never seen anything supernatural in the case of demoniac possession. To correct such 'libertine' views, d'Aubigné sent him authentic and detailed narratives of possession, sorcery, witchcraft and magic, including a graphic account of a witches' sabbat at Pau in Navarre. D'Aubigné himself had attended the trial, together with the King and the Huguenot élite. The evidence had convinced them that the sabbat was real, had led to thirty-four executions, and had corrected the mistaken scepticism of certain other physicians 'who had learned in Paris to change the crime of sorcery into mere illness'. However, even the censorious d'Aubigné respected la Rivière as a doctor: he addressed him as 'le plus grand médecin que l'Europe connoisse'.[40] Mayerne similarly described him as 'medentium omnium hodie viventium facile coryphaeus ac princeps'; and the same opinion was expressed by the English diplomatist Sir Dudley Carleton. When la Rivière and Marescot died, almost at the same time, of an epidemic then raging in Paris, Carleton deplored the loss of 'the two greatest physicians of this town, and for one of them it may be said, of this time'.[41]

La Rivière died in Paris on 5 November 1605. Jean-Baptiste le Grain, the chronicler of the reign of Henri IV, who was one of his friends and patients, tells a story of his death. When the doctor felt that his end was near (says le Grain), he sent for his servants and distributed among them his money, plate and other movable possessions. Having done so, he ordered them to leave the house and not to return. When all had gone and nothing was left in his house but the bed on which he lay, he was visited by his medical friends, who came to enquire after his health and attend his sickness. La Rivière asked them to summon his servants, to which they replied that no servant was at hand: on their arrival they had found the doors open and the house empty. La Rivière then said, 'Adieu Messieurs, il est donc tems que je m'en aille aussi, puisque mon bagage est parti', and died. The story has been doubted because it was applied, when first printed, 150 years after the event, to the synthetic la Rivière who had by then become established in the historical record; and it was known that Roch le Baillif left heirs of his body. But le Grain clearly told it of the *premier médecin*, and as we have no record that the *premier médecin* was married or had heirs, we may reasonably suppose it to be true. It is certainly compatible with those 'libertez et gayetez ordinaires' which d'Aubigné deplored in him and with the roguish character, implicit in the epitaph pronounced upon him by Pierre de l'Estoile: 'le bon larron que Dieu a regardé pour luy faire misericorde'.*

After his death, one of la Rivière's friends, unlike d'Aubigné, took some care of his papers. This was his most famous and successful disciple, Theodore de Mayerne. Mayerne came to Paris some time after taking his medical degree at Montpellier in 1597. From 1599 to 1601 he was away from Paris accompanying the young Henri de Rohan – the same Henri de Rohan to whom Roch le Baillif had dedicated his penultimate book – on his grand tour of Europe. He returned to Paris before the end of 1601, and from then until la Rivière's death in 1605 he assisted him regularly in his practice. La Rivière secured Mayerne's appointment as *médecin ordinaire* to the King and Mayerne's papers record numerous private consultations with la Rivière and several *consilia*, or letters of medical advice, from him.

In 1602 Mayerne began a list of the cures achieved by la Rivière and himself 'in certain great and desperate illnesses', and he afterwards

---

* The story was first printed by the abbé Goujet in his article in the Paris supplement to Moreri's *Le Grand Dictionnaire* (1735), incorporated in the text of the edition of 1759 (s.v. 'Bailli'). Goujet there ascribed it to a manuscript journal of le Grain which he had seen, and which he describes more fully in his article on le Grain in the same work (s.v. 'Grain'). The diary is evidently still unpublished. The story is repeated, without evidence of its source, by J. F. Carrère, *Bibliothèque historique de la médecine* (Paris, 1776), s.v. 'Baillif'. J. N. F. Eloy, who rejected it on the above grounds (*Dictionnaire historique de la médecine*, Mons, 1778, I. 248–9), took it from Carrère and was evidently unaware that it had good contemporary authority. The remark of l'Estoile is in his *Journal de Henri IV*, VIII, 194.

recorded the patients who, 'having been abandoned by the doctors of Paris, were cured by us and recovered their health'.[42] One of these was Roger de St Lary, duc de Bellegarde, Grand Ecuyer de France, the former *mignon* of Henri III, who had organized the assassination in 1589 of the two brothers the duc de Guise and the cardinal de Guise, and then, on the assassination of his master, had become the confidant of Henri IV. He was a sufferer, like so many of their patients, from venereal disease; but he recovered, Mayerne noted, adding piously 'soli Deo laus et gloria'; and twenty years later he recorded in the margin of the page, 'he is alive and well and has never, from the time of that cure, felt the slightest trace of that disease'.[43] Others included some very distinguished names. There was Antoine Séguier, *président à mortier*; Madame de Retz; 'la Concini', the wife of the *premier écuyer* of Marie de Médicis, afterwards notorious as Maréchal d'Ancre; and Renée Burlamachi, widow of Cesare Balbani, afterwards wife of Agrippa d'Aubigné. She too, Mayerne observed, lived happily ever after, not dying till 1641.[44] Another famous patient was Armand du Plessis, bishop of Luçon, the future cardinal de Richelieu. He too suffered severely from venereal disease,* and his case prompted Mayerne to write a treatise on the subject of his complaint.†

Mayerne ultimately inherited most of la Rivière's Parisian patients, including his old patron the duc de Bouillon,‡ the apostate de Sancy, the Huguenot duc de Thouars, and indeed almost the whole *haute société protestante*. He would have inherited Henri IV too, if he had been willing to become a Roman Catholic. Instead, after the assassination of the King, he emigrated to England and made a great career there. But the personal notes which he took with him to England contain more remedies derived from la Rivière than from any other source, and the

---

* MS Sloane 2089, fo. 27 v. Richelieu appears in the list as 'Mr le Cardinal'; but the list (like the other entries in this MS) has clearly been copied later, as the other titles show. That the reference is to Richelieu is clear from the reference in Mayerne's 'Ephemerides' where the patient is described as 'Mr de Lusson, Maij 1605, Gonorrhoea inveterata a vj. mensibus cum caruncula circa collum vesicae dura', and Mayerne has afterwards written in the margin 'Cardinal de Richel'. (MS Sloane 2059 fo. 45). Richelieu had begun his career as Bishop of Luçon.

† The title of Mayerne's work *de gonorrhoeae inveteratae et carunculae et ulceris in meatu urinario curatione* almost exactly repeats his description of Richelieu's complaint. Though not published till 1619, in the correspondence of Fabricius Hildanus (Oppenheim, 1619), this treatise was written before May 1607 – i.e. about the time of Richelieu's treatment (MS Sloane 2105 A fo. 17).

‡ MS Sloane 2062 fo. 1. This was on 1 October 1609 – i.e. after the death of Joseph du Chesne (Quercetanus) who had worked in partnership with la Rivière and Mayerne.

manuscript books which he treasured consisted predominantly of the medical papers of la Rivière and of la Rivière's master Fernel.* It seems, in fact, that Mayerne's extraordinary success as a physician, both in the Paris of Henri IV and in the London of James I, Charles I, and Cromwell, was based largely on the practice of his medical patron, la Rivière.

It is unlikely that la Rivière will ever receive the full study suggested by Emmanuel Philipot. He published no book and left, so far as we know, no personal papers; and without such aids it is difficult to trace even a royal doctor in the sixteenth century. But at least his name should be rescued from the taint which has clung to it for the last two centuries in consequence of the casual conjecture of Jacob le Duchat and the consequent general assumption that his quality as a doctor is to be deduced from the primitive and fanatical Paracelsianism of the provincial empiric Roch le Baillif, sieur de la Rivière.

Sources

1. J. A. de Thou, *Historiae sui temporis*, lib cxxiii.
2. Theodore de Mayerne, *Apologia* (La Rochelle, 1603), p. 13.
3. *Memoires du duc de Sully*, ed. L. R. Lefèvre, 1942, 249. Rivière's prediction concerning Louis XIII, quoted by Sully, is recorded, in the hand of J. Dupuy, in B.N. MS Dupuy 588 fo. 205.
4. Agrippa d'Aubigné, 'Confession de Sancy,' printed in Pierre de l'Estoile, *Journal de Henri III* (Hague, 1744), V, 384.
5. e.g. Joannes Renodaeus (Jean de Renoud), *Institutionum Pharmaceuticarum . . .* (Paris, 1608), *de Materia Medica . . .* lib III cap. xxxiv.
6. Mayerne, *Apologia*, l.c.; Jos. Quercetanus [du Chesne], *de Priscorum Philosophorum Vera Medicinae Materia* (1603), p. 213.
7. The two most important documents for la Rivière are MS Sloane 2089, which contains several letters to and from la Rivière, and MS Sloane 2111, which is anonymous, but which is proved by internal evidence and by the evidence of MS Sloane 2089 to be by la Rivière. MS Sloane 1996 consists largely of material from la Rivière. Other MSS in the Sloane collection containing incidental evidence from or about la Rivière will be cited as they are relevant. It may be remarked that the confusion concerning la Rivière is still further confounded by the printed index to the Sloane MSS, in which the *premier médecin* is consistently confused with the 17th-century French physician Lazare Rivière.
8. Emmanuel Philipot, *La Vie et l'Oeuvre Littéraire de Noël du Fail, gentilhomme breton* (Paris, 1914).
9. Pierre de l'Estoile, *Journal de Henri III* (Hague, 1744), V, 394.
10. *Petit Traicté de l'antiquité et de la singularité de la Bretagne armorique* (Rennes, 1578).
11. *Discours sur la signification de la comète apparue en Occident au signe du Sagittaire le 10 Nov*

---

* MS Sloane 2046 fo. 42: 'Catalogus librorum quos mecum sumpsi in Angliam'. Of 15 titles, six are by la Rivière, two by Fernel, and one by Fernel's disciple le Paulmier.

(Rennes, 1577). A copy of this rare work, which is dedicated to the duc de Mercoeur, is in the Bibliothèque Municipale de Rouen.

12. 'Edelphus', le Baillif explained, 'est qui iuxta naturam elementi pronosticat' (*Demosterion*, p. 131). Cf. Martin Ruland, *Lexicon Alchemiae* . . . (Frankfurt, 1612), 193: 'Edelphus, qui ex elementorum natura prognosticat.'

13. Paris, Ecole de Médecine, Registres de la Faculté, VIII. fos. 128ff.

14. Philipot, op. cit.; *Les Lettres d'Etienne Pasquier* . . . (Paris, 1619), I, 455; II, 752, 787.

15. C.-P. Goujet, *Histoire du Collège de France*.

16. See the depositions against the Ligueurs made before the Sénéchal de Rennes in 1589 and published by F. Joüon de Longrais in *Bulletin et Memoires de la Société Archéologique du Départment d'Ille-et-Vilaine*, tom. XLI (Rennes, 1911), 154–7, 163, 178.

17. *Traicté de la Cause de la Briefve Vie de plusieurs Princes et Grands* . . . (Rennes, 1591).

18. *La Conformité de l'ancienne et moderne médicine d'Hippocrate à Paracelse* . . . (Rennes, 1592).

19. 'Livre de Raison de Gilles Satin, sieur de la Teillaye 1591–1597' in *Bulletin Archéologique de l'Association Bretonne*, tom. XVI (St. Brieuc, 1898), 454.

20. Philipot, op. cit., 354ff.

21. Ibid., 358.

22. Pierre Bayle, *Dictionnaire*, s.v. 'Mayerne'.

23. MS Sloane 2089, fo. 78 v.

24. Haag, *La France Protestante*, s.v. Ribit.

25. Gesner records the fact in his *Bibliotheca Universalis* (Zurich, 1545), fo. 450 v., where he calls Ribit 'summus amicus meus'.

26. On Jean Ribit the Hellenist see A.-L. Herminjard, *Correspondance des Réformateurs dans les pays de langue française* (Geneva, 1866–97), IV, 288 etc.; Henri Vuilleumier, *Histoire de L'Eglise Réformée du Pays de Vaud* (Lausanne, 1927–33), I, 398, 407, 667, 734, 748, etc.

27. Helenus Ribit, *Vita Aemylii Ferretti*, (Lyon, 1553), preface; Herminjard, op. cit., VIII, 133; IX, 16, 485. I deduce that Helenus Ribit was the brother of Jean Ribit from the letters of Jean Ribit in B.N. MS Latin 8641 (see below, note 28).

28. B.N. MS Latin 8641. This is a notebook of Jean Ribit the Hellenist, containing drafts of his letters, sermons, etc.

29. MS Sloane 2089 fo. 74.

30. Ibid., fo. 74 v.

31. See Pier Giacosa, 'La medicina in Piemonte nel secolo XVI', in *Studi pubblicati dalla Regia Università di Torino nel IV centenario della nascita di Emmanuele Filberto* (Turin, 1928).

32. See Arturo Pascal, 'La Colonia piemontese a Ginevra nel secolo XVI', in D. Cantimori *et al.* (ed.), *Ginevra e l'Italia* (Florence, 1959), 114–15.

33. For Botallo see Leonardo Carerj, *Leonardo Botallo Astese, medico regio* (Asti, 1954). His *Opera Omnia* were published at Leyden in 1660.

34. MS Sloane 2111.

35. MS Sloane 2089 fo. 77.

36. Quercetanus (Joseph du Chesne), *de Priscorum Philosophorum* . . ., 213.

37. For an account of the journey from England see Historical MSS Commission, *MSS of Marquess of Salisbury*, IV, 102.

38. Quercetanus, loc. cit.; MS Sloane 2111 fo. 9; 2089 fo. 75 v.-77.

39. L'Estoile, *Journal de Henri IV* (ed. Paul Bonnefon, Paris, 1888–96), VI. 219.

40. Agrippa d'Aubigné, *Oeuvres*, I, 428–33.

41. HMC, *Marquess of Salisbury*, XVII, 454.

42. MS Sloane 2089 fo. 23, 27 v.

43. MS Sloane 1996 fo. 55 v.

44. MS Sloane 2089 fo. 35.

The Culture of the Baroque Courts

This congress, which has done me the honour of inviting me to give this opening lecture, is on the culture of the baroque courts. But what do we mean by these terms? Much ink has been spilt in seeking to define the concept of the baroque: almost as much as on that of the Renaissance. But let us not waste time in these semantic exercises. For practical purposes we all know what we mean by it. The baroque age is the era of cultural history which follows the Renaissance; which emerges out of the Renaissance, stealing upon us almost imperceptibly until we discover its distinct, individual character. It is recognizably a mutation of the Renaissance, not a foretaste of the Enlightenment. Perhaps we may call it the autumn of the Renaissance, and leave it at that. And the baroque court is the characteristic political system of that era: the organization which not only directed its political activity but also generated, organized and exploited its typical court culture.

Of course princely courts have always been important generators of culture. Instances easily spring to mind: the courts of Augustus, of Charlemagne, of Haroun al-Rashid, of Frederick II *Stupor Mundi*. But the courts of the Renaissance differ from these personal, and sometimes ephemeral phenomena. The Renaissance court is not only the expression of a personal taste or a personal policy. It is general, typical: it has a function which is bound to the society and politics of a particular era – the early modern era.

What is that characteristic political system? It is not enough to speak of monarchy. Monarchy was the normal form of government in Europe from the Dark Ages to the present century. But the monarchies of medieval Europe seemed 'barbarous' to the sophisticated city-republics of Italy, and the 'enlightened despots' of the eighteenth century were very different from their predecessors. The court-gap between the Emperors Rudolf II and Joseph II, or between Elizabeth I and George II of England, is as unbridgeable as the culture-gap between Shakespeare and Pope, Rabelais and Voltaire. As for the nineteenth century, which was as monarchical as any previous century, who can compare its competitively dull and philistine monarchs with the competitive brilliance of their ancestors? Ludwig II of Bavaria, like his sixteenth-century predecessors, patronized music and built palaces; but he was discounted as mad. Ferdinand of Bulgaria, like the Emperor Maximilian II, was interested in botany and beetles; but such undignified pursuits were held to disqualify him for a throne.

If we are to isolate the distinguishing marks of the Renaissance court, we must, I believe, begin by looking at its origin. How did that peculiar political form emerge and become general in Europe, and how was it gradually changed into its last form, the baroque court? Let me begin by trying, briefly, to describe that process.

It began in Italy. It was in Italy, the economic and cultural capital of Europe, that the previous model of government had been perfected, and it was there that it was transformed. That model was the commune, the city-republic ruled by a mercantile patriciate. Medieval Europe was, in a sense, a colony – at least an economic colony – of Italy. It was on the trade-routes to Italy that the cities of Flanders, the Rhineland and South Germany grew rich, and it was from Italy that they borrowed their culture and, to some extent, their political forms. International trade made these cities international, and being international, they looked, for their culture, to the greatest of international institutions, which was also Italian, the Church. This combination – the Guelf alliance of free cities with the Roman Church – determined the culture of the Middle Ages. It was Florence, Venice, Genoa, Milan, Ghent, Bruges, Augsburg, Nuremberg, not the feudal courts of Europe, which generated the great art, as they also generated the wealth, of that phase of history; and it was the Roman Church which determined its form.

Then, at the close of the Middle Ages, came the great crisis of the cities which was to end, almost everywhere, in the extinction of their liberties. First in Italy, then in Flanders, the old city republics were replaced by new monarchies. Almost every Italian commune became a principality. Milan was transformed into a duchy, Florence into a Grand Duchy. The cities of Flanders were swallowed up in the duchy of Burgundy. The few city republics which survived drew in their horns and ceased to assert their independence. Genoa became a client-city of the King of Spain, Ragusa of the Grand Turk. Venice retreated into permanent neutrality. Geneva survived by the protection of France, the free cities of Germany by the fragmentation of Germany and imperial guarantee. If any city sought to resist, it was crushed, as Charles V crushed the Castilian communes, the last Florentine republic, and the city of Ghent.

This take-over of the cities by the princes marked a profound social change in Europe, comparable, in its generality, with the eclipse of nineteenth-century liberalism by twentieth-century dictatorship. The princes, old and new, erected their power on a new social base and justified it by a new political philosophy. Against the urban patriciate, with its ideas of freedom and republican tradition, they relied on wider support; they mobilized the country against the city, the plebs against the patriciate; and they built up their own military force based on independent finance. Some of them, like the Medici, began as their own financiers. Others relied on international financiers, like the Fugger of Augsburg. Once in power, of course, they could impose taxes on the defeated merchants. The merchants then learned their lesson. The sons of the old patriciate turned away from the uncertainties of private commerce to the profits of office. They became courtiers, bureaucrats, farmers of taxes, court-monopolists, 'officers' of those close-knit, pro-fessional 'privy councils' which would replace the looser, more amateur 'chambers' of the old feudal princes.

At the same time, the princes also took over the other institution which had sustained the culture of the Middle Ages: the Church. In the early sixteenth century the Papacy had become worldly, the Church lax and corrupt, and the princes seized their chance. The kings of France and Spain took over the patronage of the Church so completely that they did not need to turn heretic. The kings of the north went further. If necessary in alliance with popular religion, they made themselves absolute over their churches, over doctrine as over power and wealth. By mid-century, the Church, almost everywhere, was an organ of the state. In England, the King was Head of the Church. In Spain and Portugal, the Pope was powerless. In Germany, the Prince was *summus episcopus*. Some German princes were really bishops: 'prince-bishops' as of Münster or Würzburg; elector archbishops as of Mainz, Trier, Cologne.

This shift of power from the Church to the State – that is, to the Prince – was illustrated in the world of learning. The sixteenth century was a great age for the founding of universities. But whereas the medieval universities had been founded to supply theologians for the

Church, the new universities were founded by princes to supply 'officers' for the court – or for the state-church. So, when a German principality was divided, as so often happened, new universities had to be founded, unless, as in Brunswick, the princes agreed to hold their university, like their mines, in common. It can also be illustrated in the world of art. Art in the Middle Ages had been propaganda for the Church. Now it became propaganda for the court. The artists patronized by the House of Habsburg commemorated the dynasty, its grandeur, its victories, its imperial ambitions, and only incidentally its defence of the true faith against Moors, Turks and heretics. Sometimes, as during the reign of Rudolf II, religion was forgotten altogether. The triumphs and apotheoses of secular monarchs were a more fashionable theme for court painters.

This fusion of Church and State in a new monarchy did not happen only in lay principalities. The Papacy itself moved with the times. In the Middle Ages the Papal Consistory had exercised some real power. By 1600 it had become a mere rubber-stamp for the Pope. Sixtus V changed the papal states into a modern monarchy. Cardinal Baronius wrote the Annals of the Church as the triumph of the Papacy. The principal result of the Council of Trent, wrote Paolo Sarpi, was to convert the old aristocracy of the bishops into the new monarchy of the Pope.

The very revival of religion, whether by Reformation or by Counter-Reformation, positively hastened the fusion of Church and State, which its weakness had begun. At first, in the genial days before the Flood, the princes could take their religion lightly. Those were the days of humanism, when the pagan deities seemed to have taken over the Christian altars; for society then seemed stable and the court rested sufficiently on a humanist intelligentsia united in its support. This paganism survived the appearance of those grim ayatollahs, Savonarola and Luther. It would never entirely die out. But after the great ideological crisis of the mid-century we see less of it. The intelligentsia was then fragmented, and so the new monarchies needed to put down deeper roots, to enlist the support not merely of an educated élite but of the country, the people. So the old courtly humanism withered and shrank, or was subsumed, as superficial decoration, into the new devotion. Princes now became not merely the arbiters but the populist reformers, or counter-reformers, of their countries: grim royal moralists, incarnating and inflaming popular prejudice, leaders of the hunt against ideological or social deviation or dissent. So the kings of Spain, from the protectors became the persecutors of Moors and Jews, the patrons of the Holy Inquisition; the dukes of Bavaria established, through the *Geistliche Rat,* a moral police; and even some of the most learned and cultured of German princes, like Heinrich Julius of Brunswick-Wolfenbüttel, were notorious for their persecution of witches. The intensification of the witch-craze after 1550 was the extreme form of social persecution: a sign of solidarity between prince and people, part of the price paid for absolute power.

Thus the princes of the sixteenth century took over not only the substance of power but also the arts and sciences (even the pseudo-sciences) which are the epiphenomena, or the propaganda, of power. In so doing, they concentrated, and subtly transformed, the individualism of the early Renaissance. That individualism – that heightened, competitive spirit which Jacob Burckhardt saw as the originating force of the Renaissance in Italy – was now concentrated at court. At the same time, it was formalized within relatively safe limits as competition to please the prince. But it was also competition in which the prince himself took part, and in which, naturally, he must always win. So, once art and learning have become the fashion, we find princes who are not content to be patrons but must themselves be artists and men of learning. Henry VIII would write a book to expose the theological errors of Luther and would confound his own theologians by a spectacular firework-display of 'God's own learning'. Charles V played the organ, as did his son Philip II. Philip IV painted, wrote poems, composed musical airs. The Emperor Maximilian II was a universal man: naturalist, antiquary, scholar, bibliophile, linguist, orientalist. Most of the Habsburg Emperors, from Charles V onwards, were accomplished linguists. Queen Elizabeth astonished foreign ambassadors by her extempore command of Latin. The learning of James I was proverbial. Pope Urban VIII, the most civilized and sophisticated of popes, dabbled in science – he thought himself a match for Galileo – wrote poetry, was an amateur of all the arts. Maurice the Learned of Hesse-Cassel was surgeon, philosopher, theologian, linguist, poet, musical composer, as well as patron of science, literature and drama. Heinrich Julius of Brunswick was mathematician, scientist, chemist, classical scholar, Hebraist, jurist, architect, poet and playwright. Augustus of Brunswick-Lüneburg, whom we commemorate as the founder of this great library, was scholar, builder, bibliophile, author of works on chess and cryptography, patron of learning and music, connoisseur of topography, astronomy and mechanical clocks.

Patrons of learning and the arts, founders of colleges, chairs, private academies, scientific laboratories, competitors with each other in their ostentatious patronage, sometimes themselves practitioners of learning and the arts – such, in general, is the character, or at least the ideal, of the Renaissance princes. Of course some of them were incapable of this role. There were plenty of princes, especially in Germany, who were content with the time-honoured pursuits of hunting and drinking. Even in this role, some were naturally more capable, or more competitive, than others. But is there, apart from these varieties of human temperament, any difference of type among them? I believe that there is, and that it springs, like so much else, from that polarization of attitudes caused, in the mid-sixteenth century, by the religious division of Europe, and hardened into fixity by the decrees of Trent and their consequence, the revolutionary challenge of Calvinism.

This polarization can be seen, especially, in the attitude towards learning and the arts. To the humanist of the early sixteenth century, art and nature, literature and learning, were all equally legitimate human interests, equally to be pursued without conscious limit. But after the great schism, specialization set in. Scholarship, pursued for its own sake, or for the sake of a yet undiscovered truth, had led to heresy, Erasmus to Luther, or worse. To the Catholic of the Counter-Reformation, therefore, the pursuit of learning was dangerous and had to be controlled lest it go beyond the limits of orthodoxy. Hence the need for vigilant censorship and, from the 1550s onward, for a constantly published, constantly enlarged Index of Prohibited Books. To the Protestant, on the other hand, whose doctrines had been nourished by the discoveries of scholarship and the appeal to reason, the great danger lay in the arts, in the appeal away from reason and scholarship to the senses. All through the dark ages of popery, it was said, the Church had concealed the true meaning of Scripture by pictorial commentary, 'images', which distorted those simple truths, and thereby diverted worship from God to the Virgin and the saints, even to the images themselves. This indeed had been the whole function of art. Therefore the radical preachers of Protestantism denounced art itself. With Mosaic enthusiasm, they declared war on 'images', and every national reformation was accompanied, at some stage, by outbreaks of iconoclasm: statues beheaded, sculptured tombs defaced, the crash of broken stained-glass windows, the screech of saws in carved organ lofts, altarpieces torn down and burnt.

The positive reaction to these events was obvious. In Protestant countries, the court gave a lead in the promotion of learning. Foreign scholars were invited in; university chairs or sinecures were found for them; schools, colleges, universities were founded or promoted; works of scholarship were patronized and dedicated to the prince. In Catholic countries, learning was severely controlled – even Catholic universities outside Spain were banned to Spanish students by Philip II – but the sensuous arts (carefully regulated to ensure that they represented only orthodox doctrine) were promoted as never before. The princes of the Counter-Reformation patronized art and music, not casually, as some of their predecessors had done, but systematically. The alliance of Church and State was publicized to the world by an ostentatious policy of cultural conquest.

The great agents of this reconquest, as of the Catholic reconquest in general, were those front-soldiers of the Counter-Reformation, the Jesuits. To a Catholic prince, the Jesuits were invaluable allies: only they, it seemed, could guarantee his throne. By their missionary work, they could bring back the people to obedience. By their teaching, they could win over the élite. And when they had once stabilized a tottering throne, they could keep it stable: their victories were never reversed. The prospect of being able to rely on such spiritual janissaries must have tempted many a Protestant prince, especially since they were as skilful at undermining a Protestant as at upholding a Catholic throne. Henri IV of France, while a Protestant, had hated the Jesuits. Even after his conversion, he would, for a time, hear no good word of them. But a Catholic king, he soon found, could not do without them; and within a few years, the ban was lifted and a Jesuit confessor guided the conscience of the ex-Huguenot king.

The secret of the Jesuits lay in their modernity. Like Marxist-Leninists today, they had studied the mechanics of power and understood the *arcana imperii*. They had captured, and then converted to the use of the court, the most up-to-date ideas, making them both fashionable and safe. By their teaching, the sceptical reason of Erasmus was converted into orthodox casuistry, the uninhibited statecraft of Machiavelli into ideologically justified 'reason of state', and the individual Renaissance courtier of Castiglione was replaced by the sophisticated, identikit servant of the Counter-Reformation prince. For the Jesuits, in their total opposition to the Reformation, did not seek, like their Dominican rivals, to go back to the past. They recognized that humanism had come to stay. So they mastered it, drained it of its dangerous content, and turned it into decorative learning for the Roman Church and the Christian Prince.

They also produced other kinds of decoration. The *style jesuite* in architecture may not have been their creation, but they took possession of it and extended it. The flamboyant church of the Gesù in Rome became the model for the Catholic reconquest: a model which they would establish wherever they were welcomed by a Catholic court. For without the Catholic court, they were powerless: witness their failure in England, Sweden, Russia. Their efforts there were no less heroic, but failure to capture the court was final. Their success was in the lands where political power had been recovered by a Catholic court. It was shown in the architecture of Bavaria, the Netherlands, Austria, Poland, Bohemia.

It was shown, best of all, in the reconquered Netherlands, the shop-window of the Counter-Reformation. There the iconoclasm of the Protestant 'rebels' had cleared the ground and sent out the challenge. Now the ground was filled, and the challenge met, by new and more splendid churches, new and more splendid works of propagandist art. The archducal court at Brussels, the most splendid and ceremonious court in Europe, took charge of the work. Brother Huyssens, Jesuit and architect, designed the most magnificent church of all, the church of St Ignatius Loyola, the founder of his order, and Rubens, the master-painter of court and Church alike, filled it with his great canvases. The general of the Jesuits himself was shocked by the extravagance and opulence of the work – the Order did, after all, preach Christian poverty to the people. He tried to call a halt: sent Brother Huyssens off to a monastery and commanded him to give up the practice of architecture. But the court was having none of that. The Infanta Isabel promptly got him out again and the partnership of Rubens and Huyssens was soon back at work on the archducal chapel and the great church of St Peter at Ghent. In general, Rubens was no friend of the Jesuits; but in the world of art they collaborated in the service of the Counter-Reformation Church and Court.

At the other pole from the Catholic courts which sparkled in the orbit of Spanish power were the austere courts of Calvinist princes. They were few, for although the Calvinists articulated the frontal resistance of Protestantism as the Jesuits articulated that of Catholicism, Calvinism itself – as the snobbish convert Caspar Scioppius perpetually hinted to the German princes whom he showed round the sights of Rome – was no religion for a prince, or even perhaps for a gentleman. James I of England began as Calvinist King of Scotland, but there was no court there, and the King himself was a mere puppet of barbarian nobles and insolent clergy. When he moved to London, he soon got rid of his Calvinist ideas, and of his Calvinist frugality. Henri IV of France similarly began as Calvinist King of Navarre, but at his little court at Nérac Calvinist austerity was modified by incorrigible gallantry and the seductive model of Fontainebleau. On moving to Paris he too changed his tune. The Princes of Orange, heirs to the magnificence of the Burgundian court nobility, assumed Calvinism as a religion of revolt against Spain; but their Burgundian tastes were not easily subdued. Unlike Catholicism, whose capital in Rome was a monarchy, the ideal of Calvinism was a city: a city of refuge, defensive, as all cities must be in this age of the princes: the city of Geneva. Whenever it entered the courts of princes, it was forced to compromise.

However, there were a few small Calvinist courts, most of them, like Geneva itself, little more than cities of refuge on the periphery of France. There was the principality of Sedan, ruled by the great Huguenot leader, the duc de Bouillon. There was Zweibrücken, 'une cour demi-française' ruled, as the other great Huguenot leader, the Duc de Rohan, was pleased to note, by 'un prince tout entièrement français'.[1] There was Hanau, ruled by a cadet prince of the house of Orange-Nassau. Above all, there was the capital of aggressive Calvinism in Europe, the court of the Elector Palatine at Heidelberg. The language of all these courts, as also of that of the Prince of Orange in the Netherlands, was French. Calvinism was essentially a French religion, a badge of French cultural imperialism in the Protestant fringe; and it was under French influence that it penetrated some of the German courts. Maurice the Learned, the agent of French policy among the German princes, became Calvinist in 1605. Calvinism merged with Lutheranism in Hanover and Württemberg – and even, for a very brief spell (under Christian I, 1586–91), in electoral Saxony. Other princes adopted it for more or less political reasons: Anhalt, in self-defence against the pressure of Lutheran Saxony; Bentheim, under the shadow of the United Provinces; Brandenburg, to secure the inheritance of Cleves.

What was the character of these Calvinist courts? Just as the Catholic courts extended themselves, and their finances, in the cultivation of the sensuous arts, so the Calvinist and Calvinizing courts distinguished themselves by the patronage of learning. James VI of Scotland, the pupil of the French humanist turned Scotch Calvinist, George Buchanan, was hailed as the most learned prince in Europe: he was a poet and a scholar, and in England would be able to patronize poets and scholars. All the Calvinist princes founded academies or universities in their states. The learned princes of Germany were those who ruled over Calvinist or 'crypto-Calvinist' states. The Palatinate and then Hanau became the great publishing centres of the learned world, reaching out – as did the new academy of Herborn in Hanau –

to the Calvinists (and Socinians) of the East, in Poland and Hungary.[2]

This polarization of the courts of Europe between Catholic patrons of the arts and Protestant, and especially Calvinist, patrons of learning is nicely illustrated in the opposition – the bitter political and, in the end, military opposition – of the two branches of the house of Wittelsbach: the Calvinist Elector Palatine at Heidelberg and the Catholic Duke of Bavaria at Munich. At Munich the Counter-Reformation dukes, having crushed the Protestant nobility, advertised their monarchical power and religious devotion by favouring the Jesuits, collecting pictures and patronizing musicians. The Lutheran Wittelsbachs of Neuburg, once they had been converted to Catholicism in order to secure the duchies of Berg and Mark, hastened to imitate them.* But at Heidelberg, the glory of the dynasty was its library, the famous Palatine Library which was re-ordered, in its last decades, by the Dutch scholar Jan Gruter. In 1618, when the Elector Palatine was elected Calvinist King of Bohemia, the great Habsburg collections in Prague were in danger. There were cries for the destruction of those godless, shameless, 'popish' works of art. Four years later, when the same Elector had been driven not only from Prague but also from his own capital of Heidelberg, the Bavarian army looted the Palatine Library and the orthodox Duke had it packed up and sent off, wholesale – not to Munich, to be incorporated in the fine Renaissance library which he had inherited, but over the Alps, to be buried in the great orthodox *oubliette* of the Vatican. A Catholic prince had no use for possibly dangerous books, and like a good boy he handed them over to his headmaster, who would know what to do with them.

Art versus ideas, that was the most obvious antithesis caused by the ideological division of Europe in the patronage of its princely courts. Other divisions are less striking, for there was still neutral ground on which Catholic and Protestant felt free, though with subtle variations, to borrow from each other and compete with each other. There were also intermediate parties. Though tinged with Calvinism under Elizabeth, the English court always maintained its independence and, under Charles I, would be Catholic in its aestheticism. The Lutheran courts of east Germany and Scandinavia – what we may call the High Lutherans, as distinct from the 'crypto-Calvinists' or Zwinglians of the West – never surrendered to Huguenot austerity – although the court of

---

* After his conversion in 1609, Wolfgang Wilhelm, count palatine of Neuburg, became one of the most enthusiastic patrons of Rubens.

electoral Saxony, the capital of High Lutheranism, only acquired its full flamboyance when its prince had turned Catholic for the sake of the Polish crown. Visitors from the Calvinist West were sometimes shocked by the sensuous ornament of the high Lutheran Church. Bulstrode Whitelocke, the English Puritan sent by Oliver Cromwell as ambassador to Queen Christina of Sweden, goggled with dismay at what he found there: 'None could see a difference', he wrote, on seeing the rich gilded effigies and magnificent baroque organs, the chalices and pyxes, vestments and crucifixes, 'betwixt this and the Papists' churches.'[3] Queen Christina, of course, thought differently. To her, the difference was far too great; and she left it behind her to enjoy the real thing in Rome itself.

Music itself was debatable ground. Catholic and Protestant princes alike patronized it. But there was a certain difference in the kind of music that they patronized. In the early sixteenth century, Flemish polyphony was the fashion. Flemish musicians and Flemish choirs had long dominated the church services in St Peter's, and Flemish music was played for the Emperor Charles V, and perhaps by him too. Philip II banned those frivolous exercises from his severe court. His large musical establishment was commanded to keep to simple plainsong. But that perhaps only illustrated his essentially reactionary tastes. The greatest composers of the second half of the century, Palestrina and Lassus, both served only Catholic princes: Palestrina in Rome, at the court of successive popes; Lassus in Munich, at the head of the huge and costly musical establishment of the dukes Albert V and William V. The Wittelsbach court at Munich, with over ninety musicians, Philip II's Escorial with its monastic choir and four splendid organs, were great centres of solemn church music, as reformed by the Council of Trent. The Protestant courts were full of music too. The high Lutheran courts saw nothing 'popish' in choral music, which indeed would flourish there. The Lutheran Elector of Saxony tried, though vainly, to lure Lassus away from Munich. But the Calvinist or Calvinizing courts rejected the choir and concentrated on instrumental music. There was no lack of such music at the court of Queen Elizabeth, or of the Protector Oliver Cromwell either. The duc de Bouillon loved instrumental music and patronized it, and composed it himself, at his austere court in Sedan.[4] The Calvinist court of Heidelberg delighted in the elaborate musical confections of the French Huguenot Solomon de Caus. De Caus, who had come from the English court with the Princess Elizabeth, was not a musician by profession. He was a mechanical artist, the prince's surveyor, 'an extremely brilliant garden-architect and hydraulic engineer', with a special interest in 'mathematical music', and he filled the geometrical garden which he had created at Heidelberg with 'musical grottoes, singing fountains and pneumatically controlled speaking statues'.[5] Ornamental gardens, botanical innovations, elaborate waterworks, were all encouraged at the princely courts, Protestant and Catholic alike. In Protestant courts, music served these secular diversions, while the courts of Catholic princes gave opportunities for great church music. The difference of emphasis is perceptible among the artists themselves: the botanists, engineers, engravers, even of Catholic princes, were often Protestants, while the musicians at Protestant courts, like William Byrd at the court of Queen Elizabeth, were sometimes Catholic.

One of the arts which music served at court was the drama. The drama, of popular origin, was soon drawn into the court, and courtly patronage converted it into the masque and the opera. French companies were invited by Queen Henrietta Maria to perform at the English court, and English actors carried English drama to the courts of Germany: to Heidelberg, of course; to Hesse, where Maurice the Learned had a company of English actors; to the Brunswick of Heinrich Julius; and elsewhere. In Catholic countries, the Jesuits captured the drama as they captured, and tried to corner, all the arts. Meanwhile court patronage was making masques ever more elaborate. In Inigo Jones the English court had 'one of the most original theatrical engineers of all time',[6] and Princess Elizabeth carried this fashion too to the Calvinist court of Heidelberg. Good Calvinists, of course, objected to all these frivolities. The English Puritans and the French Huguenots condemned stage-plays in general: the only exceptions they allowed were the Senecan tragedies of Buchanan, *Baptistes* and *Jephthes*, which were sound anti-clerical propaganda and had no musical frills. But these vetoes had no effect on the court. Indeed, that severe Huguenot Agrippa d'Aubigné admits that he had himself organized masques at the Catholic court of Catherine de Médicis. Spanish friars similarly denounced stage-plays in Spain. But their denunciations were vain: the reigns of Philip III and Philip IV were the golden age of the Spanish drama, and in 1630 the rebuilt royal palace in Madrid included a special *salón de comédias* for the performance of masques and plays. Seven years later, a new 'masquing house' was built in London to replace the Banqueting Hall at Whitehall and save Rubens's great ceiling-painting, 'The Apotheosis of King James', from damage by candle-smoke. Monteverdi's first operas were performed for the magnificent court of the Gonzaga at Mantua while Rubens was court-painter there, and his disciples would carry the art to the court of Vienna, its permanent home.

Like the other arts, the drama and the masque were soon converted from the entertainment to the propaganda of the court. They became, like the 'Triumphs' of Renaissance princes, elaborate allegories in honour of the ruling house: a ritualization of that courtly flattery, that 'cult of personality' which is inseparable from totalitarian monarchs. They were also taken up, developed, and given a further propagandist content, by the Jesuits. This, of course, only sharpened Puritan opposition. In England, in 1632, William Prynne published his wholesale attack on stage-plays, with tart aspersions on royalty for countenancing them. The defenders of the court struck back; Prynne lost his ears; and the court dramatists became more aggressive than ever in their propaganda. James Shirley in his *Triumph of Peace*, William Strode in his *Floating Island*, Thomas Carew in *Caelum Britannicum*, all of which were performed for – and the last by – Charles I, extolled obedience, monarchy and religious conformity, and went out of the way to lampoon stage-hating Puritans. A few years later, when the Great Rebellion broke out, the Puritans had their revenge. The last court masque was performed in January 1640. Soon afterwards, the London theatres were shut for the duration: that is, as it turned out, for twenty years. Twenty years' intermission can break any tradition, and the English theatre, like the English court, was never the same again.

The sciences too became polarized in these years. Astronomy and mathematics flourished in Catholic as well as Protestant courts, but certain sciences had, or rather acquired, a definite Protestant bias. In particular, the new medicine, Paracelsianism, and its off-shoot, the new Hermetic alchemy, became gradually a Protestant monopoly. There was nothing necessary in this: the early Hermeticists were good Catholics; but gradually Hermeticism was extruded from Catholic courts and even, in the 1590s, was condemned at Rome. There were still exceptions. The Emperor Rudolf II, who broke all the rules, was the greatest patron of Hermeticism, magic and alchemy in Europe, and it was a Catholic archbishop, Ernst von Wittelsbach, brother of the Duke of Bavaria, who, as Elector of Cologne, sponsored the first complete edition of the works of Paracelsus. But in general the patrons of alchemy, chemistry and Paracelsian medicine were the Protestant princes. Peter Severinus, the reformer of Paracelsianism, was court physician to the King of Denmark. Joseph du Chesne, known professionally as Quercetanus, the most admired of chemical doctors, listed the princes who patronized the new medicine: except for the archbishop, they were all Protestants.[7] Maurice the Learned of Hesse drew alchemists from all Europe to his laboratory at Marburg. The Duc de Bouillon at Sedan, a typical Calvinist prince, founded a library and an academy, and was cheated by alchemists. At Stuttgart the Duke Frederick of Württemberg welcomed and rewarded a whole series of adepts who promised to transmute base metal – and then, when they had failed, hanged them on a gallows of iron mockingly painted over to resemble gold.

For it was not solely an interest in science which caused princes to build laboratories and outbid each other in luring fashionable alchemists to their courts. There was also the prospect of gold. Now, more than ever, they needed it. Those lavish courts, with their centralizing councils and proliferating 'officers', each seeking to enlarge his own department, with their ever-expanding households, their conspicuous patronage, their new buildings, their ornamental or exotic gardens, their picture galleries, libraries and laboratories, all cost money. And money, in those days of inflation, was increasingly hard to come by. For we must not forget that the baroque age was an age of inflation: indeed, the baroque might be defined as the Renaissance *plus* inflation, the Renaissance under the strain of inflation. Prices, in the last half of the sixteenth century, quadrupled everywhere; and the process still went on. How then was a prince to keep his place in the competition when the purchasing power of his revenues was mysteriously shrinking? Some princes, indeed, found new resources. The King of Spain had his royalty on American silver. The King of Denmark could sustain his lavish patronage, and his mania for building, out of the tolls levied at the Sound. The Elector of Saxony had his mines. Such resources gave to those princes a certain independence. But other princes were less fortunate, and if they were to maintain extravagant courts in inflationary times, they had to resort to increased taxes. That meant, since few of them had power to tax at will, a wrestling-match with their parliaments, diets, estates.

To secure such taxes, the princes pleaded the rising cost of government. The estates responded by looking into accounts, suggesting reform of the princely household – that is, elimination of 'waste' and dismissal of superfluous officers, and especially of such 'parasites' as artists, musicians, actors. Sometimes they also demanded that less be spent on 'useless' works of art. Often the attitude of the estates took on a puritan colour. The polarization between Catholic and Calvinist, which divided Europe, was mirrored internally in the polarization of court and country. Court patronage is thus directly related to that general crisis of the seventeenth century in which, as James Harrington would put it, the princes either blew up their estates or were themselves blown up.[8]

The princes of Italy, whose power was illegitimate in origin, had never had to reckon with constitutional opposition, and now, as protectorates of Spain, they were secure. If the Duke of Mantua had to sell his famous picture gallery to Charles I, that was due not to pressure from below – his subjects protested at the sale – but to his personal tastes: he preferred to invest in dwarves. The Wittelsbachs in Bavaria and the Habsburgs in Austria were able to defeat Protestantism and constitutional opposition together, though not before one duke, the aesthete William V, had abdicated under the load of debt (those ninety musicians had been the last straw) and one Emperor, the aesthete Rudolf II, had been deposed by his family. Victory in civil war established the court of France and Spanish arms secured that of Flanders. But other courts, and especially the Protestant courts, were less successful, less prepared for the great crisis which was soon to face them all: the Thirty Years War.

The ultimate test for any society is its capacity to survive the strain of war. In general, the baroque courts, with their finances permanently strained, shrank from war. The Emperor Rudolf II, King James I of England, the Queen-Regent Marie de Médicis in France, the Archdukes in Flanders, cultivated the arts, and exploited a time, of peace. When the general peace broke down, it was not they, but their antithesis, the revolutionary Calvinist International, which gave the fatal push. The great monarchies, at first, were reluctant to come in. When the Crown of Spain at last decided to act, it began by ordering, as a painful necessity, the reform of the court. The reform proved ineffectual. Such reform almost always was, for it entailed the 'de-manning' of a powerful corporation. The courtiers were a solid 'interest', a kind of trade union, concerned not with efficiency but with job-protection, full employment and union rates. In Milan, when the courtiers, at a time of crisis, were asked to accept a cut in their salaries, they drew together and, with one voice, declared, 'No! Not a sou!' In London, when King James I appointed an outsider to rationalize and reduce his expensive household, the officers of the household similarly drew together and blocked the appointment.* Voluntary reform, self-reform, was impossible; and so, in the end, it was war or revolution which transformed

---

* The outsider was Sir Arthur Ingram. For an account of the episode see A. F. Unton, *Sir Arthur Ingram* (Oxford, 1961), pp. 69–76.

or destroyed those overblown Renaissance courts which were so ill-equipped for such a strain.

At first, some of the courts sought to exploit the war for short-term ends. The Thirty Years War witnessed an orgy of cultural cannibalism as capital cities were occupied, palaces or monasteries sacked. The sale of Charles I's marvellous picture-gallery, when, in the words of the outraged Clarendon, the kings of Europe came to imbrue their hands in the blood of a murdered monarch, was the climax of a long series of spoliations* in the course of which upstart new courts had arisen: Wallenstein's court as Duke of Friedland, the last and most outrageous imitation of the illegitimate condottiere principalities of Italy; Queen Christina's glittering robber's den in Stockholm. But these last mushroom creations rose only to burst. Wallenstein and his duchy disappeared in a night; Queen Christina carried her trophies off to Italy; and after 1660, though absolutism might continue, it no longer claimed a total monopoly of culture and religion, science and philosophy. The deposition of Rudolf II and Maurice the Learned, the ruin of the Palatine Wittelsbachs, the retribution exacted from Maximilian of Bavaria by the sack of Munich, and the tragedy of Charles I of England, taught princes that it was wiser to leave culture to private enterprise and concentrate on the duller but more necessary business of monarchy: government, power, survival.

Sources

1. A. Laugel, *Henri de Rohan, son rôle politique et militaire sous Louis XIII* (Paris, 1889), p. 37.
2. On this see R. W. J. Evans, 'The Wechel Presses: Humanism and Calvinism in Central Europe 1572–1627', in *Past and Present,* Supplement no. 2 (1975).
3. B. Whitelocke, *Embassy to Sweden,* ed. H. Reeve (1855), 187–8, 244–5.
4. Pierre Congars, Jean Lecaillou, Jacques Rousseau: *Sedan et le Pays Sedanais* (Paris 1969), p. 216.
5. Frances Yates, *The Rosicrucian Enlightenment* (1972), pp. 11–12.
6. M. B. Pickel, *Charles I as Patron of Poetry and Drama* (1936), p. 161.
7. *Jos. Quercetani . . . ad Veritatem Hermeticae Medicinae* (Paris, 1604), p. 13.
8. James Harrington, *The Oceana and Other Works* (1711), pp. 128–9.

* I have described this process in *The Plunder of the Arts in the 17th Century* (1970).

12

Robert Burton and The Anatomy of Melancholy

Robert Burton, the anatomist of melancholy, was born in 1577. Of his life we know very little, and perhaps there is little to know, for he was an academic scholar. He was born at the manor-house of Lindley, on the Warwickshire border of Leicestershire, 'the possession of Ralph Burton, my deceased father'. Of his father, who deceased in 1619, we know nothing; of his mother, Dorothy, *née* Faunt, only what he tells us himself, that she had 'an excellent skill in chirurgery, sore eyes, aches, etc., and such as all the county could testify, and wrought many famous and successful cures upon her neighbours'; and that she died in 1629. Robert Burton was the fourth of their nine children. He was sent to school locally, to the grammar school at Nuneaton three miles from his parents' home, and to the free school at Sutton Coldfield in Warwickshire. He does not seem to have enjoyed his childhood. It appears that he received little affection at home, and he hated his schooldays: 'children live in a perpetual slavery', he wrote, 'still under the tyrannical government of masters'; many of them become 'weary of their lives . . . and think (as once I did myself) no slavery in the world like that of a grammar scholar'. But by his will he left money to the school at Nuneaton.

The Burtons were a gentry family, conscious of their armigerous state. They traced their lineage to a squire of the body of King Richard Coeur de Lion. They were well educated. Robert's eldest brother William, who inherited the family estates – besides Lindley there was another property at Launde in Staffordshire – was an accomplished scholar, learned in ancient and modern tongues, and of antiquarian tastes. He is remembered as the first historian of Leicestershire. He was well versed in the niceties of heraldry and genealogy and filled his book

239

with the pedigrees and quarterings of his neighbours, not all of which were allowed by the College of Heralds.[1] He dedicated it to the most successful of the Leicestershire gentry, the court-meteor of Jacobean England, George Villiers, Duke of Buckingham. William Burton had many literary and scholarly friends, including Michael Drayton, the poet of British antiquity, and he called his own son Cassibilian after the ancient British King Cassivelaunus.

Robert Burton was very conscious of being a younger brother. As such, he was excluded from the inheritance of the estates, and would have to earn his keep. So he was less impressed by genealogies and heraldry and had less respect for the way of life of the gentry. 'Amongst us', he would write, 'the badge of gentility is idleness: to be of no calling, not to labour, for that's derogatory to their birth; to be a mere spectator, a drone, *fruges consumere natus* . . . to spend his days hawking, hunting, etc.' He would not deny that 'we have a sprinkling of gentry, here and there one, excellently well learned'; but such men were exceptional. In general 'our ruder gentry', he complains, are barbarians: they look down on libraries and books; if they read anything ''tis an English chronicle, *Sir Huon de Bordeaux, Amadis de Gaule*, etc.'; their sole discourse is dogs, horses and 'what news?'; they consume their substance in competitive extravagance and ridiculous snobbery: 'they buy titles, coats-of-arms, and by all means screw themselves into ancient families, falsifying pedigrees, usurping scutcheons, and all because they would not seem to be base. . . . Of all the vanities and fopperies to brag of, gentility is the greatest, for what is it they crack so much of, and challenge such superiority as if they were demigods? Birth? . . . it is a *non ens*, a mere flash, a ceremony, a thing of naught. . . .' And all this, he exclaims feelingly, is at the expense of younger brothers, who often, 'by reason of bad policy and idle education (for they are likely brought up to no calling) are compelled to beg or steal, and then hanged for theft'. Such were the ultimate consequences of the disastrous system of primogeniture.

In making this complaint, Burton was no doubt extrapolating from his own case; but he was not describing it. He remained on good terms with his brothers, who were certainly not enemies to learning. He mentions two younger brothers: George, a parson, whom he supplied with learned quotations for his sermons, and Ralph, whose translations he would cite; and when he died in 1640 it was his elder brother William who set up for him the fine monumental tomb, with his painted effigy, in the cathedral of Christ Church, Oxford.

For Oxford, not Leicestershire, was Burton's true home. He went there, in 1593, to Brasenose College, his father's college; then, in 1599, he moved to Christ Church, where his tutor – 'for form's sake, though he wanted not a tutor'[2] – was Dr John Bancroft. Bancroft was at that time a 'Student' of the college – that is, a college tutor, awaiting preferment. In due course he would obtain preferment: he would rise to be Laudian Bishop of Oxford. Burton himself would soon become a Student, and he too, at first, sought to rise in the Church by the normal method, that is, by patronage. 'I was once so mad', he would afterwards write, 'to bustle abroad and seek about for preferment, tire myself and trouble all my friends.' But his efforts were wasted: some of his friends died, others turned against him or shook him off, others fed him with false hopes; and in the end he gave up the struggle. He recognized that he was not agile enough to climb the greasy pole towards a bishopric, nor cut out to live as a country vicar, 'banished from the academy, all commerce with the Muses, . . . and daily converse with a company of idiots and clowns'.

So he contented himself with his studentship and his books. He wrote a Latin comedy, to be performed in the college, and a few Latin poems when occasion called them forth. He would also become college librarian (an office which suited his tastes); he would serve the university for three years as clerk of the market; and he held a college living in Oxford, to which he afterwards added two successive country livings given to him by aristocratic lay patrons and evidently treated by him as sinecures. The first of these was the rectory of Walesby in Lincolnshire, to which he was presented in 1624 by 'my noble friend and patroness' the dowager Countess of Exeter, the mother of one of his pupils. There is no evidence that he ever performed any duties there: he left them to a curate. After seven years he resigned the benefice 'for some special reason', having taken instead the living of Seagrave, just north of Leicester. This second country living was given to him by George, Lord Berkeley, to whom, by then, he had dedicated his great work. He probably saw no more of it than of Walesby, but he kept it, together with his Oxford parish, 'with much ado', as we are told, till his death.[3]

The grant of the living of Seagrave may have been connected with a particular crisis in Burton's otherwise uneventful life. For although he always represented Christ Church, in his time, as a haven of peace and scholarship, it was in fact periodically convulsed by internal struggles; and the chance survival of a letter of his brother William shows that in 1629, in consequence of these struggles, Burton actually contemplated leaving it. In order to understand the affair we must go back to the earlier history of the college, before his arrival there in 1599.

For Christ Church was not like the other colleges of Oxford. Every other college was ruled by a corporation consisting of a Head and Fellows, whose rights and duties were defined by statute. But Christ Church had no Fellows. By the Letters Patent of the Founder, King Henry VIII, the ruling corporation consisted of the Dean and Chapter of the new cathedral of Oxford; the hundred 'Students', while otherwise similar to the Fellows of other colleges, were excluded from it. They had no part in government, no proportionate share of the revenue; and although their studentships were assured to them during good behaviour, the interpretation of such behaviour depended entirely on the good will of the Dean and Canons. For Christ Church had no statutes. Henry VIII had died before any had been devised, and although draft statutes had been prepared in the turbulent minority of Edward VI, they had never been approved by the young king and were repudiated as dangerously democratic under Mary. Thus the rule of the Dean and Canons was virtually absolute. However, in times when absolutism was challenged in the state, it was challenged also in Christ Church, and in the last years of Elizabeth, shortly before Burton's arrival in the college, the Students broke out in revolt. One of those who took part in the revolt was John Bancroft, soon to be Burton's tutor.

The complaint of the Students was that the Dean and Chapter, whose rents had been secured against inflation by the Statute of Provisions of 1577, had seen to it that they alone benefited from this improvement: they had first reduced the commons allowed to the Students, and then changed them into a fixed money allowance in a declining currency. In 1596 the case was argued before the Archbishop of Canterbury, the Lord Keeper and the Chancellor of the University, and an agreement was reached or imposed; but the Dean and Canons, according to the Students, promptly broke the agreement, and in 1597 the battle was joined again. In petitions to the new Lord Keeper and to Sir Robert Cecil, the Students complained that, under the arbitrary rule of the Dean and Canons, they were kept on short commons and in a state of servitude unworthy of free men; and in order to protect them against such oppressions in future, they begged for a royal visitation and for a grant of statutes to complete the 'clearly imperfect' foundation of Henry VIII. These petitions were evidently unsuccessful, at least as far as the visitation and the grant of statutes were concerned; but peace was restored and the College was quiet when Burton was elected a Student in 1599.[4]

For nearly thirty years peace seems to have reigned in Christ Church. However, in 1628, when Charles I was locked in conflict with his

Parliament, this local battle flared up again. Once again the Students rebelled against their exploitation by the Canons; the Dean appealed to the Crown; and Charles I sent down letters commanding the Students to obey their legal governors. Thereupon the Students again petitioned for redress. The King ordered the Lord Keeper, the Chancellor of the University, and others to investigate the matter. Impartial committees were set up, evidence was collected, financial accounts were submitted. Ultimately, on 30 January 1630, both parties argued their case before the King himself and his Council at Whitehall. The result, given the character of the King and of the times, could hardly be in doubt. The Students were totally crushed. The King told them that by the Letters Patent of Henry VIII, the Dean and Canons were their legitimate governors and must be obeyed. The Students, he said, 'were but as the foot, who were not to intermeddle with the direction or government which belongs to the head'; they had no rights, no certainty of tenure; and they must be grateful for whatever allowance they were given by their masters, the Canons, whose 'good government' he went out of his way to commend.[5] That ended the controversy, for the rest of Burton's life, and indeed far beyond it.*

What part Burton played in this controversy we do not know, but we know that, at the height of the battle, he decided, 'by reason of the troubled state of the College between the Canons and the Students', to leave Oxford altogether. Probably it was simply the atmosphere of intrigue and recrimination that he found intolerable. However, his decision was evidently serious and caused grave concern to his eldest brother William, who, at precisely this time, was planning to send his son Cassibilian to Christ Church to be under his brother's care. Fortunately, when the King gave his ruling, and so composed the quarrel, 'though not altogether to the Students' content', Burton changed his mind. He decided to stay after all, and look after young Cassibilian.[6] It seems probable that it was while he was contemplating emigration from Oxford that Burton resigned his unvisited Lincolnshire living and accepted a rectory in Leicestershire, only thirty miles from his old home. If he was obliged to live in the country, and 'from a polite and terse academic turn rustic, rude, melancholize alone' like 'Ovid in Pontus', he would prefer to live in his own county within reach

---

* The matter seems to have been raised again by the Students in January 1641, when Charles I had lost his authority and the Long Parliament was in reforming mood (Ch. Ch. MSS); but without effect. The Students were not admitted to the Governing Body of the College till the 19th century. See E. G. W. Bill and J. F. A. Mason, *Christ Church and Reform 1850–1867* (Oxford, 1970).

of his friends. When he changed his mind and stayed in Oxford, his Leicestershire parishioners, or his patron, may well have regretted his appointment and made 'much ado' about his retention of the rectory as an absentee.

So Burton stayed in Christ Church. There he lived, as he would write, 'a silent sedentary solitary private life, *mihi et Musis*, in the university, as Xenocrates at Athens, *ad senectam fere*, to learn wisdom, as he did, penned up most part in my study'. After all, at Oxford he had 'the use of libraries as good as any in the world', and he made good use of them: he 'would be loth', he said, 'by living as a drone, to be an unprofitable or unworthy member of so learned and noble a society'. He also enjoyed, in that society, erudite scientific conversation; for science flourished at Oxford in the reign of James I, that learned king: a reign which saw the foundation of the Bodleian Library, the Earl of Danby's Physic Garden, and the Chairs of Natural Philosophy. In Christ Church itself – the most flourishing college of Europe, as he called it – there was the newly built college library, of which Burton had charge. There his particular friend was Edmund Gunter, a famous mathematician who refined Napier's logarithms and invented the slide-rule.[7] He also mentions Thomas Clayton, the Regius Professor of Physic, who made the neighbouring Pembroke College a scientific centre, and 'our Dr Gwinn', that is Matthew Gwinn of St John's College, the musical and medical professor who had been a friend of Giordano Bruno when he came to Oxford; and he must have known Robert Hues, the expert on terrestrial and celestial globes, who had sailed round the world with Cavendish and who came to spend his later years in Christ Church. In general, Burton seems to have been more familiar with scientists than with his fellow clergy. He was unnoticed by the Church establishment of his time, and he does not mention any of the Oxford theologians as his friends.

This unadventurous, unambitious life suited Burton. He was the archetypal college bachelor who knew everything through books. His other passions were not strong, but he loved books, and venerated, above all, the founders of libraries. 'How', he asked, 'shall I remember Sir Thomas Bodley amongst the rest, Otho Nicholson and the Right Reverend John Williams, Bishop of Lincoln . . . ?' Otho Nicholson had recently founded the Library of Christ Church, and Bishop Williams, whom few others praised – for he was a slippery Welsh politician of ambiguous loyalty – had founded libraries in Cambridge, where he had been a student, at Westminster, where he was Dean, and at Lincoln, his unvisited episcopal city: 'a noble precedent', Burton exclaimed, 'for all corporate towns and cities to imitate'. Thanks to the Oxford libraries, Burton had no need to travel in search of learning. 'I never travelled', he wrote, 'but in map or card, in which my unconfined thoughts have freely expatiated.' Yes, very freely: for through his books he travelled over the whole world, following explorers and conquistadors, merchants and missionaries, from China to Peru, from Lapland to Patagonia, and was astonishingly well informed about them all. With this sedentary, vicarious life he was quite content, as he was content with his life in general: 'I am not poor, I am not rich: I have little, I want nothing; all my treasure is in Minerva's tower' – that is, in the bank of learning.

His recreations were equally academic. He liked country life, but not the rude exercises of the gentry. However, he made an exception for fishing, provided it was not taken too energetically. 'Our gentlemen', of course, took it far too energetically. They could be seen 'booted up to the groins', 'wading up to the arm-holes', wrestling in a most exhausting and undignified manner with their rods and nets. That was what gave the sport a bad name, enabling Plutarch to dismiss it as a 'filthy, base, illiberal employment, having neither wit nor perspicacity in it, nor worth the labour'. But there is a different, more elegant kind of fishing: 'he that shall consider the variety of baits for all seasons, and pretty devices which our anglers have invented, peculiar lines, false flies, several sleights, etc.,' will think better of it, will see it as an intellectual pastime and prefer it to all other forms of sport. Hawking and hunting are laborious, even dangerous, but fishing is 'still and quiet; and if so be the angler catch no fish, yet he hath a wholesome walk to the brookside, pleasant shade by the sweet silver streams; he hath good air and the melodious harmony of birds; he sees the swans, ducks, waterhens, etc., and many other fowl with their brood; which he thinketh better than the noise of hounds, or blast of horns, and all the sport that they can make'.

Besides, fishing brings one to the water. Water, sweet, running water, had a particular attraction for Burton. Next to the founders of libraries, he revered those who provided mankind with water, 'pure, thin, light water . . . of good smell and taste': drainers of fens, builders of conduits, aqueducts, cisterns. How he loved to think of the great Roman aqueducts, the splendid public baths of Constantinople and Fez! And nearer home he would commemorate his English contemporaries, Sir Hugh Middleton, the great entrepreneur who brought water to London with his 'New River', and Otho Nicholson, who had a double title to gratitude, for he created not only a library but also 'our

water-works and elegant conduit in Oxford'.* The very noise of water
was music to Burton: how soothing to be lulled to sleep by 'a basin of
water still dropping by his bedside', or lying beside 'the pleasant
murmur of stream or weir, flood-gates, arches, falls of water, like
London Bridge'.

With clean water went clean air. The Cotswold air, Burton thought,
was best: those pastoral uplands were 'most commodious for hawking,
hunting, wood, waters, and all manner of pleasures'; but above all for
walking. He loved walking. 'The most pleasant of all outward pas-
times', to him, was to walk 'with some good companions', not too
strenuously, 'among orchards, gardens, bowers, mounts and arbours,
artificial wildernesses, green thickets, arches, groves, lawns, rivulets,
fountains and suchlike pleasant places . . . brooks, pools, fishponds,
betwixt wood and water, in a fair meadow, by a riverside'. Only
boating, another aquatic pastime, could compare with it; 'to take a boat
in a pleasant evening and with music to row upon the waters, which
Plutarch so much applauds . . . or in a gondola' – for now his mind
begins to travel again – 'in the Grand Canal of Venice to see those
goodly palaces, must needs refresh and give content to a melancholy
dull spirit'. But there was no need to be ambitious, or to over-exert one's
self, in order to enjoy country life: 'the very being in the country,' he
wrote, 'that life itself, is sufficient recreation to some men'; and he
recited the names of gardening emperors and bucolic philosophers: 'if
my testimony were aught worth, I could say as much of myself. I am *vere
Saturnius*' – a true lover of the country; 'no man ever took more delight in
springs, woods, groves, gardens, walks, fishponds, rivers, etc.'

So he reflected; but alas, even these innocent pleasures eluded him as
he sat, day after day, 'a collegiate student, as Democritus in his garden',
leading 'a monastic life, *ipse mihi theatrum*', myself my own entertainment, solitary, bookish, introspective. His tastes were simple. He did
not drink wine, that wine which, he says drily, 'so much improves our
modern wits'. Coffee, and coffee-houses, he had read of, but only in
Turkey: they had not yet come to England – although when they did,
they would come first to Oxford.† As for tobacco, 'divine, rare,
superexcellent tobacco, which goes far beyond all the panaceas, potable
gold and philosopher's stones, a sovereign remedy to all diseases', he

---

* Nicholson's 'elegant conduit' was set up at Carfax, Oxford, in 1610. In 1787 it was
taken down to enlarge the High Street and presented by the university to Lord
Harcourt. He placed it in his park at Nuneham Courtenay, where it still stands.
† II, 246–7. According to Anthony Wood, coffee was first brought to England by the
Greek priest Nathaniel Conopius, who drank it in Oxford in the 1630s.

approved of it as medicine, in small, measured doses; 'but as it is commonly abused by most men, which take it as tinkers do ale, 'tis a plague, a mischief, a violent purger of goods, lands, health: hellish, devilish and damned tobacco, the ruin and overthrow of body and soul'.

What did Burton read in his solitary study? As far as we can see, everything, anything: ancient classics, medieval chronicles, modern literature, Latin and Greek, French and English, Spanish and Italian, philosophy, philology, history, politics, travel, mathematics, astronomy, medicine. He knew the English poets and quotes them often. 'Our English Homer', Geoffrey Chaucer, is his clear favourite; then Edmund Spenser, whom he describes as our Virgil; that 'elegant poet of ours', William Shakespeare; 'our arch-poet', Ben Jonson; and 'our English Ovid', Michael Drayton; but he also quotes Lydgate and Gower, Marlowe, Sidney, and Samuel Daniel. He read light literature too – his library contained the comedies of Greene and Heywood, Dekker, Middleton and Beaumont. Of modern foreign literature he quotes Rabelais and Montaigne, *La Celestina* and *Don Quixote*. He also left a mass of ephemeral pamphlets 'now grown wonderful scarce' and 'ludicrous merry pieces'.[8] The only category of books unrepresented, or under-represented, is that of scholastic theology. He was a complete humanist scholar who was also up-to-date in all modern subjects. He could quote Machiavelli and Bodin in politics, Giordano Bruno and Campanella in philosophy, Paracelsus and Severinus in medicine, Gilbert and Bacon in natural science, Vives and Comenius in education, Galileo and Kepler in astronomy, Grotius and de Thou in law and history. Like his contemporary Francis Bacon, he took all learning for his province – but with a difference.

This became clear in 1621 when he published the first edition of his great work. It was published under the pseudonym 'Democritus Junior', and dedicated to George, Lord Berkeley. It was immediately successful. It passed through five editions in his lifetime, and before his death he had corrected a sixth for the press. Each edition contained revisions, additions and embellishments from the author's continuous reading, and the happy publisher made a small fortune. 'Scarce any book of philology in our land', declared Thomas Fuller (himself a steady source of income to publishers), 'hath in so short a time passed so many impressions.' Nor has it ever been quite forgotten. It has left traces in our literature for the next two centuries. We find echoes of it in the poetry of Milton and the prose of Laurence Sterne. It was the only book which could get Dr Johnson out of bed two hours early. It delighted Lamb. It inspired Keats. It amused the leisure of Byron.

Byron saw the *Anatomy of Melancholy* as an entertaining *omnium gatherum*, a repository of arcane erudition, very useful 'to a man who wishes to acquire a reputation of being well read with the least trouble'. This is a very common view. It had been expressed in the seventeenth century by Anthony Wood and in the eighteenth by Thomas Hearne.[9] Those who have read the book for its own sake have enjoyed it for other reasons. They have praised it as humorous, fanciful, quaint. The biographer of Burton in the *Dictionary of National Biography* allows that it is 'original', but original only in being 'one of the most fantastic works in English literature'. In general, readers are charmed by its discursive method, its arcane and voluble erudition, its unique style, which is both erudite and lively, both baroque and colloquial. As Burton himself put it, 'as a river runs . . . doth my style flow: now serious, then light: now comical, then satirical; now more elaborate, then remiss, as the present subject required, or as at that time I was affected'. Not looking behind that style, such readers are content to delight in the amiable self-revelation of an eccentric old college codger, living in an unreal world of disordered antiquarian books.

Of course, this is partly true. Burton is *naif* and transparent. 'I have laid myself open (I know it)', he writes, '. . . turned my inside outward.' He made no pretence of system: 'I have read many books, but to little purpose, for want of any good method; I have confusedly tumbled over divers authors in our own libraries, with small profit, for want of art, order, memory, judgment.' Consequently, he admitted, his work had grave faults: 'barbarism, Doric dialect, extemporanean style, tautologies, apish imitation, a rhapsody of rags gathered from several dung-hills, excrements of authors, toys and fopperies confusedly tumbled out, without art, invention, judgment, wit, learning: harsh, raw, rude, phantastical, absurd, insolent, indiscreet, ill-composed, indigested, vain, scurrile, idle, dull and dry; I confess all ('tis partly affected), thou canst not think worse of it than I do myself. 'Tis not worth the reading, I yield it; I desire thee not to lose time in perusing so vain a subject . . .' However, he had his excuses: he worked on his own, without help: he had no secretary, no amanuensis: 'I must for that cause do my business myself, and was therefore enforced, as a bear doth lick her whelps, to bring forth this confused lump. I had not time to lick it into form, as she doth her young ones, but even to publish it as it was first written.' But he published it because he had, he felt, something substantial to say: the accumulation of a lifetime of study; and it was the substance not the form by which he wished his work to be judged.

What is that substance? Behind the disorderly erudition, the tumbling cascade of recondite authorities and conflicting ideas and precariously suspended judgements, behind the grave irony and the pervasive scepticism, it is hard to isolate and define. But it is there. Let us try to disengage it.

First of all, the topic. As a divine, Burton might have been expected by the academic establishment to produce a solid work of theological controversy, suitable to the times: for we are now in the reign of James I, when such controversy was positively encouraged. However, of such works, he confessed, he saw no great need. His age, he thought, had already done enough in that line: it had produced 'so many commentators, treatises, pamphlets, expositions, sermons, that whole teams of oxen cannot draw them'. Besides, he was not himself theologically minded. No one would suppose, from his work, that he was a clergyman. Indeed, he had a positive hatred for the 'theologasters' and their squabbles. Though 'by profession a divine', he was, he said 'by mine inclination a physician'. This was a rash claim to make, for the professional physicians were a touchy breed, jealous of their status and their monopoly. However, Burton hastened to disarm his critics. Many clergy, he observed, were part-time physicians – they had to be, to make ends meet – and physicians were known to have taken orders. If the medical faculty would pardon his invasion of their field, he promised that he would afterwards 'divert the scandal' by publishing some grave treatise of divinity – which, of course, he never did. Meanwhile he let himself go, on his chosen subject: the fascinating subject, never more fashionable than in his time, of 'melancholy'.

Why melancholy? we ask. Publicly, Burton replied that he wrote of melancholy in order to occupy himself and thereby protect himself against the disease, to which, he admitted, he was liable: 'I write of melancholy, by being busy, to avoid melancholy.' For melancholy, aimless rumination, pleasing at its best – Milton's 'divinest melancholy' – but leading, if indulged, to low spirits, morbid fantasy, even lunacy, is the occupational disease of scholars, akin to the deadly medieval sin of 'accidie', so common in the cloister. But in fact Burton has a more serious purpose. He is not only a student of man: he is a would-be reformer of society. He is deeply conscious of the disorders of his age; and he believes that those disorders can be cured. They cannot be cured by public debate, religious controversy, war or politics. Those have never made anything better. They can be cured only by a change in human psychology, in the heart of man. And since the heart of man is essentially irrational, this change cannot be wrought by rational means: by exhortation, argument, preaching. Another method must be used: the method (Burton believed) of Democritus.

Democritus of Abdera, the original Democritus, was one of the most influential of those pre-Socratic philosophers who studied the physical sciences rather than, like Socrates, the nature of man. He was the first to advance the atomic theory of Nature, and the first to believe in the infinity of the universe and a plurality of worlds. But although these cosmological doctrines had been revived in his own time, it was not they which caused Burton to choose Democritus as his model: it was rather his popular reputation as 'the laughing philosopher'. In his preface Burton makes this clear. He there describes Democritus in terms which he is clearly prepared to own for himself. The philosopher of Abdera, he tells us, was 'a little wearish old man, very melancholy by nature, averse from company in his latter days, and much given to solitariness'. He was also a man of wide observation, who had examined the entire workshop of nature, and who found the behaviour of humanity irresistibly absurd: so absurd that his only relaxation from private study was sometimes to 'walk down to the haven and laugh heartily at such a variety of ridiculous objects as there he saw'. Similarly Burton himself, we are told, would sometimes suspend his studies in Christ Church, leave his books, which engendered melancholy, and his fire of juniperwood, whose smoke was calculated to dispel it, and walk down to Folly Bridge, the bridge over the river Thames, only a quarter of a mile away, there to divert himself by listening to the scolding and storming and swearing of the Oxford bargees.[10] Thus at the very beginning of his book Burton tells us that the behaviour and opinions of men are absurd, and he himself is not only an observer, 'a mere spectator of other men's fortunes and adventures', but a philosopher who has chosen to use wit, ridicule, humour in order to convey his message to the world.

That message, it soon appears, is highly critical. The society which Burton sees around him does not please him. How he hates the absurd pretensions of the religious factions which divide the Christian world! How he detests sectarian quarrels, the intolerance of religious parties: 'ruffling cardinals', 'hell-born Jesuits and fiery-spirited friars', puritan precisians! How he chastises the rulers of the world for their love of war! What, he asks, would Democritus have said to see, hear and read of so many bloody battles, the horror and barbarity of our frivolous wars, so many 'proper men, well-proportioned, carefully brought up, able both in body and mind, sound, led like so many beasts to the slaughter, in the flower of their years, . . . infinite treasures consumed, towns burned, cities sacked and ruinated'? How would he have looked on the unjust organization of our society, our absurd standards of value, our topsy-turvy priorities? The truth is, Burton concludes, we are all mad, melancholy mad: no man so wise but has seemed to some other wise men a fool: Pythagoras, Socrates, Aristotle, none is exempt. Perhaps Copernicus, 'Atlas his successor', is right who 'is of opinion the earth is a planet, moves and shines to others, as the moon doth to us. . . . If it be so that the earth is a moon, then are we also giddy, vertiginous and lunatic within this sublunary maze.'

Have we not heard such a voice before? Hatred of war, hatred of religious strife, all the world as a theatre of folly, to be exposed by wit, irony and scepticism, those subtle corrosives which alone can eat away the foundations of bigotry; is not this the philosophy of Erasmus – Erasmus in his colloquies, Erasmus in his *Praise of Folly* – and of Erasmus' friend, to whom he dedicated the *Praise of Folly*, Sir Thomas More? Both Erasmus and More are owned by Burton as his models, and praised by him; and so is the great Greek sceptic and satirist whom they both admired and whose work they jointly translated: Lucian of Samosata. Lucian is a hero of Burton too, and is constantly quoted by him; and in his wake comes that other great satirist who was a devoted admirer of Erasmus: 'Rabelais, that French Lucian'. As we read on – and we do not have to read far – this intellectual ancestry becomes even more obvious. For in order to show what a society would be like if it were freed from 'this feral disease of melancholy' which 'now domineers almost all over Europe amongst our great ones' and has brought it to its present pass, Burton looks at Jacobean England, with its national vice of idleness, its social anomalies, its neglected opportunities, and opposes to it an imaginary ideal. His model is the *Utopia* of Thomas More; to which, in later editions, he could add the *New Atlantis* of Francis Bacon.* 'Let men be as foolish and as heedless as they like', he writes, 'I will yet, to satisfy and please myself, make a *Utopia* of mine own, a *New Atlantis*, a poetical commonwealth of mine own, in which I will freely domineer, build cities, make laws, statutes, as I list myself. And why may I not? . . . You know what liberty poets ever had; and besides my predecessor Democritus was a politician, a recorder of

---

* Bacon's *New Atlantis* was first published in 1627, six years after the first edition of *The Anatomy of Melancholy*. Burton first cites it in his third edition, of 1628.

Abdera, a law-maker as some say: and why may not I presume as much as he did? . . .'

Burton's Utopia, like Thomas More's, is a remote island, known only to him. 'For the site, if you will needs urge me to it, I am not fully resolved. It may be in *Terra Australis Incognita*, there is room enough (for of my knowledge neither that hungry Spaniard nor Mercurius Britannicus have yet discovered half of it), or else one of those floating islands' in the South Sea, which 'are accessible only at set times and to some few persons; or one of the Fortunate Isles, for who knows yet where or which they are?' It will be in the temperate zone, in latitude 45° ('I respect not minutes') . . . 'the longitude for some reason I will conceal'. Then we are given a description of its organization and economy: twelve or thirteen provinces, each with its capital; regularly spaced cities, rationally sited on 'navigable rivers or lakes, creeks, havens', with broad straight streets and uniform houses, like the old free cities of the Netherlands, Switzerland, Italy, or Cambalu (Peking) in China. For Burton, like so many of his contemporaries, was fascinated by China, the great empire described long ago by Marco Polo and now again by the Jesuit missionaries Matteo Ricci and Trigault, with its orderly and peaceful society, its rational government, its scholarly mandarins. Again and again he reverts to it, and almost always with admiration. It was to him, as to so many Europeans since – to the philosophers of the Enlightenment and to the ideologues of the 1960s – a model of perfect social organization.

The organization of Burton's utopia is similarly rational, similarly beneficent. Public health, public sanitation, public education are all cared for. There are orphanages, almshouses, hospitals, asylums, not founded at random by 'gouty benefactors' out of the spoils of rapine and fraud, but publicly maintained for all who need them. There is a system of old age pensions. Thanks to such a system, poverty will be eliminated. If it survives, it will be evidence of criminality and therefore suppressed: 'I will suffer no beggars, rogues, vagabonds, or idle persons at all.' There are public granaries against times of dearth, public academies of learning, public banks – for though usury may be condemned by divines, 'it must be winked at by politicians', 'for we converse here with men, not with gods'. There are uniform weights and measures – a great *desideratum* in seventeenth-century Europe – a regular fire-service, communal playing-fields, and, particularly, 'conduits of sweet and good water aptly distributed in each town'. In the country, 'I will have no bogs, fens, marshes, vast woods, deserts, heaths, commons, but all enclosed (yet not depopulated, and therefore take heed you mistake me not) . . . I will not have a barren acre in all my territories, not so much as the tops of mountains: where Nature fails, it shall be supplied by art: lakes and rivers shall not be left desolate.'

A socialist paradise? Certainly not. Burton is keenly aware of the injustice caused by social inequality, but he is no egalitarian. Unlike More, he believes in private property, and seeks only to correct its abuses, not to abolish it. Ownership of land is to be private, but 'with a charitable division in every village, not one domineering house to swallow up all, which is too common with us' – and nowhere commoner, in those years, than in his own Leicestershire, the centre of agrarian discontent. In Burton's Utopia the landlords are to keep within their limits, and the tenants to have long leases and pay fixed rents and fines, 'to free them from those intolerable exactions of tyrannising landlords'. In government too there is to be no equality. Burton is no radical, no democrat. He is impatient of the 'witty fictions', 'mere chimaeras', of his contemporaries Tommaso Campanella and Valentin Andreae. He rejects a Platonic or 'Utopian parity' which – as More himself admitted of his Utopia – 'takes away all splendour and magnificence'.* His government is monarchical and aristocratic; but his aristocracy is different from the feudal nobility of Europe. It is to be hereditary indeed, endowed and independent, with degrees of nobility – dukes, earls, viscounts, barons – but it must be open to new men of talent: 'I hate those severe, unnatural, harsh German, French and Venetian decrees which exclude plebeians from honours.' It is also to be open internally, to younger brothers, who 'shall be sufficiently provided for by pensions, or so qualified, brought up in some honest calling, they shall be able to live of themselves'. In other words, the evils of primogeniture are to be corrected, and no discredit is to be attached to trade.

Trade, indeed, is to be encouraged. Except in luxuries, it is to be untaxed. Industry is to be specialized, controlled by gilds and fraternities; but prices are to be regulated, 'as our clerks of the market do bakers and brewers' – having himself been clerk of the market, Burton knew all about that – and there are to be 'no private monopolies, to enrich one man and beggar a multitude'. This also was a notorious abuse in Jacobean England: Burton was writing at the height of the agitation which led to the Monopolies Act of 1624.

---

* Burton's phrase consciously echoes More's own – ironical – objections to his Utopia: 'qua una re [i.e. community of goods and absence of money] funditus evertitur omnis nobilitas, magnificentia, splendor, maiestas . . .' (*Utopia*, last paragraph).

Like his state, Burton's church too is hierarchical. It is an episcopal church, under the state; but it is spared one of the great abuses of the Anglican church. There are 'no impropriations, no lay patrons of church livings'. Poor vicars are not to be starved by greedy patrons. Again and again, throughout his work, Burton denounces the system of lay-patronage and its results: the poverty and dependence of the clergy, who are forced to comply with their patron's doctrine, to make simoniacal compacts with him, to resort to menial trades in order to live: to 'turn taskers, maltsters, costermongers, graziers, sell ale as some have done, or worse'. Like Archbishop Laud, during whose rule he was revising his work, Burton would 'leave not so much as the name of a lay fee in England'; but he would also, like the puritan reformers, rationalize and decentralize the church: 'no parish to contain above a thousand auditors'. For the clergy, ideally, of course, he would have 'such priests as should imitate Christ', just as he would have 'charitable lawyers' who 'would love their neighbours as themselves, temperate and modest physicians', politicians who would 'condemn the world', etc. But since 'this is impossible, I must get such as I may'; and the best way of getting them is not by the machinery of patronage but by election by 'common societies, corporations, etc.; and those rectors of benefices to be chosen out of the universities, examined and approved as the *literati* in China'.

Reformation of law was to be as powerful a slogan in the Puritan Revolution as reformation of clergy. In Burton's utopia law is cheap, lawyers few, lawsuits brief, and judges, 'and all other inferior magistrates, chosen as the *literati* in China'. Education is reformed too: there are academies of all the sciences for learned men, and public schools teaching grammar and languages not by precept but by conversation, as recommended by Comenius and others. The ideas of Comenius were coming into England in the 1630s and would be read by educational reformers who, after Burton's death, would seek to realize them. It is one of the signs – there are many others – of Burton's constant alertness, his unfailing openness to new ideas, that he so quickly adopted them. In his utopia he also provided for 'public historiographers', so that history shall not be at the mercy of 'each insufficient scribbler, partial or parasitical pedant, as in our times'. This office would be created by the Parliament in the civil war, but without achieving the objectivity which Burton required. But then Burton never envisaged a civil war. He would have an army, but for defence only: 'I hate wars, if they be not *ad populi salutem*, upon urgent occasion. . . . Offensive wars, except the cause be very just, I will not allow of.'

Such is the ideal, rational society. But can it ever be achieved?

Theoretically, Burton believes that it can; and one does not need to go as far as China to see the evidence. Look, nearer home, at the Netherlands. There you shall see what can be done by human skill and foresight: 'those neat cities and populous towns, full of most industrious artificers, so much land recovered from the sea, and so painfully preserved by those artificial inventions . . . so many navigable channels from place to place, made by men's hands, etc.' How different from the undrained fens, the squalid provincial towns, the stagnant trade of Jacobean England: 'our still running rivers stopped, and havens void of ships'; not to speak of the swarms of lawyers, the idle gentry whose parks and forests are kept unimproved for their barbarous field-sports, the depopulated villages, the discontented peasantry. The Netherlanders showed what could be done: what could have been made of England if the will had been there. We are reminded that it was in the Netherlands, in the home of his friend Peter Gillis, that Thomas More had conceived the idea of his *Utopia*; and it was the same contrast which had caused him to conceive it. The difference was that while More discovered the orderly, rational mercantile society of Flanders through experience, as the envoy of Henry VIII, Burton discovered the orderly, rational mercantile society of Holland through books.

If the will had been there . . . why then was the will not there: why was it lacking in England? For, after all, such a will can be created. Society is not inherently static: history shows that it goes up and down. The Romans had civilized England, France, Germany, just as the Turks have barbarized Greece, Egypt, Asia Minor, Palestine, once noble and fruitful countries, now 'mere carcases' of their former selves. 'Even so might Virginia and the wild Irish have been civilised long since' if due order had been taken. One of the new books which Burton had read while meditating his *Anatomy* was Sir George Carew's *Discourse showing The True Reasons why Ireland was Never Entirely Subdued*. Carew was an expert on Ireland: he had spent most of his life there, in the royal service. But Burton was not impressed by his expert political opinion. 'If his reasons were thoroughly scanned by a judicious politician', he wrote, 'I am afraid he would not altogether be approved.' The effective means of gaining allegiance was not conquest but improvement: the true lesson of Ireland was that 'it would turn to the dishonour of our nation, to suffer it to lie so long waste'.

How is improvement achieved? To Burton two conditions are essential: good government and industry – and good government means government which encourages industry. It was the arbitrary and tyrannical government of the Turks, he wrote, which had ruined the industry, and therefore the prosperity, of the once flourishing Levant. Wise rulers had always attracted industry to their countries. 'Edward III, our most renowned King, to his eternal memory, brought clothing first into this island, transporting some families of artificers from Gaunt hither.' It was industry, often immigrant industry, that had made the fortune of medieval Italy and Flanders, as it had now made that of the United Provinces of the Netherlands: for 'the chiefest loadstone which draws all manner of commerce and merchandise' thither, and maintains their present estate, 'is not fertility of soil but industry'. So these petty provinces produce more wealth than the gold-mines of Peru or New Spain: they are 'our Indies, the epitome of China, and all by reason of their industry, good policy and commerce'. For industry draws in all good things: 'that alone makes countries flourish, cities populous, and will enforce, by reason of much manure which necessarily follows, a barren soil to be fertile and good'.

Why then should not England, which had so many natural advantages – which had peace and unity and defensible frontiers and a happy system of government – do as well, especially now, when it had the particular and unique benefit of 'a wise, learned, religious King, another Numa, a second Augustus, a true Josiah; most worthy senators, a learned clergy, an obedient commonalty, etc.'? The government of King James had indeed 'seriously attempted' to establish a new industry in England – the reference is to alderman Cokayne's project to 'finish' (that is to dye) English cloth in England instead of sending it to the Netherlands. However, this project too had failed, and the question has to be asked, what is the obstacle which frustrates progress in England and in so much of modern Europe but which, we must infer, was somehow absent from Augustan Rome, medieval Flanders and Italy, distant China, and the neighbouring Netherlands?

Before proceeding to Burton's answers, we may pause for a moment to reflect on the implications of his utopia, and of the questions which it inspires. What must strike us, above all, is his realism. Although he had never travelled abroad, and hardly at home – there is no evidence that he had been outside the Midlands of England – and although all his illustrations come from his vast reading, there is nothing 'quaint', 'pedantic', or 'fantastic' about his thinking or his conclusions. His utopia is essentially practical. He will not, like More or Campanella or Andreae, lay down a blueprint for a radically new form of society or expect a transformation of human nature. He will create his utopia within an existing pattern. He will retain the social hierarchy and the state church. He will make concessions to human weakness. He is not a revolutionary philosopher but a highly intelligent observer of historical and economic facts. Those facts may have been derived from reading, not from personal observation, but they are real, and their reality is respected: they are taken from historically attested societies, not theoretical constructions and imaginary lands.

His answer to his own questions is no less empirical. Looking for the effective difference between those societies whose dynamism he admires and the contemporary English and European society whose values he deplores, Burton, like some later sociologists, discovers it, not in merely mechanical arrangements, in political or economic systems, but in a difference of ethos, of spirit. Those admired societies, in so far as they were active and industrious, animated by a desire for improvement, were, he believed, 'free from melancholy'. From which it appears that 'melancholy' is not merely a temporary depression of spirits but a kind of pervasive social inertia, an incapacity for deliberate self-improvement and rational activity. Melancholy therefore must be cured in the individual before society can be improved: the health of the commonwealth rests ultimately on the psychology of man.

What is melancholy? To the orthodox medical profession in the sixteenth century – and Burton is fundamentally orthodox – the word had a precise meaning. Melancholy was one of the four 'humours' which were unevenly distributed in the composition of man. These four humours – the sanguine, the choleric, the phlegmatic and the melancholy – were associated with the four elements and, astrologically, with four planets. Melancholy, which was physically the result of an excess of black bile, was associated with the dullest of the elements, earth, and the most sombre of the planets, Saturn. Melancholy people were thus predestined at birth to a condition that was depressed and poor, to a character that was dull and heavy, and to a complexion that was 'saturnine', that is dark and woe-begone. That was the consequence of their birth, and could not be changed. But there were secondary developments which could be affected by treatment. In the sixteenth century there was a fashionable theory according to which melancholy, if properly tempered, could be 'revalued' – that is, in the words of Frances Yates, raised from being the lowest of the four conditions 'to become the highest, the humour of great men, great thinkers, prophets and religious seers'.[11] It is easy to see in this the rationalization of a well-known psychological fact. The pioneer of this theory was Marsilio Ficino in the late fifteenth century, who derived it from Neoplatonic philosophy. His methods of 'revaluation' included wine and aromatic foods, odours and pure, sunny air, and music.[12] Burton, as we shall see, came to some of the same conclusions. He had of course read the works of Ficino, as he had read everything. But his main concern is with a different, indeed opposite, development of melancholy: not its sublimation into genius but its degeneration into morbidity. Such degeneration was caused when the humour had either gone bad or been burnt up. This was 'melancholy adust', which, being not predetermined, is curable. Admittedly the cure is not easy, for, once established, it is 'a chronic or continuate disease, a settled humour . . . not errant but fixed; and as it was long increasing, so now, being . . . grown into a habit, it will hardly be removed'. However, we must not despair. We must use the right method, which is to study it empirically, clinically, through numerous case-histories. Only thus can we hope to discover its explanation, and perhaps its cure.

So, for the rest of his long work (for we are still only in the introduction), we are taken through all the varieties of human melancholy, their causes, their symptoms, and their cure. We begin with a discussion of diseases in general. Then there is a digression on the subject of anatomy, 'this most excellent subject', the essential basis of medicine. And then we are off, on this long, rambling, delightful excursion through the infinite varieties of human psychology, as revealed by reading and experience: vast discursive reading, necessary experience, for bookish though he is, Burton is temperamentally a Baconian, believing that it is in 'the chiefest treasures of Nature', not in the intricate subtleties of speculation, that 'the best medicines for all manner of diseases are to be found'. The proper method of discovery, he insists, is empirical: it is by examining hundreds of instances and noting parallels, coincidences and exceptions that we shall approach at least a provisional truth.

How are diseases caused? Man, we are taught, was created perfect, in the image of God, but having fallen from grace, he is liable to all kinds of ills. Some of these ills are caused supernaturally, either directly by God, or, through his permission, by the devil or his agents – spirits, witches, or magicians; others are natural, caused either directly or indirectly: directly, by the general organization of the world and the regular working of Nature (as by the stars and their influence and the processes of generation, growth and decay), or indirectly, by particular accidents and dislocations of nature, affecting both the body and the mind. So, to begin with, all these forces, in so far as they cause 'melancholy', must be examined in detail, their symptoms must be observed, their prognostics isolated, and, when these have been set out, the method of 'rectification' must be discovered. One cannot, of course, 'rectify' God or Nature, and it is questionable whether one can or should seek to rectify the operation of spirits, by dabbling in magic or superstition; nor can one do much about heredity or old age; but the disturbances of Nature, whether in the body or the mind, in so far as they are caused by environment or habit or diet, can be scientifically rectified. All that is necessary is to accumulate the evidence, to gather it out of the immense storehouse of the world's literature, to order, arrange, apply it – and, if possible, not to be overwhelmed by it, or to lose one's way in it: for of course it is impossible to be entirely systematic; nor indeed would we wish Burton to be too systematic, since it is in his digressions – sometimes explicitly admitted as such, sometimes accidental through pursuit of a particularly fascinating theme – that the layman has always found his charm.

For instance, since they may be (indirectly) the cause of melancholy in some, we have a long 'digression of spirits', bad angels or devils, what they are, whether corporeal or incorporeal, mortal or immortal, their hierarchy, kinds, number, etc. If the authorities marshalled by Burton can be believed, there are many kinds of spirits. First and most elevated are the aerial spirits, of which some cause 'tempests, thunder and lightnings, tear oaks, fire steeples, houses, strike men and beasts, make it rain stones, as in Livy's time, wool, frogs, etc., as at Vienna before the coming of the Turks . . .' while others 'corrupt the air, and cause plagues, sickness, storms, shipwrecks, fires, inundations, etc.' Then there are devils who 'desire carnal copulation with witches (incubi and succubi), transform bodies, and are so very cold if they be touched'; and water-devils, fauns, satyrs, wood-nymphs, among whom are to be classed the weird women who met Macbeth and Banquo on the blasted heath; fairies, 'that do usually walk in little coats, some two foot long', hobgoblins and Robin Goodfellows (who are a little larger), trolls, who are very common in Norway 'and do drudgery work', foliots – our poltergeists – who make strange noises in the night, howl sometimes pitifully, and then laugh again, cause great flame and sudden lights, fling stones, rattle chains, shave men, open doors and shut them, fling down platters, stools, chests; and *getuli* or *cobali*, the two sorts of spirits which live underground in mines, dressed as metal-men, to protect the treasures of the earth. These last haunt the centre of the earth, where they are employed to torture the souls of the damned; but they pop up occasionally through the craters of Etna, Lipari, Hecla in Iceland,

Vesuvius, Tierra del Fuego etc., 'because many shrieks and fearful cries are continually heard thereabouts, and familiar apparitions of dead men, ghosts and goblins'.

Another digression is a long consolatory chapter on the remedies of all manner of discontents: a moral exhortation from which Burton evidently did not expect much, for 'to what end are such paraenetical discourses? You may as soon remove Mount Caucasus as alter some men's affections.' However, if his digression did not relieve the reader, he reflected, perhaps it would relieve himself: 'if it be not for thy ease, it may be for mine own. So Tully, Cardan and Boethius wrote *de consolatione* as well to help themselves as others.' So also, in the edition of 1635, he would add his remarkable 'Digression of Air', which begins as a consideration of the effect of climate on human constitutions, and the means of rectifying it, but gradually develops into an aerial excursion through the astronomy and cosmography of the age.

Burton introduces the Digression of Air in a fine Homeric simile: 'as a long-winged hawk, when he is first whistled off the fist, mounts aloft, and for his pleasure fetcheth many a circuit in the air, still soaring higher and higher till he be come to his full pitch, and in the end, when the game is sprung, comes down amain and stoops upon a sudden; so will I, having now come into these ample fields of air, wherein I may freely expatiate and exercise myself for my recreation, awhile rove, wander round about the world, mount aloft to those ethereal orbs and celestial spheres, and so descend to my former elements again.' And mount he does, to a very great height, through all the 'hypotheses and fabricated new systems of the world' which paradoxical cosmologers have invented 'out of their own Daedalian heads'; but always he keeps a sharp eye open for 'a convenient place to go down with Orpheus, Ulysses, Hercules, Lucian's Menippus, at St Patrick's Purgatory, at Trophonius' den, Hecla in Iceland, Etna in Sicily, to descend and see what is done in the bowels of the earth: do stones and metals grow there still? How come fir trees to be digged out of the tops of hills in our mosses and marshes all over Europe', and fossil shells and fish-bones in mountains far from the sea? In the end, he duly comes down – 'my melancholy spaniel's quest, my game, is sprung, and I must suddenly come down and follow' – not to Hecla or Etna, but to more familiar spots: to Leicestershire and Warwickshire, the manor-houses of the local gentry, his family friends, and the ill effects of their situation, surrounded, too often, by stagnant moats or in foggy bottoms, which generate melancholy.

The 'Digression of Air' is an essay in itself, provoked (it is clear) by the great astronomical debate which followed the condemnation of Galileo in 1633; but there are other, less ambitious digressions, on the problems of heredity and environment, on the use of baths, and the miseries of scholars. This, of course, to any academic, is an irresistible subject, and plentifully documented. The scholar, says Burton, 'like an ass, wears out his time for provender'. 'If he be a trencher-chaplain in a gentleman's house', he may in the end 'after some seven years service' – provided he does not 'offend his good patron or displease his lady mistress in the meantime' – have half a living, paying the other half to his patron, 'or some small rectory with the mother of the maids' – that is, the housekeeper – 'at length, a poor kinswoman, or a cracked chamber-maid, to have and to hold during the time of his life'. We are reminded of Macaulay's famous picture of the seventeenth-century country parson. As for those who are not in orders – 'poets, rhetoricians, historians, philosophers, mathematicians, sophisters, etc., they are like grasshoppers: sing they must in summer and pine in winter, for there is no preferment for them'. This being so, there was something to be said for being a student of Christ Church, even under the arbitrary rule of the Dean and Canons. But indeed no class of men is exempt from these troubles: 'our whole life is an Irish sea', all mankind are, or make themselves, miserable; 'betwixt hope and fear . . . betwixt falling in, falling out, etc., we bangle away our best days', there is no peace anywhere, 'our villages are like mole-hills, and men as so many emmets, busy, busy still, going to and fro, in and out, and crossing each others' projects, as the lines of several sea-cards cut each other in a globe or map'.

Admittedly these digressions rarely lead us to any conclusions, but that is not their purpose: to digress is to digress; and anyway, if we read between the lines, we can often perceive the author's preference. For his method is to rely on the reader's perception rather than on his own explicit statements, at least in the more delicate areas of controversy. How far, for instance, do the stars influence human temperament? Burton's answer is cautious, even conventional. 'If thou shalt ask me what I think,' he replies, after marshalling and surveying his authorities, 'I must answer . . . they do incline but not compel; no necessity at all . . . and so gently incline that a wise man may resist them.' Is the universe infinite, containing a plurality of worlds, as was taught, among the ancients, by Democritus and, among the moderns, by Giordano Bruno and his English disciple Nicholas Hill? Burton is clearly attracted to the idea, to which he returns more than once, but he avoids commitment. Are chemical remedies to be preferred to traditional?

Though he clearly distrusts the extreme claims of the Paracelsian and Hermetic philosophers, Burton prefers, on the whole, not to decide: 'why do I meddle with this great controversy, which is the subject of many volumes? Let Paracelsus, Quercetan, Crollius and the brethren of the Rosy Cross defend themselves as they may.' 'Quercetan' (Joseph du Chesne) and Crollius (Oswald Croll) were two of the most famous modern disciples of Paracelsus.* Among the brethren of the Rosy Cross – the Rosicrucians who had crept so mysteriously into the limelight in 1614 and clearly fascinated him, for he makes several somewhat ironical references to 'that omniscious and only wise fraternity' and its radical plans of reform – Burton no doubt included Robert Fludd, the encyclopaedist of the macrocosm and the microcosm; but rather surprisingly (since he cites so many arcane authors), he never quotes him, although they were colleagues at Christ Church. This may be significant. Burton, though he lacked Bacon's clarity of vision, was essentially a Baconian; and, as Bacon's disciple John Wilkins would afterwards put it, 'there are not two ways in the whole world more opposite than those of Lord Verulam and Dr Fludd'.[13]

Another great controversy of the time was that concerning witches. Are witches real agents of the Devil, or are they themselves, as some maintain, the victims of melancholy? This is a very grave question to which Burton often returns. On the whole, he yields to the embattled demonologists: for how can anyone defy the combined authority of so many 'lawyers, divines, physicians, philosophers': of the Swedish pundit Olaus Magnus on the Lapland witches who sell winds and raise storms; of Cardanus on *incubi* and *succubae*; and of all those modern masters – the encyclopaedic Bodin, the oracular Lipsius – who are so eager to trounce the sceptics and chronicle the multiplication of witches in contemporary Europe? Burton may not have equal respect for all these authorities – indeed for 'old doting Lipsius', the self-styled pedagogue of the human race, who swallowed the miracles of the Virgin of Halle, he has some contempt (it was in a spirit of high irony that he exempted him, together with the Pope, since both claimed to be infallible, from the otherwise universal catalogue of fools). Still, the factual evidence which they gave had to be respected, and 'if these stories be true', the consequence could not be rejected: 'there is some probability for it'. It is not a very positive conclusion, and is at best conditional. Like Montaigne, whom he so resembles in his scepticism, his discursive style, his reluctance to commit himself, and his genial,

* See above, pp. 169–79, 181–2.

uninhibited self-exposure, Burton generally ends, in these meta-physical matters, by suspending judgement.

But let us look past the digressions and seek to isolate Burton's central message. The burden of his work is the belief that the human mind can be restored to its natural rationality by curing 'melancholy' at its base: that is, by 'rectification' of the imbalance which causes or aggravates it. That imbalance may be external or internal. It may be the effect of heredity or of environment. It may of course spring from physical defects which need to be cured by medicine: for body and mind are not distinct, one operates on the other. But in general Burton is as sceptical of purely medical cures as he is of supernatural explanations. He distrusts bleeding and uroscopy and the elaborate composite drugs of the apothecaries no less than astrology and incantations. Physic itself, he observes, is not necessary where diet is simple and healthy, as in northern countries, and even in modern England 'except it be for a few nice idle citizens, surfeiting courtiers and stall-fed gentlemen lubbers'. Although his conclusions are always tentative, safely con-veyed in the form of quotations from other authorities, he is essentially a psychiatrist who seeks, by external and internal adjustments, by physical and mental therapy, to re-create the natural harmony of the disturbed human psyche.

How is this to be done? As each human being is an individual, there can be no *panacea*, no universal cure. Drugs, palliatives, stimulants must be tempered to the person. So must the other forms of therapy. The essential task is to restore the balance. The scholar must escape from his books. On the other hand, the country squire who is melancholy through rural indolence may be cured by discovering an intellectual interest: let him calculate logarithms, square the circle, correct Scaliger's chronology, peruse the metaphysics of the Schoolmen, or, if he prefers, seek the philosopher's stone, apply his mind to heraldry, devise emblems, epithalamia, epitaphs, palindromes, anagrams, chrono-grams, acrostics upon his friends' names – no matter what. Solitude can be the cause or the cure of the disease, according to circumstances, and therefore monasteries and nunneries, which institutionalize solitude, should not have been so totally abolished. A melancholy young man should relax in the company of fair women – 'provided always that his disease proceed not originally from it, that he be not some light *inamorato*, some idle phantastic who capers in conceit all the day long and thinks of nothing else but how to make jigs, sonnets, madrigals in commendation of his mistress'. Sexual frustration – 'Venus omitted' – can be as damaging to monastic recluses as sexual excess to students, for whom it is 'one of the five mortal enemies, consuming the spirits and weakening the brain'. In general, diversity, diversion are needed, and moderate self-indulgence: 'a cup of strong drink, mirth, music and merry company' exhilarate a sorrowful heart and draw the mind out of itself. They are 'the true *nepenthes*', 'a principal engine to batter the walls of melancholy, a chief antidote and a sufficient cure of itself'.

Especially music, 'instrumental, vocal, with strings, wind, etc.' Music indeed is the nearest we can come to a universal therapy, 'so powerful a thing that it ravisheth the soul . . . and carries it beyond itself, helps, elevates, extends it'. It is effective among all men, regardless of their state. 'Sir Thomas More, in his absolute Utopian commonwealth, allows music as an appendix to every meal, and that throughout, to all sorts.' Even animals respond to it. Fishes, 'as common experience evinceth', are much affected by it, and singing-birds, 'especially nightingales, if we may believe Calcagninus'. Elephants delight in it; whales, off the coast of Cornwall, 'will come and show themselves dancing at the sound of a trumpet'; and bees, 'though they be flying far away, when they hear any tingling sound, will tarry behind'.

Such are the instrumental means of prevailing over melancholy. But, of course, they can be effective only if the patient responds: if 'he himself, or his friends' make use of them. ' "He himself" ', I say; from the patient himself the first and chiefest remedy must be had': he must be persuaded, by reason, to accept the cure. However, if that is too much to ask, if 'our judgment be so depraved, our reason over-ruled, will precipitated, that we cannot seek our own good, or moderate ourselves', then 'the best way for ease is to impart our misery to some friend, not to smother it up in our own breast', for 'grief concealed strangles the soul' but 'friends' contabulations are comfortable at all times . . . Democritus' collyrium is not so sovereign to the eyes as this is to the heart'. Ideally, of course, the friend – the external fixed point of reference for the unstable patient – should also be the physician, that is, the psychiatrist who understands the rules. Modern psychologists would agree.

Having dealt with melancholy in general, its causes and cure, Burton ends his work with two long sections on the two most comprehensive causes of melancholy: love and religion. On love and its infinite varieties, extravagances, perversions, he has a high old time. He has well-stocked chapters illustrating the power and extent of love, its causes and provocations, its symptoms and expressions. Many are the recondite and surprising details which he has discovered in the classics, the humanists, the 'priapean Popes' and self-tormenting Church

Fathers, not to speak of the Greek *Priapeia*, the writings of the Venetian pornographer Aretino, and an Italian dialogue suggestively entitled *Pornoboscodidascalio*. Sometimes he is constrained to drop into Latin: 'good Master Schoolmaster,' he adds in a marginal note on one such occasion, 'do not English this'; and his chaste editors, otherwise liberal in their translation, have obeyed. But in the end he can conclude little, for, as he says, 'there is no end of love's symptoms, 'tis a bottomless pit. Love is subject to no dimensions, not to be surveyed by any art or engine; and besides, I am of Haedus' mind, "no man can discourse of love matters, or judge of them aright, that hath not made trial in his own person", or, as Aeneas Silvius' – that is, the humanist Pope Pius II – 'adds, "hath not a little doted, been mad or lovesick himself".' 'I confess', Burton concludes, 'I am but a novice, a contemplator only . . . I have a tincture, for why should I lie, dissemble or excuse it? yet . . . what I say is merely reading . . . by mine own observation and others' relation.'

Once the forms of the disease, its causes and symptoms, have been set out, we turn to the cure. How does one cure love-melancholy? The grave philosophers and casuists ('for I light my candle at their torches') offer several remedies. One can cut down on food and drink, contenting one's self with monastic diet – 'not with sweet wine, mutton and pottage as many of those tenter-bellies', our latterday monks, 'do, howsoever they put on Lenten faces', but with vegetarian diet, 'cucumbers, melons, purslane, water-lilies, rue, woodbine, ammi, lettuce'. So the early Fathers advised, and so the famous anchorites of the desert subdued the lusts of the flesh – although they, of course, went too far, inducing another variety of melancholy, soon to be described. Or one can mortify the flesh by other external means, like the Indian Brahmins who kept themselves continent, 'lying upon the ground covered with skins, as the redshanks' – that is, the Scottish highlanders – 'do in the heather'. Then there are special diets and herbs, unguents and amulets, which positively extinguish passion or potency (here we must take refuge in Latin again): camphor and coriander, verbena and cannabis, a topaz ring, the right testicle of a wolf ground in oil and rose-water, powdered frog, etc.; not to speak of 'philtres, magical and poetical cures'.

Finally, of course, there is the more natural and socially approved remedy of marriage. Of this great temptation, and great risk, Burton cannot speak personally: it was incompatible with his studentship of Christ Church, and he was anyway wedded to his books, from which, of course, he knew all its drawbacks: 'I never tried, but as I hear some of them say . . . an Irish sea is not so turbulent and raging as a litigious wife.' However, he will be impartial; he sets out the *pros* as well as the *cons*, and at length, with the learned authorities ranged on each side, he draws to a liberal conclusion: 'the last and best cure of love-melancholy is, to let them have their desire'. 'It is', he exclaims, 'an unnatural and impious thing to bar men of this Christian liberty, too severe and inhuman an edict.' So he condemns all legal and social barriers to marriage, and particularly, as 'far more tyrannical and much worse', the barriers interposed by superstition, 'those rash vows of monks and friars and such as live in religious orders'. Think what goes on in monasteries and nunneries . . . so, for once, he is decisive. Marriage is 'the last and best refuge and cure of heroical love'. By this emphatic sentence 'all doubts are cleared and impediments removed'.

So far so good. But, alas, the problem is never finally solved; for if 'heroical love', which precedes marriage, is cured by it, there is another form of the disease, no less disturbing, which follows it. This is jealousy, 'a bastard branch' of love-melancholy and the cause of some of the most horrible crimes recorded in history and literature. Moreover, it is institutionalized in society, with unhappy results. 'See but with what rigour those jealous husbands tyrannize over their poor wives in Greece, Spain, Italy, Turkey, Africa, Asia, and generally over all those hot countries.' Hence harems, hence the thousands of eunuchs kept by 'the Grand Signior among the Turks, the Sophies of Persia, those Tartarian Mogors and Kings of China'. For this disease of jealousy, there is, alas, no medicine. Only philosophy can cure it. If the worst comes to the worst, husbands should take consolation by reckoning that they are in good company. Look at imperial Rome: 'husband and cuckold, in that age, it seems, were reciprocal terms; the emperors themselves did wear Actaeon's badge; how many Caesars might I reckon up together, and what a catalogue of cornuted kings and princes in every story – Agamemnon, Menelaus, Philippus of Greece, Ptolemaeus of Egypt, Lucullus, Caesar, Pompeius, Cato, Augustus, Antonius, Mummius etc. – that wore fair plumes of bull's feathers in their crests. The bravest soldiers and most heroical spirits could not avoid it. They have been active and passive in this business, they have either given or taken horns.' So is it not best simply to forget it, to treat it as a mere accident of life, no more serious than a papal excommunication? 'He that suspects his wife's incontinency, and fears the Pope's curse, shall never live a merry hour or sleep a quiet night: no remedy but patience . . . if it may not be helped, it must be endured.' On this all the philosophers agree. But Burton slily hints that he can improve on them. 'One other sovereign remedy I could repeat, an especial antidote against jealousy, an excellent cure, but I am not now disposed to tell it. Not that, like a covetous empiric, I conceal it for any gain, but for some other reasons I am unwilling to publish it. If you be very desirous to know it, when I meet you next I will peradventure tell you what it is in your ear.' And with that last tantalizing word he dismisses the subject of love-melancholy and moves on to the next and most speculative form of the disease, religious melancholy.

'That there is such a distinct species of love-melancholy no man hath ever doubted', says Burton: his own doubts were simply whether 'this tragi-comedy of love' was not too frivolous a subject for his grave analysis. But whether his next species of melancholy will be allowed, he is not so sure: for here he is treading on dangerous ground and might well find himself in trouble with the clergy. Is there indeed such a disease as 'religious melancholy'? Here, he admits, 'I have no pattern to follow, as in some of the rest, no man to imitate. No physician hath as yet distinctly written of it, as of the other.' However, he is not afraid to be a pioneer and open up this new subject. And what a subject! he exclaims. 'Give me but a little leave, and I will set before your eyes in brief a stupend, vast infinite ocean of incredible madness and folly: a sea full of shelves and rocks, sands, gulfs, euripes' – that is, treacherous currents – 'and contrary tides, full of fearful monsters, uncouth shapes, roaring waves, tempests and siren calms, halcyonian seas, unspeakable misery, such comedies and tragedies, such absurd and ridiculous, feral and lamentable fits, that I know not whether they are more to be pitied or desired, or may be believed, but that we daily see the same practised in our days, fresh examples, *nova novitia*, fresh objects of misery and madness in this kind, that are still represented unto us, abroad, at home, in the midst of us, in our bosoms.'

Where shall one find a safe and comfortable island from which to survey this swirling sea? Burton finds it in the established Church. He is a natural Anglican, firmly opposed to the two opposite extremes of excess and defect: that is, of superstition and infidelity, of idolatry and atheism. Of the two he hates superstition more; for whereas atheism is a private sin which can be corrected by reason – see the encyclopaedic refutation of it by that 'malapert friar' Marin Mersenne[14] – superstition is not merely absurd: it has 'lamentable and tragical' social conse-quences. 'When I see two superstitious orders' locked in furious con-troversy over trifles like the Immaculate Conception of the Virgin, 'when I see grave learned men rail and scold like butter-women, methinks 'tis pretty sport', fit for Democritus to laugh at. 'But when I see so much blood spilt, so many battles fought, etc., 'tis a fitter subject for Heraclitus to lament.' For Heraclitus was the weeping, as Democritus was the laughing philosopher.

Of superstition, whose range and variety are too vast to comprehend, for it infects all religions alike, Burton selects for treatment two kinds, both equally objectionable. On one side, his bugbears are the 'pseudo-Catholics', that is, the Romanists of the Counter-Reformation who usurp the name of Catholics although in fact they are barely Christians, since they have taken over the superstitious apparatus of paganism. Here is organized superstition, militant, powerful, aggressive. At its head is 'the bull-bellowing Pope which now rageth in the West'; around him is his cabinet of 'huffing cardinals'; under him, to execute his orders, are the 'janissary Jesuits', always 'in the forefront of the battle', and now fighting 'almost alone; for the rest' – that is, the secular clergy, the monks and friars, who merely keep the supplies flowing – 'are but his dromedaries and asses'. And what is the system which this formid-able political organization exists to maintain and extend? Erasmus before him, or Hobbes after him, is not a more devastating critic of the abuses of the Roman Church, its combination of machiavellian policy and abject superstition, its exploitation of 'counterfeit and maggot-eaten relics', pilgrimages, indulgences, etc., in order to seduce 'rude idiots and infinite swarms of people' and thereby establish a power greater than that of the old pagan empire of Rome – and incidentally create, for its rulers, similar opportunities of extravagant self-indulgence; for while 'the ruder sort are so carried headlong with blind zeal, and so gulled and tortured by their superstitions . . . their epicurean popes and hypocritical cardinals laugh in their sleeves and are merry in their chambers with their punks'.

That is one extreme of superstition. The opposite form of it is represented by the English puritan fanatics, who, to Burton, are no less insufferable, with their fussy consciences. They are 'a mad, giddy company of precisians, schismatics, and some heretics' who, in their opposition to popery, will admit no decent ceremonies, no church music, no hierarchy – all of them things which Burton valued – 'no, not so much as degrees some of them will tolerate, or universities: all human learning . . . hoods, habits, cap and surplice, such as are things indifferent in themselves . . . they abhor, hate and snuff at, as a stone-horse when he meets a bear'. This, to a university man, was a shocking perversity.

Among papists, religious melancholy finds its expression in the hallucinations of fasting friars and desert anchorites: men who, in their zeal to control the lusts of the flesh, carry the corrective virtues of abstinence too far and 'after much emptiness, become melancholy, vertiginous, they think they hear strange noises, confer with hobgoblins, rivel up their bodies . . . become skeletons, skin and bones . . .'. In the end, such men, whose brains are addle, 'their bellies as empty of meat as their heads of wit', become the instruments of scheming politicians: 'the devil hath many such factors, many such engines'. Among Protestants there is a different form which is no less absurd: it consists of sectarian pedantry. 'A company of giddy heads will take upon them to define how many will be saved and who damned in a parish, where they shall sit in Heaven, interpret apocalypses . . . and precisely set down when the world shall come to an end, what year, what month, what day.' The symptom of this alarming disease is a fanatical spirit, expressed in a willingness to impose, and to suffer, martyrdom. The natural result is fresh in the memory of men: the Spanish Inquisition in the Netherlands, the French massacres and civil wars, the 'hurly-burlies all over Europe for these many years'. If Burton had lived a little longer, he would have seen them in England too.

What is the cure of this, the worst of all forms of melancholy? 'To purge the world of idolatry and superstition', Burton admits, 'will require some monster-taming Hercules, a divine Aesculapius, or Christ himself to come in his own person, to reign a thousand years on earth before the end, as the millenaries will have him.' However, for the present, since all these events seem equally improbable, we must face the facts as they are. The idea that one true religion can be imposed upon the whole world, even upon the whole Christian world, is chimerical. That world is already irremediably divided. Nor is this division necessarily to be deplored; for after all, 'if there be infinite planetary and firmamental worlds, as some will' – Burton is thinking, once again, of Bruno and Campanella – then there must also be 'infinite genii or commanding spirits belonging to each of them; and so, *per consequens* (for they will all be adored) infinite religions'. Plurality of worlds entails plurality of religions.

Are we then to go to the other extreme and tolerate all beliefs however superstitious, or even the absence of belief: the errors of atheists, epicureans, libertines: of philosophers like Pomponazzi, who denied the immortality of the soul, or Giulio Cesare Vanini, 'lately burned at Toulouse in France'? Such a toleration is advocated by some: by the Socinians, for instance, the followers of Servetus, whom Calvin had caused to be burned at Geneva, or by the great French historian

Jacques-Auguste de Thou, whose work (for he had dared to praise Erasmus) was now on the Roman Index. It is even practised in certain places, in Poland and Amsterdam, for instance, which are 'the common sanctuaries' of heresy in Europe. Burton is himself tolerant, and can sympathize with, or at least seek to understand, even the most eccentric doctrines. He is aware of the temptation to scepticism provided by the spectacle of *odium theologicum* and 'the horrible consideration of diversity of religions which are and have been in the world'. But he cannot go quite so far as to tolerate atheism. Defect of belief is, after all, half-way to despair of salvation, which in turn will plunge a man into another form of religious melancholy; for 'those whom God forsakes, the devil by his permission, lays hold on', with fearful consequences.

No, between the two extremes of persecution and toleration 'the medium', as always, 'is best', and that means, of course, the established Church of England, exerting its legitimate discipline, reinforced by medical and psychological treatment. So Burton is not averse from occasional wholesome severities, not against the heretics, whose disease is psychological, but against their doltish followers. 'For the vulgar', he recommends, 'restrain them by laws, mulcts, burn their books, forbid their conventicles; for when the cause is taken away, the effect will soon cease.' But the 'prophets, dreamers, and such rude silly fellows that through fasting, too much meditation, preciseness, or by melancholy are distempered' – the men who 'see and talk with fiery spirits, smell brimstone, etc.' – these must be cured 'partly by persuasion, partly by physic'. 'We have frequently such prophets and dreamers amongst us, whom we persecute with fire and faggot. I think the most compendious cure, for some of them, at least, had been in Bedlam.'

So Burton stands firm in the *via media* of Anglicanism, the Anglicanism of Hooker, if not of Laud. If he hates popish superstition, he will have no Calvinist austerity either. He rejects altogether the dreadful doctrine of double predestination: 'these absurd paradoxes', he writes, 'are exploded by our Church: we teach otherwise'. Indeed, he speaks favourably of 'our late Arminians' – the Laudian party – who 'have revived the plausible doctrine of universal grace', and cites Erasmus in its favour. He is against all forms of puritanism; for is not puritanism in itself, with its scrupulosity of conscience and narrowed zeal, a symptom, or aggravating cause, of melancholy? It is by rational indulgence, not perverse self-mortification, that the disease is cured, or at least alleviated. So he will divert the too devout mind from speculation and introspection, leading it gently towards the world, the flesh, even, with moderation, the devil. Let not the pious man look too curiously into the controversies of the faith. Let him keep to the Thirty-nine Articles, newly reprinted under the auspices of Archbishop Laud, with a preface expressly forbidding such curious search and private interpretation. Does not Erasmus urge men reverently and decently to respect the rules of the established Church *velut a Deo profectas*, as if proceeding from God?

On all the sensitive issues of the time Burton was with Laud against the Puritans. He had no use for sabbatarianism or biblical fundamentalism. The Puritans' opposition to church music disgusted him, for he loved music. So did their hatred of stage-plays, to which he was addicted, and their condemnation of rustic sports and festivals, maypoles, church wakes and ales: he explicitly approved of King James's *Book of Sports* which Charles I, encouraged by Laud, defiantly re-issued. 'For my part', he wrote, 'I will subscribe to the King's declaration and was ever of that mind, those May-games, wakes and Whitsun-ales, etc., if they be not at unseasonable hours, may justly be permitted. Let them freely feast, sing and dance, have their poppet-plays, hobby-horses, tabors, crowds [fiddles], bagpipes, etc., play at ball and barley-breaks, and what sports and recreations they like best.' He is for merry England; and although he wishes to ban idleness, that sure cause of melancholy, from his utopia, he is no friend to the Puritan ethos as the way thither: 'Sir Thomas More, in his Utopian commonwealth, as he will have none idle, so he will have no man labour over-hard, to be toiled out like a horse.' Similarly, in Burton's own utopia, 'none shall be over-tired, but shall have their times of recreations and holidays'.

Burton hates the papists because they exploit superstition in order to create power; but at least by their 'mechanical devotions' they made salvation easy – indeed, too easy. He hates the Puritans because their preachers, or some of them, make it impossible: they exploit the fear of damnation, which is 'the last main torture and trouble of a distressed mind'. Thinking that they are already irrevocably damned, their auditors suffer prematurely, in their minds, the pains of Hell: 'they smell brimstone, talk familiarly with devils, hear and see chimaeras, prodigious uncouth shapes, bears, owls, antics, black dogs, fiends, hideous outcries, fearful noises, shrieks, lamentable complaints.' Despair drives them, sometimes, to suicide. But Burton bids them cheer up. All these 'terrible objects which they hear and see', all these 'devils, bugbears and mormoluches, noisome smells, etc.', come, as he has shown, from 'inward causes' and can therefore be dispersed by medical or psychiatric treatment.

Burton's medicines are the medicines of his age. Some of them are
bizarre enough to us. To induce sleep, 'anoint the soles of the feet with
the fat of a dormouse, the teeth with ear-wax of a dog' . . . To cure
redness of the face, wash with 'water of frog's spawn . . .' But these are
not his own recommendations: the former is cited from Cardanus, the
universal Platonic philosopher of the mid-sixteenth century, the latter
from Quercetanus, the most celebrated of modern Hermetic, chemical
doctors. Such remedies are to be found in the most sophisticated
pharmacopoeias and are repeated by the most advanced physicians of
the time. In general, Burton is averse from such fanciful cures, preferring
simple herbal remedies. So, in order to cure religious despair, beside
'that Christian armour which Paul prescribes', he recommends penny-
royal, rue, mint, angelica, peony and especially St John's wort, known
as *fuga daemonum*, as putting devils to flight, and betony which Antonius
Musa, the Emperor Augustus' physician, highly approved, and which
the ancients used to plant in churchyards as a holy herb, 'good against
fearful visions'. Betony, indeed, is one of Burton's favourite herbs,
overshadowed only by borage and bugloss, which contend for the first
place; for was not one or other of them, it is not quite clear which, the
famous *Nepenthes* of Homer,

> which the wife of Thon
> In Egypt gave to Jove-born Helena,

and which anaesthetized a man against any kind of grief?

As for psychological remedies, there is always the therapy of music,
'accurate music; so Saul was helped by David's harp', or cheerful fires
and lights, 'odours, perfumes and suffumigations, as the angel taught
Tobias', of odoriferous fuel – brimstone and bitumen, frankincense,
myrrh and bryony – such as good spirits are pleased with, but evil
spirits abhor: these can safely be borrowed from pagans and papists,
though their exorcisms are to be rejected as mere 'fopperies and
fictions'. Finally, if a man finds that his religious despair proceeds from
reading religious books or listening to rigid preachers – those waggon-
loads of theological books to which Burton refused to add, those puritan
preachers intoning perpetual damnation – then the cure is simpler still:
'let him read no more such tracts or subjects, hear no more such fearful
tones'. Let him give ear to sound medical and spiritual advice, 'and no
doubt but such good counsel may prove as prosperous to his soul as the
angel was to Peter, that opened the iron gates, loosed his bands,
brought him out of prison, and delivered him from bodily thraldom:

they may ease his afflicted mind, relieve his wounded soul, and take him out of the jaws of Hell itself'.

'I can say no more', Burton continues, 'or give better advice to such as are anyway distressed in this kind, than what I have given and said. Only take this for a corollary and conclusion, as thou tenderest thine own welfare in this and all other melancholy, thy good health of body and mind, observe this short precept, give not way to solitariness and idleness. "Be not solitary, be not idle."' This is the essential cure not only, directly, of that personal melancholy which would long be re- garded as the peculiarly English malady, but also, indirectly, of the stagnation and apathy of English society, at least as seen from Oxford and in Leicestershire.

So we have come full circle. It has been a long way round, and we have picked up a vast quantity of strange and delightful information on the way. The card-index in those rooms in Christ Church must have been a splendid sight. But the message is clear. It is the triumph of medical and, above all, psychological science that will restore sanity to a disordered world. The rounded human personality is the essential means of achieving the perfect society, the essential unit within it. Everything, even religion, must subserve that purpose, and the great virtue of the Anglican Church lay rather in its moral and social func- tion than in its doctrinal truth. As a clergyman, Burton was in the tradition of Erasmus, of Hooker and – since he too was essentially in that tradition, however harshly he interpreted it – of Laud. But his priorities were different from theirs. Perhaps therefore it is no accident that his best-selling propaganda for conformity, though admired by medical writers, is never cited by the clerical champions of orthodoxy. Look at his portrait in Brasenose College. That sedate, scholarly figure has a mischievous glint in his eye. If he is a pillar, it is an elaborate, baroque, perhaps illusory pillar of our national church.

Sources

1. See John Nichols, *History and Antiquities of Leicestershire* (1795–1815) III, part i, pp. 415–19; cf. II, ii, 842–5; IV, ii, 645–58.
2. Anthony Wood, *Athenae Oxonienses* (ed. P. Bliss, 1813–20), II, 154–6.
3. Wood, loc. cit. See also Paul Jordan-Smith, *Bibliographia Burtoniana* (Stanford University Press, 1931), p. 9.
4. The troubles of 1596–7 are documented in the petitions of the Students to Cecil (Hist. MSS Commission, Marquess of Salisbury XIII (Addenda) 598) and to

Lord Keeper Egerton (Huntington Library, San Marino, Ellesmere MSS, EL 1926, 1928, 1942).

5. Archives of Christ Church, Oxford: volume entitled 'Anno Dom. 1628. The writings concerning the cause between the Dean and Canons of Christ Church and the Students there'.

6. This episode is described in a letter from William Burton to Simon Archer of Tamworth, dated 7 June 1630, and quoted in P. Jordan-Smith, op. cit., p. 12.

7. II, 97. Cf. Bishop Corbett's poem, 'A Letter from Dr Corbet to Master Ailesbury', 41–2:

> Burton to Gunter writes, and Burton hears
> From Gunter . . .

(*The Poems of Richard Corbett*, ed. J. A. W. Bennett and H. R. Trevor-Roper, Oxford, 1955, p. 64). Corbett was at Christ Church at the time.

8. See the list of his books in *Oxford Bibliographical Society Proceedings and Papers*, ed. F. Madan, Vol. I; and cf. *Reliquiae Hearnianae* (ed. P. Bliss, Oxford, 1869), III, 113.

9. A. Wood, loc. cit.; *Reliquiae Hearnianae*, loc. cit.

10. White Kennet, *Register and Chronicle* . . . (1728), p. 320.

11. Frances Yates, *The Occult Philosophy of the Elizabethan Age* (1979), p. 51.

12. D. P. Walker, *Spiritual and Demonic Magic from Ficino to Campanella* (1958), pp. 3–7.

13. [John Wilkins], *Vindiciae Academiarum* (1654), cap. x.

14. The reference is to Mersenne's *Quaestiones Celeberrimae in Genesim* and *de l'impiété des déistes* (Paris, 1623).

13
The Outbreak of the Thirty Years War

Why do great wars break out? Several times in history the pattern has recurred. We see a general peace, apparently welcome to all powers. But beneath this peace we see fear and suspicion constantly threatening it. No power wants war but each fears that some incident, by disturbing the precarious balance of power, will create war. The atmosphere is combustible and therefore a spark may set the world ablaze. Consequently when a spark does fly, there is a rush to isolate or stifle it. Even those who might profit by a fire in that quarter are too frightened to exploit it; for it might spread. And so the peace is kept: the various danger-spots are guarded; even their dangers are preserved, not eliminated, for to eliminate them is to touch them and to touch them is to set them off. And then, suddenly, a spark flies which is not thus isolated; the complex system of insurance suddenly fails; the wind blows and all the danger-spots are simultaneously alight: it is general war.

Consider the 1930s. There were a number of danger-spots. There was the Rhineland, Danzig, the Polish corridor, the Sudetenland. Each in turn was guaranteed by the Powers, its anomalies artificially preserved for fear of worse trouble. Incident after incident was localized. And then, suddenly, from a small incident that was not localized, the war broke out: a general war that enveloped all the old danger-spots at once. Similarly, since 1945, in the years of 'the Cold War', in one place after another – in Berlin, in Persia, in Korea, in Indo-China, in the Middle East, a series of carefully preserved anomalies and irrational partitions testify to the uncertain balance of the powers, and the successive localization of conflict in the interest of peace. But who can say whether the next incident will be localized or whether, in an

275

unguarded moment, it will not send out a sudden, spontaneous, consuming flame?

On such occasions it is customary to say that the incidents lead to the war: they generate a fear whose pressure is irresistible and cause men to build up armaments which must be used: 'the guns go off by themselves'. In other words, the war is inevitable: it is only a question of time. This may be so, but of course it may not. Since the question is open, perhaps it is worth while to look back at the outbreak of the greatest, most destructive war in pre-industrial Europe: the Thirty Years War, which is customarily dated from the last of a series of such incidents, the Bohemian revolt of 1618.

For the Thirty Years War also followed a period of general but precarious peace. The peace was general because all the great powers wanted it: the last general war had impoverished and exhausted them all. But it was precarious too because Europe was full of unresolved tensions. Two great hostile ideologies, Catholicism and Protestantism, divided its allegiance. Protestants and Catholics were deeply suspicious of each other. By 1600 the Protestant powers had narrowly escaped reconquest. Some, indeed, had been reconquered. Those which had not knew that their freedom was not yet guaranteed: they must defend themselves against sudden attack, if necessary by forestalling it. Fortunately, though themselves weak and scattered, they had allies even in the Catholic camp. For across the ideological division of Europe lay another, and different, line of fissure: the political division. The patron of Catholicism was the Spanish monarchy, the most active partner in the great Habsburg combine which ruled in Madrid and Lisbon, Brussels and Milan, Naples and Palermo, Vienna and Prague. The Spanish monarchy drew upon the wealth of East and West Indies and dominated the Pope in Rome. But this domination had its consequences. The Spanish captivity of the Pope released the consciences of the political enemies of Spain, and European Protestants sometimes found themselves supported by anti-Spanish Catholics: by the newly restored monarchy of France or by those states of Italy which still had power to resist the Spanish domination of the peninsula.

Thus Western Europe was full of tension; but so too was Central Europe. Germany was a mosaic of nearly 400 states and cities in each of which religion might be changed at the will of a ruler. The consequences of this could be enormous. The accession of a new prince with a new religion, even in a small state, might alter the international balance of power. It could also change the composition of an electoral chamber and thereby affect the outcome of an election. For some of the German princes were elected. The prince-bishops of the Rhine, for instance, were elected by their chapters, the King of Bohemia by his Diet. And the Emperor himself was elected by those elected prince-bishops and that elected king and a few other German princes who were also Electors. So anything might happen. At present the situation was in hand. There was a precarious balance of power in Germany. The Peace of Augsburg had legally fossilized the *status quo* in 1555; a *status quo* which now left an elderly and childless member of the Habsburg family both on the Bohemian and on the imperial throne.

Such was Europe in the first twenty years of the seventeenth century. Obviously there were opportunities for incidents everywhere. But if we wish to find a pattern in these incidents, which seem otherwise so confusing, we must always look to Spain. After all, it was Spain which had made the peace of the great powers. First in 1598, then in 1604, finally in 1609, the Spanish monarchy, bankrupt but still powerful, had successively wound up the wars of Philip II with France, England and Holland. It was Spain too which kept the peace; and it was Spain which, in the end, broke it. The Thirty Years War is generally thought of as a German war; it was indeed fought out in Germany; but it was the Spanish Habsburgs who dominated their cousins in Vienna and Prague, and it was the Spanish renewal of the war against the Netherlands in 1621 which turned the German war, which might have been local and brief, into a long, general, European war. It was in Spanish interests that the war was carried to the Baltic and the North Sea; Wallenstein, who carried it thither, was general of Spanish soldiers; he stood on the shores of the Baltic as admiral of a Spanish fleet.

It follows that the significant incidents, the incidents which really threatened the peace, were all connected with Spain. Just as the danger-spots of the 1930s were on the frontiers of Germany and those of the 1950s on the frontiers of Russia and China, so the danger-spots of the 1610s were on the frontiers of the great Habsburg system which, in those years, was effectively directed from Spain. No doubt there was tension elsewhere, but elsewhere it could be localized or crushed. A revolt in southern Italy or in Brussels (there were revolts in both) was doomed to extinction. No foreign power could intervene there. But wherever the frontiers or vital communications of Spain were exposed to the rest of Europe, there revolts might spread and even trivial incidents might cause a conflagration. These points were the danger-spots of Europe, the equivalents of Berlin or Hungary or Korea today.

And what were these danger-spots? A glance at the map is sufficient to identify them. The Spanish empire in Europe consisted, essentially, of Flanders and Italy. Since its chief problem was the revolt of the Netherlands, its vital communications were between Spain and Flanders, across or around the huge, intervening body of France. In the old days the regular route had been by sea, from Laredo or Coruna to Flushing. But now that route was fatally cut. The Dutch held Flushing, the Dutch and English commanded the sea-lanes through the English Channel. So now the essential route was by land. Spanish forces – men, munitions, money – now all reached Flanders by land. They sailed from Barcelona or from Naples to Genoa (nominally free but in fact a Spanish protectorate, the financial capital of the empire), and then assembled in Milan, the arsenal of Spain in Italy. Then they marched north, over the Alps, along the Rhine. On this route there was one solid Spanish stepping-stone: Franche-Comté, a detached relic of the old Burgundian inheritance, on the borders of France and Switzerland. There were also imperial fiefs, held by the Austrian Habsburgs: such was Alsace, strategically situated on the Rhine between Franche-Comté and the Netherlands. Then there were theoretically independent states, which in fact were safely spaniolized, like the prince-bishoprics of Cologne or Liège: no trouble came from them – or if it did (as it had done in 1582 when the Archbishop-Elector of Cologne declared himself a Protestant in order to marry a wife), it was crushed. Then there were allied states like the Catholic cantons of Switzerland which, by treaty, allowed free passage to Spanish (but only Spanish) troops. This was a very useful concession, which the French tried to counter by diplomacy among the Protestant cantons.

As long as Spanish power was firm, all these could be managed. But there were other spots which were more difficult. There was Savoy, whose Duke had once been sound but was now anti-Spanish. Savoy had a mountainous terrain and the Duke had an army which could be very troublesome, especially if he were supported by France. His great ambition was to recover Geneva, the capital of international Calvinism, and in 1600 he nearly did so, by a surprise attack; but Geneva was now protected by France. Then there was the Palatinate on the middle Rhine. The Elector Palatine was a dangerous enemy: his predecessors had been a menace to Philip II. He was also a Calvinist, the titular leader of the activists among the German Protestants. And he had a vote in the making of emperors. It was most inconvenient that his castle of Heidelberg should overlook a sector of the Spanish route. Finally there were other petty German principalities which the chance of election or heredity might so easily place in the wrong hands.

Moreover there was another vital area. To the Spanish Habsburgs it was essential that their Austrian cousins rule the Empire. The Emperor was overlord of the German princes on the Rhine. He controlled Alsace. He also held legal rights over a number of princes in Italy. A non-Habsburg or a weak Habsburg emperor could be most inconvenient to Spain. The Austrian Habsburgs in 1609 were inconveniently weak; the three royal brothers – Rudolf, Matthias and Albert – were all childless and there was no agreed heir. In the next generation there was only one candidate within the family on whom the Spaniards felt that they could rely: the Archduke Ferdinand of Styria. It was important that he should be elected Emperor. In these circumstances it was doubly necessary to Spain to have means of communicating with Austria and means of influencing imperial elections. These necessities raised two other areas to the status of danger-spots. To communicate with Austria Spain needed to control the land-route from Milan to Tyrol; to influence elections it needed to control the distant and otherwise irrelevant kingdom of Bohemia.

The land-route from Milan to Tyrol ran through the Alpine passes to the south of Switzerland. These passes were called the Valtelline. The inhabitants of the Valtelline were Catholics, but they were subject to the Swiss Grisons, who were Protestant. This made matters difficult; for although the leaders of the Grisons were weak and corruptible, they could be corrupted by others too. To secure the pass, in spite of the unreliability of its rulers, the Spanish governor of Milan had built a fort near Lake Como. This had provoked the Grisons who had looked for sympathy. They found it in France, the traditional enemy of Spain. They also found it in Venice.

Venice was the last of the independent republics of Italy, the only really independent republic. It was conscious of its historic greatness and proud of its independence. It had just made a famous and successful defiance of the Pope and the Jesuits, the allies of Spain. Now it felt itself being strangled by the Habsburgs. By land, the Austrian Habsburgs overhung it from north and east, from Tyrol and Carinthia, the Spanish Habsburgs from the west, from Milan. By sea, the Austrians encouraged its enemies, the Bosnian pirates or Uskoks, within the Adriatic, and the Spaniards, from Naples, dominated the outlet of the Adriatic by Apulia. To the Venetians the Uskoks were a permanent nuisance, and they waged an intermittent and sometimes a regular war against them; but the outlet of the Adriatic was their lifeline and its safety had always been regarded as a prime interest of state. They had no desire to see the last gap closed and two powerful enemies joining hands in the Valtelline to encircle them.

As for the kingdom of Bohemia, its claim to be a danger-spot was purely political, not strategic. At present the Emperor was also King of Bohemia. Therefore if the Emperor should die, the throne of Bohemia would become vacant together with that of the Empire. But the King of Bohemia was an Elector to the Empire, and in the present balance of power he might even control the decisive vote. It was therefore essential to Spain that the new King of Bohemia be elected before the imperial election took place – and of course that the new king so elected should be the Spanish candidate. This candidate was the Archduke Ferdinand, who would then, according to the Spanish plan, help to elect himself as Emperor. In 1609 this plan was not yet complete, least of all in Madrid, but the Spanish ambassador had built up a solid party in Prague and was prepared for the future. He had built up his party in the usual way of Spanish ambassadors: by lavish distribution of favours, honours, promises and pensions.

Thus all the danger-spots name themselves: the Rhineland, the Palatinate, Savoy, Venice, the Valtelline, Bohemia. Incidents that occurred elsewhere could be settled locally, on their merits, or at least by the balance of local force; but incidents in these places invariably endangered the peace. And indeed, throughout the second decade of the seventeenth century the peace was endangered by a succession of incidents in precisely these places.

The first trouble came in the Rhineland, in 1609. Scarcely had the truce between Spain and Holland been signed, and the last great war wound up, when a disputed succession in Jülich-Cleves, on the Lower Rhine, launched a general crisis. The Duke of Cleves who had died had been a Catholic, but two rivals now claimed his throne, both Protestants. A Protestant prince on the lower Rhine! To Spain such a thought was impossible, and one of the claimants, to ensure Spanish support, promptly turned papist. But the dispute remained and soon engaged all Europe. It seemed a re-run of the affair of the prince-bishopric of Cologne twenty-seven years ago. That contest had brought Spanish troops into action. Then there had been no one to resist, so it had been a walk-over. But now Henri IV of France would not allow a walk-over. He allied himself with the German Protestants and with the Duke of Savoy, and the Duke of Savoy wove plots with his kinsmen on lesser Italian thrones. There was general mobilization. Savoy prepared to pounce on Milan. Henri IV had his queen crowned as regent in his stead and set out to the Rhineland front. Then, quite suddenly, all was over. In the streets of Paris an assassin sprang into the royal coach, and stabbed and killed Henri IV. With that sudden *coup* the course of history was stayed. The anti-Spanish coalition collapsed. The Queen Regent of France accepted the guidance of the ultra-Catholic party, the party of peace, even appeasement. Isolated, the Duke of Savoy had no chance against the Spanish governor of Milan. He was forced to surrender and send his son to make abject apologies to the court of Madrid. Afterwards the greatest of Spanish commanders, the Genoese Ambrogio Spinola, as easily chastised the Rhineland cities which had prematurely committed themselves, and made a triumphal progress through the Palatinate. The Rhineland crisis was over. There was no general war.

Thus the first international crisis passed off without an explosion. It had been a narrow squeak, and perhaps only the assassin's knife had saved the peace of Europe; but at least it had been saved for the time. However, the tension remained and other crises soon followed. In 1613 there was another disputed succession. This time it was in Montferrat, an exposed enclave lying between Milan and Savoy. The Duke of Savoy claimed control over it, refused mediation, occupied it, defied Spain, expelled the Spanish ambassador, sent back his Spanish decorations. Successive Spanish governors of Milan made war against him. He was defeated in the field, forced to submit, but bobbed up again. He had foreign support, unofficial but valuable: military support from the neighbouring French governor of Dauphiné, disowned by his 'appeasing' government in Paris; secret financial support from the republic of Venice; moral support from all Italians who lamented their country's subjugation by Spain. It was in the war of 1613–17 that the house of Savoy founded its claim to liberate Italy from the foreigner: a claim which it would ultimately make good in the nineteenth century.

If the voice of Italy, calling for freedom, was not yet effective, the ducats of Venice were. For Venice had its own battles to maintain and welcomed a fighting ally. While Savoy was engaging the Spanish army by land, Venice was occupied in a fierce struggle by sea against the Bosnian pirates who enjoyed the protection of the Archduke Ferdinand. Before long Venice found itself at war with the Archduke himself on land, and a Dutch fleet brought Dutch soldiers through the Straits of Gibraltar to fight on its side. And then another force entered the ever-widening fight. The Spanish viceroy of Naples, the Duke of Osuna, was a man of wild visions and ruthless methods. Extravagant, demagogic, aggressive, inflated by a sense of his power and his naval successes against the Turks, he despised the distant, inactive court of Spain and sought to make peace and war almost as an independent sovereign. He sent troops by land through a protesting Italy to assist his

colleague, the Spanish Viceroy of Milan, against Savoy. He sent a fleet
– his own fleet, flying his own personal flag – into the Adriatic to destroy
the ships of Venice, with which Spain was not even at war. Within
Venice, he had an ally in the Spanish ambassador there, the Marquis of
Bedmar, who was equally self-willed and independent. There can be no
doubt that Osuna and Bedmar were making plans – at least contingen-
cy plans – to destroy Venice. Bedmar, like so many Spanish ambassadors, had a huge spy-system in the state to which he was accredited,
and distributed pensions freely. He made no secret of his contempt for
the Republic and described the ease with which it could be conquered.
Osuna agreed with him. With a new fleet poised at Brindisi, he declared
that he would strike at Venice itself 'in spite of the world, in spite of
God, in spite of the King'; if the Venetians should resist, 'I shall deal
with them once and for all.'

    And yet in fact the Italian crisis came to nothing just as the
Rhineland crisis had done. The great powers were never engaged. The
governor of Dauphiné might make war in Savoy, but the government of
France was still. The Archduke Ferdinand might be at war in the
Adriatic, but the Emperor, his sovereign, did not stir. The governors of
Milan and Naples might plot and act and demonstrate, but Madrid
remained uncommitted. Dutch soldiers fought in Italy, but the Dutch
government remained at peace. It seemed as if the great powers would
only fight through agents. And then, in 1617, there was peace, peace on
all fronts. In Madrid, Savoy and Spain settled their quarrel; in Wiener
Neustadt, Venice made terms with Austria. The second crisis, though it
had spread so far and threatened to involve all the powers, had passed.

    Immediately it was followed by a third, a fourth, a fifth. 1618, the
year after the peace of Madrid, was a year of continuing crisis. On 18
May it broke out in Venice. On that morning the inhabitants of Venice
awoke to see two corpses hanging upside-down from the public gibbet.
Their legs were broken, a sign that they were guilty of treason. Five
days later a third corpse joined them, mutilated by torture. No
explanation was given: the Venetian Inquisitors of State never explained: they acted, and left the public to guess. But all agreed that
there had been a deep plot against the independence of the Republic. In
spite of the peace of Madrid, Osuna and Bedmar had planned a sudden
coup: Bedmar had organized the fifth column within, Osuna had his
fleet ready to strike without. But Venice had struck first. In indignation, Venetian crowds attacked Bedmar's palace and the ambassador,
without waiting for orders from home, fled to Milan. Osuna was burnt
in effigy in Venice; so was his secret agent, the Spanish poet Francisco

de Quevedo, who, since he was in Venice at the time, was lucky not to be burnt alive. Somehow he escaped (he had escaped in very similar circumstances from Nice, which Osuna had also tried to seize, five years before); but he never explained precisely what he was doing in Venice on that fatal date.

'The Spanish Conspiracy' against Venice caused a *furore* at the time and has perplexed historians since. There is still no final agreement about it. Was it real, a carefully laid plan to seize the city, or a fantasy generated in the heated atmosphere of the time? We do not know; but whatever it was, it led nowhere. Osuna and Bedmar of course protested their innocence; but whereas the cautious Bedmar continued his diplomatic career, and would be made a cardinal of the Church, the impetuous Osuna would afterwards be recalled, accused of seeking to make himself king of Naples, and die in prison. On all sides the matter was dropped. As the Spaniards disowned the plot, the Venetians did not publish anything which would exasperate them. Once again the crisis had passed – at least in Venice. Instead, it broke out in another, remoter nerve-centre of Europe: in Prague, the capital of the kingdom of Bohemia.

For in the Empire, meanwhile, the Spaniards had won a great victory. There too, as in Venice, they had been represented by resolute, independent, aggressive ambassadors. First there was Balthasar de Zúñiga, who had held that post since 1608, and was the constant advocate of a forward policy in Germany. By 1617, when he was recalled to Madrid, Zúñiga had prepared the ground, and in that year his successor, the Count of Oñate, was able to pick the fruit. The old Emperor Matthias then persuaded the Bohemian Diet to pre-elect the Spanish candidate, the Archduke Ferdinand, as his own successor as King of Bohemia. That ensured that the crown of Bohemia would be on the right head. Indirectly, it also ensured that the imperial election should go as the Spaniards wished. And further, by a secret treaty signed between Oñate and the Archduke at the Archduke's palace of Graz, the Spaniards agreed that the next emperor should be the Archduke himself. The King of Spain himself had claims, but by this treaty he renounced them. He could afford to do so, for they were not very powerful claims, and he renounced them in exchange for solid assets: for Alsace, an essential stage on the route to Flanders; for Tyrol, which linked Italy with Germany; and for the imperial fiefs in Italy. Thus at one blow Spain had secured Bohemia and the Empire for the most dependable of its allies and fastened its own hold over its European communications. At least, it had done so on paper.

In fact it had not. In fact, on 23 May 1618, three days after the ruin of the Spanish conspiracy in Venice, the Spanish conspiracy was ruined in Prague also. On that day the Protestant nobility of Bohemia revolted, threw the hispanophil Catholic ministers out of the window of the Hradschin castle, and set up a revolutionary government. The first act of this new government was to expel those constant allies of Spain, the Jesuits. The second was to look round for a Protestant heir to replace the pre-elected Archduke. Only a radical prince would accept such a revolutionary throne, and therefore their eyes lit on the most radical of all German princes: the Calvinist Elector Palatine whose own capital of Heidelberg was such a nuisance on the Spanish Rhineland route.

The revolution in Prague, coinciding with the delivery of Venice, sent a thrill of excitement through all Protestant Europe. All the enemies of Spain were roused. Two months later, in July 1618, the Protestant party in the Valtelline murdered their Catholic enemies whom they accused of 'Hispanismus', appeasement of Spain. Then they seized control of the pass, and so cut Milan off from Tyrol. At the same time Savoy and Venice made a formal alliance against future aggression. Next month, Maurice of Nassau, the leader of the Dutch war-party, overthrew, arrested and would soon judicially murder the Advocate Oldenbarnevelt, the maker of the truce of 1609. Olden-barnevelt was accused of 'appeasement' both of Popery and of Spain. Next year Venice and Holland made a defensive alliance against Spain, the estates of Austria joined the Bohemians in revolt, and the death of the Emperor gave the signal for a general rebellion: while the Hungarian Prince of Transylvania marched on Vienna, the Bohemian Diet formally elected the Elector Palatine as their king.

From now on, historians say, general war was certain. The pattern is clear, at least in retrospect. Incident after incident had increased the alarm; the pressure had been built up; it must be discharged. Of course it is easy to say this now because we know that in fact war did break out: the Thirty Years War is conventionally dated from the Bohemian revolt. But in fact did these events inevitably cause the general war? The causes of war are so important that we ought to take nothing for granted. Let us look a little more closely at the course of events after that revolt. We may find that the easy answer is not necessarily the true or only answer.

The first fact to notice is that the Bohemian revolt was far less fatal than might appear. It did not in fact lead to the loss of the Empire. In 1619, while the Bohemian Diet was electing its new Protestant king in

Prague, the Archduke, as legally elected King of Bohemia, was in Frankfurt helping to elect himself as Emperor. Therefore the major part of Spanish policy was undamaged. The imperial crown was secure. So the secret treaty of Graz would stand. All that was lost was Bohemia. But Bohemia in itself was not a direct Spanish interest. And anyway, if Bohemia could only be isolated, the position there could surely be recovered without general war. Moreover, it seemed that Bohemia could be isolated. The election of the new king was illegal: the Archduke had been legally pre-elected and his election could not be thus superseded. Therefore who would now defend the usurper? In fact his own father-in-law, the King of England, refused to support him, and a French envoy succeeded in persuading the two German leagues, the Catholic League and the Evangelical Union, to remain neutral. It seemed that the European great powers were determined merely to hold the ring, to localize the struggle. The Bohemian rebels had overplayed their hand. They had even given a moral advantage to Spain and the Catholic cause.

It was an advantage which Spain was prompt – or rather prompted – to seize. For although the Spanish government was passive, the Spanish governors in Europe insisted on action. The Archduke Albert in Brussels, the ambassador Oñate in Vienna, his predecessor Zúñiga, now back in Madrid, the Duke of Osuna, still in Naples, all pressed for decisive intervention; and they had their way. In 1620 a Spanish army under Spinola marched from the Spanish Netherlands and occupied the Palatinate. The Elector could hardly complain: he had put himself in the wrong: he had deserted his own country to usurp a crown elsewhere and deserved what he got. That was the general view, even of the Rhineland princes, who accepted defeat and made peace. In the same year the Spanish governor of Milan carried out a successful coup in the Valtelline. Under his patronage the Catholics in the valley suddenly rose and in the Sacro Macello, or 'Holy Butchery', massacred their Protestant rulers and placed the vital corridor, for a time, under Spanish protection. A few months later a Bavarian army, acting for the Habsburgs, totally defeated the usurping King of Bohemia and drove him headlong from Prague. It was the Battle of the White Mountain, the end of the historic independent kingdom of Bohemia. By the spring of 1621 all, it seemed, was over; the *status quo* had been restored; the danger of general war was past. There was victory in Bohemia, *fait accompli* in the Valtelline, truce in the Palatinate. All that was necessary now was a general settlement. Everyone wanted a settlement: at least all the governments did. As if to emphasize its wish for peace, the

Spanish government went out of its way to meet French demands for a peaceful partnership in the Valtelline.

Thus when we look closely at the facts we see that the last of the 'incidents' did not, of itself, precipitate a general war. The revolt in Prague no more created the war than the conspiracy in Venice had done, or the war in the Adriatic, or the war over Montferrat, or the affair of Jülich-Cleves, or the Palatinate or the Valtelline. Each of these incidents had been localized and finally ended because the great powers, valuing peace and dreading the cost of a general war, had refused to be involved; and now exactly the same thing had happened over Bohemia. And yet, in 1621, real war broke out: war which immediately re-inflamed all the sensitive danger-spots I have named and gradually involved all the great powers, bringing devastation and revolution to Europe for the next twenty-seven years. How, then, did this happen? To seek an answer to this question we must turn away from the facile assumption that war rises spontaneously out of 'incidents' and look instead at the men who create incidents and are the real makers of history.

The European war which broke out in 1621 was caused not by accumulated accidents but by human decisions. Those decisions were taken in Madrid. Theoretically the war was renewed because the twelve years' truce of 1609 had run out, but in fact, of course, that truce could have been prolonged. The refusal to prolong it was a positive decision, deliberately made. The questions we must ask are, who were the men who made that decision and why did they make it? I believe that it is possible to answer these questions. The men were a party of Spanish officials who came to power in Madrid in 1621, and they made war deliberately because, unlike their predecessors, they believed that war would now be more profitable, or at least less unprofitable, to Spain than peace.

For in 1621 two deaths changed the government of the Spanish Empire in Europe. The first was of Philip III. He expired in March, just ahead of the truce which had been made in his name. Throughout most of his reign this indolent, peace-loving king had allowed the great questions of policy to be decided by his *válido* or 'favourite', the indulgent, peace-loving peace-profiteer, the Duke of Lerma. But in October 1618, just as the European crisis was blowing up, Lerma had been driven from power. Thereafter, while the fortunes of the House of Habsburg in Central Europe trembled and Spanish viceroys and ambassadors pressed for decisive action, the King had gone on a long, ceremonial visit to his other kingdom of Portugal, where the affairs of

Europe were little regarded. There he had contracted the illness which was to prove fatal on his return to Spain.

The second death was that of his brother-in-law the Archduke Albert, in July. The younger brother of the Emperors Rudolf and Matthias, he had been a cardinal of the Church before he had been married to Philip II's favourite daughter, the Infanta Isabel, and sent by his father-in-law – it was almost the last act of Philip II's reign – to govern the Netherlands – that is, the 'reconciled' Belgian provinces – as an 'independent' sovereign. His death was of great significance, for two reasons. First, he had always been the greatest advocate of peace in the north. As an Austrian archduke, he had favoured decisive action in Germany where the fortune of his house was at stake; but as governor of the Netherlands, he knew that war would be fatal to the loyal provinces. He knew that Spain was incapable of financing such a war; he doubted the possibility of decisive victory; and he sided with his subjects. It was he who had negotiated, or imposed, the successive treaties which had wound up the three wars in the north – with France, with England, with Holland – and so ushered in the era of general peace. His death therefore removed a main obstacle to the renewal of the war. Secondly, by the terms of his original appointment, on his death the sovereignty of the Netherlands returned to the King of Spain. Thereafter, Belgium was no longer, even in theory, independent. This might not have mattered if the king had still been Philip III. With the change of ruler in Madrid, the change of rule in the Netherlands gave the power of decision to new men, whose ideas were very different.

And who were these new men? Essentially they were two. First there was Balthasar de Zúñiga, whom we have seen as the advocate of a forward policy in Germany. As a young man, he had sailed in the Armada against England. Later, he had been ambassador, first to the Archduke, then to the King of France, and finally to the Emperor. He was now the most powerful figure in Madrid. Secondly there was the new King's young tutor, Gaspar de Guzmán, the nephew of Zúñiga, who would dominate Spain for the next twenty-two years as the Count-Duke of Olivares. These men were not mere court-figures. Behind them stood a whole party: the party of the pushing, powerful, uncontrolled governors and ambassadors throughout the empire who had long been openly impatient of the restraining peace which all the great powers were conspiring to keep: men like the Duke of Osuna, now fallen, and the Marquis of Bedmar, now ambassador in Brussels itself, who had wished to liquidate Venice; like the Marquis of Villafranca, governor of Milan, who had wished to annihilate Savoy, or his successor the Duke of Feria who had sponsored the 'Holy Butchery'; like the Count of Oñate who was even now pressing the Emperor into war in central Europe. For years these men had fretted at the weakness of politicians in Madrid. They had longed to throw into action the armies which they commanded and maintained, the fifth columns which they had created and nursed. They were the 'experts', and if politicians would not use their expertise, they were willing to break into politics themselves. Fortunately, with the change of government, they found politicians who shared their views.

But why, we may ask, should anyone, and particularly any Spanish statesman, positively want war in 1621? Had not Spain been forced into peace by the sheer impossibility of continuing the war, by financial bankruptcy and military failure? And had not the peace, in spite of this defeat, been a Spanish peace? Had not Spain in fact gained more by that peace than it had ever done by war? From 1609 to 1621 Spain had dominated Europe; it had set a pattern to other governments, drawn other governments into its orbit, drugged those governments into quiescence while it gained one local victory after another. In France, since the murder of Henri IV, the government had been entirely pro-Spanish. The Queen Mother, Marie de Médicis, had been in league with Spain. The old Huguenot minister of Henri IV, the Duke of Sully, had been dismissed at the request of the Spanish ambassador, whose liberal bribes and pensions ensured him a strong party at court. Even the young Richelieu, in his first brief ministry, was regarded as completely spaniolized. And this Franco-Spanish alliance, blessed by the Church, cemented by the Jesuits and the *dévots*, was consummated by a double marriage between the two crowns: two marriages celebrated with a prodigality of magnificence staggering even in that Indian summer of Renaissance splendour, the Spanish peace.

France was a Catholic country: it could be spaniolized with the help of the Church. But even Protestant governments, in that decade, were seduced by Spain. By 1612 King James I of England had emancipated himself from his Elizabethan ministers and their policy. His court was filled with Catholic ministers, rotted by Spanish pensions. Interest and *snobisme* drew him towards Spain, the source of unearned wealth, the pattern of absolute royal power. In 1613 a new Spanish ambassador, the Count of Gondomar, arrived in London and completely captivated the court. For ten years the English court hung attentively on Spanish wishes while another royal marriage was dangled as a bait before the King. In 1618 Gondomar achieved his greatest public triumph when, at his request, the old Elizabethan Sir Walter Ralegh was sent to the block for trespassing in the now closed transatlantic empire of Spain. Even Protestant Holland, in those years, was under a pacific administration: the rule of the 'Arminians' who found the commercial interest of Holland in peace and were accused of indecent subservience to Spain. It was because France, England and Holland all moved in the Spanish orbit that Spain had been able to win those bloodless victories, and in 1621 France and England moved obediently in that orbit still. Why then were the ambassadors and viceroys so determined to break the Spanish peace?

The answer is not difficult to find. It is to be found in their own statements. It can be expressed briefly. These men believed that, in spite of appearance, Spain was losing the peace. It might be winning politically, but on a wider front it was losing, and every year was increasing its loss. And this loss was not a loss of territory (Spanish territory had been constantly increasing), nor even merely a loss of trade (Spanish trade had never been much). It was something far greater than this. Beneath the surface of spectacular peaceful triumphs the whole Spanish 'way of life' was being undermined. It was being undermined by a more successful rival 'ideology'. Moreover, to add to the humiliation of it, this rival ideology had its headquarters in Amsterdam, the capital of those insubordinate, invincible, unpardonable heretics and rebels, the Dutch.

For the Spanish peace did, in some respects, represent the victory and spread of a 'way of life'. Wherever we look, in Italy, or in Flanders, we can see it. It is the triumph of princely bureaucracy, of an official class in a monarchical society, constantly growing both in numbers and in appetite, and living to a large extent on taxes, which also grow as it grows. This official class had by now an official ideology, an ideology of 'the court'. This ideology was shared even by the merchants who handled the great monopolies, farmed the taxes, and felt themselves half-courtiers. It was consecrated by the Church, which was a court-church, and particularly by the religious orders: most of all by the courtliest of all orders, the Jesuits, who at this time were the invariable allies of Spain. Such a system had its outward charm, of course. The bureaucracy patronized official art and architecture; it advertised itself and its solidity through magnificent buildings which we admire today and magnificent shows and pageants which dissolved overnight. But it also had its weakness. Though it created a form of 'state-capitalism', it discouraged private trade and industry. If we wish to see the system at its best we may look at Flanders: the Flanders of 'the Archdukes', where the gaps created by war and iconoclasm were being filled with splendid baroque palaces and churches, decorated by the greatest genius of the Counter-Reformation, Rubens. If we wish to see it at its worst we must look at the economic life of what had once been the industrial capital of Europe – the towns of Flanders and North Italy. Everywhere we see the same spectacle: industry and commerce crushed under the weight of bureaucracy; merchants shifting their capital into the purchase of land, titles or offices; peasants oppressed by taxes; craftsmen fleeing to other lands.

This 'Spanish' way of life was not confined to the Spanish empire, or even to Catholic countries. It was the system of most of Europe. But nowhere was it more obvious than in Spain, and wherever Spanish influence was felt it was encouraged. We see it in France, the France of Marie de Médicis; we see it in England, the England of James I and the Duke of Buckingham. But over against it there was another 'way of life', another 'ideology'. It was the ideology of the 'country', opposed to the 'court'; of country landlords opposed to court-magnates, of lesser merchants opposed to the great 'monopolists' of the court, of taxpayers opposed to tax-eaters. This ideology was conservative, for such men regarded the swollen court as a mushroom-growth: it appealed to old history against new government; it was nationalist, for it opposed an international system; it was anti-Spanish and anti-clerical, for that system was operated by Spain and Rome; and against the ostentatious consumption of the court, it was 'puritan'. This ideology had been suppressed, indeed could hardly exist, in Spain and Spanish Italy; it seethed below the surface in England and France; but in Venice and Holland, in different forms, it ruled. Against Venice and Holland therefore all the hatred of Spanish officialdom was directed. In 1618 the Spanish officials in Italy had wished to destroy Venice. They had been prevented partly by Venetian firmness, partly by lack of support in Madrid. By 1621 they were in power in Madrid and they were resolved to destroy Holland.

Of course, if time had been on the Spanish side, if the Spanish peace had really been consolidating Spanish power in Europe, there would have been no need for action: Spain could have waited till the dwindling 'puritan' generation had died out. But the Spanish officials were convinced that time was not on Spain's side. They might recognize that Spain had needed peace, but what had been the purpose of peace? To rest, sit back, to exploit the resources and live on the spoils of an undiminished empire? That was what the court of Philip III had done. But the officials abroad did not hold that view. They believed that the purpose of peace was to recover from the bankruptcy of war, to renew military strength, to create new resources for final victory. And that, it was only too clear, had not been done. Spain, under Philip III, in spite of its apparent wealth and strength, had, behind the façade of its wealth and strength, sunk deeper into bankruptcy, deeper into feebleness. Meanwhile its old enemies were using the peace to grow in power and prosperity. The courts of England and France might be sound, but beneath them the country was gathering strength. At any moment the brittle restraints of the court might dissolve, and this force would break through. And the new power and prosperity of Holland was terrifying. The courtly, clerical, aristocratic system of Spain might be magnificent; but it did not work. The ideology of the Dutch might be heretical, rebellious, vulgar, but it did work. Time therefore was on their side. Fortunately, said the Spanish officials, the balance of power was still on the side of Spain, provided Spain struck, and struck now.

Listen to the voices of these men. Here is the greatest of them all, the Count of Gondomar, ambassador in England. Gondomar's whole task was to neutralize England, to keep it at peace, and his triumph consisted in doing so. But in 1616 he wrote home expressing his views at length. Unless the Spanish government made better use of the peace, he said, 'I consider that war would be much better for the Catholic religion and the state and monarchy of Spain'. For what in fact were the fruits of peace? Thanks to the peace the English were increasing their trade and wealth and at the same time ceasing to do very little of what they did in war. They were becoming rich at the expense of Spain which, for all its American mines, was now the poorest country in Europe: Spain brought gold and silver from overseas 'only to distribute it among all the nations of the world, whose ships wait to carry it home'. If Spain wished to win the peace, said Gondomar, it must adopt a new and positive policy. It was not enough merely to enjoy the respite, to relax and maintain a static system. Spain must invest in commerce, encourage shipping, found trading companies, abolish inland tolls, give a new status and new facilities to merchants. In this way trade and wealth would grow, shipping would be increased, and sea-power would give ultimate victory in war, 'for the world today is such that whosoever rules the sea rules the land also'. But if Spain would not adopt this policy, then, said Gondomar, the proper course was war, and war at once. King Philip must send 'invincible Armadas to conquer this Kingdom'. The conquest, after all, was easy. All who had ever landed in England had conquered the country. Philip II would have conquered it but for the winds and waves. A landing should be made in Scotland; after the first pitched battle the way to London would be open; and once London, 'the arsenal for all the enemies of God and Spain', had fallen, 'the King our Lord will be true monarch of the world. For till then we risk losing the East and West Indies and cannot hope to reduce Holland, but thereafter all is ours and the rest is easy.'

That was in 1616. Next year, when the Dutch sailed through the straits of Gibraltar, and the year after, when he himself went home on leave, Gondomar was disillusioned with Spain. He could hardly recognize his country, he said: the poverty and depopulation of Spain compared with the wealth and activity of England and Holland was terrifying. He now despaired of mastery of the sea. 'England and Holland have won the peace: we have lost it.'

But if the Spanish navy was rotted with disuse, the Spanish armies were still invincible. So we may turn to other, more military-minded, speakers. Such was Carlos Coloma, governor of Cambrai, a veteran of the wars of the Netherlands, who submitted his views in 1620 and 1621. By that time the great question concerned the truce: should it be renewed or should it be allowed to lapse? To this question Coloma's answer was clear. It should lapse. For what was the original purpose of the truce? In 1609, wrote Coloma, the Spaniards had made it because they supposed that peace would relieve the Treasury and gradually dissolve the martial spirit and rickety government of the Dutch. But had it done so? Not at all. On the contrary, the Dutch had made covert war on Spain in Venice and Germany, had captured the trade of East and West Indies, and had built up in twelve years an empire such as had cost the Portuguese and Spaniards 120 years. Amsterdam, forty years ago 'an almost unknown village', had become a world-city eclipsing Genoa for wealth, Lisbon for merchandise, Venice for situation. 'I conclude', wrote Coloma, 'that if in twelve years of peace they have undertaken and achieved all this, we can easily see what they will do if we give them more time. . . . If the truce is continued, we shall condemn ourselves to suffer all the evils of peace and all the dangers of war.' Therefore, he urged, let Holland be destroyed. To destroy it would be easy. (Osuna had thought it would be easy to destroy Venice, Gondomar to destroy England.) With England and France neutral, one campaign, one *Blitzkrieg* would do it; but it must be done now.

On the Council of State in Madrid, Coloma's arguments were driven home by Balthasar de Zúñiga himself. In 1619, during the Bohemian crisis, when he had been pressing for action in Germany, Zúñiga had urged renewal of the truce, but on impossible terms: as the price of peace, the Dutch were to surrender almost everything that they had gained by war. He had even hoped to convert the Prince of Orange into a real ruling prince, but a client of Spain. That was a counsel of despair. But now that the Bohemian crisis was over, he spoke out for war. 'If the Republic of these rebels goes on as it is', he said, 'we shall succeed in losing first the two Indies, then the rest of Flanders, then Italy, and finally Spain itself.' It seemed to him as if the Spaniards had shed their blood only to fill the veins of subject nations: 'we have left our own country deserted and sterile in order to people and fertilise the lands we have conquered'. Therefore let the truce be ended. The Carthage on the Zuider Zee must be destroyed, the treasure of Spain that had been secretly drained away to the north must be brought back by force. Was it not for this day that Zúñiga himself and his fellow imperialists had so long been waiting? Why else had they worked so hard, throughout the Spanish peace, to secure the vital corridors – the Valtelline, Alsace, the Palatinate? Now they had secured them all. Were they, then, not to strike?

When these arguments were first advanced in Madrid, there was resistance. How, men asked, could Spain face the cost of war? With his dying voice, the Archduke in Brussels urged that the truce be pro-longed. 'We must suppose', he protested, 'that even if all Europe is destined to be subject to one monarch, that time is not yet.' But as the old rulers died off, the new prevailed; and besides, they had other allies. The Councils of Portugal and the Indies, representing the East and West India trades, agreed with Zúñiga and Coloma. These men had long suffered from the Dutch. In the years of war the Dutch had seized half the East Indies from Portugal; in the years of peace they had stolen the trade of the West Indies. It was vain to hope of defeating them now at sea, but a well-aimed blow by land would solve the problem. Struck in the heart, the octopus would loosen its distant tentacles. . . . Thanks to this argument, and this support, the party of war prevailed. The truce was denounced. The half-settled troubles of Germany were swept up into a general war.

Thus we can answer our question. The Thirty Years War, as a general war, was not created by the Bohemian and German incidents which officially began it. These could have been settled, or at least localized, as so many other such incidents had been. It was not even created by the lapse of the Twelve Years Truce. That truce could have been prolonged, as the Belgians themselves (in whose interest, osten-sibly, it was denounced) wished it to be. Perhaps no general war ever arises out of mere incidents. General wars arise because the govern-ments of great powers, or the men behind such governments, choose war, and exploit incidents. It used to be said that no government wanted war in 1914. Indeed, August 1914 has long been the classic case of muddled governments sliding accidentally into unwanted war. Now, since the work of Fritz Fischer, we think differently. Not the Kaiser indeed, but the German government, and the interests behind it, wanted war, or at least chose it. They chose it because they thought that they could win it, if they made it now, and that victory would solve their problems, which delay would increase. In 1939 Hitler wanted war, more positively, but essentially for the same reasons. And in 1621, in the greatest power in Europe, behind the politicians of the peace, there was a group of men who positively chose war because they believed that they could win the war whereas, in the modern world, they could not win the peace.

It only remains to say that (as in 1914, as in 1939) they did not in fact win the war either. They began well, of course. They were prepared and their enemies were not. And they had chosen a good time. In the next few years the House of Habsburg would win triumph after triumph and Spanish statesmen would dream of dominion over the Baltic and the conquest of England. But then, slowly but effectively, the other great powers would be roused; war would reveal new forces, new techniques; once again Spain would be forced to make peace; and this time it would not be a Spanish peace: it would be the end of Spain as a great power.

Index

16.95